PLAS

PITT
LATIN
AMERICAN
SERIES

Illusions of Conflict

//

Illusions of Conflict

Anglo-American Diplomacy
Toward Latin America, 1865–1896

//

Joseph Smith

University of Pittsburgh Press

Published by the University of Pittsburgh Press, Pittsburgh, Pa. 15260
Copyright © 1979, University of Pittsburgh Press
All rights reserved
Feffer and Simons, Inc., London
Manufactured in the United States of America

Library of Congress Cataloging in Publication Data

Smith, Joseph, 1945-
    Illusions of conflict.

    (Pitt Latin American series)
    Includes bibliographical references and index.
    1. United States—Foreign relations—Latin America.
2. Latin America—Foreign relations—United States.
3. Great Britain—Foreign relations—Latin America.
4. Latin America—Foreign relations—Great Britain.
I. Title.
F1418.S64   327'.098   78-53602
ISBN 0-8229-3387-X

For Rachael

//

Contents

//

Acknowledgments

I wish first to express my gratitude to Professor R. A. Humphreys who directed me to the subject of Anglo-American diplomatic rivalry. I am also indebted to Professor John Lynch for his constant encouragement and advice. For the financial assistance which facilitated my research in London and the United States I wish to thank the William Waldorf Astor Foundation and the Universities of Durham, London, and Exeter. The helpful attitude of the staffs of the following libraries made research considerably easier: in England, the Public Record Office, the Institute of Historical Research, the British Museum, the University of London Library, the University College London Library, and the University of Exeter Library; in the United States, the Library of Congress, the National Archives, and the libraries of the University of Texas at Austin and Princeton University.

//

Introduction

For almost three centuries Spain enforced international isolation upon her American colonies until events thrust them into world politics at the beginning of the nineteenth century. British and American diplomats took a special interest in Latin America's struggle for independence, but their appreciation of the outcome showed a radical divergence. The British foreign secretary, George Canning, boasted that he had "called the New World into existence to redress the balance of the Old World." The concept of Latin America as an integral part of the international relations system centered on Europe was, however, challenged by the Monroe Doctrine, which asserted the idea of a separate Western Hemispheric system.

The system that emerged conformed to neither image. The Latin American nations were able to preserve their political independence from European interference, but they lacked the power to become a force in world affairs. On the other hand, their commercial value compensated for their slight international significance, and Canning's hopes were fulfilled to the extent that the new nations remained open to European economic and cultural penetration. In this respect it was Britain, the world's leading economic and maritime power, that established the most substantial relationship. American diplomats could do little to prevent this development. For much of the nineteenth century the people of the United States were preoccupied with their own internal progress and paid little attention to external affairs.

But the sense of hemispheric conflict between Europe and the United States was never totally absent. The outbreak of the Civil War in 1861 brought the United States to the verge of disintegration, and France sought to exploit this by launching an ambitious scheme for aggrandizement in Mexico. Britain chose not to become involved. By the mid–nineteenth century the process of British political disengagement from Latin America was well under way and British diplomats attached little strategic importance to the area. Moreover, they were well aware of the sensitivity shown by the United States in all questions relating to the Western Hemisphere. Anglo-American economic rivalry in Latin America was a reality, but on the diplomatic level British policy toward Latin America stressed conciliation and cooperation with the United States rather than confrontation or conflict.

This policy was fully put to the test after 1865. The United States emerged from the Civil War united and imbued with an increased consciousness of its own power and inherent virtue. Secretary of State William H. Seward unveiled an expansionist policy designed to promote American political and commercial influence throughout the Western Hemisphere. This aim was pursued by succeeding administrations and reflected the growing American interest in Latin America. Under James G. Blaine the concept of a separate Western Hemispheric system was once again vigorously revived. But the implementation of this policy was inconsistent. Internal political factors continually thwarted expansionist aims and American business lacked the economic base to compete effectively with well-established European interests in Latin American markets.

The economic struggle between Britain and the United States in Latin America continued into the twentieth century, but the political battle was concluded in 1896. In practice, British policy had long respected the predominant interest of the United States in political matters relating to the Western Hemisphere. But this policy was implicit rather than explicit, and despite this conciliatory attitude American expansionists continued to regard Britain as the primary obstacle to the achievement of their aims. In 1895 direct confrontation could not be avoided when the Venezuela boundary dispute was transformed into the simple but explosive question of whether or not Britain recognized the validity of the Monroe Doctrine. Beset by its own internal political difficulties and other pressing diplomatic problems, the British government acquiesced. In British eyes Latin America was of marginal international importance, and the price of political disengagement, however visible, was a small one to pay in order to avoid conflict with the United States. This policy would later be justified as a calculated effort to secure the friendship of the United States, but it had been the characteristic feature of British policy throughout most of the nineteenth century.

For the United States Britain's acceptance of arbitration in the Venezuela boundary dispute represented a satisfying diplomatic victory and a resounding affirmation of the Monroe Doctrine. It was, however, only a partial success for the concept of a separate hemispheric system. European commercial and cultural ties with Latin America remained strong. Moreover, Latin American nations distrusted American idealism and suspected the sincerity of American diplomatic motives. They admired the achievements of their great neighbor, but also feared its power. The outcome of the Venezuela boundary dispute underlined the inherent dangers for Latin America. Decisions taken by diplomats in London and Washington determined that Latin America must fall even further under the sway of the United States. From 1865 onward British diplomacy was the barometer showing the rise of the United States to world power status and to political preeminence within the Western Hemisphere.

The study that follows is divided into two parts. The first presents an overview of British and American foreign policy and describes the nature of the diplomatic relationship established by these powers within Latin America. The second examines the specific British and American responses toward the various diplomatic events occurring in the Western Hemisphere between 1865 and 1896.

I /The Diplomatic Relationship

//1//

British Policy
Toward Latin America

In the nineteenth century Britain was the world's leading economic power. The basis of this power lay in her headstart in industrialization and also in the release of a dynamic and constructive energy that maintained her in the forefront of industrial technology for much of the century. An international economy came into being with London as the financial capital. British exports dominated world markets and few countries remained unaffected by British capital investment. In 1815 Britain had an accumulated credit abroad of around £10 million. By 1895 the figure was £2,195.3 million.[1]

This economic strength formed the basis of Britain's assumption of the role of a great world power. British citizens and interests spanned the globe and their protection was the concern of the Foreign Office. British rights were secured by the negotiation of commercial and consular agreements between Britain and the other sovereign states of the world. On paper the agreements were between equals, but in practice Britain often gained the most advantage. Economic strength, political prestige, and military power in the shape of the ubiquitous British navy ensured the extension of British political and commercial influence over weak and less-developed states.

Some of these states were ultimately incorporated within the British empire. Many of those that remained outside the confines of "formal" empire have been described as part of Britain's "informal" empire, and Latin America is often cited as a conspicuous example.[2] British political and commercial interest in Latin America had, in fact, extended over several centuries. This interest was, however, greatly stimulated by the independence of Latin America that marked the end of the Spanish mercantilist system and opened the new nations to British economic and political penetration. The new economic relationship flourished because Britain could supply what these countries needed: cheap manufactured goods in large quantities and capital for economic and political purposes.

Although the Latin American relationship was not as important to Britain as trade with Europe, North America, or Asia, British trade with Latin America was still substantial. Between 1865 and 1895 annual British exports to that area averaged £20.6 million and annual imports averaged £20.3 million.[3] As a supplier of raw materials and foodstuffs, Latin America was also of increasing value to the British economy. The rapidly developing British relationship with Argentina was the prime example of this.[4]

Latin America was also a major field of British financial investment. Such investment has been estimated at just over £80 million in 1865 and at more than £552 million in 1895.[5] The sum was considerable, but Latin America was only a part of a global picture.[6] Moreover, in contrast to Africa or Asia, British investment in Latin America was not accompanied by political involvement. There was no "scramble" for Latin American territory in the late nineteenth century. The foreign secretary, Lord Castlereagh, had warned against such ideas as early as 1807 during the disastrous British expedition to the River Plate.[7] British policy was to suffer a second humiliation in the same area in 1845 when his guideline was departed from. The mistake was not repeated again.

Yet, the assertion of political influence is not limited to merely annexing territory. French and German statesmen talked of "perfidious Albion," and American politicians frequently protested that Britain had selfish designs on Latin American territory. The public outcry in the United States in 1895 over Britain's alleged encroachment upon Venezuela was merely one more illustration of how many Americans suspected the intentions of British foreign policy.

Such perceptions were perhaps distorted by the fact that the last quarter of the nineteenth century witnessed an intensification of international political and economic rivalries among the great powers. One consequence was the scramble for empire, but despite American apprehensions this did not occur in Latin America. By the end of the century the independence, authority, and sovereignty of most Latin American states was firmly established, not only in a legal but also in a military sense.[8] Furthermore, Britain gave a virtual public recognition to the Monroe Doctrine in 1896 and thereby acquiesced in United States political preeminence in the Western Hemisphere.[9]

Yet British economic interest in Latin America was still greater than that of any other power and, indeed, from the mid–1890s onward a new boom period of British trade and investment in Latin America was initiated. The economic balance sheet was therefore exceedingly healthy while the political balance sheet showed a distinctly adverse trend. Britain was alleged to have backed Chile during the War of the Pacific (1879–1883), but Chilean hemispheric influence was in decline in the 1890s. The Brazilian republic survived the rumors of British plots, and reports of British designs on Nicaragua and Venezuela evoked American diplomatic protest. Did this represent the failure of British policy or could it be that such designs were mere allegations based on circumstantial evidence? British economic interest in Latin America was considerable, and diplomatic and naval action was employed for its protection. But this did not constitute an "informal" empire because Foreign Office officials manifested little interest in Latin American affairs. Where official action was judged to be necessary it was exercised with moderation, legalistic concern, and a determination not to upset the susceptibilities of the United States.

The Nature of British Diplomacy

The salient characteristic of the nineteenth-century British foreign policy establishment was its aristocratic ethos. The foreign secretary was invariably an aristocrat and officials were recruited on a class basis. The result was an elitist and exclusive foreign service attuned and equipped for the "drawing room diplomacy" of Europe but unrepresentative of British society as a whole.[10] Moreover, the number of actual personnel was inadequate and their function tended to be limited to the writing and copying of diplomatic dispatches.[11] The formulation of policy and the immediate instructions for its implementation depended primarily upon the foreign secretary and his permanent undersecretary. One was a politician and the other a professional diplomat, although possessing little personal experience of the diplomatic world outside London. The foreign secretary's staff was recruited on social grounds, and whatever diplomatic expertise an official might later develop was unlikely to be utilized, given the hierarchical structure and procedures of the Foreign Office. The diplomatic service and the Foreign Office were regarded as separate services, and the skills gained in London were rarely transferred to overseas diplomatic missions and vice versa.[12]

There was, however, no great pressure for change. The social exclusiveness of the foreign service contributed toward an internal resistance to change that extended to policy itself. For example, although the Foreign Office was not indifferent to the importance of British commerce, it was not in the nature of the aristocratic mentality to become too actively involved in such matters. Within the Foreign Office there was, therefore, a distinct preference for "political" work and a clear downgrading of "commercial" business. The same attitude prevailed in the diplomatic service. Commercial work was assigned to commercial attachés or more usually to the officials of the consular service. Consequently, it was not the diplomat but the consul who involved himself in the mundane problems of British citizens and their claims in the industrial cities and ports throughout the world.

If the charges of government-inspired British economic imperialism are to be substantiated then it must be shown that these men were truly the agents of the policy emanating from London. In fact, consuls belonged to a veritable "cinderella service." They were appointed not on merit but by the patronage of the foreign secretary. They possessed therefore some social influence, but the rewards for this were meager. Consuls were lowly officials and treated as such. A social gulf divided the diplomat and the consul both at home and abroad. The Foreign Office maintained written contact with the consuls, but since few consular dispatches were ever passed on to the foreign secretary, a consul could expect neither to influence policy nor even to come into direct contact with the men who might bring about his promotion.[13]

A further limitation upon the effectiveness of the consular and the foreign service was the inadequacy of its funding by Parliament. The Victorian period was characterized by a preoccupation with government expenditure, and financial retrenchment was a popular theme in every parliamentary session.[14] On the other hand, although Parliament and its agent in this matter, the Exchequer, might raise difficulties over finance, Parliament did not tend to inquire too closely into diplomatic matters. In fact, the Foreign Office rarely made extravagant claims upon the Exchequer,[15] and sought to involve Parliament in its affairs as little as possible. Nor were Parliament, the major political parties, the cabinet, or even the other departments of government anxious to involve themselves in foreign affairs. They were concerned with domestic matters and their own internal business; except in a matter of international crisis they showed little interest in foreign policy.[16] Moreover, their influence over such matters was limited. The foreign secretary was invariably a prominent political figure in his own right, and within the cabinet he was second only to the prime minister. Furthermore, such was the secretive and special nature of foreign policy that certain questions could not be asked in public. Adequate information was also lacking, and that which was available had usually been presented and edited by the Foreign Office. Only if a foreign policy issue had considerable domestic ramifications could it become a significant domestic political issue and thereby mobilize the force of public opinion to demand changes in policy itself.[17]

The lack of legislative and public interference with the formulation and execution of British foreign policy enhanced the role of the individual decision-maker. Consequently, the personalities of successive foreign secretaries from 1865 to 1900 stamped upon British diplomacy their own characteristics of hard work, moderation, and caution. With the possible exception of Granville, these men became so immersed in their work that their concentration on minutiae most likely obscured many of the major diplomatic issues. They all believed in the greatness of Britain and that it was its due and in its interest to exercise an important influence in world affairs.[18] But what that influence should be was not clear except that it should be used to ensure peace. The Victorian concern over unnecessary expenditure ruled out extravagant policies, and the traditions of British diplomacy dating from Castlereagh and Canning underlined the need for freedom of diplomatic maneuver and the avoidance of constricting foreign alliances.

Nineteenth-century foreign secretaries rarely departed from these guidelines. "We are the Parliament of the United Kingdom, and not the Parliament of the world," summed up the foreign secretary, Lord Stanley, in 1867 when he rejected proposals that Britain officially condemn the execution of the archduke Maximilian in Mexico.[19] The tradition of caution and moderation plus the resistance to change, or perhaps inertia, of those in control of policy and the institutions that they represented produced a conservative if not negative foreign policy. This was encouraged and indeed partly justified by Britain's powerful international position even though this position was based primarily on economic rather than political factors. But given the prevailing attitudes and the nature of the Foreign Office, with its emphasis on political rather than commercial work, officials paid minor attention to economic matters, especially when there was little public demand for a change of attitude.

During the last quarter of the nineteenth century, however, there was growing public concern that falling British exports were causing economic depression at home. The increasingly bitter competition in the international economy was attributed to the rise of nations such as Germany and the United States and their lack of scruples in using diplomacy to "push" their own commerce.[20] In 1886 a royal commission investigated the state of British industry and also inquired into how the foreign service might assist British trade. The final report reaffirmed the traditional view that diplomatic and commercial functions were not easily mixed in that any official who used his position to further private commercial transactions must inevitably compromise not only his own diplomatic standing but that of his country too.[21]

One foreign secretary who saw the danger to British trade in the rise of "a hungrier, more tenacious, perhaps even less scrupulous competition" believed that foreign policy could do little; only "individual effort and stronger self-denial" by British merchants could effectively counter the threat.[22] The argument that merchants remedy their difficulties by their own efforts was not an abnegation of government responsibility; it faithfully reflected the prevailing economic doctrine of the time. Just as foreign service officials represented the exclusive values of their own social class, so did they reflect the faith in laissez faire and free trade that was such a feature of Victorian society.

These doctrines were adhered to by both politicians and businessmen. "It is not to the Government and its agents," declared the *Times* in 1886, "that our traders must look for their real support in the struggle against foreign competition."[23] British chambers of commerce also advocated that the government pursue a policy of laissez faire in commercial matters.[24] Free trade, the corollary of laissez faire, inspired a similar allegiance. Its value in producing economic progress was enthusiastically affirmed although this view came under increasing criticism in the last decades of the nineteenth century as British commercial dominance in world markets visibly declined.[25] The supremacy of laissez faire and free trade had become part of the heritage of the Foreign Office mind and was not to be broken until the twentieth century.

The belief in free enterprise and minimum government interference accorded well with British diplomatic traditions and provided an ideological justification for a policy of nonintervention that might otherwise be interpreted as inaction or inertia. For example, British statesmen stressed the necessity of preserving the European balance of power, but their response to Germany's disruption of that balance showed that the concept was defensive and rhetorical rather than positive or assertive. British diplomats clearly preferred the role of spectator summed up by the description "splendid isolation." The British diplomatic perspective embraced, however, more than just Europe; the aim of British foreign policy was the preservation of an ill-defined and vague status quo throughout the world. This policy reflected not only Britain's substantial international interests but also the conservative attitudes of its foreign policy establishment. Moreover, as long as Britain remained the world's unchallenged leading naval and commercial power, it was a policy that could be pursued with little effort and at minimum expense.[26]

At certain times British policy did assume a much more positive aspect, especially in areas of British political and strategic sensitivity. Thus, Britain was active in the affairs of the Ottoman empire in the 1870s and of Egypt in the 1880s. Economic factors influenced this policy, but the "Eastern question" was also considered an issue of national security. "It is not a question of upholding Turkey," summed up Queen Victoria. "It is a question of Russian or British supremacy in the world."[27] In such cases the Foreign Office was prepared to act vigorously. But after the death of Canning the Western Hemisphere provided no such spur to action. Britain did possess considerable colonial possessions, substantial economic interests and certain diplomatic obligations in the area, but the distorted Foreign Office image of the Western Hemisphere combined with the organizational structure and traditions of the Foreign Office to produce an essentially cautious and negative foreign policy.

Anglo-American Relations

The conduct of diplomatic relations between Britain and the United States was the task of the American Department of the Foreign Office. The title was something of a misnomer since this department embraced not only the affairs of the United States but also those of China, Japan, Siam, and after 1882, Central and South America.[28] Moreover, this vast task of administering relations with a considerable area of the globe was allotted to no more than five or six permanent officials. To an extent this was a reflection of the lack of political and strategic importance accorded by the Foreign Office to American affairs, although there was the awareness that the United States could disrupt the European balance of power.[29] Furthermore, the heritage of the ideology of the American Revolution posed a constant threat to Britain's continued possession of colonies in Canada and the Caribbean.

Conflict was, however, averted. Even though British governments stressed their determination to maintain Canada within the empire, its ultimate loss to the United States was privately conceded. "Nearly all the ministers were of the opinion," noted Kimberley after a cabinet meeting in 1869, "that it would be impossible to defend Canada successfully against the Americans."[30] An effective defense required a permanent policy of fortifications and garrisons that involved too much expense and too many political difficulties. In the interests of peace and financial retrenchment, British policy after 1865 quietly completed an almost total military withdrawal from Canada.[31]

A similar attitude of political and military conciliation of the United States was evident in British policy toward Central America and the Caribbean islands.[32] The special interest of the United States in Cuba was recognized from the late 1820s onward, and the negotiation of the Clayton-Bulwer Treaty in 1850 indicated British recognition that the United States had an equal claim to political influence in Central America.[33] The desire not to upset American sensitivity influenced the British decision in 1861 not to participate in the French scheme to coerce Mexico. This consideration remained a feature of British policy after 1865 and was to receive its most public illustration during the Venezuela boundary dispute.

The stress on nonintervention, minimum political involvement, and, especially, the rejection of territorial expansion in the Western Hemisphere produced just the policy most suited to allay American sensitivities. Nevertheless, this policy was frequently tested because the late nineteenth century saw the emergence of a vigorous and positive United States foreign policy in the Western Hemisphere. The British aim of maintaining the status quo clashed with this assertive policy. Open friction was avoided not only by Britain's conciliatory attitude but also by the skill of British diplomats. Memories of the *Alabama* dispute had soured Anglo-American relations after the Civil War, but this was resolved by the Treaty of Washington in 1871.[34] Agreement rather than conflict was fostered by the tradition of diplomatic compromise between the two nations and by the fact that both nations desired, above all, peace and prosperity. Their ultimate goals, therefore, coincided rather than clashed.

Consequently, despite Irish propaganda or the agitation of anti-British politicians such as Blaine, Anglo-American diplomatic relations were amicable rather than unfriendly. Among political leaders there were enough anglophiles to balance the anglophobes. "Twisting the British lion's tail" was a regular feature of American electoral campaigns, but support for an anti-British policy was not automatically forthcoming from Congress. With the exception of the *Alabama* dispute there were few occasions during the late nineteenth century of sustained anti-British feeling in the United States. In fact, admiration if not veneration for Britain and all things British was just as much a part of American culture as was suspicion and hostility toward what many Americans regarded as the home country.[35]

Successive American administrations also had to contend with public indifference on foreign policy issues. After the Civil War the United States concentrated on internal economic development, and political interest was confined to domestic matters such as Reconstruction, the tariff, and civil service reform. In general, foreign affairs attracted little public attention. The debate over the tariff raised the question of foreign commercial relations, but trade between the United States and Britain prospered throughout the late nineteenth century and did not become an issue of diplomatic negotiation. Consequently, Anglo-American relations assumed a subdued key and this reinforced the inertia of the Foreign Office toward extra-European affairs.

The neglect of American affairs was justified by their lack of political or pressing strategic importance for Britain. The threat to Canada remained, although Canada successfully maintained its independence and the danger posed by American military power was much more potential than actual. Another reason for British indifference was the pressure of work upon the inadequately staffed American Department plus its general disdain for American affairs and style of politics. "It is surprising," commented Pauncefote when ambassador in Washington, "how few public men in this country can carry on a discussion like a gentleman." The recall of Lionel West in 1888 was another example of how politics were conducted in the "great republic."[36]

The fact of geographical distance between London and Washington also imposed a certain degree of caution upon British policy toward the United States. Most official correspondence was dispatched by sea mail rather than by telegraph so that communications between the Foreign Office and its minister in Washington took weeks rather than days.[37] An added argument in favor of caution and delay was the awareness by Foreign Office officials of the unpredictability of American foreign policy. After Grant's victory in 1872 no president won reelection until McKinley in 1900. Consequently, American administrations experienced wholesale changes of personnel at four-year intervals; this produced a basic element of uncertainty and change in foreign policy. Moreover, congressional action frequently intervened to undermine executive policy. For example, several administrations favored the construction of an American-controlled canal across Central America, but Congress would not vote the necessary funds or ratify the treaties negotiated by the State Department for this purpose. As for the interminable congressional debates of the 1890s on the tariff, a Foreign Office Official minuted that "it is no use to go through the Tariff . . . as it is changed almost every day."[38]

The luxury of delay could therefore be applied by British diplomats to almost all American questions. In fact, precipitate action was most unwise given the distance of London from Washington and the nature of American foreign policy itself. But while Foreign Office officials attached a low political and cultural value to the United States they did not underrate its commercial significance and potential. It was clearly in British interests, both political and economic, to maintain good relations with the United States. This would not only ensure that British commerce would prosper but also that Canada would remain independent. Nor was there any great public pressure upon the Foreign Office to change this policy.[39] In fact, British public opinion, like American, was usually supremely indifferent to foreign policy issues. Noting the anti-British hysteria produced in the United States by the incident involving Lionel West in 1888, the *Economist* admonished Americans to "recognize the fact that we are far too busy with our home difficulties to occupy ourselves with the private affairs of foreign nations."[40] Rivalry and antagonism did indeed exist, but Anglo-American relations were marked by friendship rather than discord. The desire of British diplomats to compromise and to conciliate did much to assuage the bitter American memories of the *Alabama* dispute, and the close of the nine-

teenth century was marked by a new emphasis on Anglo-Saxon fra-
ternity and diplomatic rapprochement.[41]

Diplomatic Relations with Latin America

If there were few reasons requiring an active British policy toward the
United States, the same applied even more so with regard to Latin
American affairs. While Foreign Office officials would always consider
American susceptibilities in questions involving the Western Hemisphere, they showed little interest in the views of the Latin American
governments. As far as Britain was concerned, Latin America lacked
strategic and political importance. Because there was no hostage such as
Canada to complicate diplomatic relations, Latin American questions
did not involve questions of imperial security.[42] There was substantial
British economic involvement in Latin America, and British diplomacy
sought to safeguard and protect this interest, but in general British policy
avoided involvement in Latin American political affairs as far as possible and sought to maintain a relatively uncomplicated and apolitical
relationship.

This cautious attitude was partly the result of experience. The failure
of British interventions in the River Plate during the first half of the
nineteenth century provided a constant reminder against a repetition of
similar policies, and the example of the French humiliation in Mexico
further underlined this lesson. A protest was usually forthcoming in
cases of perceived insult to British honor or dignity, but the degree of
response varied according to how soon it was reported to London and
how close a British warship might be to the scene of disturbance.
Examples of British "gunboat diplomacy" after 1865 were few and
confined to the Caribbean area.[43] British diplomats were extremely
reluctant to intervene in Latin American affairs and doubted the value of
forceful action.[44] For example, the destruction of a large amount of their
property in Valparaiso by the Spanish bombardment of 1866 provoked
British merchants to criticize bitterly the inaction of the local British
naval force. The Foreign Office disagreed. British interference in the
conflict was not contemplated and the British captain had been right to
confine his actions to advising British residents to remove their property
from the designated area of hostilities. Ample time had been allowed for
this removal.[45]

On such occasions as the outbreak of revolution or major civil disturbance, a British warship would be ordered to the nearest port. The
purpose was not to intervene in local affairs, but to provide reassurance
to British citizens in the area. Local British officials were bound by their

standing instructions to remain neutral at all times, but in cases of political disturbance they requested the presence of a British warship as a protective agency for British citizens and property.

The British fleet was not as omnipotent in Latin American waters as was often thought. The Disraeli administration had withdrawn the only British ironclad on the South American station for service in the Mediterranean. Consequently, when British merchant shipping was disrupted in 1877 by the piratical activities of the Peruvian ironclad *Huascar*, the Admiralty secretary confessed that a British ironclad should have been sent, but that none were available.[46] During the Chilean revolution of 1891 British military inadequacy was similarly revealed. The insurgents threatened to cut a British-owned telegraph cable, and the company concerned requested some form of protection. This drew the admission from Sanderson that Britain could not send "a sufficient force to the Chilean Coast to overpower the Chilean Fleet." He also declared that it was not the "business" of the Foreign Office to undertake such action.[47] In cases of revolution and political change in Latin America, British policy sought to steer an impartial and neutral course. Certain action was necessary to protect British citizens and their property, but the Foreign Office acted cautiously, preferring to await developments and to observe the responses of the other foreign powers involved.

Britain lacked, therefore, the need and frequently the resources to intervene actively in Latin American affairs. The resulting policy of nonintervention was also reinforced by the structure and prevailing attitudes of the Foreign Office and its officials. British diplomacy was concerned primarily with European affairs and it was a natural corollary that these were regarded as much more important and worthy of attention than events in Latin America. The remoteness of Latin America and the lack of knowledge and expertise regarding the area contributed further to this attitude of neglect. Foreign Office officials had usually traveled widely in Europe, but there was no similar personal acquaintance with Latin America. No doubt, officials in the American Department could have overcome this deficiency by their own intelligence, aptitude, and experience and by the use of the Foreign Office library, which contained considerable information on Latin American affairs. Given the tedious nature of Foreign Office work and the fact that the American Department was inadequately staffed, it is, however, doubtful whether there was much background reading of the Latin American files.

These files consisted of the collected dispatches of the British diplomats and consuls who had served in Latin America. Whatever the individual merits or demerits of these men, their status within the foreign service was low. This was, as we have seen, because much of their work was commercial rather than political in nature and also because the vortex of diplomacy revolved around the highly prized embassies of Europe and did not extend to the other continents of the world.[48] Latin American posts, whether diplomatic or consular, were not regarded as socially attractive and were in fact considered a dumping ground for the incompetent and the unfortunate.[49] "It is a great disappointment to me," went a typical British lament, "to have to remain any longer among these Spanish Americans of whom I have had more than my full share."[50] Nor did the Foreign Office feel that the Latin American legations warranted any major upgrading in rank. Despite the growing military and economic power of Chile in the 1880s, it was decided not to raise the rank of the Santiago legation to that of second-class status, an honor enjoyed only by Rio de Janeiro, Buenos Aires, and Mexico City among Latin American nations.[51]

Opinions on Chile were, however, usually complimentary. One consul as early as 1873 described her as "the model Repulic of South America," although a later view added that Chilean society was "poor, proud, capricious, ignorant, and much addicted both to drunkenness and violent crime."[52] In general, the statements of British diplomats on Latin American affairs and politicians were very scathing. In a well-publicized speech in 1891 Salisbury talked of wars, sudden disturbances and recklessness as characteristics of South America.[53] Pauncefote once noted that Colombia was "a country so ill-governed that the ordinary rules which regulate and limit the functions of consular officers may be departed from."[54] His successor, Sanderson, described the Central American republics as "semi-savage."[55] The leading British periodical on Latin American affairs, the *South American Journal,* complained that the Foreign Office regarded Latin America as "unworthy of particular consideration."[56]

The same attitude tended to prevail among officials serving in diplomatic and consular posts in Latin America. A special correspondent of the *Times* touring Latin America in 1891 reported the "practical absenteeism" of British officials in most of the legations that he visited.[57] This was not surprising in view of London's indifference toward these places, the financial frugality that limited office space and furniture, and the frequency of inclement weather and disease.[58] "Bolivia, as a residence presents so few attractions," remarked a British diplomatic visitor in 1875, "that everyone appeared anxious to leave it."[59] Reports from Peru continually emphasized the political and economic bankruptcy of successive governments.[60] It seemed to one minister that

Britain "did far too much honour to the Spanish American Republics," which in his opinion were "retrograding rather than advancing in morality and civilisation."[61]

The fact that the Foreign Office was inclined to neglect Latin America and that diplomats and consuls abroad shared the same social attitudes and beliefs as officials in London did not mean that the latter were allowed to act in an independent or irresponsible manner. In general, the low esteem accorded to Latin American postings reflected itself in a low esteem for the abilities of the men serving in those regions. These officials were bound by their standing instructions and were required to report their actions in regular dispatches to London. No official was left in any doubt that decisions were made solely by his superiors at the Foreign Office.

On the other hand, the official serving abroad was still the man on the spot and was therefore allowed a certain discretion to act independently should the need arise.[62] On occasion this was done with skill and the results were pleasing to the Foreign Office. For his work in Lima during the closing period of the War of the Pacific, Alfred St. John was commended for acting "very well."[63] During the Chilean revolution of 1891, the "great discretion" of the British minister, John Kennedy, was praised by his superiors in London.[64] Certain other appointments did not inspire the same confidence. The repeated requests from one minister in Central America for additional funds to make a trip to Nicaragua were treated with the utmost suspicion.[65] The British chargé at Bogotá, Robert Bunch, was described by a Foreign Office official as "a man spoilt by being raised beyond his proper sphere, and consequently too much impressed with the sense of his own dignity."[66]

Another influence on British policy was the action of Latin American diplomats, both in Latin America and, on occasion, in Britain. Most Latin American nations maintained diplomatic representatives in London and thus facilitated the transaction of business there as much as in Latin America. The Foreign Office was, however, very careful in its dealings with these diplomats because of their frequent association with European capitalists and their basically propagandistic purposes. The persistent attempts of Tomás de Mosquera to persuade Britain to guarantee Colombian sovereignty over the isthmus of Panama provided one example. In this case, the British chargé at Bogotá was warned to beware of the "troublesome" president of Colombia.[67] During the War of the Pacific both the Peruvian and the Chilean ministers in London sought to influence the Foreign Office by their respective propaganda. The Foreign Office maintained its cautious and legalistic attitude and took particular care to avoid the recurrence of another *Alabama* dispute by preventing the departure of British-built warships already ordered by the Peruvian and Chilean governments.[68]

Diplomacy and Economics

British official indifference toward and even ignorance of political events in Latin America was sustained by the belief that these events had virtually no impact on the state of European politics and rivalries. But what could not be so easily ignored or neglected was the massive amount of British economic involvement in Latin America. The public speeches and statements of British diplomats frequently stressed that commerce was the basis of British greatness, but the traditional aristocratic attitude of the Foreign Office and its disdain of commercial work resulted in a low priority for such interests. Commercial policy was further complicated by the fact that it was not exclusively the province of the Foreign Office. The negotiation of commercial treaties was the responsibility of the Foreign Office, but their drafting was done by the Board of Trade. The creation of a new Commercial Department within the Foreign Office in 1865 was intended to remedy this, but its function soon degenerated into the receipt and dispatch of consular reports on commercial conditions to the Board of Trade. The potential for conflict between executive and advisory services presented an obvious barrier to administrative efficiency.[69]

Despite the administrative defects and their own personal disdain of commercial work, Foreign Office officials took up the myriad commercial and consular problems that constantly arose from Latin American affairs with seriousness and responsibility.[70] While the Foreign Office paid scrupulous attention to all British claims, this did not imply automatic official intervention on the claimants' behalf. Officials insisted that they first seek redress of their grievances in the local courts, and only when this had been denied was the matter likely to be taken up formally by the Foreign Office. This cautious and legalistic attitude derived from the fact that the British government had played no direct role in the formation of these economic ventures, nor was it regarded as a function of government to promote them.[71] Moreover, official involvement on behalf of economic interests always carried the risk of weakening diplomatic influence by compromising the integrity of the foreign service. On the other hand, the Foreign Office could not ignore cases of injustice to British citizens. The responsibility of providing protection for British citizens and their property abroad was accepted, but a distinction was drawn between a policy of promotion and one of protection. The Foreign Office played no part in the promotion of British contracts and concessions in Latin America, but once they had been established it could not disregard its responsibility to protect them.[72]

Examples drawn from Brazil during the late 1880s illustrate the response of, and the difficulties faced by, the Foreign Office in the settlement of claims. Three major claims were involved. First, the cancellation of a railway concession held by Messrs. Waring; second, the cancellation of a water drainage contract held by Joseph Hancox; and third, the imposition of increased customs duties upon the goods of Bowman's Heirs. In each case the Foreign Office was initially satisfied that a denial of justice had occurred. The Waring claim was considered "a serious act of injustice," and the British minister at Rio was instructed to press for the payment of compensation "without further delay." The British representative carried out his instructions in a rather zealous manner and when his "somewhat forcible language" was publicly revealed in Brazil, an anti-British demonstration resulted. Nevertheless, the vote to pay compensation passed the Brazilian Senate by three votes. "How awkward would have been our position," remarked a British official, "if two of these votes had been the other way."[73]

The constraints upon British policy were demonstrated by the initial Foreign Office attitude to the Hancox claim. It was decided that Hancox had not exhausted all the legal remedies available to him in Brazil and so, asserted Davidson, the Foreign Office legal adviser, "we have no right, according to the ordinary diplomatic usage to press his claim officially upon the Government of Brazil," since such action would imply that the Brazilian courts were "corrupt and impotent." Official protest was therefore ruled out although it was hoped that some means might be found of privately bringing "strong pressure" upon the Brazilian government.[74] The assistant undersecretary, Philip Currie, later defended what appeared to be official indifference in this matter by pointing out that "when once these cases are taken up by Her Majesty's Government nothing short of war is likely to settle them."[75]

The Hancox claim has some bearing upon the question of "influence" in British policy because Hancox's son-in-law was William Haggard, a former British secretary of the legation at Rio. Haggard had since left the diplomatic service, but he pursued his father-in-law's claim with vigor. Nevertheless, his suggestion that "extreme measures" were necessary was not taken up by his former colleagues.[76] There was a certain sympathy for Hancox's claim, but officials seemed relieved when he was able to enlist the support of the Rothschilds. "I don't think it is desirable," minuted Davidson, "that we should interfere more than we can help while Haggard is negotiating privately for a settlement. And moreover I do not think such interference on our part would advance his own private negotiations."[77]

In the case involving Bowman's Heirs, it appeared that they had been illegally fined £3,000. Pauncefote advocated unofficial action in support of the claim. But the question involved the interpretation of a Brazilian ministerial decree and the foreign secretary, Lord Salisbury, later urged caution, arguing that "the general doctrine that a foreign state has a right to compensation if its nationals are injured by a blunder in the drafting of a law—would carry us very far."[78] The claim was, however, considered to be "deserving of great sympathy," and the British minister at Rio was instructed to apply unofficial pressure on the Brazilian government to recognize its validity. The matter was also complicated by the activities of the company's London agent, Ghewy, who pushed the claim in a manner that Davidson regarded as "impolitic in his own interests."[79] Ghewy eventually succeeded in raising the issue in Parliament and secured a government statement of support for his claim.[80]

British policy was, no doubt, restrained by traditional inertia and also by an inbuilt suspicion that claims were rarely as strong as they appeared on first reflection. Reports of certain disparities in the figures presented by Hancox prompted Sanderson to advise care in pressing the claim, and the British minister at Rio later confirmed that the claim had always been "a weak one."[81] In the case of Bowman's Heirs, the most extreme proposal advocated was that the Brazilian government might be reminded as a "dernier resort" that adverse publicity would "injuriously affect" the standing of Brazilian credit in the London money market.[82] When it was learnt that the goods of Bowman's Heirs had not in fact been illegally taxed by the Brazilian government, the Foreign Office withdrew its support. "I do not think," minuted Sanderson, "that Bowman's Heirs have got any real case against the Govt. or that they have suffered much hardship."[83] The Foreign Office now advised the company to appeal *ad misericordiam* to the Brazilian government and to accept arbitration if granted. "It may be worth the while of the Brazilian Government," suggested Davidson, "to get rid of a troublesome claim by paying a moderate sum without prejudice and as an act of grace."[84]

In respect to the claims by Hancox and by Bowman's Heirs, official action was thus not undertaken. But the Foreign Office had not neglected its responsibility to protect British interests in Latin America. In the Brazilian examples this responsibility took on a decided sympathy for the British claimants although a certain amount of official caution was always in evidence. The issues involved legal investigations and counsel and inevitably the claims were long drawn out. But force was never considered to expedite matters and, as some of the facts emerging from the Brazilian claims demonstrated, the policy of caution and moderation was fully vindicated. Above all, the Foreign Office recognized that Brazil was a sovereign nation with its own legal system and courts of law. Unless there had been a denial of justice in these courts or an infringement of any existing treaty rights, official action was not justified.

Foreign Office officials were prepared to give support in an unofficial manner to legitimate British claims. But such support was not automatically forthcoming in all cases. It was refused the Western and Brazilian Telegraph company, which complained that the Brazilian government was in breach of contract because it intended to supplement the company's submarine cable by a land one. "Although it is hard upon the Company," argued Davidson, "it is good for the public that the government and the Company should be trying to undersell each other and that in consequence the public should be able to send its telegrams at a cheaper rate."[85]

These examples from Brazil suggest that the Foreign Office took a sympathetic though legalistic approach toward Latin American claims and adopted a policy in keeping with the prevailing concepts of laissez faire and minimal government intervention. The lack of interest shown by the Foreign Office toward Latin America also reflected that of British public opinion in general. "Considering the sums of money which Englishmen have lent to the Spanish American states, and the interest taken in them by commercial men," commented the *Economist*, "it is remarkable how little is known of their daily history." The leading British journal on Latin American affairs noted a few years later: "To the general public the mention of South America suggests the ideas of mere republican turbulence, culminating, as a rule, in conspiracy, bloodshed, and revolution."[86]

British public opinion was not sufficiently aroused by Latin American issues to influence government policy toward that area. The same might be said of the activities of Parliament. Although the formulation and execution of foreign policy was primarily the task of the Foreign Office, foreign secretaries could be called to account by Parliament for their policies. M.P.s could also raise questions in Parliament, and this was regarded as the best means of speeding up government action on a particular issue. In the case of the claim by Bowman's Heirs, their agent had received a favorable reply in the Commons. When the Foreign Office later learned that the claim was extremely doubtful, Davidson drew attention to the difficulty:

> We must be prepared for great indignation on the part of Ghewy and perhaps for some small parliamentary agitation on the subject. This he has threatened us with before and as he succeeded in getting an MP to take the case up and ask a question about it to which at the time a not unencouraging answer was returned, he will

probably now return to the charge on the strength of that answer and of the other assistance given him by Her Majesty's Government and now suddenly withdrawn. But we can't help this under the circs.[87]

Parliament could, therefore, exercise some influence on foreign policy and there were many M.P.s whose opinions on these matters commanded attention and respect. A few M.P.s concentrated on Latin American affairs and regularly raised questions on this subject.[88] There were also extraparliamentary means of exerting pressure upon the government in the form of private conversations, letters,[89] and public petitions. Most active in this respect were the organized lobbies, and foremost among those interested in Latin America were the various chambers of commerce and especially the Corporation of Foreign Bondholders.[90]

A major activity of these lobbies was to inform the Foreign Office and Parliament of the benefits of increased trade with Latin America and to ask for government assistance to promote or, if necessary, to protect this trade. For example, the passage of the McKinley Tariff followed by the conclusion in 1891 of a reciprocity treaty between the United States and Brazil aroused considerable alarm in a number of chambers of commerce. Questions were raised in Parliament and the Foreign Office received petitions from chambers of commerce throughout Britain requesting that the government act to remedy the situation.[91]

The Foreign Office showed concern, but adopted a legalistic approach. Britain had no treaty grounds for protest and therefore could not justify interference in a treaty concluded between two sovereign nations. This response might appear unsatisfactory, but even less sympathy was shown toward the Corporation of Foreign Bondholders despite the massive growth in volume of British investment in Latin America during the late nineteenth century. Since the first Latin American bonds had been floated in London during the 1820s, the Foreign Office had refused to act on requests made by the bondholders for official assistance in the settlement of their claims against Latin American governments.[92] In 1867 Edmund Hammond argued that bondholders were involved in "a hazardous speculation expecting to make their fortunes" and should they fail "they must not expect their Government to quarrel for their redress."[93] A quarter of a century later another permanent undersecretary demonstrated that British policy toward the bondholders had not changed. "Our general line," noted Sanderson, "is to confine ourselves entirely to giving the representatives of the Bondholders such unofficial support and assistance as seems judicious."[94]

On occasion, support took the form of "tied" loans or the giving of government guarantees, but these were exceptions to the general rule and did not involve Latin America.[95] British officials in Latin America were sometimes allowed to act as unofficial agents for the bond-holders,[96] but the Foreign Office chose to involve itself as little as possible in the activities of the latter. In general, officials had little sympathy for speculators who were diverting funds from domestic uses to overseas speculation and were, consequently, accepting higher risks in the hope of higher profits. There was also the traditional disdain toward commercial matters, a feeling possibly reinforced in 1875 by a parliamentary inquiry that reported the exploitation by financiers of the "credulity and cupidity" of investors.[97] More practically, officials clearly understood that the giving of guarantees or intervention to collect debts would result in British policy becoming the instrument of a particular interest, in this case that of the bondholders. Not only would British diplomacy lose the flexibility which it possessed and which Victorian officials considered essential, but bondholders would be encouraged to risk vast sums with impunity, safe in the knowledge that the British government would protect their investments. Such a policy also immeasurably increased the chances of war.[98]

Appeals from bondholders were therefore treated with care by the Foreign Office. The customary procedure was to send them for examination by the law officers of the crown, who invariably recommended that recourse be had first to the local courts. This was sound advice but was tantamount to a refusal of help and demonstrated that British diplomacy was not the servant of the financiers in Latin America.[99] On the other hand, the Foreign Office would support the bondholders in cases that transcended mere financial considerations. After the end of the War of the Pacific it acted to protect British interests in Peru, including those of British bondholders, because the French government was giving official support to its own bondholders and because the question of the Peruvian debt raised important points of international law. British diplomatic intervention was justified on grounds of international legal equity and not as support for particular bondholders' claims against a foreign government.[100]

British policy toward Latin America was thus a combination of indifference, ignorance, and neglect based on the reality that Latin America possessed no political or strategic importance for Britain. But the sheer size of British trade and investments in the area required that the Foreign Office concern itself actively with Latin American commercial and consular business. The policy that emerged was influenced and shaped by the demands of this business although the organizational structure and traditional attitudes of the Foreign Office imposed a cautious and legalistic approach that greatly inhibited positive action. The last two decades of the nineteenth century did, however, witness certain qualitative changes in the nature of British policy toward Latin America and toward the United States too, insofar as that nation became directly involved in the affairs of the Western Hemisphere.

Most visible was the sheer growth of British economic involvement in Latin America, multiplying consular and commercial business. Events in Latin America such as the failure in 1890 of the Baring Brothers merchant bank in Argentina threatened financial ruin not only to individual speculators, but also to prominent merchant banks in the city of London. The resolution of this crisis required the attention of the highest levels of government. This was a demonstration of the increasing interdependence of world finance and a sign that obscure events in such places as Latin America could no longer be treated with the same amount of indifference as previously. The shock when the Venezuela boundary dispute turned into an international crisis in 1895 showed that this lesson had not been fully appreciated by British diplomats.[101]

Within Britain itself there was growing pressure from commercial interests for a more positive government policy to assist what was felt to be Britain's stagnating export trade. It was feared that Britain was losing valuable export markets to the Germans and the Americans, and many of these markets were located in Latin America. This adverse trend was most frequently attributed to the official government support that both Germany and the United States gave to the promotion of their export trade, and it was suggested that the British government should adopt a similar policy.[102]

This was not, however, a unanimously held view. British businessmen were not only believers in laissez faire; they were also doubtful of the practical value of government support in what were primarily commercial matters. James Bryce declared that the Foreign Office fully recognized the need for increased trade and did not "snub" commerce. But he believed that only complications would result from a policy that "pushed English commerce in a grasping and exclusive spirit."[103] The *Times* presented a similar view later in 1886:

> It is not to the Government and its agents that our traders must look for their real support in the struggle against foreign competition. The gigantic fabric of English trade was not built up by Governments; it was built up by the enterprise, the energy, the watchfulness, the self-denial, the laborious efforts of individuals. Moreover, if it was built up by these, by these it must be sustained.[104]

The British share of the Latin America export market was falling in the closing decades of the nineteenth century although British exports to Latin America were increasing in total volume.[105] While no one could deny that international competition was becoming more intense in such markets, there was still a continuing faith in laissez faire and in the abilities of British businessmen to overcome their difficulties. There was also the comforting argument that the foreign challenge was perhaps more imagined than real. As a counter to predictions of gloom there were the heartening comments of men such as the Manchester M.P., Colonel Howard Vincent, who visited South America in 1893 and reported:

> The English have beyond doubt the most influential position in South America. In their hands are the banks, the railways, and the higher commerce. Germans only seriously rival us in detailed commerce and in clerical departments. The French do not appear to interfere with any of the branches of our trade, . . . and as for the Americans, their influence and competition is scarcely appreciable. Englishmen will only have themselves to blame if they are deprived of the advantageous position they have held so long and still occupy, and it will not be so easy to defeat them as some writers seem to imagine.[106]

But Colonel Vincent was not totally complacent and he did recommend more positive action from British officials in Latin America to assist British trade. The Foreign Office continued to resist such suggestions on the grounds that government policy should not favor particular commercial groups at the expense of others. This objection did not apply to more general forms of assistance, and the closing years of the nineteenth century were marked by a systematic effort to provide the public with more accurate and up-to-date business information drawn from the commercial and consular dispatches.[107]

The international pressures that required the British government and the Foreign Office to take more note of commercial developments applied also to political matters. The attention of British diplomacy remained preoccupied with events in Europe, where the rise of Germany resulted in new alliances and an arms race that increased Britain's strategic vulnerability. By requiring an increased allocation of military resources in the North Sea and the Mediterranean, the new strategic balance further reduced Britain's already limited capability for military action in Latin American waters. As long as there was no major military threat to Britain in the Western Hemisphere, however, this weakness and deficiency was not clearly apparent to other nations.

But a threat was materializing, and it took a political and economic rather than an overtly military form. It derived from the growing economic power of the United States combined with a political determination among many American political leaders that the United States should assert itself much more actively in events that directly affected the Western Hemisphere. While Foreign Office officials discounted the extent of the threat to well-established British economic interests in Latin America, they could not ignore its political and military implications. Conscious of Britain's increasing vulnerability in Europe and the logistical imperatives of the Western Hemisphere, British diplomats wanted, above all, to maintain friendly relations with the United States. This was illustrated by Britain's conciliatory policy toward the isthmian canal, the reciprocity treaties, the Brazilian naval revolt, the Mosquito Reservation, and, ultimately, the Venezuela boundary dispute.

The result was increased British diplomatic friendship with the United States and the creation of a peaceful and stable environment in the Western Hemisphere to the benefit of British trade and investment. This was, however, achieved at the cost of recognizing the political preeminence of the United States in the Western Hemisphere, thereby undermining the diplomatic status quo in that part of the world. This trend toward differential change in power relationships had been occurring throughout the late nineteenth century. It had been sustained by Britain's basic lack of political interest in Latin America and had been accelerated by the rapid rise in economic and military power of the United States.[108] British diplomatic prestige and influence in Latin America had been based on economic power combined with the display rather than the direct exercise of military power. The United States was a newcomer to world power and was inclined to be much more assertive and more directly involved in Latin American affairs than Britain had ever been. The scene was thus set for the troubled United States–Latin American relations of the twentieth century. The situation was not one that greatly troubled Victorian Foreign Office officials. Their function was to conduct policy on a day-to-day basis, and the assumption by the United States of responsibility for the behavior of the Latin American states was considered to be to Britain's benefit. The concentration on European affairs and the inbuilt conservatism and hierarchical structure of the Foreign Office meant that officials had neither the will, the need, or, perhaps, even the energy to try to understand the full significance of what was happening in the Western Hemisphere. It was for later generations of Foreign Office officials to experience and grapple with the implications of the changes.

//2//

United States Policy Toward Latin America

Historians might debate the question of to what extent the United States was a "world" or a "great" power in the nineteenth century,[1] but in the system of states located in the Western Hemisphere the "great power" status of the United States has been unquestioned. Vast territorial and natural resources, an expanding and vigorous population, and a stable political and economic system propelled the "colossus of the north" into a position of prestige and leadership within the Western Hemisphere. Nor did the nations of Latin America possess the means to challenge or reverse this development.[2] For most of the nineteenth century these nations lacked political stability and economic unity so that, in terms of relative power, they were dwarfed by their northern neighbor. The geopolitical facts were clear: The United States was a massive and therefore potentially dominant power in a system of weak states.

The most overt challenge to American predominance came from the European powers who attempted to penetrate the system. The Latin American wars of independence had not inaugurated a new era of "America for Americans." They marked a rejection of European political control but not of continued European economic, social, and cultural influence. During the nineteenth century Britain in particular came to exercise considerable economic influence and prestige throughout the hemisphere. Whatever its motive or extent, European penetration was a reality and was regarded as a permanent challenge, if not a threat to the United States itself, by a succession of nineteenth-century presidents and secretaries of state. The long saga of Anglo-American rivalry in Latin America and the evolution of the Monroe Doctrine reflected this.[3] But American confidence in ultimate victory was unshakeable. "The time is not probably far distant," affirmed President Grant in 1870, "when, in the natural course of events, the European political connection with this continent will cease."[4] The issue appeared to be resolved in 1895–1896 when the political preeminence of the United States in the Western Hemisphere was officially acknowledged by Britain and, by implication, the rest of Europe too. The reaction of the Cleveland administration to the Venezuela boundary dispute was therefore much more than a simple response to perceived British aggression. It reflected the long-held consciousness of American hemispheric power brought to the surface by the interaction of diplomatic events with the inherently expansionist nature of American society itself.[5]

The American Diplomatic Tradition and Latin America

The development of the United States from a nation "born in revolution" to a nation of continental extent in the mid–nineteenth century was accompanied by a grass-roots sense of mission and destiny. Diplomatic strictures and warnings were issued against European meddling in the Americas while large areas of territory were annexed from the Indians and the Mexicans under the justification of "manifest destiny."[6] Trade and economic development were also part of this process. Economic expansionism, characterized by large-scale production and the creation of vast markets both at home and abroad, was not only seen as a necessary ingredient of America's success, but also as the fulfillment of American destiny. "The nation that draws most materials and provision from the earth, and fabricates the most, and sells the most of productions and fabrics to foreign nations," asserted William H. Seward in 1853, "must be, and will be, the great power of the earth."[7] Four decades later, at the 1890 Washington conference of American states, John B. Henderson declared that the United States had entered its third stage of national growth. "The same restless energy, the same enterprise, and the same inventive genius which gave success to agriculture and manufactures," he predicted, "will mark the development of commerce."[8]

Allied with this mood of economic determinism was the similarly powerful and pervasive sense of ideological commitment to the ideals of the American Revolution. The Declaration of Independence had thundered a worldwide message that "all men are created equal" and the advancement of democracy throughout the world became a characteristic feature of the rhetoric of American diplomacy. This was initially neither a purely utopian nor an idealistic objective, for the early years of the American republic were a precarious period in which the survival of democracy and of American independence were regarded as inextricably linked. This sense of mission was sustained and reinforced within the Western Hemisphere by the outbreak of movements for independence in Latin America during the first quarter of the nineteenth century.

Perceived strategic, economic, and ideological needs resulted, therefore, in an expansionist, assertive, and frequently arrogant American foreign policy. Geopolitical factors facilitated its most direct and effective exercise within the Western Hemisphere. Moreover, it was also a policy that could be readily justified and rationalized. "Comprehensive national policy," declared President Johnson in 1868, "would seem to sanction the acquisition and incorporation into our Federal Union of the several adjacent and insular communities."[9] In fact, American national security was conceived not just in terms of the continental United States but of the whole of the Western Hemisphere. "It is impossible," President Monroe warned Europe in 1823, "that the allied powers should extend their political system to any portion of either continent without endangering our peace and happiness."[10] In 1895 Secretary of State Olney reminded European statesmen that Americans were still acutely aware of "the disastrous consequences to the United States" should they allow European aggression in Latin America.[11] The Monroe Doctrine thus symbolized the concept of a separate hemispheric system of nations whose security and welfare were protected and promoted by the United States.

The strategic argument was also supported by the perceived economic and ideological requirements. During the wars for Latin American independence Americans had formed a profitable trading relationship with Latin America, but this gradually fell into neglect. The United States continued to import large quantities of sugar and coffee from its southern neighbors, and during the period from 1865 to 1895 total imports from Latin America averaged $180 million a year, amounting to about 25 percent of all imports into the United States. American exports to Latin America for the same period, however, averaged only $75 million annually, little more than 10 percent of total American exports.[12] This imbalance of trade and the imperative need to correct it became a prominent feature of the speeches of the Republican leader, James G. Blaine. A similar theme was expressed by many Democrats. In one message to Congress, President Cleveland stressed that Latin America offered "natural markets" that demanded "special and considerate treatment."[13]

Increased trade with Latin America not only brought financial profit; it also promoted the advance of democracy. The result was greater political stability so that the Western Hemisphere became more secure and less vulnerable and tempting to foreign interference. Even more satisfying to Americans was the sense of both assisting and leading their Latin American "sisters" from the shackles of Old World imperialism to the freedom of New World democracy, as exemplified by the United States. Olney informed the British government of this in 1895: "The people of the United States have a vital interest in the cause of popular self-government. They have secured the right for themselves and their posterity at the cost of infinite blood and treasure. . . . They believe it to be for the healing of all nations, and that civilization must either advance or retrograde accordingly as its supremacy is extended or curtailed.''[14]

Some thirty years earlier another secretary of state had issued similar reminders to the governments of France and Spain to desist from their intervention in the affairs of the New World. Seward's words were not challenged, and the collapse of the European adventures reflected a triumph for American diplomacy. Nor did any European nation lodge a formal protest against President Grant's addition to the Monroe Doctrine in 1870. ''I now deem it proper,'' he informed Congress, ''to assert the equally important principle that hereafter no territory on this continent shall be regarded as subject of transfer to a European power.''[15] In European eyes such statements appeared brash and self-righteous, but they were nonetheless worthy of respect. In 1857 the British foreign secretary, Lord Palmerston, explained why: ''These Yankees are most disagreeable Fellows to have to do with about any American question: They are on the Spot, strong, deeply interested in the matter, totally unscrupulous and dishonest and determined somehow to carry their Point.''[16]

Latin American diplomats also fully appreciated the geopolitical reality of American economic and military power. In particular, the annexation of Mexican territory and the activities of American filibusterers in Central America aroused acute alarm and led to mid-nineteenth-century Latin American protests and conferences to discuss defense against American aggression. Examples of such aggression were, however, limited both in location and duration. They were confined to Central America and the Caribbean islands; South American countries were in fact relatively immune from direct American military action throughout the whole of the nineteenth century.[17] On the other hand, despite their fear of the United States, a number of Latin American nations sometimes encouraged American diplomatic interference in their affairs by seeking assistance from Washington, either to counter European imperialism or, perhaps more accurately, to promote their own national interests. For example, Venezuela assiduously cultivated good relations with the United States as a means of resolving its boundary dispute with Britain. Similarly, representatives of Central American governments lobbied Washington vigorously for support in their respective boundary quarrels with neighboring states; this tactic was particularly influential when couched in terms of defense against alleged European intrigues.

Positive diplomatic support was often forthcoming, but not because American diplomats were easily manipulated. An active policy was attractive on grounds of hemispheric defense, protection of republican and democratic institutions, and, in the background, the prospect of material advantages to be gained from a country grateful for American assistance. Moreover, such a policy fully accorded with and helped to fulfill the American sense of destiny in which the United States would both protect and lead all the nations of the Western Hemisphere. The traditional American suspicion of and hostility toward Old World conspiracies gave added impetus to the policy of asserting American preeminence in the Western Hemisphere at the expense of Europe.[18]

This development was not completely to the benefit of the Latin American nations. The reduction of European influence simply reaffirmed and reinforced the trend toward their political and economic subordination to the dictates of the United States. An increase in Yankeephobia accompanied this development, for American diplomats appeared to pay little attention to Latin American desires or sensitivities. For example, Harrison's response to the *Baltimore*[19] incident and Gresham's instructions during the Brazilian naval revolt of 1893–1894 firmly placed their interpretation of American rights above those of the Latin American countries. In part, this was the consequence of the American political system, which rendered American foreign policy subject to so many conflicting domestic pressures. It was also a reflection of America's sense of cultural superiority and prejudice toward its Latin neighbors. The *Nation* described the Latin American delegates to the Washington conference as "travelled gentlemen," but a scholarly pamphlet critical of the reciprocity policy emphasized the paucity of the Latin American market, which was based upon "a race of which the bulk is composed of a low caste and rather ignorant half-savage type."[20] While few American politicians would subscribe openly to such racialist views, the travails of their Latin American colleagues were greeted with a sympathy that often bordered on contempt. Latin Americans were "incapable of preserving order and stability among themselves," declared Congressman James Blount of Georgia. "Bring them into connection with us, with all these troublesome questions, and the equipoise of our institutions which we enjoy and preserve to-day by reason of the splendid character of our population, will be endangered."[21]

Latin American weakness and instability encouraged and reinforced this great power mentality. Moreover, jealous of its freedom of maneuver in foreign policy and acutely suspicious of Europe, the United States stressed a unilateral diplomatic role. This manifested itself not only in diplomatic noncooperation with Europe, but in a failure to consult Latin American nations in policy decisions. The Western Hemisphere idea proclaimed a New World that contained new values and new hope for humanity, but however sincerely American diplomats might believe this, their actions all too often belied this elevated sentiment.[22] President Monroe did not seek the agreement of the Latin American states when he delivered his message in 1823. Nor did Grant discuss his 1870 declaration prohibiting the transfer of Latin American territory or Hayes his canal message with those countries who might be vitally affected by the consequences. As long as American diplomacy emphasized words rather than action, the threat of United States preeminence in the Western Hemisphere might be disregarded by European and Latin American nations alike. On occasion, a proud and powerful nation such as Chile could even resolutely resist American diplomatic pressure, but the implications for Latin America were clear even though not officially stated until 1895, when Olney ominously proclaimed: "To-day the United States is practically sovereign on this continent, and its fiat is law upon the subjects to which it confines its interposition."[23] Resounding words, perhaps, but the Cleveland administration appeared ready to back them up with force if necessary. The Monroe Doctrine was to be "something more than a mere declaration of principles."[24]

The Constraints Upon Diplomacy

The style of nineteenth-century American diplomacy was unilateral, ambitious, and moralistic; within the context of the Western Hemisphere it was also assertive and, on occasion, forceful. But when that style is equated with substance, American diplomatic achievement fell short of its aspirations. Nor is this surprising, for American foreign policy, both in its formulation and execution, had to withstand the searching and frequently obstructive requirements of a democratic and open society. It also had to contend with the inherent difficulty faced by all diplomats of attempting to influence situations outside their own nation's area of control and authority. This constraint upon policy was not always fully appreciated by politicians based in Washington.

Nevertheless, the claim of the United States to political preeminence in the Western Hemisphere was never openly disputed. Infringements of the Monroe Doctrine occurred before the Civil War but not afterward. The United States emerged from its internal conflict with increased military power and a renewed, although temporary, sense of hemispheric mission. But the assumption of diplomatic conflict between the United States and Europe over Latin America was illusory. Despite frequent American alarm there was little substance to the allegations of European political intrigues and territorial ambitions in the Western Hemisphere. European governments adopted conciliatory policies toward the United States and showed a distinct aversion to provoking clashes with that nation. Their strategic priorities lay primarily in Europe and, although there was great interest in areas of colonial rivalry outside Europe, this did not extend to the Western Hemisphere. From the occupation of Buenos Aires in 1806 to the Mexican and Pacific coast adventures of the 1860s, European armed interventions in Latin America had proved not only costly but also futile and diplomatically humiliating. Regardless of the many rumors to the contrary, similar expeditions were not repeated in the late nineteenth century.

The major concern of the European powers in Latin America was not territorial aggrandizement, but the promotion of their trade and investment. Consequently, the primary European objective complemented that of the United States and also of the dominant political elites of Latin America itself in that they all sought political stability and order as the means of facilitating economic development and the creation of wealth. The relative political stability and economic achievement of Latin America in the late nineteenth century[25] testified to the lack of need for outside intervention.

Europe and the United States were therefore economic rather than political rivals in Latin America. Moreover, the policy of American expansionism in Latin America did not seriously undermine European economic interests. In 1870 Secretary of State Fish had deplored the fact that Latin Americans purchased twice as much from Britain as they did from the United States.[26] Despite the efforts of merchants and expansionist-minded politicians in the meantime, twenty-five years later a congressional report still bemoaned the small share that Americans possessed of the Latin American import trade in contrast to that held by the British.[27] In fact, the economic rivalry for the Latin American market during the last quarter of the nineteenth century was at its most intense among European exporters; the American share of the trade was rising but remained relatively small. Diplomacy proved an inadequate substitute for the economic enterprise of the individual merchant. "So long as Europe comes here with its millions and Americans come here with itinerating commissions," summed up the *Buenos Ayres Herald,* "the business supremacy of Europe in this country will be seen."[28]

American diplomacy also had little direct influence over the actions of the Latin American states themselves. While the French and Spanish governments heeded Seward's warnings, the members of the Triple Alliance ignored American efforts to mediate their conflict with Paraguay. Despite the unequivocally hostile attitude of Washington, the Colombian government allowed the de Lesseps canal project to proceed. Most notably, Chile assumed a defiant and independent attitude toward the United States during the War of the Pacific. This tradition of resistance to American pretensions was succinctly expressed by Sáenz Peña at the Washington conference in 1890 when he countered the slogan of "America for the Americans" with the plea of "let America be for humanity."[29]

On the other hand, the Latin American nations, with the sole exception of the Dominican Republic, did not refuse to attend the Washington conference. Quesada, the Argentine minister in Washington, informed the British chargé that though he personally disapproved of the conference there would be "some difficulty" in declining an invitation "when made by the United States Government."[30] For similar reasons a number of Latin American nations later complied with the forceful reciprocity policy pursued by the Harrison administration. Moreover, in sharp contrast to its attitude of ten years previously, Chile retreated in the face of American threats during the *Baltimore* incident of 1891. The course of the Brazilian naval revolt and of Nicaraguan designs upon the Mosquito Reservation were also considerably influenced by American naval and political action during 1894. The momentum provided by these events presented a suitable context for Olney's ringing declarations of 1895.

The active assertion of American political preeminence in the Western Hemisphere was thus more apparent at the close of the nineteenth century. This did not, however, mean that the basic objectives of American diplomacy had altered. In the 1860s Seward sought hemispheric peace and security, the expansion of American trade, and the preservation of democratic institutions. The expansionists of the 1890s pursued similar goals, as did Fish and Evarts, the men at the helm of American foreign policy during the 1870s. The Grant administration declared the "no-transfer" resolution to the Monroe Doctrine and attempted to annex the Dominican Republic. Under Hayes the world was informed of prior American rights in the isthmian region, and a presidential message to Congress in 1880 stressed the "unrelaxed" efforts of the State Department to increase American trade.[31] The aims of American diplomacy toward Latin America during the 1860s and 1870s were thus not so different from those of the 1890s.

Although successive administrations from Johnson to Arthur pursued outwardly expansionist goals in the Western Hemisphere, a variety of internal and external reasons determined that these goals were not realized. For example, Latin America enjoyed relative peace and calm throughout this period. After the end of the War of the Triple Alliance in 1870 there was no major military upheaval until the outbreak of the War of the Pacific in 1879.[32] There was therefore little reason for American diplomatic involvement in Latin American affairs. Nor was the calm disturbed by external threat. European powers deferred to American political preeminence in the Western Hemisphere, a belief confirmed and reinforced by the diplomatic successes of Seward. This comfortable situation was not visibly challenged until the de Lesseps canal project of 1879. Even then, both de Lesseps and his government allayed American fears and sensitivities by strenuously disavowing any official partici- pation by the French government in the venture.

Even if a forceful hemispheric policy had been necessary, it would have been difficult to implement before the late 1880s. In part this was a consequence of geographical and logistical factors. The Latin American nations were regarded as neighbors of the United States, but in terms of actual distance and especially of steamship communications, most of those nations were closer to Europe. Even without these difficulties of distance and delays in communications, the instruments of American foreign policy were deficient in both quantity and quality. In particular, effective military power was lacking for much of the late nineteenth century. The huge Civil War army and naval establishment was soon in decline after 1865. The size of the army was severely limited while congressional parsimony and an obstinately traditional naval attitude that preferred sail power to steam power even into the 1880s resulted in a navy that was ridiculed as "an alphabet of floating washtubs."[33]

The presence of a powerful American naval force was a prominent feature of the dispute between Chile and Spain in 1866, but a similar demonstration of American naval force could not be repeated in South American waters until the 1890s.[34] Even in the much more strategically sensitive area of the Caribbean, American naval action after the mid- 1860s was limited to "showing the flag" and to surveys and explorations of potential canal routes and naval harbors. For much of the nineteenth century naval thinking was based on a dual strategy of commerce raiding and passive coastal defense. Consequently, for much of the late nine- teenth century the United States Navy lacked the capability to serve as an effective instrument of American hemispheric diplomacy.[35]

Nor was American policy always ably served by its foreign service establishment. Like the armed services, the State Department suffered from congressional parsimony and neglect. At each congressional ses- sion the debate on the diplomatic and consular appropriation bill aroused widespread criticism of the foreign service and resulted in frequent demands for retrenchment of expenditure. "It is the same old subject," remarked Congressman William Robinson of New York in 1885, "of taxing the toilers at home to enable the fops and dandies of our diplomacy to make fools of themselves and of us abroad."[36] This atti- tude had strong support because the American democratic tradition resisted both the concept of and the need for a professional and selective foreign service fashioned on European lines.[37] A long-serving official such as Alvey A. Adee[38] provided much-needed expertise and con- tinuity in the technical matters of diplomacy, but in general State

Department officials lacked diplomatic experience and security of tenure. "It is a well-known fact," alleged William E. Curtis, "that the diplomatic service of the United States is small in numbers and receives less compensation than that of any other of the great nations of the world."[39]

Moreover, the State Department was highly vulnerable to the vicissitudes of the American political system since appointments to the foreign service were an essential and integral part of the spoils system. The selection by the president of his secretary of state was a maneuver dominated by political and not diplomatic considerations; the same procedure applied to the appointment of even the most minor consular official to serve abroad. Each new administration was inundated with pleas and entreaties for political office. Four hundred men a day personally waited upon Hamilton Fish for this purpose during his first few weeks as secretary of state in 1869.[40] The selection of officials was therefore dictated not so much by questions of merit but by prevailing political considerations. "At present, as in the past," complained one critic in 1889, "it cannot be said that consuls are selected by our government with sole or, in very many instances, with prevailing reference to their fitness to fill their offices efficiently."[41]

Although the rhetoric of American diplomacy attached great significance to Latin American affairs, this did not apply in practical terms to the diplomatic and consular officials resident there. Such posts were referred to as "the Botany Bay of broken-down American politicians."[42] Length of office was uncertain and was determined by political favor and the life of the administration that had made the original appointment. Nor were the offices particularly remunerative or prestigious, and some appointments in Latin America might be described as positively hazardous. Congressman Hitt pointed out in 1892 that eight American consuls had died at Colón during the preceding twenty-five years.[43] Working conditions in Latin America were uniformly bad. The offices were inadequately furnished and legations tended to be permanently short-staffed. "The watchword of the American is economy," complained a former minister to Chile. "He has no such staff as the European and even pays a translator out of his own funds."[44] Most American officials were further handicapped by their inability to speak or understand Spanish. When John W. Foster was offered the Mexican mission in 1872 he confessed his inexperience in diplomacy and his lack of foreign languages, but he related that his patron, Senator Morton of Indiana, "only smiled at my hesitation, reasserted his confidence in my ability, and said I was much better fitted than most of those who were appointed to our diplomatic service."[45]

For Foster the appointment marked the beginning of a distinguished diplomatic career. For other men, the lack of experience and skill, and sometimes of good moral character, resulted all too often in social isolation, frustration, inefficient work, and, on occasion, diplomatic blunders. For example, the inexperience of Judson Kilpatrick contributed to the humiliation of American diplomacy in Chile in 1866. A similar consequence arose from the activities of Stephen Hurlbut, who had acquired a reputation for "rough and ready diplomacy" during his service as minister to Colombia in the early 1870s.[46] But as a friend of Grant and a campaign manager for Blaine he was duly rewarded with a return to diplomatic duty as minister to Peru in 1881. His partisan attitude combined with the use of his official position to promote his own private business enterprises reflected little credit upon American policy. Another official with a dubious sense of ethics was William L. Scruggs. Scruggs had earned a high reputation as minister to Colombia, but after moving to Venezuela he was dismissed from the foreign service in 1892 for bribing the Venezuelan president. Ernest Dichman, who also served in Colombia, left the State Department for other reasons. He was described as "full of extraordinary and extravagant projects" and his blustering style of diplomacy provoked the Colombian government into demanding his recall to the United States.[47]

Tactlessness and bluster was not confined to a few isolated foreign service officials. Blaine reprimanded Hurlbut for his unethical activities in Peru, but both minister and secretary of state thought very much alike on the broad objectives of American policy. "I, myself," proclaimed Hurlbut in 1881, "am a profound believer in the right and duty of the United States, to control the political questions of this continent, to the exclusion of any and all European dictation."[48] These views were echoed by many other officials from Kilpatrick in the 1860s to Egan in the 1890s and accurately mirrored the expansionist concept that Americans held of their nation's role in the Western Hemisphere. On the other hand, the inadequate pay, low prestige, and poor working conditions of the American foreign service reflected the practical aspect of American diplomacy in which political and economic constraints undermined the effective implementation of policy.

The conduct of American foreign policy could not be divorced from domestic political considerations. The Constitution made the distinction between executive, legislative, and judicial powers, but the jurisdictions were overlapping and subject to continual debate and controversy. This was especially characteristic of the period immediately after the Civil War, when President Johnson and the radical Republicans battled over whether it was the executive or the legislature who initiated policy. The impeachment proceedings against Johnson and the weak personality of his successor signified and made possible the temporary ascendancy of the legislature in domestic affairs. The nature of diplomacy, with its requirement of central control and a certain degree of secrecy, gave the executive a wider latitude for maneuver and control than in domestic policy, but not completely so. Congress had, after all, its committees on foreign affairs and foreign relations in the House and Senate respectively. These committees might support administration policy, but they could also oppose it, as Bayard noted in 1888. After three years as secretary of state he remarked that "no suggestion of comity or cooperation has come to me from the Foreign Relations Committee of the Senate."[49]

American foreign policy was also formulated and debated in much more open and public conditions than in Europe. For example, diplomatic papers were frequently leaked to Congress or the press. Secretary of State Frelinghuysen arranged the publication of much of the diplomatic correspondence on the War of the Pacific in order to discredit Blaine, but Frelinghuysen himself was embarrassed in similar fashion when the *New York Tribune* published his "secret" treaty with Nicaragua in December 1884.[50] Moreover, congressional involvement in the foreign policy process was necessary, if not vital, because Congress had the final say in such decisive matters as appropriations and the ratification of treaties. The failure of the Arthur-Frelinghuysen treaties in 1885 prompted the young political scientist Woodrow Wilson to write:

> We can readily believe that foreign governments are often greatly confounded by the discovery that in dealing with our federal administration they have been dealing only with titled individuals, not with governmental authorities; that the President or Secretary of State may exert a powerful lobby influence upon the Senate, but can hardly do more than that to secure a ratification of their engagements.[51]

A similar constraint upon foreign policy was the frequent denial by the House of adequate appropriations for the foreign service. This might have been electorally popular, but at times it resulted in diplomatic difficulties. For example, financial retrenchment in 1876 brought about the temporary closure of three American legations in Latin America, one of which was in Colombia. This coincided with the beginning of an important period of canal diplomacy in which French influence appeared to take advantage of American diplomatic absence from Bogotá.

Conflict between executive and legislature hindered the development of a consistent and effective foreign policy. This did not, however, imply that foreign policy issues were clearly perceived or understood. There was in fact little consensus on these issues within either major political party. Republican leaders often appeared to be bitterly divided. Both Seward's and Grant's schemes for territorial annexation provoked intraparty disputes and Blaine's advocacy of a vigorous Latin American policy was criticized more on grounds of partisan party politics than on its particular merits or demerits. Many Republicans also found the policy of commercial reciprocity hard to reconcile with their avowed adherence to the doctrine of protection and opposition to tariff tinkering.

Even if the Republicans had agreed on foreign policy matters, the reemergence of the Democratic party as a national political force during the 1870s deprived them of working majorities in Congress. Up to 1877 the Republicans controlled both houses of Congress and the presidency. After that date such control was rare and was held only for short periods until the presidency of McKinley. The consequences of this electoral stalemate were uncertainty and, on occasion, paralysis in both domestic and foreign policy. In the House, Democratic congressmen were persistent critics of Republican proposals to increase naval or foreign service appropriations, while the votes of Democratic senators did much to defeat the expansionist policy of the Arthur administration.

Political factors placed powerful constraints upon the exercise of nineteenth-century American diplomacy, but this was only part of the explanation for the failure to implement expansionist goals in the Western Hemisphere. Although American society subscribed enthusiastically to the Monroe Doctrine, manifest destiny, and the sense of mission, there was clearly never enough grass-roots support for an expansionist policy that would offset or even overcome the objective realities that made the exercise of foreign policy so difficult and so uncertain. With American hemispheric preeminence so apparently secure and with the internal preoccupations of industrialization and westward expansion before them, Americans manifested an attitude of general indifference toward foreign affairs from 1865 to the late 1890s. They were inherently expansive in attitude, but they also linked the concept of an active foreign policy with the Old World practices that they had so decisively repudiated as a nation. The United States had no need of large standing armies and navies or professional foreign offices and denounced the imperialist and colonial policies pursued by European powers. Washington and Jefferson had warned against "entangling alliances" and had thereby established a tradition of American isolationism in foreign affairs. The decisions taken to reject the acquisitions proposed by Seward and Grant signified that this tradition remained in the ascendancy during the 1860s and 1870s.

The geopolitical realities of power and the disinclination of European nations to challenge that power posited the United States as the preeminent political power in the Western Hemisphere. The rhetoric of

American expansionism and, on occasion, its aggressive and actual assertion, reinforced this position, but in general throughout the two decades following the Civil War the United States pursued an ineffective and inconsistent policy that belied its hemispheric status and prestige. In such circumstances Europeans could go about their business in Latin America and the Latin American governments could conduct their own affairs with little fear of hindrance or interference from the United States. This situation began, however, to change from the late 1870s onward.

The Rise to Preeminence

American opinion had been apathetic toward foreign affairs during the 1870s, but events after 1879 contributed to an increasing awareness of the rest of the world and, in particular, of Latin America. Domestic political and economic considerations strongly influenced the official American response to these events and formed the basis for a change in the foreign policy attitudes of both the public and politicians. Consequently, the last two decades of the nineteenth century were marked by the forceful assertion of American political preeminence in the Western Hemisphere.

International relations during the last quarter of the nineteenth century were dominated by the build-up of military alliances and armaments in Europe and by the scramble for overseas colonies. Despite its anti-militaristic and anti-imperialist tradition, the United States could not completely ignore these developments. After decades of apparent invulnerability Americans began to consider the dramatic possibility of naval bombardment of their coastal ports and cities. The British bombardment of Alexandria in 1881 demonstrated what a great naval power might accomplish, but it was the threat of a Chilean attack upon the California coast that was taken most seriously by Americans. This alarming scenario was a rather exaggerated tribute to Chilean naval capability, but it provided naval lobbyists with a powerful and emotive argument in favor of increased appropriations for the United States Navy. Congress showed some initial reluctance to vote these, but the issue was kept in the forefront by a succession of vigorous secretaries of the navy, beginning with William E. Chandler in 1882. Public support was also gradually aroused by the writings of Admiral Mahan emphasizing the strategic and commercial necessity of a powerful American navy.[52] The debate continued throughout the 1880s and 1890s, but the change in its terms of reference indicated a victory for the advocates of a big navy. During the 1860s and 1870s the major issue had concerned the relative merits of sail over steam power; from the late 1880s onward the question revolved around how much armor the new battleships would require. The "new" American navy that came into being not only gave international prestige to the United States; it also provided American foreign policy with the availability of much greater military power. Latin American nations experienced many examples of this in the 1890s.

Another influential argument in favor of a strong American navy was the need to counter possible European imperialistic designs on the Western Hemisphere. Vast areas of territory in Africa, Asia, and the Pacific had fallen under European control, and there were constant rumors of similar European ambitions in Latin America. Successive administrations from Hayes to McKinley were acutely suspicious of the de Lesseps canal project and continually warned against the establishment of a French protectorate on the isthmus. British complicity in hemispheric intrigues was suspected wherever disturbances occurred, from Chile to Venezuela and from Nicaragua to the Hawaiian Islands. Germany was also credited with expansionist ambitions and even the cautious Bayard responded firmly to rumors of German designs on Cuba by reaffirming the traditional American attitude that "we cannot see with indifference foreign dominion pushed to our very door."[53]

Support for a more active policy toward Latin America was also caused by a sense that American influence in that region had diminished while that of Europe was increasing. This theme was often stressed by James G. Blaine throughout the 1880s, and it formed the basis of the policy known popularly as *Pan-Americanism*. In Blaine's opinion, the requirements of national security and material interest made an activist policy imperative. "If these tendencies are to be averted, if Spanish-American friendship is to be regained, if the commercial empire that legitimately belongs to us is to be ours," he argued in 1882, "we must not lie idle and witness its transfer to others."[54] The approval of appropriations for the Latin American Trade Commission in 1884 and for the Washington conference in 1888 demonstrated the growing political support for this idea.

Blaine talked of the "reconquest" of the Latin American commercial market, and American policy toward Latin America frequently adopted the characteristics of aggressiveness implicit in that word. Anticipating by twenty years the views of Theodore Roosevelt, Blaine emphasized the necessity of maintaining peace in the Western Hemisphere and the role of the United States in achieving this. The Latin American nations, he noted, "require external pressure to keep them from war; when at war they require external pressure to bring them to peace."[55] Blaine contemplated an association of all the nations of the Western Hemisphere in which the United States would act the part of a friendly sister. In practice, the role worked out differently as goodwill and benevolence became intermingled with force and bluster. The Harrison administration did seek to promote hemispheric peace, but American power was also used to extract commercial concessions and to apply diplomatic pressure in the internal affairs of several Latin American countries. Commercial diplomacy proved quite successful, as the negotiation of reciprocity treaties demonstrated. But political developments were not quite so pleasing. The outcome of the 1893–1894 naval revolt in Brazil was regarded with favor by American diplomats, but not so the Chilean revolt of 1891. Moreover, despite considerable diplomatic pressure, American diplomats failed to bring about a change in Colombian policy toward the French canal project.

It was, however, the economic question that attracted most attention and political concern. "The old nations of the earth creep on at a snail's pace," declared Andrew Carnegie, while he noted confidently that "the Republic thunders past with the rush of the express."[56] But such a state of affairs was not achieved without effort, and the economic imperatives of the last quarter of the nineteenth century were demanding a greater effort than ever before. American foreign policy had consistently regarded the promotion of American trade as one of its functions and, consequently, the State Department responded vigorously to the growth of world competition in overseas markets.[57] Domestic factors also played an important part in this. The American economy grew steadily throughout the late nineteenth century, but not without periods of economic recession and, in the case of the years from 1893 to 1897, severe depression. Agrarian discontent was particularly vociferous, for even though the farmer produced more and more, the general decline in price levels resulted in shrinking incomes. The reason seized upon rather simplistically for this apparently abnormal state of affairs was chronic overproduction. Added to this was the traditional agrarian distrust of the "East," especially of the machinations of eastern bankers, symbolized by the maintenance of the gold standard.

Solutions were simple too. The economist David A. Wells stated the problem clearly in 1884: "There is no sufficient market for our surplus agricultural products except a foreign market."[58] Goods that the home market could not absorb should therefore be exported. The force of this argument was undeniable, but it evoked considerable political controversy because it raised the question of tariff protection. Nevertheless, the basic principle was rarely lost sight of because economic expansion suited the American temperament and promotional activities came easily to American officials, many of whom were recruited directly from business.[59] The State Department stressed the preparation of commercial reports for public use and the assertion of American trading rights wherever they might be violated or infringed. Most ambitious and novel was the development by the Republican party of the concept of reciprocity as a means of maintaining the protective tariff and, at the same time, satisfying the requirement of more exports. A Republican spokesman such as Senator Washburn of Minnesota was merely reiterating the views of Wells when he stated in 1894: "We have been engaged since 1884 in endeavoring to extend our foreign trade. The product of the industry and the genius of our people have so far outstripped the requirements for home consumption that we will be compelled to seek new markets for the surplus or close our factories and let a portion of our harvests rot upon the ground."[60]

During the 1880s and 1890s most politicians of both parties firmly endorsed the need for more exports as a means of resolving the problem of overproduction. Agrarian interests had, however, become identified with a more practical proposal, but one that was not so easily acceptable. This was the replacement of the gold standard by a bimetallic currency of gold and silver in order to inflate the economy and thus bring about a rise in prices. Such a policy was supported by American farmers and silver interests and was also attractive to the silver-based currencies of Latin America. "Free silver" not only satisfied domestic needs; it also pointed to a closer relationship with Latin America. Morris Estee asserted at the Washington conference in 1890: "An international coin would give new force to American finance, uniformity in prices, and business confidence to all. With this done, no one is great enough to call a halt to American progress in its march southward, or successfully oppose closer friendly and commercial relations among the people of all the American States."[61] While both the Harrison and Cleveland administrations entered into monetary discussions with European and Latin American governments, no action was taken. As one of its obligations arising from the Washington conference, the United States agreed to stage an International American Monetary Commission in Washington in 1891. But it was soon apparent that the United States had no constructive intent. "It is useless," complained the delegate from Haiti, "to continue in the present commission a discussion which can not reach any issue."[62] The Monetary Commission quickly terminated its activities with face-saving but empty phrases and resolutions.[63]

The question of the coinage of silver was first and foremost a domestic rather than a foreign policy issue and as such it dominated American politics in the mid-1890s. But it was such a political "football"[64] that affirmative action on it was virtually precluded. The issue was ultimately resolved in the late 1890s when the return of economic prosperity combined with Republican political ascendancy ensured the maintenance of the gold standard. Much less bitterly fought but still politically controversial was the debate over reciprocity. This question was not given the same political significance as "free silver" although the strenuous efforts of Blaine and Harrison made it an integral aspect of official Republican policy. Its attraction lay in the mixture of its appeal to economic nationalism and its assistance in exporting the domestic surplus. "The alarmed attention of our European competitors for the South American market," noted Harrison in 1892, "has been attracted to this new American policy and to our acquisition and their loss of South American trade."[65] Since they exported large amounts of sugar and coffee to the United States, a number of Latin American countries were extremely vulnerable to American economic pressure. The negotiation of reciprocity agreements became therefore a means not only of promoting American trade and thereby alleviating domestic distress, but also of advancing American influence in Latin America. The example of how the German *Zollverein* had assisted the rise of Prussia did not go unnoticed and congressmen such as Richard Townshend of Illinois and Senator Frye of Maine frequently talked in terms of a similar association in the Western Hemisphere.

Increased trade between the United States and Latin America was also seen as a means of strengthening both the bonds and the security of the nations of the Western Hemisphere. "It is the history of all diplomacy," declared Frelinghuysen in 1884, "that close political relations and friendships spring from unity of commercial interests."[66] The stress was economic, but the policy was viewed in a much wider perspective than merely assisting American exporters. The description *Pan-Americanism* was coined to describe a policy that sought a hemisphere of prosperous, secure, and democratic sister nations. The assembly of these nations in Washington in 1889 appeared to mark the beginning of the realization of this ideal. The conference itself and the reciprocity treaties that followed demonstrated that American politicians and American society in general were showing a growing interest in their southern neighbors. The influential preacher Josiah Strong declared that Anglo-Saxons had a "genius for colonizing" and he prophesized that they would "move down upon Mexico, down upon Central and South America, out upon the islands of the sea, over Africa and beyond."[67] This reawakened sense of mission and ideological necessity combined with strategic and economic considerations to overcome the resistance to expansionist policies that had been so evident during the 1860s and 1870s. In fact, the dictates of party politics now focused congressional and public attention more and more upon Latin American affairs.

After the failure of Grant's scheme to purchase the Dominican Republic, Latin American questions aroused little public interest until the announcement of the de Lesseps canal project in 1879. This interest was further sustained by the political controversy surrounding Blaine's policy toward the War of the Pacific. Partly in self-defense and partly to promote his own presidential ambitions, Blaine issued public statements designed to push Latin American issues into the forefront of domestic political debate.[68] While the new Arthur administration appeared initially to reject Blaine's ideas, it soon appeared to adopt his recommendations when it asserted a hemispheric policy stressing the negotiation of commercial treaties and the construction of an isthmian canal under American control. The statements of Benjamin Harrison during the presidential campaign of 1888, and later as president, further demonstrated that Blaine's concept of a vigorous Latin American policy had become widely accepted within the Republican party.

The compromise over the reciprocity amendment in 1890 gave a tangible direction to this policy and the Republican platform of 1892 enthusiastically claimed: "We point to the success of the Republican policy of reciprocity, under which our export trade has vastly increased and new and enlarged markets have been opened for the products of our farms and workshops."[69] Led by Cleveland, the Democrats were critical of reciprocity and favored in principle the free importation of raw materials. Commercial agreements thus found little support in Cleveland's first administration. However conservative its ideology and sympathies, the administration could not ignore the growing need and pressure for a positive foreign policy. Bayard felt compelled to forestall German designs on Samoa, and while he rejected the idea of annexation of Central American territory by the United States, he did resolutely protest alleged British intrigues in that region.[70] The administration also affirmed its wider interest in Latin American affairs by approving the congressional appropriation for the Washington conference, and despite Cleveland's electoral defeat in November 1888, Bayard sent a special commission to several of the Latin American countries to confirm that the conference would take place as scheduled.

During the last quarter of the nineteenth century Latin American affairs therefore intruded into the very essence of American domestic politics. In previous decades Latin America had appeared as remote and unworthy of much attention, but the strategic implications raised by the de Lesseps canal scheme and the political controversy generated by Blaine thrust hemispheric matters into the American political consciousness. The simultaneous sense of economic gloom and the awareness of the value of the Latin American market as a means of resolving this ensured that the new interest of America in its southern neighbors increased rather than diminished.

Moreover, during the 1890s a series of events occurred in Latin America that prompted a vigorous American diplomatic response. The long strained relationship between the United States and Chile suddenly changed into friendship, although this was abruptly reversed by political revolution in 1891. In the process American diplomacy became compromised and the resulting state of bad diplomatic feelings was intensified by the *Baltimore* incident. It was an awkward diplomatic situation and President Harrison chose to react in an assertive and aggressive manner. In a similar fashion, his imposition of retaliatory duties under the McKinley Tariff upon Colombia, Venezuela, and Haiti indicated that he would exert forceful pressure where he judged it necessary to uphold both American honor and diplomatic objectives, and that Latin American nations might expect no special privileges or favorable treatment from his administration.

The return of a Democratic administration in 1893 appeared, however, to signal a more cautious and restrained foreign policy. Harrison had been eager to annex the Hawaiian Islands when the opportunity arose in 1893, but the new Cleveland administration rejected this policy as morally wrong. The secretary of state, Walter Q. Gresham, explained that he was "unalterably opposed to stealing territory, or of annexing a people against their consent."[71] The disavowal was sincere, but it did not preclude a vigorous policy toward Latin America. The Cleveland administration actually went one step further than its Republican predecessor by undertaking direct though limited military intervention in Brazil and Nicaragua and by demanding that Britain take action to resolve its boundary dispute with Venezuela. Each of these actions involved a degree of diplomatic conflict with Britain and the ultimate outcome was interpreted as a victory for the United States and an affirmation of American political preeminence in the Western Hemisphere. The Latin American nations were regarded as the beneficiaries of this policy, but the events actually implied their further political and economic subordination to the United States within a system of conferences and reciprocity treaties. The events also gave warning that an occasional show of force could be used to coerce possible recalcitrants and deter potential adversaries. Within the United States itself this policy was sustained by a growing consciousness of Latin America's strategic, economic, and ideological importance. The simultaneous development of American economic and military power provided a further cause-and-effect sequence in which the United States embarked on an activist policy toward its southern neighbors, leading in 1898 to direct military intervention in Cuba.

American political preeminence in the Western Hemisphere did not, therefore, suddenly arrive in 1898, for it had been clearly in evidence from the 1860s onward. Its vigorous assertion was restrained by internal factors that placed obstacles in the way of expansionist aims. Enforcement was also unnecessary because after 1867 European powers saw little or no advantage in pursuing ambitious political schemes in Latin

America. Led by Britain's example these powers demonstrated a decided propensity to avoid possible clashes with the United States over Western Hemispheric questions.

Indeed, the conciliatory attitude of British diplomats did much to defuse potentially explosive Latin American issues. But if American political preeminence was the result, it was also a result that was not so bad for European interest. For example, the American right of intervention in the isthmian region provided European merchants with a welcome reassurance that law and order would be maintained. The economic implications of American preeminence in the 1880s and 1890s also differed significantly from those of American "dollar diplomacy" in the twentieth century. The distinction lies in the fact of American economic weakness in nineteenth-century Latin America in contrast to the well-established and substantial European economic interests in that area. Unlike Britain, the United States was not a major exporter of capital investment and, excluding Mexico and Central America, Americans had relatively little capital invested in Latin America. Surplus capital was absorbed in internal development and in paying the foreign interest and service charges on foreign investment in the United States itself. Nineteenth-century American economic strength lay predominantly in the export of primary products to Europe; commercial links with Latin America were much less significant.[72]

Despite the efforts at commercial diplomacy, American economic expansion into Latin America during the last quarter of the nineteenth century was not particularly successful. As the British minister to Washington noted in 1885: "The inauguration of an American hemispherical policy does not seem to meet with much favour. . . . The channels of trade cannot be so easily diverted by insisting on national exclusiveness as was anticipated."[73] Dispatches from several other British officials continually alluded to the internal political difficulties that hampered American policy and the lack of success of American schemes even when implemented.

Pan-American conferences and reciprocity agreements were a beginning, but they were no substitute for the essential ingredients of economic success that the United States conspicuously lacked in Latin America. Whether foreign service officials were hard-working or incompetent mattered little. "Do what he may to make an opening for American manufactures abroad," judged a former diplomat, "a consul cannot overcome in this respect the inertia and obstinacy of American manufacturers."[74] Indeed, the lack of shipping services,[75] banking and credit facilities, and business branches, as well as the added difficulties of linguistic and customs barriers, all interposed severe obstacles toward the expansion of American trade in Latin America. A typical consular report noted in 1891: "It can not, nevertheless, be too often urged upon our people that we are fearfully handicapped in the race. Until the lack of rapid and frequent steam communication, banking facilities, and distinctively American houses shall be supplied, we must be laggards. The atmosphere here is charged with European influences. There are few Americans and less Americanism."[76]

In such circumstances, the American economic threat to well-established European interests in Latin America was not serious in the short term. Moreover, the reality of European economic strength was reinforced by the evident desire of Latin Americans to maintain close links with Europe. The late nineteenth century saw the emergence of a world economy in which Europe exported vast quantities of manufactured goods, capital, and people to areas such as Latin America and in return imported essential raw materials and primary goods. Latin Americans admired "the colossus of the north," but they admired Europe too and were very much aware that their economic fortunes were tied as much to Europe as to the United States. The mutual economic benefits of increased inter-American contact were not disputed, but Pan-Americanism made Latin Americans even more aware of their bonds with Europe. "South American travel and social and intellectual intercourse," commented Pauncefote in 1890, "are with Europe and not with North America."[77]

Finally, the implications of American political preeminence in the Western Hemisphere were not disturbing or threatening to European nations, who attached, after all, marginal strategic significance to this area. Throughout the nineteenth century colonial powers such as Britain, France, Holland, and Spain[78] continued to exercise their traditional authority over their possessions in the Americas. After 1865 the influence of the Jeffersonian tradition in foreign policy and, more practically, public indifference and the anti-expansionist attitude of Congress, pointed to the improbability of an American policy of territorial aggression; despite the expansionist rhetoric of American politicians, overt attempts at such expansion were uniformly unsuccessful. From the European and especially the British point of view, the Western Hemisphere provided an excellent opportunity for the exercise of laissez faire diplomacy. The reckoning was, however, to come symbolically for Britain in 1895–1896, and more painfully for Spain in 1898. For thirty years American political preeminence in the Western Hemisphere had been tacitly deferred to by both European and Latin American nations. Lack of a consistent and assertive American attitude toward Latin American affairs had allowed these countries a much wider latitude in the conduct of hemispheric affairs than squared with the existing geopolitical realities. By the mid-1890s this reality had been decisively affirmed and a new era opened in hemispheric relations.

II / Diplomatic Events

//3//

Divergent Responses to Conflict

Political disturbances most often brought Latin American affairs to the attention of diplomatic officials in both Washington and London. In the "great republic of the north," observers were disappointed that democratic institutions were still not yet firmly planted, and apprehensive that monarchical institutions might be restored. Such sentiments were not shared by British officials. Britain had no Monroe Doctrine to defend or to propagate. Political disturbance and change in Latin America did not affect British national security, but it did affect British trade and investment, a fact of which Foreign Office officials were frequently reminded by the activities of economic pressure groups in Britain itself. When political disturbances became transformed into war between various of the Latin American countries, the issues involved assumed even greater importance and urgency. In such cases, humanitarian questions often became as pressing, if not more important, than those of commerce. This was illustrated by the British and American responses to events in the two decades after the close of the Civil War, especially by their respective policies toward the war between Spain, Chile, and Peru in 1865–1866 and later toward the War of the Pacific, 1879–1883.

In each case, both powers sought to end the conflict by volunteering their good offices as a means of facilitating peace talks between the belligerents. Whereas the United States preferred to pursue an independent policy, Britain desired a policy of concerted diplomatic action with the other interested powers. At the same time, both powers dispatched sizable naval forces to the area of conflict for commercial and humanitarian reasons, but these naval detachments assumed negative rather than positive roles.[1] Communications between Washington and London were usually friendly throughout these incidents, though an element of Anglo-American rivalry was never absent from the relations of the British and American officials attached to the Latin American capitals. In this respect, American diplomacy was badly served by its representatives abroad, who too often proved to be men lacking in judgment and diplomatic skill. British officials tended to be superior in this respect, mainly because their standing instructions restricted their freedom of action and inhibited them from making rash decisions. These instructions reflected the habitual caution and realism of the Foreign Office in London. In each of the wars in the Pacific, the British government wished to see a quick end to the hostilities, but could see no way of achieving this except by agreement between the belligerents themselves. Intervention was ruled out in favor of a cautious, low-risk policy, which though rarely winning friends, did not make enemies. It was a policy that emphasized neutrality and was rarely influenced by considerations of commerce or rivalry with the United States. After all, in an age of free trade and laissez faire, British commerce could be allowed to take care of itself.

American officials had different ideas. Though their actual experience of Latin American affairs was little different from that of British officials, they believed that the United States possessed a special role and influence in the affairs of the Western Hemisphere. There was some truth in this, but Washington invariably overestimated its influence on events. In both the wars in the Pacific, American policy found itself in a position where imminent American intervention was anticipated by the Latin American belligerents. In each case, American policy promised too much and lacked the military resources and political will to implement these promises. The consequence was all too frequently Latin American disillusionment with the United States and the criticism that American policy was hypocritical. In reality, neither the United States nor Britain could really expect to direct affairs in a continent as far away and as vast as Latin America. Even if the commitment to do so was present, the resources were certainly lacking. This was doubly so when the powers at the center of events, especially the rapidly emerging power of Chile, were not prepared to be dictated to by outside powers, be they European or even North American.

Attempted Mediation of Latin American Conflicts, 1865–1878

From 1861 to 1866 Spain attempted to regain part of its former American empire. In the Dominican Republic a long and bitter struggle was waged until Spain recognized defeat in 1865. Anti-Spanish feeling was aroused throughout Latin America, especially in the west coast republics of Chile and Peru where the presence of a Spanish naval squadron increased tensions and resulted in Chile's declaration of war on Spain in September 1865. The scale of hostilities was not great, for Spanish power was represented solely by its naval squadron, then on a tour of the

Pacific coast of the Americas. Land battles were therefore absent as Spain employed the traditional policy of naval warfare: the blockade and the threat of naval bombardment. Such a policy had grave consequences for foreign and especially British commerce in the region. Commercial operations were severely restricted as the Spanish squadron attempted to institute a blockade of the major Chilean ports.[2]

The *Times* described Spanish policy of this period as "undignified and discreditable" and believed that Chile was justified in declaring war.[3] At the Foreign Office the matter was considered an "unhappy dispute" that could only be disastrous for both Chile and Spain. The danger to British residents and commerce in Chile was keenly appreciated by the new foreign secretary, Lord Clarendon. He expressed concern and considered it the duty of his government to raise the matter with the Spanish government and to express "their earnest hope that measures may be taken for bringing this state of things to a pacific termination."[4]

British naval reinforcements were also ordered to Chilean waters, though with instructions not to interfere with the hostilities in progress. The British chargé in Santiago was instructed to recognize the Spanish blockade where he judged it to be effective, and while he might exert his "friendly influences" in favor of peace he was to be "careful not to transgress the limits of intervention permissible to the agent of a neutral power."[5] As the instructions were dispatched, the editorials of the *Times* recommended British intervention to end the conflict.[6] Such a course of action was out of character with Foreign Office policy. When war had broken out between Spain and Peru in 1864, British officials had been concerned not so much with the immediate commercial problems, but whether Spain sought to reconquer territory in South America. Spanish denials of this had, however, resolved these apprehensions.[7] In the Chilean situation as well, commercial interest was not the motivation for British action. Instead, the obligations arising from its status and influence as a world power prompted British efforts. "The matters in dispute between the two Governments," noted Clarendon, "seem to be peculiarly fitted for the friendly interposition of other Powers to bring about a reconciliation between the parties who are at variance with each other."[8]

In November 1865 Britain therefore proposed its good offices to both Spain and Chile in the hope that this might bring about peace negotiations. This was not a unilateral policy; it was carried out in full consultation and cooperation with the French government.[9] Instructions to this effect were also sent to the British and French chargés in Santiago.[10] In point of fact these diplomatic efforts were concentrated not in Santiago but in the European capitals of London, Paris, and, especially, Madrid. In this sense, the war was regarded as a European rather than purely an American question. It involved a European government and one whose domestic instability had long been a problem for European balance-of-power politics.[11] Communications within Europe were also much faster, and this both facilitated and encouraged diplomatic activity. A dispatch from London to Madrid took no more than five days in contrast to the six to eight weeks from London to Santiago. Furthermore, contact with the Chilean government could be maintained through the Chilean minister in London.[12]

The "drawing-room" diplomacy of Europe was therefore put into action and from the European point of view the effort seemed successful when Spain accepted the Anglo-French offer of good offices in December 1865. But wars are rarely settled by proxy. By 1866 news reached Europe of Spanish naval losses in the Pacific and of the suicide of the admiral in charge of the Spanish squadron.[13] Spanish policy now put aside thoughts of peace and determined on retaliation. The acceptance of the Anglo-French good offices was withdrawn though the efforts of the two powers to bring about a peaceful settlement still continued. The situation was, however, further complicated by the entry of Peru into the war on the Chilean side in January 1866, an action that considerably diminished hopes of immediate peace.[14]

The time lag in communications in the days before the telegraph now produced an ironic development in January 1866. While hopes of peace were collapsing in Europe, the British and French chargés in Santiago received the instructions dispatched to them in late November. They now proceeded to volunteer the good offices of their governments as a means of bringing an end to the war. The offers were rejected by a Chilean government flushed with the recent naval successes and the alliance with Peru[15] and rejected too by the new Spanish admiral, who explained that he was awaiting instructions from Madrid.

The activities of diplomatic officials serving abroad were, however, not insignificant. They were the men on the spot with the capacity to influence directly the course of events. As was the custom in such matters, the British chargé in Santiago, Taylour Thomson, was under instructions to maintain a neutral attitude. Nevertheless, his personal view of the dangers to British commerce and property posed by the war had prompted him in September to advise the Chilean government to pursue moderate policies that would not invite destructive Spanish retaliation.[16] He was also empowered to judge the effectiveness of the Spanish blockade. His opinion that the Spaniards had instituted an effective blockade meant that British ships and merchants would have to recognize it too.[17] In practice this was not greatly to the detriment of foreign commerce. Though the blockade was initially gravely damaging to foreign commerce at Valparaiso, the restrictions on foreign vessels were later much more leniently applied. For example, the Spanish admiral agreed to allow the landing of mail from the British mail steamers. Moreover, because the squadron could not adequately enforce a blockade of the other Chilean ports, business was restored to former levels by the end of the year.[18]

While Thomson was concerned over the consequences of the war for British commerce, he was not particularly sympathetic to the losses of British merchants. "These are losses," he noted, "to which foreign merchants are in all countries occasionally liable."[19] Thomson was in fact under instructions not to give official support for compensation should British property be destroyed during any forthcoming hostilities. The Foreign Office believed that the danger of Spanish bombardment of Valparaiso was ever present and that foreign property should therefore be removed from the customs house area, the area most vulnerable to attack. On the advice of the law officers of the crown, Thomson was instructed to inform British merchants that goods not removed from the customs houses were left at their own risk, and "they are not to expect that, in the event of any injury accruing to it from the operations of the Spanish belligerent, Her Majesty's Government will hold the Chilean Government responsible for that injury."[20]

This was a policy based upon legal and not political or commercial considerations. Nor was it a policy arising from weakness, for Britain maintained a considerable naval presence outside Valparaiso consisting of two frigates and one gunboat. Admiral Denman, the British commander-in-chief, had stated that he would prevent any Spanish bombardment of the city unless prior warning of at least twenty-four hours was given.[21] It was also local public information that he was in communication with the United States commander, Commodore Rodgers, and that they would act together if the need should arise. Denman's views, however, were his own and not official British policy. In early March 1866 Thomson informed Denman of Clarendon's instructions concerning the protection of British property in Valparaiso and the necessity for maintaining a neutral policy. When London learned of the admiral's views, instructions were dispatched in mid-April warning against any action that "is likely to lead to serious complications in our relations with Spain."[22]

That Anglo-American cooperation was not greatly in evidence throughout the war was a consequence of circumstances, the personalities of various diplomatic officials, and, most of all, the desire of the United States to pursue a unilateral and independent policy. The United States was greatly concerned by its own domestic preoccupations arising from the Civil War and the resulting problems of reconstruction. It was also a period of general American hostility toward Europe. Britain was greatly disliked for its pro-Southern attitude during the Civil War, France was criticized for its intervention in Mexico, and Spanish policy in both Santo Domingo and on the Pacific coast of South America was viewed with suspicion.[23]

On the official level, the State Department had received a number of assurances from Madrid that Spain had no desire to regain territory in the Americas.[24] Secretary of State Seward has often been viewed as an avid territorial expansionist, but he in fact showed little desire to be involved with the war.[25] His initial opinion was that the conflict had been caused by a point of honor and that, with some "good sense," it might be brought to "a speedy and harmless end."[26] In the meantime American policy would fulfill its international obligations by pursuing neutrality and in no way give material support to either of the belligerents.[27] The United States would also volunteer its good offices in favor of a peace settlement, but without wishing to impose its views on either side.[28]

Despite this cautious approach of Seward's, American influence upon peace attempts was very evident. At this time, the military and naval power of the United States was well recognized, as was demonstrated by the French withdrawal from Mexico. The American ministers in Madrid, Lima, and Santiago were instructed to try to use the influence of the United States to bring about peace negotiations, and consequently, American diplomacy became active rather than passive.

Instructions to tender American good offices were dispatched in August and again in December 1865. On each occasion the offers were welcomed profusely but ultimately rejected. In Madrid, the Spanish government preferred to accept those of Britain and France;[29] and in Santiago, both the Chilean government and the Spanish admiral failed to agree on any basis for discussion of peace terms. A joint effort at mediation involving concerted action with Britain and France might have achieved more success, but this was ruled out by Seward. While he had no objection to the Anglo-French efforts, he did insist "that representations made by the United States alone, without concert with other powers, are more in harmony with our own national character and institutions."[30]

But such a policy was not so easy to put into practice. In Chile, the situation was somewhat complicated by the fact that since the American minister was the highest-ranking foreign official,[31] he was therefore doyen of the diplomatic corps. This meant that he alone could summon and preside over meetings of the corps and that official business addressed to the corps was directed through him. Both the Chilean government and the Spanish admiral had to communicate with the diplomatic corps by way of the American minister.

This fact may explain the failure of the diplomatic corps to visit

Admiral Pareja immediately on his arrival at Valparaiso in September 1865. The Spanish foreign minister later criticized the diplomatic corps for its delay and, in particular, accused the American minister, Thomas Nelson, of adopting a pro-Chilean attitude.[32] Nelson denied that he was anything but strictly neutral, but his speech on his departure from office on March 12, 1866, indicated a certain bias. In a reiteration of the Monroe Doctrine he informed his audience, which included the Chilean president, that the United States "cannot consistently consent to the permanent subjugation of any of the independent states of this continent to European powers, nor to the exercise of a protectorate over them, nor to any other direct political influence to control their policy or institutions."[33]

Nelson's views were warmly supported by his successor, General Judson Kilpatrick. But whereas Nelson was an experienced diplomat who had served in Chile for almost six years, Kilpatrick was a Civil War general without diplomatic experience and just thirty years of age. Nor was he unaware of his own lack of qualifications. As he wrote to Seward in June: "I still feel that want of confidence and knowledge which time, hard study, and experience alone can give. In consequence of this I have been obliged to feel my way most carefully."[34]

Nevertheless, within a few days of assuming office the young and inexperienced Kilpatrick faced the most acute diplomatic crisis of the war. On March 23 the new Spanish commander, Admiral Mendez Nuñez, announced that unless the Chilean government accepted his terms he would bombard Valparaiso on the 31st. Days of frantic diplomatic activity ensued, but all without success. Valparaiso was an unfortified city,[35] but despite this the bombardment duly took place on the appointed day. Kilpatrick believed that resolute action by the British and American squadrons in the harbor would have averted the bombardment, but that Thomson and Denman had refused him the necessary support.[36] In similar fashion, Thomson attached much of the blame for the failure of the diplomatic efforts to Kilpatrick, whom he criticized for using his rank to visit Mendez Nuñez alone on the 27th and not informing the admiral that the other members of the diplomatic corps also wished to confer with him afterward.[37] In reality, both the Spanish admiral and the Chilean government resolutely rejected compromise and no amount of diplomatic activity by Kilpatrick and Commodore Rodgers could alter this. On the other hand, their strenuous exertions and the proximity of six American warships in the harbor no doubt raised Chilean hopes of intervention on their behalf. It was not therefore surprising that after the bombardment Kilpatrick noted that "cordiality" for the United States had been replaced by "ill-will." "Chili looked upon the United States as her best friend," reported Kilpatrick, "and that friend has failed to assist her in her hour of trial."[38]

The events of late March had placed Kilpatrick in a position of "no ordinary embarrassment," and he very much felt the lack of clear and precise instruction on how to act in cases of emergency.[39] His sincere though perhaps disorderly efforts to avert the bombardment had merely raised local hopes of American intervention, resulting in disappointment and a certain amount of anti-American feeling.[40] By contrast, his British counterparts, Thomson and Denman, were under strict instructions to remain neutral. Adherence to those instructions did not, however, spare them from the wrath of the resident British merchants in Valparaiso and their associates in Britain. "I regret to say," wrote Denman, "that several of the English merchants have endeavoured to excite the feelings of the inhabitants against their own country."[41]

The damage to neutral property was estimated by Thomson at $10 million,[42] but as his instructions of January 11 had foreshadowed, there would be no official support for compensation. Despite considerable efforts from commercial pressure groups, Henry Layard[43] reaffirmed in the Commons that British merchants who had refused to remove their property "must themselves bear the responsibility of any damage."[44] While approving the actions of Thomson and Denman as being in conformity with their instructions, the British government was in fact deeply critical of the Spanish action. Clarendon complained of a "want of candour" on the part of the Spanish government and was convinced that such acts of "wanton destruction" would merely prolong and embitter the war.[45]

The Spanish squadron did go on to attempt a similar bombardment of Callao in May, though this time without much success, for Callao was not a defenseless city. This action brought an end to actual hostilities though the nominal state of war continued. Rumors that Spain might retake the Chincha Islands provoked vigorous protests from Seward asserting the Monroe Doctrine.[46] Spain needed little persuasion: The war had become not only a political embarrassment but also a financial disaster for that country. In December 1866 Spain agreed to accept the good offices of the United States and to attend a peace conference in Washington scheduled for April 1867.[47] The Chilean government accepted the American offer, but raised a number of reservations that effectively delayed the conference. The Spanish Revolution of 1868 introduced a further delay, and it was not held until April 1871.[48]

United States mediation might therefore be described as being ultimately successful though the time lag involved in holding the peace conference somewhat undermined any cause for self-congratulation. The war had demonstrated the difficulty, if not impossibility, of decisively influencing events by diplomatic means. Both Britain and the

United States deplored the war for its loss of life and its dislocation of commerce. "We have nothing to gain," summed up the *Times,* "and everything to lose by the continuance of hostilities between Spain and Chili."[49] A considerable British and American naval presence was maintained in the area of hostilities, but unless the respective governments were prepared to use this power its impact was purely negative. The potential for "gunboat diplomacy" existed, but the will to exercise it apparently did not. While Clarendon was concerned by the risk to British commerce and investment that the war posed, his policy was strictly neutral and legalistic and, in practice, tended to harm rather than promote British interests. American policy had less to protect in Chile, but was more assertive, at least from the point of view of American foreign service officials. The result was not a speedy end to the war but the arousal of anti-American feeling. No doubt the difficulties in communications hindered and restricted effective diplomatic action. On the other hand, although the war occurred during a period of internal political chaos for Spain and grave territorial difficulties for Chile,[50] neither government was prepared to defer to the wishes of the great powers. The markedly independent attitude of Chile would soon recur in succeeding diplomatic events. Clarendon described Spanish policy as wanting candour. It was a complaint against Spain that many American diplomats echoed throughout the nineteenth century. The diplomatic lesson of the war in the Pacific was that unless the outside power is prepared to intervene actively, the belligerents will decide what is in their own best interests and will go to the conference table only when they are ready and perceive it will benefit them.

The other major Latin American conflict taking place, across the Andes, illustrated this lesson even more forcibly. The congressional resolution of December 1866 that instructed Seward to mediate in the war then occurring in the Pacific also applied to the War of the Triple Alliance of Argentina, Brazil, and Uruguay against Paraguay, which had begun in January 1865. The resulting attempt at mediation, and succeeding attempts, were all rejected by the allies so that the proposed peace conference in Washington never took place.[51] There were many reasons for this. American foreign policy under Seward was much more interested in overcoming congressional opposition to schemes for the purchase of Alaskan and Caribbean territory than in South American affairs. As was the case with the war in the Pacific, the United States had no intention of intervening to end the hostilities, and so the allies determined to continue a war whose outcome promised to be beneficial to themselves.[52] Indeed, peace talks could only interrupt hostilities and afford Paraguay an opportunity of reinforcing if not consolidating its defenses. The allies were not therefore agreeable to this suggestion or to the idea of a peace conference in far-off Washington.[53]

American peace efforts were also handicapped by the activities of the various United States officials. The minister in Paraguay, Charles Washburn, was described at one stage as a "nervous wreck."[54] In Buenos Aires, Alexander Asboth's tender of good offices was coupled with his own personal criticism of the domestic policies of the Argentine government, a style that did little to encourage acceptance.[55] The standing and reputation of the American minister in Brazil, James W. Webb, was even lower than that of his colleagues.[56]

In contrast to the United States, the British government was under no strong parliamentary pressure and had no desire to come forward as an uninvited mediator in Western Hemispheric disputes. British policy pursued a much more cautious and prudent approach based on dispatches from South America that emphasized the unlikelihood of an early end to the conflict.[57] The *Times* regarded the war as a "wretched" one and advocated concerted action by the great powers to mediate in the dispute. While the British government was not opposed in principle to this, it would only act when requested to do so by the belligerents.[58]

In fact, it was the opinion of the British minister in Brazil that the Americans might perform "the thankless task" of mediation better. While Anglo-American commercial and diplomatic rivalry did exist,[59] there was no disposition in London to compete with or hinder American attempts at mediation. Acting in concert with the French government, Britain had attempted to use its influence to bring an end to the war between Chile and Spain. In late 1866 these efforts were withdrawn in favor of American mediation that seemed to have a better chance of success. The same attitude prevailed at the Foreign Office throughout the War of the Triple Alliance. Britain did not oppose American efforts to mediate in the war, but would not itself come forward in that capacity unless requested to do so by both belligerents. Latin American affairs could only elicit a legalistic and negative response from the nineteenth-century Foreign Office.

It was also a realistic and sensible attitude. This was well illustrated by British reaction to the expansionist moods in foreign policy of both the Johnson and Grant administrations. Despite, or perhaps because of, the tense state of Anglo-American relations arising from the *Alabama* claims, little positive response was forthcoming from the Foreign Office. "The Americans," commented Stanley on the Alaskan purchase, "have bought a large amount of worthless territory." Nor would the purchase annoy Britain for, in his opinion, it was a matter of public and press indifference.[60] The opposition of the Senate to other schemes by Seward regarding the Caribbean islands and later the furor over Grant's proposal to annex Santo Domingo reinforced and justified the British attitude that caution bordering on indifference was the best response to alarmist reports of aggressive United States policies.

On the other hand, there was an awareness that United States influence and power gave that country an increasingly significant role in the diplomatic events of the Western Hemisphere. This was seen in the attempts at mediation of the Latin American wars of the late 1860s and even more clearly in British diplomacy toward the civil war in Cuba, 1868–1878. As was the case with most Latin American affairs, this was an issue that aroused little sympathy or concern in Britain.[61] The British government was willing to use its influence in order to mitigate the horrors of the war, but implied that it would not act without the cooperation of the United States government.[62] Such cooperation was in evidence in August 1870 when Fish persuaded London to join the United States in a joint tender of good offices. In late 1875 Britain refused, however, to support his proposal for extreme measures against Spain. This latter action was not to be interpreted as British support for Spain against the United States. The British government recognized that the United States was powerful enough to seize Cuba and considered that such action might even be beneficial to British commerce. The matter of concern was not so much who controlled Cuba, but the disastrous consequences for British commerce that a United States–Spanish war would inevitably entail. In this sense British apprehensions were greatly alleviated by the statesmanship of Fish, who sought to avert war. British policy therefore concentrated on reducing the effects of the conflict on British lives and property in the area. Even so, as the case of the *Virginius* demonstrated, Britain allowed the United States to assume the leading role in protesting the matter to the Spanish government. Throughout the struggle Britain pursued a cautious, neutral, and legalistic policy.[63] Despite protestations from various American spokesmen in the 1880s, this was also to be the basis of British policy toward the next major Latin American conflict, the War of the Pacific.

The Outbreak of the War of the Pacific

Many of the characteristic features of both British and United States policy toward Latin America were well illustrated by the diplomatic events of the War of the Pacific. This war marked the rise of Chile to predominance on the west coast of South America through the defeat of its archrival, Peru. The conflict had originated as a dispute over nitrate export taxes between Bolivia and Chile. Fighting broke out in February 1879, and Peru joined Bolivia against Chile in March 1879. The story that followed was one of virtually uninterrupted Chilean military success, culminating in the occupation of Lima in January 1881. A peace settlement was delayed until October 1883 as a result of the ambiguous Chilean attitude over war aims, the chronic instability of Peruvian politics, and the misguided efforts of American diplomacy.[64]

The War of the Pacific directly involved the great powers because it affected the lives, property, and trade of their citizens. This was especially true of Britain, whose trade, investment, and number of citizens in both Peru and Chile was substantial.[65] In this respect, the British fleet performed valuable protective services. "The constant presence of H.M.S. *Turquoise* off the province of Tarapacá," wrote Spenser St. John in mid-1879, "has been of considerable service to our consuls there."[66] The threatened Chilean attack upon Lima in late 1880 aroused much apprehension both within that city and abroad. In general, however, the victorious Chilean troops showed considerable respect for foreign rights and property. This respect was possibly influenced by the threat of Admiral Stirling, commander of the British fleet, to blow up the Chilean fleet if their troops failed to respect neutral property in the assault upon Lima. Pauncefote approved this action and considered that but for it, there was "no saying what further horrors might have been perpetrated."[67]

Such naval actions were not infrequent in nineteenth-century Latin America and were justified not by superior force but by humanitarian arguments and by appeals to international law.[68] Though approving actions like that of Admiral Stirling, the Foreign Office sought also to maintain an attitude of strict neutrality in the actual conflict itself. This attitude had wide ramifications. Construction of warships under foreign contract in British naval yards came under careful government scrutiny so as to avoid the emergence of another *Alabama* case.[69] A Chilean request that British influence be used to prevent Peru from purchasing warships from Turkey was rejected on the grounds that this would be a departure from Britain's professed policy of "strict neutrality."[70] The refusal of the British minister to grant asylum to Peruvian refugees after the fall of Lima was approved in London. The minister had argued that to harbor the fugitives would be "an open breach of neutrality and would constitute an act of hostility towards the present occupiers of the country." Pauncefote agreed that to grant asylum would be an act of "interference between belligerents."[71] The British government scrupulously sought to avoid such interference throughout the war.

On the other hand, Britain did make a number of attempts to mediate between the belligerents. In contrast to the previous war in the Pacific of 1865–1866, the focus of these attempts was in Santiago and Lima rather than in the European capitals. This was because the war was predominately an American question and, no doubt, also a consequence of the introduction of the telegraph, which greatly assisted diplomatic communication. What still remained, however, was the Foreign Office's preference that these efforts at mediation be made in concert with those of the other neutral powers. In this respect, the end result was unchanged. The European powers were generally acquiescent while successive American administrations and ministers refused to cooperate in such concerted action and preferred a separate and unilateral policy.

Although the idea of a unilateral policy was in keeping with American traditions and was therefore popular, American diplomacy toward the War of the Pacific was not without its critics. Much of this criticism was leveled at James G. Blaine, who was secretary of state from March to December 1881. Reasons of American party politics were considerably responsible for this, but Blaine did earn a reputation for jingoistic and irresponsible diplomacy and also incurred charges of bribery and corruption that were never satisfactorily explained away. Moreover, the American ministers in Peru and Chile did little to contribute to a peace settlement, and in fact contributed to the prolongation of the war.[72]

American diplomacy in the War of the Pacific rejected concerted action with the other powers, but neither individual nor joint efforts at mediation had much success. The first attempts at outside mediation came in mid-April 1879 shortly after the outbreak of the dispute. The Peruvian minister in London was informed by the Foreign Office that Britain could not offer its mediation unless specifically requested to do so by one of the belligerents. This was forthcoming, and the next day the British ministers at Lima and Santiago were instructed to volunteer their good offices. Lord Salisbury summed up the British attitude: "Telegram might be sent offering our friendly offices to restore peace, and arrange differences. I don't believe they will accept: but there is no harm proposing."[73]

While Chile was disposed to accept under certain conditions, Peru refused the British offer. Salisbury's opinion was thus confirmed. Spenser St. John explained that the Peruvians were confident of victory and were determined to drive the Chileans from the territory that they had occupied in southern Peru.[74] The Foreign Office was confused by the turn of events. Officials found it difficult to understand Peru's involvement in the war. One clerk, Jervoise, could only comment that "we may at present claim to be as impartial as ignorance can make use."[75] The *Times* considered that few Englishmen were interested in the events of "the prolonged and desultory war," but the situation was serious and could not be ignored by the diplomats.[76]

Attempts at mediation were also being made by most of the major European governments, but with no more success than the British effort. In June 1879 the German minister in London, Count Munster, advocated sending a commission to the United States to discuss a joint effort at mediation. Pauncefote believed, however, that the American government would oppose any suggestion of European interference.[77] This judgment was confirmed when the British minister in Washington, Edward Thornton, reported the answer given by Evarts, the secretary of state. Evarts was prepared to tender the good offices of his government, but he opposed premature action or what he described to Thornton as an effort that would "carry the impression of dictation."[78]

Evarts rejected association with European diplomatic methods and proclaimed an independent American policy reminiscent of Seward's response to the similar Pacific crisis in 1865.[79] But he also suffered the same problems as his predecessors in controlling the activities of subordinate officials overseas. This was vividly illustrated in the summer of 1879. While the American ministers in Lima and Santiago awaited instructions on mediation, the minister in Bolivia, Newton D. Pettis, undertook on his own authority an unofficial mission to both those capitals.[80] Spenser St. John gave this attempt but a "slight chance of success,"[81] and in this he proved correct. The Foreign Office was surprised by the development and instructed Thornton to make inquiries in Washington. He replied that the move had no official backing. Evarts was still prepared to volunteer American good offices, but he had also reaffirmed that the United States would pursue a unilateral policy.[82]

Concerted action with the United States was therefore ruled out, and the British ministers in Lima and Santiago were instructed to renew their offer of good offices when a suitable opportunity should present itself. The offers were made and were received very cordially by Peru and Chile, but not accepted by either government. The obstacle to a peace settlement had already emerged: Chile was determined to retain possession of its newly conquered territories while Peru stipulated Chilean evacuation of these areas as a precondition of negotiations. The Foreign Office was well aware of this development, and as early as November 1879 an official minuted that "the Chileans who have it all their own way are not likely to agree to this proposal."[83]

This view was confirmed throughout 1880 as continued Chilean victories gave that country an even stronger bargaining position. In spite of this, the new ruler of Peru, Piérola, declared his utmost determination to regain the lost territory and thus made the possibility of peace talks even more unlikely.[84] Even if Piérola was disposed to negotiate peace terms, St. John reported from Lima that the Chileans, "flushed with victory," would be unwilling to respond favorably.[85] Nor could the neutral powers do much to promote a peaceful settlement. On a petition from British merchants in May 1880, Pauncefote summed up the difficulties of the situation: "friendly overtures . . . have hitherto been unavailing. In the meanwhile Her Majesty's Government are taking all the steps they properly can for the protection of British life and property."[86]

Political changes were also occurring in Britain at this time. In April 1880 a Liberal government came to power, and Granville replaced Salisbury at the Foreign Office. The change in personnel involved no basic change in policy: Britain still sought to concert its attempts at mediation with those of the other neutral powers. In July 1880 this was reaffirmed by Granville in a talk with the Italian ambassador. Granville later suggested to Count Munster that Germany should join Britain, France, and Italy in proposing mediation jointly should a favorable opportunity arise. This was, however, declined by Berlin.[87]

The European powers, therefore, were not seeking to impose a settlement upon the belligerents. The result was a flexible though rather ineffective policy that tended to be at the mercy of the turn of events. During the late summer of 1880 it seemed that the Chilean threat to attack Lima might bring about the emergence of a Peruvian peace party.[88] This was interpreted in Europe as the opportunity for outside mediation. But the tender of European good offices was not made because in September 1880 St. John reported with some surprise and perhaps annoyance that the belligerents had accepted the mediation of the United States. It was his opinion that "the interference of the United States will retard, rather than advance the negotiations for peace."[89] It was a prophetic insight.

This was the first real sign of a tone of antagonism toward the American ministers that was beginning to appear in dispatches from British officials in Lima and was not to end until Hurlbut's death in 1882. For example, when Isaac Christiancy, the American minister at Lima, mentioned in June 1880 that Evarts feared foreign intervention, St. John riposted that "no foreign power has ever thought of intervention in the affairs of these Republics, and we can not imagine at what Government this warning is especially aimed."[90] The note of rivalry continued in St. John's reports on the attempt at American mediation. He considered that the American ministers had chosen Arica as the site for the peace talks because it was a place "beyond the influence of the European members of the diplomatic corps." When he came to report the failure of the talks, St. John reiterated his previous opinion that the American mediation attempt had been doomed to fail from its inception. Both Christiancy and Osborn, the minister in Santiago, had deceived their respective sides, and St. John remarked that their object had not been in the interests of peace but merely to have the glory of having peace signed under their auspices.[91]

Similar views were echoed in London. Pauncefote was well aware that the United States was "jealous of European intervention."[92] The British government, however, regretted that this should be the state of affairs and at no time attempted to provoke Washington. At the beginning of the war, Britain had sought the cooperation of the United States and this had been refused. The American attitude remained unaltered, and there was nothing that Britain could do to change it. Nor had the Foreign Office any reason to oppose American efforts which, if successful, would bring about a peace that was in the interests of British merchants.[93]

There was no doubt that the American government feared European intervention in the war and was particularly suspicious of European efforts at mediation. Yet the diplomatic record shows that those powers rarely manifested unity of purpose or action sufficient to constitute any form of real threat.[94] This was clearly demonstrated by the diplomatic activity arising over the imminent Chilean attack on Lima in December 1880. Apprehension over the damages and loss of life that such an attack would entail stirred the Foreign Office into action. A circular telegram was sent to the major European governments proposing a renewal of their good offices. Favorable replies were received from France and Italy, but Germany once again opposed the plan. Though he expressed little hope of success, Pauncefote felt that every diplomatic effort must be made to save Lima from destruction. He suggested therefore that the United States be invited to join the European powers in a concerted offer of good offices. This was not acted upon. The negative attitude of the German government and, more significantly, the rapidity of the Chilean military movements, rendered the suggestion obsolete.[95]

On account of their economic interests, the European powers had much more at stake in the conflict than had the United States. Britain, France, and Italy were generally in agreement over policy, but Germany remained aloof and its position was equivocal.[96] Italian policy adopted an aggressive tone, but Italy realized that Britain, on account of its naval power and commercial interests, exercized the leading influence.[97] The French government appeared to cooperate actively with Britain, but both sides were acutely suspicious of each other. To a great extent this was a reflection of matters other than the War of the Pacific. Both powers were simultaneously and intensely involved in African affairs, especially in Tunisia and Egypt, where they were more often rivals than partners. Moreover, their policies toward the War of the Pacific were complicated by the activities of various financial pressure groups. Each country had its own committee of bondholders whose interests were affected by the war, and each of these committees opposed the other and sought the assistance of its own government. The huge French banking house of Dréyfus also exerted its considerable political influence. Pauncefote was to observe in 1887 that Piérola owed his rise to power in 1880 to the gold of the Dréyfus Company. Salisbury appreciated the influence wielded by the company when he minuted that "it seems that Dréyfus is a very intimate personal friend of President Grévy."[98] This was the crux of the problem: The Dréyfus Company had considerable influence on French policy and was not averse to exploiting it.

The concert of the European powers was therefore most fragile. In fact, during the summer of 1881 the French government made a private approach to the new American secretary of state, James G. Blaine.[99] President Grévy asked the American minister in Paris, Levi Morton, to urge Blaine to intervene in the war in order to prevent further damage to neutral property. Though he agreed that such property was at risk, Blaine rejected the idea of intervention and took the opportunity to declare his opposition to European interference in the affairs of the Western Hemisphere.[100] It was the signal for a series of American diplomatic initiatives to bring an end to the war.

The Failure of American Diplomacy

A conviction that the Old World of Europe was corrupt and sordid, and that the American continent must remain inviolate from these influences, dominated much of the diplomacy of James G. Blaine. Though by birth a Pennsylvanian, Blaine was an adopted political son of the state of Maine, and the local politics of that state colored his political views.[101] In particular, Blaine exhibited a strong anti-British bias, and a good deal of his national popularity lay in his reputation for "twisting the British lion's tail." After he had left office Blaine was to describe the War of the Pacific as "an English war on Peru, with Chile as the instrument."[102] In a letter published in the *New York Times* he was even more explicit. England was accused of supplying Chile with ironclads, uniforms, and muskets. "English sympathy," continued the former secretary of state, "has stood behind [Chile] at every step in her conquest. . . . This Peru-Chilean war destroys American influence on the South Pacific coast and literally wipes out American commercial interests in that vast region. . . . Chile's victory throws the whole Peruvian business into English hands."[103]

Lionel West, the British minister in Washington, believed that Blaine was using anti-British feeling to launch an attack not upon Britain but upon the new Arthur cabinet for its apparent reversal of his policies.[104] There was much truth in this, but it was also true that Blaine sincerely sought to promote American commercial expansion and that he saw Britain as the primary obstacle to this expansion. His first term as secretary of state was limited to just over nine months and his achievements were comparatively meager, but within this short space of time he aroused considerable alarm throughout the American continent.

Blaine was without doubt a strongly partisan politician, but his diplomacy proved to be flexible. He had no rigid notions as to policy, and it is not surprising that Blaine in office was quite different from Blaine the public orator.[105] Nevertheless, traditional American concepts were strongly in evidence in his reply to President Grévy.[106] Blaine did not doubt that intervention had proved beneficial in Europe, but such practices did not belong to American affairs. The American republics he considered to be "younger sisters" of the United States and "far removed from the European system."[107]

In his attitude toward the War of the Pacific, Blaine translated these general views into specific policies. His instructions of June 1881 declared sympathy for Peru, but also expressed a realistic recognition that the Chilean right of conquest might necessitate the cession of Peruvian territory. Since Chile had denied that it was involved in a war of conquest, Blaine argued that Peru should be allowed to pay an indemnity to Chile rather than cede territory.[108]

In short, Blaine's aim was to make the cession of territory a subject of negotiation rather than a precondition. This aim was not so different from that pursued by Evarts, but since then the Chilean victories had so transformed the political and military situation on the Pacific coast that, his disclaimers to the contrary, Blaine's objective could only be favorable to Peru.

Furthermore, the new secretary of state's policy could not count on full domestic support, for his tenure of office was clouded by rumors of financial scandal. In the days of Grantism, spoils, and the robber barons, few American politicians were free of the taint of bribery and corruption.[109] As Speaker of the House of Representatives Blaine had earned a reputation for honesty, but this had been besmirched in 1876 by the scandal of the "Mulligan Letters."[110] Blaine survived the scandal, but his reputation only partially recovered and his political enemies readily exploited the weakness. Even within his own party, his position was weakened by his feud with the senator from New York, Roscoe Conkling.[111] The allegations of "guano diplomacy" affecting Blaine during the War of the Pacific were therefore widely publicized and readily believed by a receptive audience. In 1882 Blaine's successor, Frederick Frelinghuysen, appeared to accept the allegations as proved and used this as a justification for the reversal of his predecessor's policies.[112]

The basis of these allegations arose from Blaine's connection with three financial claims arising from Peru's loss of nitrate territory to Chile. The claimants were first, a French banking company, the Crédit Industriel; second, the rights of Cochet, a pioneer in the guano industry, which had been bought up by an American company headed by Jacob R. Shipherd; and third, the claim of the Landreau brothers. Even though the congressional investigation of 1882 publicly exonerated Blaine from all allegations that he had used his official position to promote these guano interests, as in the incident of the "Mulligan Letters," Blaine did leave himself vulnerable to these charges by his own imprudence. Initially, Blaine had indeed been sympathetic to the claims of the Crédit Industriel because the scheme it proposed would have enabled Peru to find the funds to pay Chile a war indemnity.[113] By contrast, he rejected the Cochet claim, though Shipherd was able to gain personal hearings at the State Department, thereby giving the impression that he had secured official support for his claim. The third claim, that of Landreau, was strongly supported by Blaine.[114]

A common feature of these claims was that they all sought to preserve the territorial integrity of Peru and proposed to raise money to pay an indemnity to Chile. They coincided, therefore, with Blaine's own basic aim and provided the means of achieving it.[115] The Chilean minister in Washington, Marcial Martínez, was alarmed and reported that Blaine was colluding with financial interests in a conspiracy against Chile.[116] These rumors of official American intervention on behalf of the claimants not only aroused the fear and resentment of Chile toward the United States, but also raised Peruvian hopes of American assistance, thus ultimately prolonging the war. When Peruvian hopes collapsed, one result was the discrediting and humiliation of United States diplomacy.

As with previous American initiatives in the late 1860s, the unfortunate consequences were not entirely the fault of officials in Washington. According to the practice of incoming administrations, Garfield and Blaine had decided to replace the American ministers at Lima and Santiago with men of their own choice. Thus in May 1881 Stephen Hurlbut was appointed to replace Christiancy at Lima, and Judson Kilpatrick once again assumed charge of the Santiago legation. This change of personalities was to have a significant impact upon the diplomatic situation. Both ministers were to adopt partisan positions in favor of the countries in which they served, and their intrigues did much to handicap American policy and to delay a peace settlement.

Illness prevented Kilpatrick from exercising a direct influence upon events though his pro-Chilean sympathies were never in doubt.[117] Hurlbut was described by the *Nation* as "grossly ignorant of the elementary principles of international law, and completely indifferent to the decorum of diplomatic intercourse."[118] His aim appeared to be to prevent the cession of the nitrate areas of southern Peru to Chile, an aim that distinctly favored the defeated nation. Hurlbut's impact was immediate. Spenser St. John reported that Hurlbut was informing Peruvian politicians that the United States sought to bring about peace without the cession of territory. St. John concluded that the Peruvians, after apparently coming to accept the inevitability of ceding territory, now reverted to their former position of no cession whatever.[119]

Far from aiding a peace settlement, Blaine's policy, as interpreted and implemented by his new ministers, was having the opposite effect. This was made apparent by the growing hostility between Hurlbut and the Chilean occupational authorities, headed by Admiral Lynch. In the opinion of the British minister, the Chileans had become "very jealous of the interference of the United States" and were especially annoyed by Hurlbut's close association with President García Calderón, the leader of the Peruvian provisional government, which only the United States had granted official recognition.[120] In like manner, Hurlbut's dispatches were exacerbating Blaine's anti-British bias, for he pointed out the frequent and long conversations between St. John and Admiral Lynch. As for the Chileans, Hurlbut categorically stated that "the purpose, end and aim of this war, declared by Chili against Peru and Bolivia, was in the beginning and is now the forcible acquisition of the nitrate and guano territory, both of Bolivia and Peru."[121]

Hurlbut had no doubts as to the rights and wrongs of the dispute and which side merited American assistance. In late October 1881 he wrote to Blaine that the "dominant influence of the United States in Peru is now a fact." The United States was obliged to assist Peru in its extremity, and a refusal to do so would amount to "almost a breach of national faith." Hurlbut ended his dispatch with a strong appeal to expansionist sentiment: "I, myself, am a profound believer in the right and duty of the United States, to control the political questions of this continent, to the exclusion of any and all European dictation. This belief I understand to be held also by the American people, and to have been asserted by Congress. This I also understand to be the doctrine of the administration which sent me to this place."[122] It was a strong statement and one that might have been deliberately calculated to stir Blaine into action. There was reason for this. The attack upon President Garfield in July 1881 and his slow death had deprived Blaine of all his accustomed energy during the months of September and October.[123]

In the meantime Hurlbut had openly linked the United States to the Peruvian cause. The danger of such rash diplomacy became clear in early November when President García Calderón was removed from office and taken as a prisoner to Chile. Hurlbut had no doubt as to the Chilean motive, which was to prevent the emergence of constitutional government in Peru and to use the resulting anarchy as a justification for continued occupation. That the arrest might also be considered a Chilean reply to the known support given to García Calderón by the United States was not overlooked by the American minister.[124] The minister who came to bring peace now raised the specter of an extension of the war that would involve the United States itself.

Nor was the British minister pleased by the Chilean action. "No sooner was there a prospect of Peru being united under one government with which Chile could treat," wrote St. John, "than the authorities of that Republic destroy the work of months by arresting the Provisional President." It might be that the Chileans intended the arrest to be a calculated provocation aimed at the United States, with the intention also of proving to the Peruvians the hollowness of Hurlbut's promises. Hurlbut himself had hinted at intervention, but St. John did not think this very likely.[125]

In fact, it was beginning to appear to St. John that in spite of Hurlbut's known friendship with Blaine, he did not quite enjoy the secretary's full confidence. In late November it was rumored from Chilean sources that Hurlbut had misunderstood his instructions. St. John could only conclude that Hurlbut had departed from his original instructions because of financial inducements offered to him by the Peruvians. "It is thought," he noted, "that Mr. Hurlbut is acting under the conviction that the immense advantages offered by the Provisional Government to American commerce and naval interests, will induce the Washington Cabinet to reconsider their policy, and that eventually they will decide to intervene."[126] But St. John was not greatly alarmed; with characteristic British caution and pragmatism he judged that time alone would reveal what the attitude of the United States government would be.

In the United States itself, Hurlbut's activities were coming under strong criticism from the press. The *Nation* in particular referred to his "strange performance" and described the resulting American diplomatic position as "untenable, humiliating and irrational."[127] The British chargé in Washington, Victor Drummond, predicted imminent official disapproval of the minister's actions.[128] This was forthcoming from Blaine on November 22, 1881. He could only believe that the minister must have had "some strange and perhaps prejudiced misconception" of his instructions. His actions had given a misleading impression of American policy and the various conventions entered into were disavowed. "As our sole purpose," wrote Blaine, "is to be allowed, in a spirit of the most impartial friendship, to act as mediator between these two powers, I would prefer at present to ask no favors of the one and to excite no possible apprehension in the other." He ended the dispatch by informing Hurlbut of the decision to send a special mission to attempt to bring about a peaceful settlement.[129] Hurlbut was not to be recalled, but his effective diplomatic powers were to be taken away from him.

The British government was not particularly alarmed by these developments in American policy. It was recognized that the United States could pursue a unilateral policy if it so wished. Concern was expressed when this seemed to involve extracting political and economic concessions from Peru. The fears aroused by rumors of "guano diplomacy" proved groundless, however, as did the rumor of the lease of Chimbote to the United States Navy. The diplomatic situation had probably become even more intractable. The Foreign Office had placed little hope in the mediation attempts of 1879; they had even less optimism in 1881. Reports from Lima stressed that the Chileans were preparing for a long occupation.[130] Even if they desired peace, the arrest of García Calderón meant that there was no Peruvian government in existence with which to discuss peace terms. Nor could the United States break the impasse. St. John reported that the Chileans would not give way to any pressure short of war and he did not think the Americans would go this far.[131]

It was also evident that with the military aspect of the war almost at an end, save for police action within Peru, the state of affairs was not now so bad for British interests. The Chilean victory had brought an end to the dislocation of trade in the area, and it was well appreciated that it was the presence of Chilean troops in Lima that prevented the Peruvian mob from running riot in that city. In the disputed nitrate areas to the south, St. John noted that the inhabitants were mostly Chilean by origin and that continued Chilean possession was "to the advantage of the commerce of the world."[132] Moreover, the interests of the British bondholders in the region were not ignored by the Chilean government. Recent Chilean proposals had received a favorable acceptance from the bondholders, a development affording considerable relief to the Foreign Office after the seemingly unresolvable disputes over Peruvian bonds during the 1870s. No doubt, Chile was seeking to play off Britain against the United States by this financial arrangement. It was a game not difficult to win. After all, St. John was on excellent terms with the Chilean authorities in Lima. British sensitivity had already been aroused by the activities of Hurlbut, and the rumors surrounding the scheme to lease Chimbote had not lessened British suspicions of the possible motives of American diplomacy.

Blaine was, in fact, attempting to break the diplomatic impasse by dispatching a special commission to Santiago. It was headed by William H. Trescot, an experienced State Department official, and Blaine's own son, Walker Blaine, was included as Trescot's secretary. Their instructions were, first, to satisfy themselves that the arrest of García Calderón had not been meant as a calculated insult to the United States. Second, they were to aid peace efforts on the basis that Peru had the right to pay an indemnity rather than cede territory. Finally, in a proposal reminiscent of the congressional resolution of December 1866,[133] they were to invite the belligerents to attend a Pan-American conference to be assembled in Washington and at which their differences might be settled.[134]

Spenser St. John regarded the idea as an attempt to create a federation of the American republics under the protection of the United States. He wrote, "The whole of Peru is tranquilly awaiting the result of the American interference. The Peruvians feel assured that the result will be a peace advantageous to Peru without any loss of territory."[135] That Trescot had no instructions to bring about such a settlement was, however, clear from his dispatches to his new superior, Frederick Frelinghuysen.[136] His initial impression was one of surprise at being regarded as "the bearer of a positive and imperious demand from the United States that Chili should make an immediate peace upon such terms as my government deemed just and proper." He was aware that the Chilean government did not hold "this exaggerated apprehension" though it was somewhat uneasy about the purpose of his mission. In his opinion, Chile sincerely desired peace and what he described as the "friendly intervention of the United States" could secure this. He believed his immediate task was to dispel the illusions of armed American intervention and, by so doing, to put an end to the "extravagant hope" extant in Peru that the United States would secure a settlement without the cession of territory.[137]

While the professional diplomats were attempting to unravel the disorderly situation largely created by their own ministers, they themselves became the victims of the vagaries of the American political system. The newly appointed assistant secretary of state, Bancroft Davis, had investigated the diplomatic correspondence on the war and uncovered what he regarded as improper diplomatic responsibilities undertaken by Blaine. Davis believed that Blaine's policy had been dictated by disreputable financial interests and that the Trescot mission might well bring war with Chile.[138] Trescot was therefore informed: "The President wishes in no manner to dictate or make any authoritative utterance to either Peru or Chili as to the merits of the controversy existing between those republics, as to what indemnity should be asked or given, as to a change of boundaries, or as to the personnel of the Government of Peru. The President recognizes Peru and Chili to be independent republics, to which he has no right or inclination to dictate."[139]

This was a sensible and diplomatic statement and in essence was very similar to the attitude of the British Foreign Office. But after the activities of Blaine and especially of Hurlbut, it did imply something of a reversal of American policy. In an attempt to make political capital out of the situation, the new Arthur administration brought the matter before Congress, and consequently much diplomatic correspondence of a very confidential nature was leaked to the press, including the recent dispatch to Trescot. Upon its publication the Chilean minister in Washington telegraphed the substance to Santiago. The official dispatch to Trescot, on the other hand, was mailed by sea via Panama and did not reach him until January 31. The Chilean government was thus aware of the new instructions even before the minister to whom they were directed.[140]

Domestic political considerations gravely weakened the Trescot mission. With their fears of American intervention allayed, the Chileans, who at first had been apprehensive about the mission, now assumed indifference.[141] Spenser St. John summed up these developments in his reports to the Foreign Office. In his opinion, "the firm attitude of Chili" had forced the reversal of the Blaine policies with a consequent loss of American prestige. In March 1882 he concluded that the United States had given up its attempt to interfere in the war; though this was "prudent diplomacy" it was also "most humiliating." The British minister even felt justified in requesting a leave of absence on the grounds that "the American intervention appears to be for the present abandoned, and no other nation is likely to interfere actively to bring about peace."[142] The sudden death of Hurlbut on March 27, 1882, added a further argument in support of his request.[143]

Trescot's mission had been under severe handicaps from its inception. By the time the mission reached South America, Blaine was already out of office and his policy was under careful scrutiny by his successor, who was later to revise it. The Chileans were soon aware of this and could therefore put aside their apprehensions and ignore both the veiled threat of censure from a Pan-American conference and the possibility of armed intervention. As St. John had remarked, the results were "most humiliating" for American diplomacy. Such events had occurred before—in the rejection of Seward's Danish West Indies treaty, in the failure to mediate the War of the Triple Alliance, and in the Santo Domingo fiasco—but now the humiliation was apparent on an international scale. Further, while Blaine may have believed that his actions had successfully forestalled European intervention in the war, he had incurred a reputation for aggressive and reckless diplomacy that was to last throughout his lifetime and that was to affect the future course of United States–Latin American relations. It was also ironic that with the failure of American mediation, the field now lay open, as it had done in 1879, for the mediation of the European powers.

The diplomatic situation in Peru remained confused. From his headquarters at Arequipa, Admiral Montero claimed to be the successor of García Calderón, but the Chileans refused him recognition. This only created further confusion and aroused even more suspicion as to the Chilean government's real motives since it had declared a willingness to negotiate with any Peruvian leader. When a settlement had been worked out, it would then be submitted to a Peruvian assembly for approval. But it was well understood that the Chileans regarded the area of Tarapacá as nonnegotiable, and as the British chargé in Lima noted, any government that accepted such terms would be overthrown "the moment the support of Chilean bayonets was withdrawn." He could only interpret Chilean policy as "an indication that they entertain no present wish to relax the firm hold they have fixed upon their prostrate foe."[144]

In London, the Foreign Office hesitated to recognize Montero, probably waiting for the Chileans to do so. The arrival of a minister from Montero in August 1882, seeking accreditation to the courts of Paris and London, created further complications. France was disposed to extend him recognition, but the Foreign Office held back. Bondholder interests in London urged Pauncefote to take the initiative and recognize Montero.[145] Pauncefote was inclined to favor recognition but not because of pressure from the bondholders. He was greatly sympathetic to the fact that Peru was without an established government and that consequently it was unable to make peace. The decision to recognize was, however, not to be taken lightly for the other European powers were waiting and would be guided by British action. Pauncefote therefore counselled caution and recommended that both St. John and Graham be sounded before any action was taken.[146]

News from Santiago in October seemed to point to a turn in events. The acting British minister, James Drummond-Hay, reported that Chile could "ill-spare" fresh reinforcements for Peru, and rumors that the government desired to withdraw from Peru as soon as possible began to circulate. It was also noted that the Chilean government was seeking an understanding with the former Peruvian leader, Piérola, now resident in Paris. This development was confirmed in a dispatch from Lima reporting conversations with Admiral Lynch to the same effect.[147]

At the same time, the Dutch minister in London proposed a renewal of joint mediation by the European powers. The Foreign Office acted by asking the opinion of Spenser St. John, then on leave in Germany. He alluded to the question of Dutch financial interests in Peru, and warned that after the recent failure of American mediation, a similar European attempt would be "unadvisable." St. John believed the internal political situation in Peru must be allowed to stabilize until the Peruvians made peace of their own accord. Otherwise, "any interference of foreign powers would tend to strengthen the illusions of the people and thus prolong a useless struggle."[148] The Foreign Office concurred and judged that the time was not opportune for a tender of British good offices.

British policy was, therefore, cautious and negative, but it was based upon the advice of diplomatic officials serving in, or with experience of, the area in question. Furthermore, even though American influence was in eclipse, Britain was making no attempt to exploit the situation to its own diplomatic advantage. It was the government in Santiago that was dictating events, and the Foreign Office clearly understood this. Chilean war aims were not clear, but there was no doubt that Chile was determined to pursue its own way regardless of outside pressure. But what Chile wanted was uncertain. This ambiguous attitude merely reinforced the basic dilemma preventing peace. There was no stable government in Peru, and with García Calderón a prisoner in Chile, Piérola a refugee in Europe, and Montero in isolated Arequipa, there was no one with whom the Chileans could hold substantive talks. Well might the British chargé in Lima lament in October 1882 that "the prospects of peace being made shortly are . . . far from hopeful."[149]

Dispatches from Santiago confirmed this gloomy analysis, thus justifying the cautious attitude of the Foreign Office. With the same information at hand, however, the United States government launched another initiative at mediation. In September 1882 the new American minister in Chile, Cornelius Logan, opened up talks with García Calderón. So well did Logan keep his British colleague informed of developments that the British chargé described the American as a friend rather than a rival. This did not prevent him from expressing some satisfaction when he reported the failure of Logan's efforts in December 1882. In his view, the Chilean government now believed that it could make peace on its own terms and did not need foreign mediation.[150]

Although disappointed by his talks with García Calderón, Logan did not give up his peace attempt. Without consulting his colleague in Peru, he switched direction and wrote to Montero urging him to accept the Chilean terms. This was harsh advice, but Logan also hinted at payment of $10 million as compensation to Peru for the cession of Tacna and Arica to Chile. The new British chargé in Lima, Alfred St. John, suspected that Logan had some part in the financial arrangement and he noted that the American minister in Lima resented his colleague's "improper" interference in Peruvian affairs.[151] When asked for his views in London, Spenser St. John wrote to Pauncefote that "it is curious to notice how completely the American Agents have abandoned the cause of Peru."[152]

The temptation to act independently and unofficially now affected Hurlbut's successor in Lima, James Partridge. No doubt annoyed by Logan's invasion of his sphere of influence, Partridge initiated his own policy of mediation. His first step was to be a personal meeting with Montero. Alfred St. John believed that this effort would meet with no more success than those of previous American ministers.[153] Partridge, however, continued his efforts and requested a meeting of the Lima diplomatic corps. This dramatic change in American policy induced St. John to speculate that the proposal for concerted action might now be renewed with better hopes of success. At the same time, he still did not believe that a Peruvian government was yet in existence that could negotiate successfully with the Chileans.[154]

In March 1883 Frelinghuysen learned of Partridge's initiative and immediately exercised Washington's ultimate, if not only sanction. He disavowed Partridge's action and presented him with his virtual recall from office.[155] It was certainly not an edifying spectacle for any government to repudiate the actions of two of its ministers in succession. Even before this action St. John had already reported to London that Partridge was advocating the withdrawal of the American mission in Lima as its position was becoming untenable. The failure of American diplomacy had turned the Peruvians against the United States, while the Chileans had lost all fear of possible American intervention.[156]

Whatever the intentions, activities, or influence of the American or European diplomats, the fact was that the war had been in progress for almost four years. A peace settlement was, however, soon to be arranged between the Chileans and the Peruvians without the mediation of, or even prior consultation with, the neutral powers. It was merely one more assertion of the independence of action that Chile had enjoyed and maintained ever since the beginning of the war. The one restraint to this had been the fear of United States armed intervention, but this had never materialized. At no stage in the war had such intervention been seriously contemplated by the European powers, but now that a legitimate government seemed to be returning to Peru and as the chaos of war gave way to a superficial sense of political stability, the European powers began to put forward their own various financial claims. Their involvement in events became now very much more in evidence though this did not mean that they acquired any more influence over the outcome of these events.

One reason for this was that Britain, the most important of the European powers, still maintained a cautious policy, preferring concerted rather than unilateral action. For example, a Peruvian Congress under Montero assembled at Arequipa and in July 1883 requested the good offices of the European powers in order to bring about a peaceful settlement. Like the question of the recognition of Montero in 1882, here was another opportunity for Britain to interfere. But the Foreign Office did not even deign to reply. "The Peruvian government declare their anxiety for peace," minuted an official, "but do not appear to be prepared to accept the only terms on which it is possible."[157] Nor was any action taken on a suggestion from the British minister in Washington that the State Department might be now more amenable to proposals concerning joint mediation.[158] The Foreign Office view was that neither proposal promised much chance of success.

American policy gradually came round to very much the same point of view. In August 1883 a new American minister, Seth L. Phelps, arrived in Lima just as events were moving strongly toward a peace settlement. It was then apparent that the Chileans were actively supporting the effort of the former war minister, Iglesias, to form a Peruvian government.[159] American interference was, however, not to be anticipated from Phelps. The State Department had issued instructions to the new minister very similar to the standing instructions that directed British diplomatic officials. In a note dated July 26, Frelinghuysen informed him: "It is not for this Government to dictate to sovereign belligerent powers the terms of peace to be accepted by them, nor is it the right or duty of the United States in the premises to do more than to aid by their unprejudiced counsels, their friendly mediation, and their moral support the obtainment of peace—the much desired end."[160] In the case of Phelps, these instructions were adhered to.

In September 1883 Iglesias took the major step of forming a government, though one described by St. John as "composed with one exception of obscure persons."[161] This weakness was offset by Chilean military pressure upon Montero, who grudgingly announced his willingness to negotiate with the new leader. In Lima an Assembly of Notables declared its support for Iglesias. The tide was turning, and in October the Chilean plenipotentiary, Luis Alduñate, arrived in Lima for the purpose of speeding up the peace negotiations. Rapid progress ensued and peace was signed on October 20, thus bringing an end to the war.[162] The British chargé remarked that Peru was "temporarily united" for the first time since January 1881. He admitted that this had been achieved by Chilean force of arms, but he added that "it may truly be said that this country was as incapable of making peace of its own free will as it was of carrying on a war with any hope of success."[163]

Even though Iglesias had achieved supremacy in Peru only through Chilean support, a new government had come into being and the question of its recognition was therefore raised. At the Foreign Office Jervoise realized that British action could be decisive. Immediate recognition of Iglesias would give him "moral support and contribute towards the stability of his Government." The alternative was to first consult the other powers and to wait for Peruvian popular confirmation of Iglesias. Another official, the assistant undersecretary, Currie, came out strongly in favor of immediate recognition. He did not see any need to consult the other powers and argued that "we should probably best increase our influence and serve the interests of the British creditors of Peru by taking the initiative."[164] A proposal as aggressive as Currie's was out of character with British policy toward the war, and it is not surprising to find that it was not taken up by senior officials. The traditional policy was adopted instead. Legal advice was requested and the other powers were consulted as to their attitudes. In April 1884, some four months later and only after being informed of the confirmation of Iglesias's powers by the Peruvian Congress, Britain recognized the new president in concert with the other powers. It was a victory for caution, moderation, and respect for the customs of international relations.

The years immediately following the peace treaty[165] did not bring stability to Peru. After the withdrawal of the Chileans, internal conflict broke out again between the various Peruvian factions. British policy still adhered to a policy of scrupulous neutrality. In 1885 the new British minister, Colonel Mansfield, was approached by his Spanish colleague in Lima, who tried to convince him of the necessity of British intervention to end the civil strife. While admitting the damage to British interests caused by the disturbances, Mansfield considered that such intervention would be inevitably misrepresented, that he would become identified with the cause of the revolution, and would thus awaken the anti-European prejudices of the Peruvians. Later in the same year Mansfield justified his refusal to grant belligerent rights to the faction led by Cáceres on the grounds that it would "throw so advantageous a weight into the scale of the Revolutionists" that it must be "under the present circumstances, a virtual interference in the internal struggle of the Republic."[166]

There can be no doubt that Blaine was in error if he meant to suggest that the British government backed the Chilean war effort. Certain private British interests did support Chile, but official policy did not. "Mr. Blaine," asserted the *Times,* "pays more honour to British diplomacy than Englishmen are prone to render when he envies and extols it as always bold, energetic, and vigilant in spreading the commercial power of England."[167] The salient fact was that throughout the war Chile maintained complete freedom of action, and when the powers became resentful at the terms of the peace treaty, this resentment was expressed against Chile and no attempt was made to exploit Peruvian weaknesses. In contrast to the United States, the European powers had little interest in the disposition of Peruvian territory. Their concern was with the financial claims presented by their citizens, including the claims of the holders of Peruvian bonds, the security for which had now been annexed by Chile.[168] It did not really matter who controlled the territory so long as the financial obligations were respected.[169]

The proposed Treaty of Ancón stipulated that the bondholders were to receive half the new proceeds from the existing but not from future nitrate operations in the territories annexed by Chile. It was not very clear as to what was to become of the Peruvian national debt and whether Chile was to assume a proportionate share. The Foreign Office was concerned because Pauncefote had information that the nitrate deposits were "nearly exhausted" and that the Chilean proposal was therefore inadequate. Furthermore, the question of the Peruvian national debt was an important one, involving all manner of international financial complications. Pauncefote was also aware that France had already lodged a protest over the Chilean proposals and that Britain could not therefore remain inactive.[170]

In January 1884 the Foreign Office came under pressure from the governments of France, Italy, and Spain to join in intervention on behalf of the rights of the bondholders. After seeking legal advice the Foreign Office agreed that the bondholders had a claim "of a special character," and the British ministers were instructed to lodge official protests.[171] Lord Granville was disturbed by this apparent departure from the traditional policy of dealing with bondholders' claims until Pauncefote informed him that this was not an operation in support of bondholders' claims pure and simple. Britain was not pressing for payment, but insisting that the rights of its citizens be respected and that they should not be deprived of those rights "because they happen to be 'Bondholders.' "[172]

Iglesias, however, resented the long delay in securing his recognition as president by the foreign powers and he was further angered by their attempts to put pressure on him to change the financial terms of the peace settlement. He decided to break off even unofficial relations with those powers and to go ahead with the peace treaty as it stood. The French reaction was sudden and critical. The French ambassador called at the Foreign Office and proposed Anglo-French armed intervention.[173] In fact, there was little likelihood of such joint action. Even though he agreed with the French analysis of the situation, Pauncefote would never consent to what he described as "this wild programme." In his view, the Chileans must be given a chance to state their own side of the case, and in the meantime he suggested the Foreign Office could "easily answer this note with some cooling and sedative language."[174] Without British support the French scheme was impractical, and a few weeks later harmony with Iglesias was restored when the powers granted him the recognition that he had desired for so long.

Although the question of the claims of the bondholders drifted on for several years, the Foreign Office never considered intervening on their behalf, and its support gradually became even more lukewarm than it had been during 1883–1884. The purpose of British policy was to avoid becoming entangled in discussions between the bondholders and the Peruvian and Chilean governments. Official diplomatic support would be given to reasonable claims, but the Foreign Office would not interfere in matters between foreign governments and their creditors.[175] The whole issue was further complicated by the intrigues of the Dréyfus Company, which had enlisted the support of the French government. This caused acute division between the British and French bondholders, further delaying a settlement.[176]

It was all a far cry from the supposed intrigues of Britain, alleged by American politicians such as Blaine. No doubt private British financial interests may have had some influence on Chilean policy, but without documentary evidence this remains a subject for speculation. The *Times* summed up the contemporary view that "British trade has suffered, not gained, by the deplorable civil war which has desolated Peru."[177] Blaine might talk about "an English war" and newspapers such as the *New York World* might run headlines entitled "The English Hand in the Chilian Game,"[178] but in reality Britain exercised no control over the events of the war. Communications were slow, and the Foreign Office was imperfectly informed of what was happening or what might occur.[179] If there were any priorities in British foreign policy, they lay in Egypt and the Near East, and not in South America.

Nor did events favor British or, indeed, any country's efforts to mediate the conflict. The rapidity and scale of the Chilean victories startled contemporaries and, moreover, startled the Chileans too. Their tone became imperious and their precise aims and intentions became obscured. Concessions in the former Peruvian nitrate fields might be falling into the hands of British promoters, but at no time did British official action direct Chilean policy. The Chileans feared American intervention not because they revolved in a British orbit, but because they feared it might rob them of what they considered to be justly earned gains. To maintain their freedom of action it became Chilean policy to play off the United States against Britain and vice versa. This proved highly successful.

Britain had never contemplated armed intervention in the war. There would have been no advantage in doing so, and in fact the Chilean victories brought with them a certain element of political and economic stability that had been previously lacking in the Pacific region. British policy was to observe strict neutrality and to act only after consultation with and in concert with the other interested powers. An attempt was made to include the United States in this scheme of things, but this was consistently rejected by Washington. British ministers in Peru and Chile were critical of the American attempts at mediation, but there was never any calculated British obstruction of these peace efforts.[180] Britain sincerely desired an end to the war and, as in 1865–1866 and during the War of the Triple Alliance, realized that this must be done primarily by the belligerents themselves and that foreign mediation would only help in specific circumstances. Even when the Foreign Office was aware that it had a number of legitimate grievances against Chile arising from the war, the French proposal concerning joint intervention was disparagingly and immediately rejected.

In the long term Britain gained no apparent benefits from its cautious diplomacy during the war. Neither Peru nor Chile was to manifest any special friendliness toward Britain, but it had never been intended that they should. On the other hand, the United States suffered a good deal of diplomatic humiliation, and the war provoked a legacy of bitterness between America and Chile that was to color their relations for some years. Peru would balance this by siding with the United States, not because of any belief in an "American" system, but rather with the ulterior motive of enlisting American influence to regain Tacna and Arica. Evarts, Blaine, and Frelinghuysen attempted to maintain an outward neutrality throughout the war, but they were badly served by their ministers, who acted much too independently and, on occasion, irresponsibly. As had been the case at Valparaiso in March 1866, the military state of affairs could only be altered by an armed United States intervention that could only be interpreted, in this case, as favorable to Peru and Bolivia. This was never expressly formulated by the State Department, but ministers such as Christiancy and Hurlbut implied that it was under consideration. Peru seized the opportunity to commit the United States to its side, but nothing could be done against a resolute Chile, which refused to give way to diplomatic pressure. Would-be mediators could not resolve complex diplomatic situations by appeals to sentiment or by aggressive bluster. The Foreign Office understood this very well and proceeded cautiously, as it had done in similar incidents since 1865. Certain politicians in the United States might interpret developments as being the result of British intrigue and machinations, but in fact the United States had continually misjudged the situation and had overplayed its hand. Nor was this a particularly exceptional state of affairs, for it had happened before, during the War of the Triple Alliance. The influence of the United States in the Western Hemisphere was not negligible, but during the War of the Pacific the Chileans showed no willingness to respond to empty words and phrases. They called the American bluff and were successful.

//4//

The Isthmian Canal

In 1869 Secretary of State Seward justified his canal policy by declaring that the destiny of America "can only be attained by the execution of the Darien ship canal."[1] Eleven years later, President Hayes noted in his diary:

> The United States will not consent that any European power shall control the railroad or canal across the Isthmus of Central America. With due regard to the rights and wishes of our sister republics in the Isthmus, the United States will insist that this passageway shall always remain under American control. Whoever invests capital in the contemplated work should do it with a distinct understanding that the United States expects and intends to control the canal in conformity with its own interests.[2]

In 1896 the Republican campaign platform declared that "the Nicaragua Canal should be built, owned and operated by the United States."[3] Nor were these isolated or unrepresentative views, for American opinion during the late nineteenth century did not doubt the potential value and strategic significance of an isthmian canal for the United States. The implementation and completion of the project was, however, another matter and in spite of the rhetoric of expansionism, the opening of the canal—under the control of the United States government—had to await the twentieth century.[4]

The idea of a canal through the isthmus of Central America had a long history,[5] and in the nineteenth century various American administrations undertook diplomatic initiatives and even commitments so that work might be begun. The question was considered so important in Washington that, in spite of its tradition of "no entangling alliances," the United States government negotiated and ratified treaties with New Granada (1846) and with Britain (1850). By Article 35 of the former treaty the United States guaranteed Colombian[6] sovereignty over the isthmus of Panama and the protection of the isthmian transit from external or internal interference.[7] The 1850 treaty with Britain was popularly known as the Clayton-Bulwer Treaty and its terms amounted to an Anglo-American undertaking to respect and to guarantee the neutrality of projected isthmian communications with a joint disclaimer that neither power would ever acquire exclusive privileges or control over such communications.[8]

In spite of these treaties the canal came no nearer to actual realization. The problems of engineering and of finance posed apparently insuperable obstacles, and American interest was distracted by the political tensions that resulted in the Civil War. After 1865 further canal treaties were negotiated but not ratified between the United States and Colombia in 1869 and 1870 and with Nicaragua in 1884. At the same time, both houses of Congress established committees to investigate canal projects, and appropriations were voted for extensive surveys of the whole isthmian region. Numerous politicians and newspapers stressed the necessity of an "American" canal[9] and American canal companies were formed to carry out the work.

One such company, the Maritime Canal Company of Nicaragua, actually began construction work in Nicaragua in 1890, but this was terminated by the bankruptcy of the company in 1893. Much more effort and expense was undertaken by the French promoters of the Panama project, although this was an enterprise devised and financed with minimal American support and encouragement. The Panama scheme ultimately failed not so much as a result of the attitude of the United States government, but because of lack of sufficient capital, corrupt and sometimes incompetent administration, and, most of all, because the original scheme involved too many engineering problems. The adoption of a more feasible scheme might indeed have resulted in the actual completion of a French canal across the isthmus.[10]

Why was American canal diplomacy so unproductive and why did the United States adopt a negative policy that belied its expansionist pronouncements and declared intentions? The reasons were many and ranged from practical political and economic considerations to the difficulties of conducting foreign policy in a world of sovereign nation states.

There were strong grounds for caution and delay. Any canal scheme was a massive undertaking and involved major engineering, geographical, and financial problems. The history of all canal ventures up to the mid–nineteenth century was one of failure, and the question of whether an isthmian canal was feasible or not remained unresolved. Both the executive and Congress understood the consequent need for thorough surveys of possible canal routes. An Interoceanic Canal

Commission was established for this purpose in 1872. The findings of the surveys, however, were not unanimous in their recommendations. The strongest arguments were in favor of a canal through Nicaragua, but alternative routes such as Panama or Tehuantepec also had their advocates. Added to this uncertainty over location was the question of finance. An isthmian canal would undoubtedly bring great commercial benefits to the United States and to the world, but such benefits lay in the future when the canal had been completed. In the meantime the needs of commerce were provided by the Panama railroad and the construction of transcontinental railroads in the United States. In such circumstances the vast capital required for the canal project was not forthcoming.

Private capital had proved capable of building a canal at Suez and major railroads and canals throughout Europe and North America, but not without some form of government support. In an age of laissez faire and limited fiscal resources, governments were unable and unwilling to provide the funds necessary for such a project as the isthmian canal. A possible solution in this sort of case was to attract private investment by giving a government guarantee of a fixed return on capital. Such guarantees were straightforward in matters of internal projects but not in far off and uncertain enterprises such as the isthmian canal. Governments could involve themselves in projects in distant sovereign nations only with the agreement of those nations. Consequently, the canal question came to involve diplomatic negotiations between the United States and the Central American governments.

By reason of its geographical proximity and its military and economic power, the United States possessed considerable influence in any negotiations with the nations of Central America. This was reflected by their constant fear of American military intervention, whether real or unfounded. Robert Bunch, the British chargé at Bogotá, reported in 1870 that the American minister "must have threatened the Colombians with the loss of the Isthmus if they do not accede to his terms whatever they may be."[11] On the other hand, impoverished Central American governments were attracted by the prospect of American money, which would be spent not only on a work of national importance but, no doubt, also on the purchase of political favors. In 1868 Bunch noted that in spite of the opposition of the Colombian government to a treaty, the American minister "will push matters through, which is not difficult if he be prepared to spend money."[12] Such negotiations were, however, not totally one-sided for although the United States had the money, it was the Central Americans who controlled the land on which the canal would be built. The more the United States wanted a canal agreement, the greater the price to be exacted. When the Interoceanic Canal Commission reported in favor of the Nicaraguan route in 1876 the foreign minister of that country came to Washington expecting very generous terms for his country. Secretary of State Fish proved unyielding in this instance, but a later secretary of state, Frederick Frelinghuysen, granted Nicaragua very favorable terms in 1884 in return for a canal treaty.[13]

Diplomatic negotiations also exposed some of the weaknesses resulting from the American diplomatic establishment's dependence upon political appointments rather than permanent career officials. The actions of certain American ministers impeded rather than assisted canal negotiations. In November 1869 Caleb Cushing was sent to Bogotá to speed up negotiations. Seward was critical of his resident minister, whom he considered "not quite up to the business."[14] Ernest Dichman, who served in Colombia from 1878 to 1881, also came to lose the confidence of his superiors in Washington. "Mr. Dichman," wrote the British minister in Washington, "is full of extraordinary and extravagant projects, which seem to be treated with ridicule and contempt by the Department of State."[15] Dichman's habit of "loose language" and his aggressive attitude so alienated the Colombian government that his recall was requested in June 1881.[16]

Officials in Washington also appreciated the difficulties of canal diplomacy. Treaties invariably took a long time to negotiate and then were subject to lengthy procedures of ratification by both sides. Frequent changes of governments and political conflicts in Central America sometimes disrupted negotiations. Even when Central American governments appeared favorably disposed toward American requests, officials in Washington tended to act cautiously.[17] This reflected a basic reluctance to become involved in internal Central American politics. Seward had recognized this in 1869. While he admitted that the 1846 treaty conferred certain responsibilities upon the United States, he also argued that the "employment of force" would be "a question of grave expediency to be determined by circumstances" and that on no account was the United States intended "to become a party to any civil war in that country by defending the Isthmus against another party."[18]

An even greater restriction upon American canal diplomacy was the existence of the Clayton-Bulwer Treaty, which appeared to preclude the policy of a canal constructed, owned, and operated exclusively by the United States government. The treaty could only be abrogated with the mutual consent of both signatories and, though the United States never formally raised the question of abrogation, the British government made it clear that it had no wish to rescind or even to modify the treaty. In fact, on a number of occasions in the nineteenth century, the British minister in Washington was instructed to remind the United States government of the stipulations of the 1850 treaty.[19] The State Department under Blaine and his successor, Frelinghuysen, responded in the early 1880s by opening up a diplomatic correspondence designed to convince the Foreign Office that the treaty was null and void, but London rejected all such contentions. In 1884 Frelinghuysen negotiated a canal treaty with Nicaragua, giving the United States canal rights in violation of the Clayton-Bulwer Treaty. But the Senate was not so ready to ignore the international obligations of the United States, and this provided one of the strongest reasons for the failure of the treaty to secure ratification.

Engineering and financial difficulties in the way of constructing an isthmian canal were massive, but were not beyond the entrepreneurs of the nineteenth century. Diplomatic negotiations were lengthy and sometimes exacting, but treaties could be agreed upon. The fate of these treaties illustrated, however, the major and insuperable obstacle to the implementation of an "American" canal in the nineteenth century. This was the negative response of American opinion, business, and especially Congress to all such proposals. While it is true that most administrations from Johnson to Cleveland favored building a canal, there were varying degrees of enthusiasm. For example, President Grant was eager, but his secretary of state, Fish, appeared to lack interest.[20] Similarly, while Hayes spoke aggressively on the issue, Evarts pursued a much more cautious policy.[21] The Cleveland administration was averse to entangling alliances and therefore to canal treaties; the Harrison administration, which included Blaine as secretary of state, showed a surprising moderation that belied its party's campaign platform of 1888.[22]

The lack of a clear and consistent administration policy undermined the chances of an "American" canal, especially when most administrations also experienced difficulties in their relations with Congress and could not count on congressional support for their foreign policies. With the exception of the purchase of Alaska, Congress defeated the expansionist proposals of the Johnson administration, including the 1869 canal treaty negotiated with Colombia. The 1870 treaty with Colombia took a very secondary place as the administration and the Senate clashed over Grant's proposal to annex the Dominican Republic. The Nicaraguan treaty of 1884 was submitted at a most inauspicious time by a lame-duck Republican administration with the inauguration of a Democratic president only weeks away.

Lack of harmony between executive and legislative branches obstructed canal policy, but this should have been offset by congressional support for an isthmian canal. This support was frequently demonstrated by numerous resolutions, canal bills, and survey appropriations introduced and, in some cases, passed throughout the last third of the nineteenth century.[23] On the other hand, Congress failed to bring the

1869 and 1870 canal treaties to a vote and did not ratify the 1884 treaty. Furthermore, in spite of the activities of canal enthusiasts such as Senator Morgan of Alabama, Congress refused to give a financial guarantee to the American promoters of the Nicaraguan canal scheme, even though this proposed an American canal to rival the French scheme at Panama.

There were many reasons for the failure of Congress to support a positive canal policy. The separation of executive and legislative functions made the ratification of treaties difficult, especially when Congress had played no part in their negotiation or when the executive, as in the case of the Johnson administration, lacked support in Congress. Moreover, Congress became uncomfortably aware of the constitutional implications of canal treaties. The terms of these treaties included American control over the proposed canal site and thus raised the question of the administration of noncontiguous areas and, ultimately, the assimilation of foreign and colored peoples. The *Nation* outlined some of these apprehensions in 1882: "We shall have enough to do for fifty years at least in assimilating the population we have already got, and which Europe has still to send us, and in developing the resources of the territory we already occupy, without saddling ourselves with the management of large bodies of Catholic Latins."[24]

The existence of the Clayton-Bulwer Treaty also served as an obstacle toward the ratification of canal treaties. If the United States voided the treaty without British consent, this would be not only a flagrant violation of treaty obligations, but it would also release Britain from those terms of the treaty prohibiting the colonization of territory in Central America. The treaty was therefore of some value to the United States. A former secretary of state, Thomas Bayard, argued in 1894 that abrogation would only "create diplomatic difficulties from which this treaty has been potentially useful in saving us."[25]

Bayard also put forward another reason for lack of congressional action. "With our own experience of the transcontinental railroads (with their credit-mobiliers, land grants, and infinite corruption)," he noted, "I recoil from embarking the Treasury and Government of the United States in the work of constructing the Canal at Nicaragua or anywhere else."[26] This attitude had been evident in congressional hostility to Frelinghuysen's request in 1884 for a secret appropriation of $250,000. The request provoked charges of a "slush fund" and made congressmen reluctant to support his Nicaraguan treaty.[27] Moreover, because canal treaties involved the appropriation of funds, they needed the consent not only of the Senate but also of the House of Representatives. For a variety of reasons ranging from jealousy of the Senate's prerogative in foreign affairs to the practical consideration of how to raise vast sums of money, the House proved reluctant to endorse canal schemes involving public money. When public opinion was aroused by the de Lesseps scheme, Congress responded by debating resolutions reaffirming the Monroe Doctrine. Congress was similarly responsive to economic fluctuations, and during periods of business depression canal interests received no special consideration. The House closed the American legation in Bogotá in 1876 as an economy measure and refused assistance to the Maritime Canal Company of Nicaragua when that company went bankrupt in 1893.

The canal diplomacy of the United States from 1865 to the end of the nineteenth century was therefore barren of actual results. In spite of the strictures of President Hayes, de Lesseps went ahead with his scheme of constructing a Panama canal. But the rhetoric of expansionism did have one positive result in that it made other powers aware of the American attitude on this question and warned these powers against interfering in canal affairs. While the European powers recognized the preponderating position that the United States exercised in the Caribbean region, they also had interests in that region. Of these powers Britain was the most involved, because as the world's leading commercial nation it would benefit most from an isthmian canal. Britain was also the world's leading naval power and could not ignore the strategic implications of a canal that linked the Atlantic and Pacific oceans. Moreover, Britain was an "American" power too, possessing vast territories in Canada and the Caribbean islands and on the Central American mainland. Finally, by the Clayton-Bulwer Treaty of 1850, Britain had assumed a vested interest, and specific rights, in the question of the isthmian transit.[28]

"Central America, although a considerable region, extending over some fifteen degrees of latitude," noted the *Times* in 1885, "does not fill a very large place in the thoughts of the people of this country."[29] Trade and investment figures confirmed this. The Central American economies were based on modest production and export of precious metals, coffee, and sugar. In the early nineteenth century Colombia had attracted considerable British mining investment, but the initial speculative fervor was soon replaced by gloom and failure. Colombian foreign trade fluctuated and was never very valuable to either Britain or the United States, amounting to around £4 million annually to Britain in the early 1870s and rarely more than an annual figure of $10 million to the United States.[30]

Nor was British investment very substantial in the Central American region, in contrast to the other areas of Latin America.[31] This must have afforded a certain amount of satisfaction to Foreign Office officials who found dealings with these republics particularly difficult. An official remarked in 1884 that the government of Panama was "notoriously bad," and Pauncefote concurred by describing Colombia "as a country so ill-governed that the ordinary rules which regulate and limit the functions of consular officers may be departed from."[32] Even so, the appeals of the bondholders evoked little sympathy from Foreign Office officials. "The parties to it [capital investment] embark in a hazardous speculation expecting to make their fortunes," remarked Edmund Hammond in 1867, "and if they fail they must not expect their Government to quarrel for their redress."[33] Over twenty years later official policy toward such appeals remained unchanged. On the suggestion that action be taken to vindicate the rights of British investors involved in certain Colombian mining and railroad claims, the Foreign Office legal adviser argued:

> I agree generally but the practical difficulty is considerable. It is a matter of common knowledge that these South American Republics are financially and politically unstable and people who invest money under their auspices take their capital in their hands seduced thereto by spurious promises either of huge profits or a very high rate of interest both of which things are incompatible with first rate security as a rule.
>
> When they are subsequently disappointed in their hopes, or even absolutely swindled (as I fear it must be admitted they sometimes are) it is very difficult to give them anything much more effective than sympathy unless we are prepared to go to war on their behalf.[34]

Foreign Office officials were uncomfortably aware that the chronic political instability of Central America might somehow involve Britain. This eventuality they assiduously sought to avoid. When the British minister in Bogotá suggested intervention in Colombia in 1875, an official wrote:

> I think it wd have been better if Mr Bunch had not written this Circular to the Consuls. It is not their business to interfere in the Presidential contests and it wd be wiser not to threaten the intervention of England and the United States for the preservation of the Union, since it is most unlikely that any such intervention by force (the only kind of intervention worth threatening) wd ever take place. Indeed we have no sort of right to intervene that I can see. These Central American and S. American States were not constituted by us or under our protection or guarantee and they have a right to separate or amalgamate or do as they choose and as

their instincts for civil war prompt them. All we have a right to do is to demand that our Treaties shd. be complied with and our trade not improperly harassed and the transit kept open so far as our Treaties provide.[35]

Only on one occasion after 1865 was there serious consideration of intervention by force in Colombia.[36] In 1867 the Colombian government insisted that British mail be delivered to the Colombian post office prior to transportation across the isthmus of Panama and also that the British mail steamers pay increased tonnage dues. Legal advice given to the Foreign Office pointed out that the rights assumed by the Colombian government in this question had been invalidated by that government's charter with the Panama Railroad Company. Moreover, this action was judged to be "clearly framed in a spirit of direct hostility to British interests" since the United States and France appeared to enjoy immunity. The matter was therefore serious, and intervention by force received consideration but was rejected. The British minister was instructed instead to emphasize that the problem was regarded as "serious" in London and to issue a "friendly warning."[37]

The Foreign Office was also aware that any forceful British intervention might lead to complications with the United States, but, as was so often the case in these matters, the passage of time made forceful measures unnecessary.[38] A dispatch written by Hammond concisely expressed the Foreign Office attitude:

The interest we have in Colombia is merely indirect. For the Country, its Government and people we need care nothing, and its commerce probably is very unimportant. . . . Colombia is valuable to us as a transit route for our commerce, and in this respect it is becoming more valuable every day; and our policy is to keep on good terms with the ruling Powers to avoid seeking or taking up occasions of quarrel, and rather to attribute to innate barbarism engrafted on Spanish absurdity, and so deal forbearingly with, any proceeding which in a more civilized State of society it would not become us to pass over. A serious difficulty with such a State as Colombia, involving all the paraphernalia of War would be too ridiculous to be thought of, and too injurious to our own interests if magnified into a positive rupture.[39]

While the Foreign Office abstained from involvement in the internal affairs of Central America, there was, however, the necessity of paying attention to the question of isthmian transit and also of replying to frequent Colombian proposals for negotiation of a treaty with a British guarantee of Colombian sovereignty over the isthmus of Panama.

The 1856 disturbances at Panama[40] had resulted in the first American military intervention on the isthmus under the terms of the 1846 treaty between Colombia and the United States. Thereafter, Colombian governments sought to offset their fear of the United States by inviting Britain to give similar undertakings to those given by the United States in the 1846 treaty. Official approaches for this purpose were made in 1857, 1865, 1868, 1870, and 1881, but all were rejected by the Foreign Office. The British government was not unduly concerned over the 1846 treaty or the possibility of American intervention on the isthmus. The treaty was in fact recognized as a force for stability in the isthmian region and therefore in British interests. In any event, these interests were already safeguarded by the Clayton-Bulwer Treaty, and this treaty needed no reinforcement. Furthermore, British policy, in general, was to refuse to give guarantees, especially when Colombia would probably use such a guarantee to involve Britain in its disputes with the United States.[41]

The lack of a positive British canal policy was also influenced by official scepticism that an isthmian canal would ever be completed. Canal promoters sought to interest the Foreign Office in their ventures, but were invariably rejected. In 1865 the Foreign Office dismissed one such scheme proposed by Edward Cullen as "utterly impracticable" and cited an official Admiralty survey of 1853–1854 that had judged such schemes a "useless and expensive waste of time."[42] This attitude was repeatedly upheld as numerous canal projects collapsed or failed to materialize. In these circumstances British policy was particularly cautious and realistic. "This is a big question," summed up Pauncefote in 1886, "and . . . should not be touched until the Canal is near completion, when some international action is pretty sure to be set on foot."[43]

Hasty and impulsive action was not only out of character in late nineteenth-century British policy toward the Western Hemisphere, but would also have been counterproductive and have involved numerous difficulties of implementation. The Foreign Office could only give verbal or moral support to canal ventures for, as in the American system, financial support or guarantees required the assent of Parliament. "To do what is here asked," minuted an official on a canal scheme proposed in 1892, "would saddle the Foreign Office with very serious responsibility." Another comment stated categorically that the British government was "not prepared to countenance any scheme involving a subsidy from the British Exchequer to a canal across Nicaragua."[44]

The Foreign Office also clearly appreciated the sensitivity of the

United States government on this question. The negotiation of canal treaties by the United States did infringe the Clayton-Bulwer Treaty, and the Foreign Office reminded Washington of this, but no official protests were lodged. It was well understood in London that these treaties had little chance of ratification in Washington and that expressions of British displeasure would increase rather than decrease that chance. In 1885 the British minister in Washington noted that Frelinghuysen had expected a British protest against the Nicaraguan treaty and hoped that this would strengthen support for the treaty. The "judicious silence" of the British government had, however, "greatly disconcerted" the secretary of state.[45] The same view was reiterated in 1895. "Any interference on the part of Her Majesty's Government," minuted the Foreign Office clerk, Francis Villiers, "would probably cause an outcry in the States and have a result contrary to that intended."[46]

Nor was Britain eager to enter into a diplomatic debate with the United States over the Clayton-Bulwer Treaty. The Blaine and Frelinghuysen notes on the subject only proposed modifications of certain of the clauses of the treaty and did not request its formal abrogation. The Foreign Office could therefore avoid giving a direct reply and simply stand on the letter of the treaty. In this way the status quo was effectively maintained. When it was suggested in 1889 that an official note be issued in defense of the 1850 treaty, Sanderson wrote that the British position had been clearly stated in 1881 and that further debate would "simply place again on record a divergence of views, which will not facilitate negotiation on more pressing questions."[47]

British policy was therefore influenced by a decided disinclination to become involved in Central American affairs and by a desire to maintain good relations with the United States. Practical constitutional difficulties and awareness of the engineering problems involved further induced Britain to decline to give official support to canal ventures. On the other hand, the Foreign Office appreciated the potential value of an isthmian canal and placed no obstacles in the way of its completion with the exception of reaffirming the Clayton-Bulwer Treaty. The Foreign Office view was clearly summed up in 1870:

> Her Majesty's Government entertain no jealousy as to the construction of the Canal by the United States, or by a Company under their sanction. It would be a work of interest and utility for the whole world, but for the United States more than for any other country. All that Great Britain desires is, that she may have the use of it on the same terms and to the same extent as the United States or any other country, unfettered by the condition of any

engagement or guarantee which it is contrary to the policy of Great Britain to give, and which from her geographical position with regard to Colombia it would be difficult for her to enforce.[48]

Both the United States and Britain were in favor of an isthmian canal and in this sense their goals coincided. The clash that emerged over the Clayton-Bulwer Treaty was somewhat deceptive in that executive and Congress were divided over the issue and because habitual British caution and understanding of American politics prevented the inflaming of American susceptibilities. Should a canal treaty have been ratified and canal construction begun under American governmental direction, then the Clayton-Bulwer Treaty would indeed have been infringed. But such an eventuality never arose and in spite of the rhetoric of American expansionism, British and American isthmian diplomacy were remarkably similar in the sense that both policies were basically negative and, therefore, unproductive.

The Emergence of an "American" Canal Policy, 1866–1879

William H. Seward had shown interest in isthmian canal projects since the early 1850s. Initially, he appeared to think of the question in non-exclusive terms. As secretary of state he negotiated a commercial treaty with Honduras in 1864 and a convention with Nicaragua in 1868 in which the United States laid no claim to any special canal rights or privileges should a canal ever be constructed through either country.[49] But another treaty, negotiated with Colombia in January 1869, marked a distinct change in Seward's thinking and indicated the emergence of a unilateral United States policy designed to produce a canal whose construction, operation, and ownership would be largely determined by the views of the United States government.

This idea of an "American" canal was a natural corollary of Seward's expansionist attitude, which flourished immediately after the Civil War. In fact, an isthmian canal was an integral and essential part of Seward's concept of America's global destiny since it would both bridge and stimulate the development of the new possessions that he envisaged for the United States on the Pacific coast and in the Caribbean. Moreover, action on the canal question was both necessary and opportune. Seward feared that the new Suez canal would reduce American economic independence[50] and that an isthmian canal would guarantee it. There were also a number of practical considerations that directed Seward's attention to the isthmus. The 1846 treaty with Colombia lapsed in 1868 and might require renewal. The American-owned Panama Railroad Company was also seeking to renegotiate its contract with the Colombian government.[51] This latter question was given added significance by reports of European intrigues to bid for the contract against the American company.[52]

The recent examples of French activities in Mexico and Spanish designs on the Dominican Republic had made Seward very sensitive to reports of European conspiracies in Latin America. In 1866 the Colombian government had invited applications for canal concessions and several tenders had resulted, mostly from European promoters. These ventures were, however, European in name only and sought to attract capital from whatever source it might be available. One of these schemes, that of Edward Cullen of Ireland, gained Seward's own support. Furthermore, Congress was showing an interest in the whole question. The Senate passed a resolution requesting information on the subject in March 1866, and a few months later the House voted $40,000 for a survey of the isthmus of Darien.[53]

In spite of all these factors favoring a positive American policy, it was the Colombians who took the diplomatic initiative. This was an unofficial discussion of the canal question by Estorijo Salgar, the Colombian minister in Washington, with Seward in March 1866. Seward responded warmly, but the Colombian minister suddenly dropped the question for a whole year. When formal negotiations were opened in April 1868, Seward was not hopeful of the outcome. In his view, neither American public opinion nor business interests believed that the canal was a feasible proposition.[54]

The situation suddenly changed in the late summer. In consultation with Seward, a New York–based group of businessmen formed the Isthmus Canal Company in September 1868 and it now appeared that the funds for the canal would be available. The next step was the negotiation of a treaty with Colombia to enable the work to go ahead. Talks for this purpose had been in progress since April and had never been satisfactory from the American point of view. The Colombian government required too definite an American commitment, too large a share of the projected profits, and unsatisfactory conditions regarding the opening of the canal.[55]

Despite the renewal of American diplomatic activity in October 1868 no further progress was made in either Washington or Bogotá. Seward acted in late November by dispatching Caleb Cushing on a special mission to Bogotá. The secretary of state was undoubtedly anxious to conclude a canal treaty before his term of office expired in March. "It would seem," commented the British chargé in Bogotá, "that the Government of the United States must attach great importance to this question from its selection of a man of such prominence as General Cushing to conduct the negotiations."[56]

The presence of Cushing secured rapid agreement in early January 1869. The treaty negotiated contained special canal privileges for the United States government and its citizens but also favorable financial terms for Colombia.[57] Cushing returned to Washington with the treaty in February, and it was quickly brought before the Senate. But a lame-duck administration, whose chief executive had narrowly escaped removal from office only a few months before, had little political capital in a hostile Congress. Despite Seward's euphoria and the formation of the Isthmus Canal Company, neither public nor congressional opinion showed much support for expansionism.[58] Nor had sufficient ground-work been laid in Colombia. In Washington the treaty never even came to a vote. The Colombian Senate did vote, but only to defeat it. Bunch explained: "The real cause of the rejection of the Treaty is the absence of any ready money payment to Colombia. Had this been promised the other objections would have disappeared."[59]

The 1869 treaty envisaged a canal to be constructed and operated by the United States government or by a company to which it might transfer the contract. Official government involvement was, however, tempered by the fact that the funding of the project would come from private sources. This policy was continued by the Grant administration. Like Seward, Grant had long been interested in the idea of an isthmian canal. He had crossed the isthmus himself in 1852 and appreciated the need for improved transit facilities. As president, he reopened canal negotiations and ordered further surveys of potential isthmian routes.

Stephen Hurlbut, the new American minister to Colombia, opened discussions with the Colombian government in November 1869. His forceful attitude[60] achieved results, and a treaty was concluded in January 1870 reaffirming the terms of the previous arrangement.[61] But this new treaty enjoyed no more success than that of 1869. The Colombian Senate did ratify the agreement in July 1870 but only after attaching seventeen amendments, among which was a stipulation that future treaties concerning a guarantee from other countries of Colombian sovereignty over the isthmus were to made without the participation of the United States. Hurlbut lodged an immediate protest and Bunch predicted that the American Senate would oppose the amendment.[62] Other factors had also emerged to dampen hopes of ratification. The completion of the first transcontinental railroad in May 1869 diminished the attraction of all isthmian projects and, ultimately, produced power-ful vested railroad interests opposed to alternative transit systems. The preliminary reports of the official survey of the Darien region also implied that a canal was not practicable by that route. Added to this was the growing friction between the Grant administration and the Senate over the proposed treaty to annex the Dominican Republic. In these circumstances the canal treaty received a very low order of priority, and Fish commented to the British minister in Washington that there was "little probability" of Senate approval of the canal treaty. The treaty, in fact, never even came to a vote, and the canal question gradually receded into the background.[63]

The canal policy of Seward and Fish implied a challenge to established British interests and treaty rights in the isthmian region. To an extent, the policy was prompted by suspicions of British designs and intrigues. Allan Burton, the American minister to Colombia, reported British moves to gain control of the Panama railroad, and his successor, Peter Sullivan, noted the "unkind and unjust jealousy" of Britain toward the United States.[64] It was true that British private interests sometimes worked against the United States, but this was an expression of straightforward economic competition rather than of official policy emanating from London.

Though the Foreign Office was interested in all canal projects, it was decided not to put any obstacles in the way of the United States–Colombian negotiations.[65] One reason was lack of information resulting from the time lag in communications sent from Bogotá to London.[66] Both treaties were concluded so quickly after months of apparent deadlock that there was little time for a British protest. There was also the widely held belief among British officials that an isthmian canal was not really feasible. Moreover, it was known that Seward's canal plans were influenced by the Irish canal promoter, Edward Cullen, whom the Foreign Office regarded as extremely unreliable. "Dr. Cullen has been for years engaged in the project in question," noted the foreign secretary, "and always unsuccessfully."[67]

Protest was also unnecessary because the British chargé in Bogotá reported that the Colombian government would not grant exclusive privileges to the United States.[68] The Colombian government withdrew this assurance in 1870, but even so, the Foreign Office was well aware that the treaties were unlikely to be ratified. "This is an extraordinary Treaty," wrote an official concerning the 1869 treaty, "and I can scarcely think the United States Congress will ratify it."[69] In 1870 the Foreign Office was well aware of the difficulties between the Grant administration and the Senate and also of the survey report critical of a Darien canal. "If the canal cannot be made," commented the chief clerk, Henry Bergne, "the Treaty loses its interest." The foreign secretary concurred that no action need be taken.[70]

British policy was not, however, completely negative. The British chargé in Bogotá had been drawn into giving his views on the United States–Colombian canal talks in November 1868. "The maritime Powers of Europe," he informed the Colombian finance minister, "would never consent to the realization of a plan which would inflict great injury on them and be productive only of benefit to the United States." The Foreign Office approved Bunch's language and further instructed him to caution the Colombian government against the "injudicious" policy of conceding exclusive canal privileges. On the other hand, Bunch was informed that Britain could neither promise nor guarantee Colombia support "in any contingencies that may arise."[71]

In fact, the United States–Colombian canal negotiations did not proceed in a vacuum. The Colombian government simultaneously sought a guarantee from Britain similar to that given by the United States in the 1846 treaty. During 1865 Mosquera had made this the focal point of his activity as Colombian minister in London and he continued these efforts when elected to the presidency in 1866. The question was reopened by his successor in 1868 but again without success. The British foreign secretary discouraged the idea by pointing out "the extreme improbability of all or any of the Powers taking upon themselves a responsibility which would entail no corresponding advantage."[72] A further opportunity for British involvement in canal diplomacy came in January 1869 when Santos Acosta, the chief Colombian negotiator in Washington, requested that the European powers guarantee the neutrality of the isthmian transit. The British minister in Washington gave some support to this request since he considered that Seward had gone back on his assurance that the canal should be open to all nations on equal terms.[73] A similar approach had been made by the Colombian minister in London, but he was informed: "The policy of this Country is opposed to engagements bearing the nature of a guarantee, and it is very certain that Parliament would not sanction any appropriation of public money for the construction of such a work as a canal undertaken in a Country not under the Sovereignty of the British Crown."[74]

Though the British government was not willing to give the Colombians the guarantee that they desired, it was still prepared to act on another front. Although both the Foreign Office and the Admiralty regarded a Central American canal as impractical, they could not completely rule out its ultimate completion. The implication of exclusive control by the United States over such communications could therefore directly affect British interests should a canal ever prove practical. These interests were to be safeguarded by an instruction to Thornton to remind Seward of the stipulations of Article 8 of the Clayton-Bulwer Treaty, by which Britain and the United States disclaimed any such exclusive rights.[75]

As a means of further strengthening the British position, the British ambassador in Paris inquired in February 1869 whether the French government would act in concert with Britain to counteract any American attempt to acquire exclusive canal rights. The French reply proved negative. Unlike Britain, the French government did not have any treaty to form the basis of a protest and did not consider the question important enough to provoke a controversy with the United States.[76]

The French attitude thus ruled out a combined protest. The whole diplomatic maneuver reflected British caution and had been no more than contingency planning. Nor was such action ever necessary. The 1869 treaty made no progress in the Senate and the "Seward episode" in the history of the canal came to an end. But within a year an almost identical situation reemerged, when at the request of the Colombian negotiators, Article 25 of the 1870 canal treaty invited other nations to join the United States in guaranteeing the projected canal.

Bunch believed that the interest now shown by Washington in the matter made the canal "probable" and that this new consideration might warrant a change in British policy.[77] The Foreign Office responded as in the previous year. It was felt that Article 8 of the Clayton-Bulwer Treaty was being disregarded, and Thornton was instructed to ascertain the precise intentions of the United States government and, if necessary, to remind Fish of the provisions of that treaty.[78] Approaches were again made to Paris. The British ambassador reported that the "unfortunate expedition" to Mexico had lowered French prestige and weakened French influence in the United States. France feared a new defeat on an American question and would not enter into a controversy over the canal treaty.[79]

At the Foreign Office the issue was carefully examined by the Treaty Department under Bergne. He was surprised by the revival of the Colombian request for a European guarantee contained in Article 25. Britain had always declined to give this and, in his opinion, the Colombian government had no reason to expect Britain to change its policy in this respect. Nor did Bergne believe that the treaty called for British interference. Citing the example of the orderly administration of the Panama railroad by the American-owned company, he did not think that American control of the projected canal would be "inconvenient" to Britain "so long as peaceful relations" prevailed between Britain and the United States.[80] In fact, no positive British action against the treaty was required for it was already coming under attack in both Washington and Bogotá. Not only the question of constructing a canal but also that of even ratifying a canal treaty was obviously much more difficult than Seward had imagined in 1868. Under these circumstances the Foreign Office need take no action.

In spite of the nonratification of the 1870 treaty with Colombia, the Grant administration maintained its interest in the canal question although a much more cautious canal diplomacy now resulted. Emphasis was placed not on the negotiation of treaties but on establishing the most practicable location. Further surveys of the whole isthmus were ordered and the Interoceanic Canal Commission, under the chairmanship of Admiral Ammen,[81] was established in 1872 to study and investigate possible canal routes. "I have no doubt," wrote Bunch," that the trouble given by Colombia in the matter of the Canal Treaty will act as a powerful inducement to the United States to look for some route which shall not pass through her territory."[82] Possible alternatives were Nicaragua, Costa Rica, and Tehuantepec.

The opening surveys did not prove very encouraging. A canal was believed to be practicable near Panama, but the expense involved was estimated as enormous.[83] Secretary of State Fish began to show less and less interest in the question. He had informed Thornton in 1870 that the treaty with Colombia would not receive Senate approval,[84] and his actions throughout his remaining years in office indicated that he had little faith in any isthmian canal at all. When Hurlbut negotiated a new canal treaty with Colombia in 1872, Fish disavowed his minister's actions.[85] Moreover, tentative approaches to reopen the question by the governments of Colombia, Nicaragua, and Costa Rica received no encouragement from Fish.[86] Indeed, the actual state of United States–Colombian relations left much to be desired. When the Colombian government refused to pay compensation over the *Montijo* incident in 1871, Fish threatened the termination of the guarantee contained in the 1846 treaty.[87] The absence of a Colombian representative in Washington from 1874 to 1876 and the withdrawal of the American minister from Bogotá in 1876 further reflected the deterioration of relations.

Nor was the British government any more receptive to canal proposals from Colombia. In 1873 the Foreign Office rejected a scheme made jointly by the Colombian minister in London and a Danish-American canal promoter. The Foreign Office maintained the view that the project was impractical;[88] there was no intention of becoming involved in either Colombian affairs or in complications with the United States. On the other hand, Thornton reported in 1874 that interest in the canal question was reviving in Washington. This time attention was directed toward Nicaragua rather than Colombia. The Nicaraguan government was maintaining a special commissioner in Washington to advocate the Nicaraguan route, whereas Colombia apparently remained indifferent. As Grant's second term of office was drawing to a close, the question was also becoming more of a political issue in the United States.[89]

Fish had justified his lack of response to canal proposals on the grounds that action was premature until the Interoceanic Canal Commission had indicated the most practical and feasible route.[90] In February 1876 the commission issued its report and recommended a canal to be constructed through Nicaragua. The report added that the project would be facilitated if all nations intending to use the canal would join together to guarantee its neutrality and protection. This recommendation, if accepted, would have reversed the "American" canal policy initiated by Seward and continued by Grant. Since that policy had not been successful, the Grant administration declared in favor of an internationalized canal.[91]

This decision was communicated by Fish to Thornton in March 1876. The secretary of state stressed that his government was anxious to begin construction as soon as possible. The canal was intended to benefit all nations and no exclusive privileges were desired by the United States. He hoped that Britain would give the project "all the encouragement and protection which it be in its power to afford."[92] The Foreign Office "appreciated" the American communication, but held that action should be guided by the Clayton-Bulwer Treaty. The existence of a British treaty with Nicaragua dating from 1860 was also raised. Any concession made by Nicaragua would therefore have to be examined by the British government in case British rights under the 1860 treaty were in any way affected.[93] The British response to the concept of internationalized control was thus not encouraging.

Fish had meanwhile begun canal negotiations in Washington, first with Costa Rica and then with Nicaragua, when that government's minister arrived in the capital. Canal discussions with these governments proved just as difficult as the previous negotiations with Colombia. The result was deadlock, and the canal proposals of 1876 came to nothing. Positive British support for Fish's proposal in March 1876 might have altered the situation, but responsibility for the failure lay with the American and Nicaraguan negotiators. As had Colombia, Nicaragua tried to drive too hard a bargain. In an attempt to safeguard protection of the canal and to make it attractive to private enterprise, Fish sought to insert too many political considerations into the proposed treaty. Finally, it has been argued that Fish was preoccupied with other matters and was not really enthusiastic about the canal project.[94] No treaty was therefore concluded, and like those of Seward before them, the efforts of Grant and Fish to construct an isthmian canal had ended in failure.

Nor was American public opinion particularly concerned by the outcome. Even though an isthmian route had now received official sanction, there was no great demand that the project be treated with any urgency.[95] The new administration of President Hayes reviewed the matter leisurely and appeared to accept the policy of an internationalized canal through Nicaragua, but nothing was done to implement this.[96] Over a decade of canal diplomacy thus ended with the record of two unperfected canal treaties. But events at Paris in 1879 were suddenly to reopen the whole question and to revive the "American" canal policy of 1868–1870.

Panama and Nicaragua, 1879–1895

Just as American canal interest shifted to Nicaragua, a new project involving the isthmus of Darien was making its appearance. Anthony de Gogorza had been involved in various abortive canal schemes since 1864, but it seemed in 1876 that he had finally secured substantial support from French sources. A French survey under Lucien Wyse declared the Gogorza route to be impractical, but at the same time claimed to have discovered a feasible route. Wyse secured a concession from the Colombian government to begin work on a canal, and with the backing of the celebrated entrepreneur Ferdinand de Lesseps,[97] invitations were sent to interested parties throughout the world to attend an international congress to discuss canal projects at Paris in May 1879. Wyse had discussed the proposed congress during a visit to Washington in March 1879, and this resulted in the attendance of a number of American delegates.[98]

Various routes were debated at the congress. The official American delegates, led by Ammen and Menocal,[99] argued in favor of Nicaragua, but the congress ultimately voted for a canal at Panama. The vote was the result of pressure from Wyse and de Lesseps, and the Americans left Paris alleging that the congress had been "packed" in favor of Panama. Nonetheless, a new company[100] was formed in which subscriptions for shares would be invited from all over the world. The company was to begin actual construction in 1881 and it was estimated that the work would be completed by 1889 to coincide with the hundredth anniversary of the French Revolution.

The proceedings of the Paris congress were not highly regarded within the United States. On June 25, 1879, Senator Burnside of Rhode Island introduced a resolution affirming that any attempt by the European powers to construct an isthmian canal under their protection would be a violation of the Monroe Doctrine. This brought a statement from de Lesseps that the canal would be entirely independent of the control of any and every government.[101] The resolution was withdrawn at the next congressional session, but the House showed a revived interest in the question by creating a special committee to investigate interoceanic canals.

American opinion was aroused, and the new mood was well expressed by an article in the *New York Herald* of July 1879:

The only interest which European commerce has in the Darien Canal is limited to its trade with the Pacific coast of America, a trade which, small at present, will decrease with the progress of events. . . . It is perfectly absurd to suppose that our people will ever permit the nations of Europe to have any share in the control of a route. . . . It is certain that our government will not only enter into no entangling alliances with European powers for the protection of the proposed canal, but that it will neither recognise nor respect or tolerate any European interference in the matter. . . . We shall never admit Europe to share in the control of a route of commerce in which we have so paramount an interest.[102]

Congress and American press opinion were alarmed by the turn of events, but their criticism was directed not against the idea of a canal, but against the possibility that the Panama project might result in a future French protectorate over the isthmus. Memories of Louis-Napoleon's expedition to Mexico were still extant and it was pointed out that the closest associates of de Lesseps were Bonapartist adventurers.[103]

The Hayes administration was also somewhat startled by the speedy implementation of the French project. Secretary of State William Evarts had been aware of the proceedings of the Paris congress, but he had considered them as "without political authority or diplomatic faculties." What astounded him was the information that the French company had a concession from the Colombian government. Although his predecessor had discouraged all canal proposals from Bogotá (the American legation there had been closed from 1876 to 1878) and his own administration had shown minimal interest in the question, Evarts now judged that the Colombian government "may not have been as frank as we had reason to expect."[104]

Despite receiving assurances from the French government disavowing any intention of becoming involved in the affairs of the isthmus,[105] the Hayes administration gradually evolved a positive policy. Ammen and Menocal returned from Paris and began to advocate an alternative canal by way of Nicaragua. The administration appeared to support this scheme and announced that the United States would explore the possibility of establishing coaling stations in the isthmian region. "It may be that the efforts now being made by M. Lesseps," suggested Thornton, "have incited the United States Government to take steps to encourage the establishment of such a communication by the Nicaraguan route."[106] This was confirmed by President Hayes in his annual message to Congress in December 1879. The president also referred, however, to the recent arrival in Washington of a special envoy from Colombia, implying that canal negotiations were being conducted on more than one front.[107]

From 1868 to 1870 the administration had pursued an ambitious canal policy. By contrast, in 1879 the administration showed more caution than did Congress. A speech by Senator Bayard of Delaware in January 1880 particularly surprised Thornton. The senator had advocated an American-owned canal and suggested that preparations for war might be necessary. "That such language should have been used by so moderate, serious and intelligent a man as Mr. Bayard," commented Thornton, "has caused some surprise and has made a great impression upon the public mind." There was also growing public criticism that the administration was neglecting national interests by its apparent indifference to the de Lesseps project. Evarts sought to counter this by his announcement of the French disavowal of any involvement in the project, but his own statements were undermined by rumors that there were divisions in the cabinet over canal policy.[108]

In early 1880 President Hayes was indeed giving the matter considerable thought, especially in view of the expected arrival of de Lesseps in New York in March to attract American support for his project. On February 18 Hayes presented his views at a meeting of his cabinet. He believed that action was urgent in order to inform the world of American opinion on the isthmian question. The French scheme threatened the national security of the United States. If the canal passed into European control, he considered that "our security, our peace, our commercial and general prosperity, and our commanding and natural position among the nations would be endangered." The cabinet agreed with this analysis, and on February 20 Hayes wrote in his diary what was to be substantially his special message to Congress of March 8, 1880: "The true policy of the United States as to a canal across any part of the Isthmus is either a canal under American control, or no canal. We cannot allow the geographical relations of the North American continent to be essentially changed. European control of this thoroughfare between the different parts of the United States is wholly inadmissible."[109]

The administration thus declared itself unequivocally in favor of an "American" canal. Congressional, press, and public opinion appeared to be strongly in support of such a policy. A feasible canal route had been recommended by the Interoceanic Canal Commission in 1876 and a company[110] had been formed in 1879 to construct a canal through that route. The President's special message to Congress had been timed to coincide with de Lesseps's tour of the eastern states and to discourage possible American support for his project. Presidential messages and congressional resolutions had informed the world of the American views. "But the world is entitled to ask of the United States," queried the *Times* in March 1880, "that they should make up their mind either to let M. de Lesseps do the thing himself by the resources at his command or to charge themselves with the task."[111]

In spite of this apparent favorable combination of circumstances no "American" canal was forthcoming during the life of the Hayes administration. The major effort of the administration was to exert diplomatic pressure upon Colombia both in Bogotá and in Washington.[112] In Colombia, the American minister encountered resentment and hostility. "The position of the United States," he wrote, "tends to dispel the fairy vision of happiness and wealth which were confidently expected to flow from the realization of the de Lesseps Canal scheme."[113] Not surprisingly, no diplomatic progress was made in Bogotá. A similar situation prevailed in Washington until February 1881, when a protocol was suddenly agreed to by the departing Colombian minister, Santo Domingo Vila, and the State Department official, William Trescot.[114] The protocol reaffirmed the American guarantee contained in the 1846 treaty and made any change in the Wyse concession dependent upon American approval. In this way, Evarts believed that American isthmian rights were both reaffirmed and reserved for the future.[115]

For all its expansionist rhetoric the Hayes administration left office with the solitary achievement of a protocol negotiated with the Colombian minister in the United States. As with the Cushing treaty of 1869, any administration satisfaction[116] was soon dashed by the seemingly intractable difficulties of ratification. The protocol proved unacceptable to the Colombian government because it gravely undermined Colombian sovereignty over the isthmus of Panama. Santo Domingo Vila was sharply criticized for his actions, and no further action was taken on the protocol. The fact that no Colombian representative was sent to Washington until 1884 further indicated Colombia's disinclination to negotiate a canal treaty with the United States.[117]

As the Hayes administration came to an end in March 1881 French survey teams were beginning to determine the exact location for their canal operations in Panama. Within a year actual construction work was underway. De Lesseps had not therefore been deterred by administration statements, adverse congressional resolutions, press criticism, or lack of financial support from the United States. The Panama project was going ahead in spite of the American attitude and, furthermore, without American competition, for neither the administration nor Congress had given endorsement or financial backing for alternative American canal schemes.

In spite of the alarm raised by the de Lesseps project, American attitudes toward the canal question remained basically negative. Like Johnson in 1869 and Grant in 1876, Hayes had begun to propose active policies too late in the life of his administration. His failure to secure his party's renomination in 1880 further reduced his political influence and created a lame-duck administration. Not only was the administration politically weak, but it had also long maintained an ambiguous attitude on the canal question. The secretary of state was responsible for this. Although Evarts had been a strong supporter of Seward's canal policy,[118] his negative attitude while secretary of state provoked public criticism, and the rumor arose that he was in the pay of railroad interests who feared competition from an isthmian canal.[119]

In reality, the options available to Evarts to prevent the French canal were limited. There was no treaty right to do so, and the attempt to negotiate one with Colombia ultimately failed. Nor could the use of force be justified against a private commercial enterprise, especially when the United States lacked a strong navy.[120] The extensive implications of the Hayes message were emphasized by the *Times:*

> The claim is not even to a sole title to guard the future canal's neutrality from violation by all and any. It is a claim to an indefinite suzerainty from Mexico to Patagonia, though throughout the vast region the Government at Washington exercises no power, and though to its populations it acknowledges no duty.
>
> Europe could not recognize so gratuitous a demand. An interoceanic canal would for every practical purpose form as much, or as little, a part of the European coast line as that of the United States. Even had America itself alone to be considered, British Columbia and Mexico in the north, Peru and Brazil and Chili and Bolivia in the south might justly exclaim against the autocracy arrogated for the United States. But while Europe cannot concede the bare principle asserted by the President and the Committee, Europe has no objection to the United States acquiring all the power they can want over the canal by subscribing the capital necessary to create it.[121]

The Hayes administration sought to achieve the opposite by discouraging American support of the French project. But this policy had to contend with the personality and incredible energy of de Lesseps. In order to dispel the objections raised against his scheme, de Lesseps was only too willing at the age of seventy-four to visit Panama itself and then embark on an arduous public relations tour of the United States from coast to coast. On this tour he stressed the private and nongovernmental nature of his scheme. If American investors took up a majority of the subscriptions, then the headquarters of the canal company would be in New York. He added that he had no objections to the Monroe Doctrine and welcomed Hayes's message of March 8 as adding to "the political security of the canal."[122] Although American financial support proved ultimately very meager, de Lesseps compensated for this by cultivating support in other ways. His company established an American advisory board of which the presidency, involving an annual salary of $25,000, was offered to ex-President Grant. He refused, and it was then accepted by the secretary of the navy, Richard Thompson, who resigned from the cabinet. De Lesseps also undermined his critics by offering very generous financial terms for the purchase of the Panama Railroad Company and by indicating that much of the material and machinery for the construction of the canal would be bought from the United States.[123]

Although he considered it an inferior scheme to his own, de Lesseps even suggested that Americans construct their own canal through Nicaragua. "I should be well satisfied with such a course," he wrote, "for every new highway is a step forward."[124] The American Congress was considering giving financial support to just such a scheme and to another, involving a "ship-railway" across the isthmus of Tehuantepec.[125] Criticism of de Lesseps became peripheral as the Nicaragua and Tehuantepec schemes lobbied furiously against each other in their struggle to win congressional favor. The result was only further confusion and fragmentation of congressional support for a positive canal policy. Moreover, rivalry between the House and the Senate and between various congressional committees for jurisdiction over the matter resulted in no decision being taken on either scheme.[126] As in 1869 and 1870 no positive action was forthcoming from Congress.

A similar situation prevailed in London for, in the absence of a direct challenge to British interests, no progress on the canal issue was to be expected from the Foreign Office. The Foreign Office had been aware of the Paris congress, but no official delegates had been sent. Instead, Stokes, a British engineer who had been invited to the congress, was allowed the use of the Foreign Office library so that he might be fully informed on the subject. But when Stokes reported after the congress that Britain should take "a special interest" in the scheme, the Foreign Office declined to act.[127] In Washington, Thornton discussed the canal question with Evarts and mentioned the Clayton-Bulwer Treaty, but Evarts kept silent on this.[128] In general, the Foreign Office did not regard the problem as pressing. When a dispatch from Bogotá reported that the Colombians feared that the United States planned to annex Panama, an official minuted: "This alarm seems quite unnecessary as the United States want the Canal made in Nicaragua not in Colombia."[129]

The British response was a characteristic one, no doubt affected by the excited state of internal British policies at that time.[130] The Conservative government was replaced by the Liberals in April 1880 and although the new government was considerably concerned by canal developments, this concern applied to Suez and not Panama.[131] The isthmian question could not, however, be completely ignored, especially when a joint resolution was introduced into the United States Congress in April 1880 requesting the president to take steps to abrogate the Clayton-Bulwer Treaty. The resolution was not adopted, but it prompted an investigation of the whole question by the Foreign Office. The Foreign Office librarian, Edward Hertslet, reported that if the treaty should be abrogated, then Britain might reassert its claims to occupy any portion of Central America, should it so desire, and also enter into any arrangements to construct a canal that it thought appropriate.[132] These would be extremely difficult options to execute, but they were possibilities and ones that the American Congress was aware of.

The inaction of the Hayes administration over the canal issue rendered any British measures unnecessary. This situation was to change after March 1881. At his inaugural address, the new president, James Garfield, echoed his predecessor's opinion when he declared that it was "the right and duty of the United States to assert and maintain such supervision and authority over any interoceanic canal across the isthmus that connects North and South America as will protect our national interests."[133] This statement, coming on top of the Santo Domingo–Trescot protocol, heightened the alarm of the Colombian government, and the request for a British guarantee of Colombian sovereignty over the isthmus of Panama was revived in April 1881. The same answer was returned as on previous occasions. Pauncefote considered that no change in British policy was required. He believed that there was no advantage to be gained from a new treaty with Colombia and, in fact, that such a treaty might cast doubt upon the existing Clayton-Bulwer Treaty.[134]

The Foreign Office was, however, concerned by reports that the Garfield administration was seeking to establish naval and coaling stations on either side of the isthmus. At the same time, the Colombian minister in London confirmed that his government had rejected the Santo Domingo–Trescot protocol, but that "they would hereafter probably have to give way if not supported by the European Maritime Powers, especially by England."[135] The question assumed added urgency when the French ambassador visited the Foreign Office on July 5, 1881. Though his government was unwilling to take the first step, he believed that there should be an expression of European views on the subject of the canal and it was hoped that Britain might take the initiative in this. The French attitude was in sharp contrast to that adopted in 1869, and Granville cautiously replied that he would give the matter "careful consideration."[136] But later in the day, in conversation with the Italian ambassador on the same subject, the foreign secretary doubted whether the European powers should declare their opposition to the United States. On the other hand, he believed that the Colombian government had done "quite rightly" in rejecting the protocol.[137]

From being a minor issue, the canal question had suddenly assumed major diplomatic significance. The Colombian attempts to obtain a European guarantee in the late 1860s and 1870s had failed because of resolute British opposition. At that time the canal had been mere speculation, but the de Lesseps scheme appeared to be practical, and prospects of success were high. American opinion had been violently stirred by the scheme and American policy became increasingly aggressive toward Colombia. The leading European powers, especially France, were now prepared to consider some form of action, but waited for Britain to take the lead. Naval and commercial power guaranteed Britain this leading role, but there was also the Clayton-Bulwer Treaty, which made Britain an interested party in any incident affecting the isthmian transit. In fact, the next few years of canal diplomacy were to revolve around a debate over this treaty.

The Garfield administration knew that the European powers were discussing the canal question. Dichman had reported from Bogotá in May 1881 that copies of the protocol were being sent to London and Paris to inform those governments of the "unusual pretentions" of the United States and to request guarantees of Colombian sovereignty over the isthmus.[138] Secretary of State Blaine responded on June 24 by addressing a circular note to the European governments stating that the United States would resist any interference by European powers in the isthmian area. This was not intended to imply that the United States sought any exclusive privilege for itself nor to interfere with the activities of any private company. Having thus disavowed the bases of the Seward and Fish policies, Blaine provided another one. The circular was not part of a new policy, but was "nothing more than the pronounced adherence of the United States to principles long since enunciated by the highest authority of the Government."[139] American canal rights were now sanctioned by the Monroe Doctrine.

The note was communicated to the Foreign Office in July 1881 at a time when the isthmian question was already under consideration. A further complicating dimension was thus added to the situation. The French ambassador informed Granville that his government could not admit the American claims, and Granville agreed that exclusive American political control of the canal could not be accepted. On the other hand, Britain was extremely reluctant to open up a diplomatic correspondence with the United States on this question when affairs at Suez were so critical and when it was known that the government at Washington had been thrown into confusion by the shooting of President Garfield. The matter required more consideration, and the circular was passed over to the law officers for a "thorough examination."[140]

The law officers reported on August 15. While they recognized the "force" of many of Blaine's arguments, they pointed out that Britain's position on this question differed from that of the other European powers. One reason was the magnitude of British commercial interests, but more significant in their opinion was the existence of the Clayton-Bulwer Treaty. That treaty regulated the respective rights of Britain and the United States in the region, and it was felt that the United States should acknowledge this fact.[141]

This was no more than a restatement of the customary British position, but before replying to Blaine, the Foreign Office decided to consult further with the leading European governments. They were informed that the British government considered the American intention to establish naval stations in the isthmus to be a violation of the Clayton-Bulwer Treaty and that Britain would notify the United States of this. Replies from Paris and Berlin were critical of Blaine's note, but although expressing agreement with the British position these governments stressed their desire to avoid complications with the United States.[142] There was therefore no likelihood of concerted European action on this issue and the idea of a collective European guarantee to Colombia was consequently completely ruled out.[143]

The threat of European intervention, which had so much alarmed Blaine, had little substance in reality. Even if Hayes's special message or Blaine's note had never been delivered, the European powers would still have recognized American preponderance in the isthmian area. Moreover, the cautious attitude of Britain set the tone of the European response and precluded any impulsive action. The Foreign Office was, however, ready to launch a diplomatic counterattack, albeit low-key, to maintain British rights by holding the United States to the Clayton-Bulwer Treaty. This was included in the reply to Blaine's note which was presented to the American chargé in London on November 10, 1881. It pointed out that the position of Britain and the United States with reference to the canal question was "determined" by the Clayton-Bulwer Treaty and that the British government relied "with confidence upon the observance of all the engagements of that Treaty."[144]

The American chargé sent Granville's reply not by telegraph, but by mail steamer to Washington. On its way it crossed a dispatch from Blaine to Granville written on November 19. No doubt irritated by London's apparent failure to answer his June circular and aware that he was soon to be replaced in office, Blaine now directly requested a modification of the Clayton-Bulwer Treaty so as to secure American control over potential canal projects. The sudden arrival of Granville's reply to the first note now caused the State Department "considerable embarrassment." Acting impulsively, Blaine dispatched a third note to London on November 29 arguing that by the 1846 treaty with New Granada, the United States had assumed a special position in the area and the Clayton-Bulwer Treaty had in no way been intended to infringe this status.[145]

"It is quite necessary to remember, in considering Mr. Blaine's diplomatic papers," noted the *Economist,* "that the American Government . . . is allowed by European diplomacy to take liberties in despatches, that such documents are often mere speeches to the people, and that discourtesy is in no way an American fault."[146] The Foreign Office was aware of Blaine's political motives,[147] but its primary concern was to understand the full implications of the communications that had been received from the secretary of state. An examination by Hertslet suggested that the United States did not object to the Clayton-Bulwer Treaty itself, but only to the terms of Article 1 disclaiming exclusive rights for either country.[148] This was the crux of the problem and was something that Britain would not concede.

The British reply to Blaine's second and third notes was communicated to the State Department at the beginning of January 1882. While the extent of the American interest in the isthmian canal question was appreciated, it was pointed out that Britain's large colonial possessions and commercial interests rendered a canal project of "the greatest importance" to that country too. The British government was "anxious" that no single nation should acquire a "predominating influence or control" over the canal and suggested that an international convention signed by all the maritime powers might provide a solution.[149] The British notes were received, however, not by Blaine but by his successor, Frelinghuysen. Nor was this change initially harmful to the British position, for it represented a repudiation of Blaine and, apparently, of his policies as well. The British minister in Washington reported reassuringly that the Arthur cabinet would not support Blaine's policy "to its full extent."[150]

Frelinghuysen did indeed show considerable caution during his early months in office. In conversation with West he was "reticent" on the canal question and expressed the opinion that the Panama project was "altogether premature." But West predicted that the personality conflicts within the Republican party would lead to "inopportune complications."[151] This was confirmed on May 8, 1882, when Frelinghuysen reopened the diplomatic debate by dispatching a note to London declaring that the Clayton-Bulwer Treaty had been violated by Britain on a number of occasions and, furthermore, was not meant to apply to Panama.[152] In London, the dispatch underwent the scrutiny of the law officers, and a British reply was delivered on December 30, 1882, denying the validity of the American arguments and declaring that there was no reason to justify a denunciation of the treaty.[153]

The correspondence continued throughout 1883. A dispatch from Frelinghuysen in May virtually restated his arguments of the previous year and was countered by a similar reaffirmation of the British position in August. On November 22 Frelinghuysen answered by repeating his previous arguments and, in default of an official American request for the abrogation of the treaty, the Foreign Office chose not to reply and thus closed what had been a "very undesirable" correspondence.[154]

As with Colombia in 1880–1881 the United States had sought to exert diplomatic pressure upon Britain to acquiesce in a policy that violated existing treaty stipulations. This was unsuccessful because Britain preferred to maintain the status quo and was not offered anything constructive in its place. The State Department adopted the technique of adversary debate rather than negotiation. This proved successful in 1895–1896 but not in 1882–1883. The Foreign Office would not surrender to weak American arguments, especially when it was known that Frelinghuysen lacked support within the United States itself. In his own party his policies were criticized by the aggrieved and ambitious James G. Blaine.[155] Nor did Congress or American opinion in general uphold the position taken by Frelinghuysen. In spite of the participation of ex-President Grant in the Nicaraguan canal scheme,[156] Congress had shown no marked interest in assisting either that scheme or any of the others. Furthermore, the alarm raised by the de Lesseps scheme was being assuaged by reports that it was running into increasing difficulties.[157]

Such was the lack of support from within the United States that the American promoters of the Nicaraguan route began to look for financial assistance from Europe. West concluded that this showed "how soon the national character attached to the Nicaragua scheme has fallen to the ground upon the failure of the financial complications." In contrast to his assertive position on the Clayton-Bulwer Treaty, Frelinghuysen refused to endorse the Nicaraguan canal company. While he had come to accept by 1884 the need for a canal and that Nicaragua provided the most suitable location, he did not believe that private enterprise could construct the canal. In his opinion, the United States government must exercise direct control over the project. Negotiations were therefore begun with the Nicaraguan government on this basis and, after protracted discussions, a canal treaty was signed in December 1884. The treaty gave the United States a virtual protectorate over the projected canal strip on its undertaking that a canal would be completed within ten years.[158] In a sense, this agreement was the logical implication of the policy inaugurated by Seward in 1868, that if private enterprise could not build the "American" canal, then the United States government must and would do so.

The immediate question was, however, whether American public opinion, or, more particularly, whether two thirds of the Senate would support the treaty. This had not occurred in 1869 and 1870, and in spite of the public interest in the canal question aroused by de Lesseps and the Clayton-Bulwer correspondence, the 1884 treaty also failed to secure ratification.[159] The reasons were not very different from those that had caused the previous failures. Once again, a lame-duck administration, whose president had been repudiated by his own party, attempted to push through a major measure in the last weeks of its life. Opposition was quite substantial. The defeated Republican presidential candidate of 1884, James G. Blaine, refused to support the treaty.[160] Nor did the president-elect, Grover Cleveland, show any enthusiasm for the measure. Senators were therefore reluctant to compromise the new president, and Democratic senators were in fact given instructions to vote against the treaty as a party measure.[161]

There were also more specific objections to the treaty. The proposed acquisition of territory in Nicaragua raised a number of constitutional and administrative questions. There was also the problem of how the money for the canal would be raised and spent. The Arthur administration was under something of a handicap in this respect because Frelinghuysen had asked Congress for an appropriation of $250,000 in the summer of 1884 to assist his canal negotiations. The request was refused because it was suspected that the money was destined to purchase certain Nicaraguan concessions held by private American citizens including ex-President Grant, who was known to be in financial difficulties.[162] The *New York Sun* concluded that the whole scheme involved "sinking public money in a ditch in Nicaragua."[163]

There was also the added difficulty that the treaty included no mention of Costa Rica even though the proposed canal would pass through territory claimed by that country.[164] A much more substantial obstacle was the existence of the Clayton-Bulwer Treaty. The *New York Times* queried whether Britain had been informed of the negotiations. If not, then it "must be looked upon as a flagrant violation of our treaty obligations."[165] The debates in the Foreign Relations Committee and in the Senate itself emphasized the widespread concern over the implications of such an act. In conclusion, the nonratification of the treaty demonstrated that neither the Senate nor, by default, American society, was prepared to undertake the task of constructing an "American" canal.

The Nicaraguan treaty was withdrawn by President Cleveland, representing a defeat for "American" canal diplomacy and a victory for the forces of inaction and negativism. It also marked a victory for the Foreign Office in the debate over the Clayton-Bulwer Treaty. According to West, Frelinghuysen had anticipated a British protest against the Nicaraguan treaty. Such an act would have stirred anti-British feeling and might have persuaded some senators to vote for the treaty. The "judicious silence" of the British government had, however, dashed Frelinghuysen's hopes. The failure of the treaty was a virtual reaffirmation that the Clayton-Bulwer Treaty was still binding.[166]

The high point of American interest in the canal question had been in the rather alarmist reaction to the announcement of the de Lesseps project in 1879. Even then, a positive "American" policy had not materialized until the 1884 treaty with Nicaragua. In the next few years reports of the insuperable difficulties facing the French project became confirmed and American interest in the canal and the Clayton-Bulwer question further diminished. The new Cleveland administration expressed an interest in the idea of an isthmian canal, but pursued a cautious policy, stressing the desirability of an internationalized canal and the avoidance of involvement in Central American politics. "The prosperity and independence of the Central American States we very much desire," noted Bayard, "but no entangling alliances with them or any other power."[167] When riots on the isthmus of Panama in 1885 prompted the intervention of American marines under the 1846 treaty, the American minister at Bogotá, William L. Scruggs, recommended: "The present seems to me to be the opportune moment for which our Government has long and patiently awaited, and that unless it contemplates the abandonment of its traditional policy of exclusive control of the Isthmean transit, now is the time to strike."[168] The analysis was in the tradition of statements made by Seward and Hayes, but it did not reflect the practice of American foreign policy. The marines had been withdrawn from the isthmus even before Scruggs's dispatch was received in Washington.[169] In spite of continual rumors of American intervention to force payment of American claims for damages resulting from the 1885 riots, the Cleveland administration adopted a moderate and legalistic approach.[170]

This was not, however, a policy of weakness or inaction, for this approach appeared as considerable firmness in other isthmian matters. In 1885 Italian marines were landed in Colombia to secure the release of Cerruti, an Italian citizen who claimed to have been illegally arrested.

The question became something of a diplomatic incident when the United States came forward as the protector of Colombia under the 1846 treaty. As a result, the Italian attitude softened and the question was decided by arbitration.[171] A similar incident occurred in 1888 when alleged British intrigues on the Mosquito Coast were condemned by Bayard as an infringement of the Clayton-Bulwer Treaty. A conciliatory reply was issued by Salisbury.[172]

Indeed, the collapse of the "American" canal policy had not encouraged any British initiative in isthmian affairs. Good relations with the United States were highly valued in London, and even though a protest was considered at American action in the Cerruti case, the foreign secretary, Lord Rosebery, rejected this as "blowing on the embers unnecessarily."[173] Nor was Britain particularly sympathetic when Colombia expressed fears of imminent American intervention to demand compensation for the 1885 claims. President Nuñez revived the question of a European guarantee of Colombian sovereignty over the isthmus and asked the British minister for advice on his country's possible abrogation of the 1846 treaty. In London, one Foreign Office official doubted whether the United States had "territorial designs" on Colombia and devastatingly added that if there was any real cause of alarm the Colombians could remove it by simply granting compensation for the 1885 damages. Hertslet believed, however, that Colombia was "justified" in seeking a "reform" of the 1846 treaty, but he considered that it was a question that did not "specifically concern" the British government or "call for an expression of their views." The British government remained confident that the Clayton-Bulwer Treaty would restrain American policy. There was no intention of either arousing American sensitivities or of becoming involved in Colombian politics. "This is a big question," summed up Pauncefote in August 1886, "and . . . should not be touched until the Canal is near completion, when some international action is pretty sure to be set on foot."[174] In the meantime, Britain would give no support either to canal ventures or to proposals of guarantees of sovereignty.

Nevertheless, events at Panama in 1887 and 1888 once more began to stimulate international and especially American interest in the canal question. The Foreign Office had acknowledged the failure of the Panama scheme in 1887, and the bankruptcy of the French company was confirmed in 1888. The financial repercussions were enormous, not only for the directors of the company but also for the hundreds of thousands of French investors now facing the loss of their money. West had earlier reported from Washington, in December 1887, that there was great concern that the imminent collapse of the project would result in intervention by the French or some other government in an attempt to gain some return on the work already completed. The United States would not tolerate such intervention and would consider it "an unfriendly act." A later dispatch confirmed that while the United States would resist the intervention of the French government in the matter, it had no intention of "obtaining a footing on or near the Isthmus of Panama."[175]

During the period of the Cleveland administration Congress had shown only a limited interest in the canal question. The death of Eads in 1887 removed his "ship-railway" from consideration, but a new Nicaraguan company was formed in 1887 in which Menocal now assumed a prominent role.[176] The rumor of possible French government intervention to take over de Lesseps's company revived congressional interest and renewed the hopes of the advocates of the Nicaraguan canal. In January 1889 a resolution reaffirming the Monroe Doctrine[177] passed the Senate with only three opposing votes.[178] In February Congress granted a charter to the Nicaragua company, which was renamed the Maritime Canal Company of Nicaragua.[179]

These events coincided with the election in 1888 of a new president, Benjamin Harrison, who was reported to be in favor of the Nicaraguan scheme and who included the expansionist-minded James G. Blaine in his cabinet as secretary of state. The Republican platform of 1888 had denounced Cleveland for his failure "to charter, sanction or encourage any American organization for construction of the Nicaragua Canal, a work of vital importance to the maintenance of the Monroe doctrine and of our national influence in Central and South America."[180] But the Cleveland administration pursued a consistent policy to the end, and in contrast to previous administrations, it made no effort to revive the canal question during its last weeks in office.

What was surprising was that, in spite of their apparent commitment to a positive canal policy, neither Harrison nor Blaine showed much interest in the question. During the period of the Harrison administration no canal treaties were negotiated. To an extent this was because the fear of French intervention at Panama proved completely unfounded. On the other hand, diplomatic pressure was exerted by the administration upon Colombia not to renew the French concession, but this failed. The decline of American influence in Colombia was further underlined by the failure to negotiate a reciprocity trade treaty while that government signed commercial agreements with France and Germany.

Congress did not manifest any positive support for an "American" canal in spite of the Edmunds resolution and the incorporation of the Nicaraguan company. Even though the Maritime Canal Company began construction work in Nicaragua, its efforts to secure either a financial guarantee or any form of financial assistance from Congress were unavailing. The Senate, cajoled and driven by Senator Morgan of Alabama, was sympathetic, but the House was invariably hostile. The *Nation* outlined the reason in 1891: "It cannot be said that the present company has put forth any great exertions as yet. It has not spent any large sums of its own money. It has not strained its credit. It has apparently come to the conclusion that the easiest way to get on is to 'lie down' on the public Treasury."[181] In these circumstances, Congress was no more ready to endorse an active canal policy in the 1890s than it had been in the 1880s, the 1870s, or the 1860s. This was clearly illustrated in 1893 when Congress ignored the pleadings of the canal advocates and allowed the Maritime Canal Company to go bankrupt.

The revival of congressional interest in the canal question was especially noted in London when a resolution was introduced in the Senate in 1894 requesting the abrogation of the Clayton-Bulwer Treaty. The Foreign Office pursued, however, its traditional policy of not interfering in American political affairs. In 1889, when the incorporation of the Nicaraguan company seemed to warrant a British reaffirmation of the Clayton-Bulwer Treaty, Hertslet had sounded a note of caution. He believed such action would reopen the debate on the treaty and produce the reiteration of American objections that Britain believed had been "satisfactorily settled."[182] Nor was the Foreign Office alarmed in 1893 by reports that the United States would force a canal treaty upon Colombia. An examination of the issue by Sanderson concluded that the Colombian government was asking too high a price and that agreement was unlikely. "Open opposition on our part to manoeuvres which after all are only suspected," argued Sanderson, "would have the contrary effect to which we wish."[183] Impulsive action in these matters was both uncharacteristic of the Foreign Office and unnecessary.

British ministers in Washington had always kept the Foreign Office closely informed of canal developments within the administration and Congress, and British policy had been careful to avoid any semblance of interference in these matters with the exception of the reminders to Seward, Fish, and Evarts of the existence of the Clayton-Bulwer Treaty. The policy that had been pursued in the 1860s persisted into the 1890s. In January 1895, when a letter in the *Times* raised the problem of the rights of transit through the projected Nicaraguan canal, the Foreign Office showed its reluctance to act. "Any interference on the part of Her Majesty's Government," minuted an official, "would probably cause an outcry in the States and have a result contrary to that intended."[184] This was a somewhat passive and negative attitude, but it was one that had been justified and confirmed by long personal experience and by accurate reports from Foreign Office officials abroad that positive canal developments were unlikely to emanate from Washington. Indeed, the wheel had turned full circle in the 1890s in the sense that American and

British officials shared a more identical view on the canal issue than at any time since the 1860s. Pauncefote reported in 1894 that Secretary of State Gresham favored not exclusive American control but the neutralization of the Nicaraguan canal on the lines of the arrangement at Suez. In London, Bayard, the American ambassador, informed the foreign secretary that he favored the construction of a canal by a private company under proper conditions of neutrality and freedom of transit. Lord Kimberley "entirely agreed" with what was in substance basically the British position on the canal question.[185]

British canal diplomacy was therefore vindicated by events. Little faith had been expressed in the feasibility of the various canal projects and this had been proved correct. In spite of American objections against the Clayton-Bulwer Treaty, that treaty remained in existence and unchanged. Britain had no compelling strategic, political, or commercial need to build an isthmian canal. Such an objective, even if feasible, could only be enormously expensive and must involve complications with the United States. The Clayton-Bulwer Treaty proposed cooperation between Britain and the United States to construct the canal, but American sensitivities and desire for a unilateral policy and lack of British interest meant that this possibility was never considered. The American attitude was clear but negative and was well summed up by the *South American Journal:* "The Americans have been talking about this business for more than half a century, and up to now have done nothing but 'fool' with it. Their's [sic] is a dog-in-the-manger policy; they will neither build the canal themselves nor allow other people to do the work."[186] This was not quite true, for the French had tried and failed at Panama. But the argument was correct in that the record of nineteenth-century canal diplomacy showed that the United States spoke loudly on canal matters, but in the last resort was unwilling to undertake the responsibility of constructing an isthmian canal. The diplomats led, but Congress and the American people would not follow. Action would come when a strong president was in office and a chain of historical events culminating in the secession of Panama convinced Congress that an "American" canal had become a national priority.

//5//

Expansion and Reciprocity

The cautious and legalistic attitude of the British Foreign Office toward isthmian canal schemes and Latin American conflicts reflected a sense of realism and indifference toward events in the Western Hemisphere. With no pressing strategic or political questions to be concerned over and imbued with the principles of laissez faire, Foreign Office officials gave little attention to Latin American affairs. Business lobbies sought to arouse officials from this lethargy and, for example, prompted consideration of the renewal of diplomatic relations between Britain and Bolivia in 1875 and with Mexico in the early 1880s as a means of assisting British commerce with those countries. In the case of Bolivia, a mission was dispatched in 1875, but no action concerning recognition was taken. The resumption of diplomatic relations between France and Mexico in 1880 encouraged similar Anglo-Mexican discussions, but agreement was not finally reached until 1884. Speedy or decisive diplomatic action to support British trade was not therefore forthcoming from the late nineteenth-century Foreign Office.[1]

On the other hand, British officials paid much more attention to the series of American diplomatic initiatives from the late 1870s onward that posed a definite threat to established British interests in Latin America. On the political level, this threat could be contained by a policy of conciliation tempered with firmness or simply by waiting for American policy to flounder either from internal or external weaknesses. Thus, the canal treaties so laboriously negotiated by the executive were defeated by Congress without any need of British action. Similarly, Blaine's diplomatic bluster was blunted by Chile and not by Britain. Under Blaine, however, the State Department had begun to evolve a vigorous policy aimed at displacing European and especially British influence in Latin America by that of the United States. This was demonstrated by the Clayton-Bulwer correspondence and by the proposal to hold a Pan-American conference in Washington, from which Canada would be pointedly excluded. The replacement of Blaine by Frelinghuysen in December 1881 appeared to signal the reversal of these policies. The most immediate victim was the Trescot mission to Chile, and later the invitations to the proposed Washington conference were cancelled. But the reversal was only temporary, for the new secretary of state differed from his predecessor on personal rather than policy grounds. The energies of the American republic were beginning to look further afield, a development already illustrated by Blaine. In particular, his emphasis upon increased commercial contact with Latin America was a theme that attracted growing support throughout the 1880s and was firmly supported by Frelinghuysen himself. Consequently, although Blaine's policies appeared to have been repudiated in 1882, the Arthur administration soon formulated a policy of commercial expansion within the Western Hemisphere that was even more ambitious than that of the former secretary of state.

The British minister in Washington, Lionel West, saw the aims of this policy as the exclusion of European influence from the Western Hemisphere and the control of Latin American markets as an outlet for domestic overproduction.[2] The threat to Britain was, however, much more potential and distant than either real or immediate. Not only did internal American political factors do much to defeat the Frelinghuysen initiatives, but, with the exception of Central America and the Caribbean islands, American commercial enterprise was so lacking in Latin America that it could not effectively compete with well-established European businesses. Diplomatic efforts could hardly build a trade where none existed, but despite its setbacks in 1884–1885 the vigorous exercise of commercial diplomacy was resumed in 1889 by the Harrison administration. The holding of the Pan-American conference at Washington in 1889–1890 and the large number of reciprocity treaties that followed indicated the extent of American influence and power within the Western Hemisphere. Even though Britain might gain temporary comfort when these policies were abruptly undermined by the Cleveland administration in 1893–1894, the series of events from 1881 to 1893 demonstrated how vulnerable Latin America, and, by implication, established British interests in that continent, were to political and commercial pressure from the United States.

The Formulation of the Policy of Commercial Diplomacy

American secretaries of state throughout the 1860s and 1870s often stressed the desirability of more foreign trade and, in particular, more trade between the United States and Latin America. In 1870 the cautious and conservative Fish informed Congress that Latin America conducted most of its trade with Britain rather than the United States despite "the American idea which has been so prominently and so constantly put forward by the Government of the United States."³ In 1882 Blaine explained that his Latin American policy had been motivated by a desire to achieve peace and "to cultivate such friendly commercial relations with all American countries as would lead to a large increase in the export trade of the United States."⁴

In practical terms little was achieved during this period. The Grant administration did secure the ratification of a reciprocity trade treaty with Hawaii in 1875, but for political and strategic reasons as much as for commercial ones.⁵ Treaties with Latin American countries, such as those with the Dominican Republic and Colombia, were humiliatingly rejected by Congress. Nor did the Hayes administration achieve anything more substantial. Evarts ordered the publication of consular reports of commercial interest, but the value of such material for the businessman was doubtful.⁶ Moreover, for an administration that stressed increased commercial contact with Latin America, Evarts manifested little interest in negotiating commercial agreements with the countries of that area.⁷

Similar criticism may be leveled against the Garfield administration. Blaine later implied that Garfield's untimely death prevented the implementation of a carefully prepared policy of commercial expansion in Latin America, but the fact is that such a policy was not forthcoming until Frelinghuysen's tenure at the State Department. Such an outcome was surprising, for the Arthur administration appeared weak in diplomatic experience and political influence. Arthur had become president by accident, and his political record was not an inspiring one. As a close associate of the notorious Roscoe Conkling, the former senator from New York, Arthur's own reputation was clouded by corruption and scandal. His influence within his own party and in Congress too was therefore very tenuous. While the new secretary of state, Frelinghuysen, was a man of undoubted integrity he was also regarded as something of a safe and noncontroversial choice after the dynamic Blaine. Initially Frelinghuysen confirmed this assessment by reversing several of Blaine's policies, but in time he formulated a Latin American policy that by implication was even more farsighted than that of his predecessor.

This policy reflected the personal views of the officials in control of the execution of American foreign policy. It was also a response to political and economic pressures and a consequence of the events set in motion by the negotiation of the reciprocity treaty between the United States and Mexico in January 1883. The general direction of policy was indicated by President Arthur in his annual message to Congress in 1884:

"The countries of the American continent and the adjacent islands are for the United States the natural marts of supply and demand. It is from them that we should obtain what we do not produce or do not produce in sufficiency, and it is to them that the surplus productions of our fields, our mills, and our workshops should flow, under conditions that will equalize or favor them in comparison with foreign competition."[8]

This policy was to some extent direct action to alleviate economic depression, for the final two years of the Arthur administration were years of industrial recession and of a sudden decline in American agricultural exports to Europe. Overproduction was perceived as the problem, and increased exports appeared to be an acceptable solution. Further, if the European market was falling off, then alternative markets must be sought, and Latin America was seen as providing a ripe field for American commercial penetration. Thus, business groups put pressure on the administration to improve economic relations with Mexico and to send a diplomatic commission to investigate the means of expanding trade with Latin America.[9] Similar pressures were exerted in Congress, where legislators discussed such matters as a customs union of all the American nations, reciprocity treaties, the improvement of rail and steamship communication with Latin America, and the dispatch of a special commission to promote trade with that area. From one such discussion in 1884 came a statistical report showing that in 1883 the United States possessed only 18.9 percent of total Latin American foreign trade.[10]

In such circumstances it was not surprising that Arthur and Frelinghuysen showed an active interest in promoting American trade by diplomatic means. Moreover, in striking contrast to British policy, political factors strongly reinforced the economic imperatives. The midterm elections of 1882 were disastrous for the Republican party, and this stirred Arthur and his cabinet into more vigorous political activity. Positive positions were taken not only on foreign policy issues, but also on explosive domestic questions such as the tariff and civil service reform. Nor had Arthur given up hope of securing his party's nomination in the 1884 presidential campaign. In this struggle his chief opponent was Blaine, and the Arthur administration sought to steal some of Blaine's thunder by pursuing its own spirited foreign policy.[11]

Nevertheless, Blaine secured the Republican nomination with ease. Much of his campaign literature emphasized closer relations with Latin America. While the Democratic platform of 1884 deprecated Republican policy in general, it also advocated the extension of American trade. The need for more trade was widely appreciated and prominent Democrats such as Senator John T. Morgan had consistently given the Arthur administration support and encouragement in the pursuance of its Latin

American policy. British journals frequently confirmed the "marked disposition" of the United States to increase its exports and, in particular, the "energetic and practical interest" of Americans in Latin American trade.[12]

For Frelinghuysen, who talked "by the hour"[13] of increased hemispheric trade, this was the opportunity to pursue a policy that would satisfy not only the commercial but also the strategic and ideological requirements raised by isthmian canal problems and the War of the Pacific. Two statements in 1884 illustrated the direction of his thinking. In August he instructed the men appointed to the Latin American Trade Commission that "an identity of material and political interests between the American Republics should be fostered and advanced by the influence and action of the United States."[14] A few months earlier he had informed the Senate Foreign Relations Committee:

> I am thoroughly convinced of the advisability of knitting closely our relations with the states of this continent, and no effort on my part shall be wanting to accomplish a result so consonant with the constant policy of this country, and in the spirit of the Monroe doctrine, which, in excluding foreign political interference, recognizes the common interest of the states of North and South America. It is the history of all diplomacy that close political relations and friendships spring from unity of commercial interests. The merchant or trader is the forerunner and aid to diplomatic intimacy and international harmony.[15]

Such views reflected the traditions of American expansionism by asserting American political, commercial, and ideological hegemony in the Western Hemisphere. Immediate questions such as the problem of overproduction, domestic political difficulties, and diplomatic imbroglios such as the de Lesseps canal scheme and the continuation of the War of the Pacific provided the spur to action.

Frelinghuysen could not halt the Panama scheme, and the dilemma posed by the War of the Pacific was solved by the protagonists themselves without American mediation. A much more promising area for American diplomatic action was that of increasing trade with Latin America by means of the negotiation of reciprocal trade agreements. The idea of reciprocity treaties was not new. The United States had negotiated such agreements with Canada in 1854 and with Hawaii in 1875 although these treaties were the exception rather than the rule. Opposition to reciprocity came from traditional sentiment in favor of protection joined by business interests, which felt threatened by the treaties. Anglophobic opinion soon undermined the agreement with Canada and contributed toward its early termination, while the agreement with Hawaii was also under considerable attack from its very inception.

Reciprocity was therefore neither a well-tried nor particularly successful policy. Moreover, Seward, Fish, and Evarts had shown little interest in the idea. But one area of Latin America provided an opportunity for a change of policy. This was Mexico, where political instability and vexatious customs regulations had long irritated American merchants into requesting some form of diplomatic assistance from Washington. Closer relations with Mexico were also desired by influential American railroad interests strongly supported by Republican party leaders, of whom ex-President Grant was the most prominent.[16] Furthermore, there was the initiative of the Mexicans themselves. A commercial agreement had been signed in 1831 between Mexico and the United States, but it had been rendered largely inoperative by the later passage of protectionist regulations in both countries. In November 1880 the Mexican government announced its intention of terminating the 1831 treaty and gave the requisite twelve months notice of this. By selecting the pro-American Matías Romero as its minister in Washington, the Mexican government indicated its desire to conclude a new agreement,[17] but Blaine's displeasure at Mexico's attitude in its boundary dispute with Guatemala prevented progress in 1881.

Frelinghuysen expressed his willingness to open discussions in March 1882, and although Mexican suspicion of American motives provided a further delay, formal negotiations were held in Washington in January 1883.[18] A treaty was speedily concluded in which the United States removed duties on a number of Mexican products, including coffee and certain categories of sugar and leaf tobacco, while Mexico gave significant concessions, especially to American manufactured goods. Frelinghuysen regarded the treaty as merely the first step in the creation of "more cordial feeling and closer relations."[19] The British minister in Washington confirmed that the State Department considered the treaty as an experiment rather than as an attempt to obtain special advantages for American commerce. He forecast that the opposition of the protectionist lobby would be aroused, especially the sugar planters of Louisiana and the California-based Hawaiian interests. He also referred to the railroad holdings of General Grant and his well-known interests in Mexican concessions, a fact that would raise misgivings in Congress.[20]

Therein lay a major stumbling block of all nineteenth-century expansionist-minded American administrations. The executive had the power to negotiate treaties, but their ratification was the function of the Senate. Frelinghuysen could talk of closer relations with Latin American nations, but to give this practical effect he also had to secure congressional assent and cooperation. Unfortunately for the administration, the Congress that assembled in December 1883 was no longer Republican-controlled, and its agenda was dominated by lengthy and enervating tariff debates. The Mexican treaty received no special attention, and the opposition of the protectionist and sugar lobbies further delayed its progress. Even Frelinghuysen came to regard ratification as doubtful,[21] although a favorable vote was eventually secured in March 1884. The winning votes were, however, gained only by the addition of an amendment requiring implementing legislation by the House of Representatives before the treaty could take effect. The treaty was therefore sent to the House, where action was deferred until the following session.

The British Foreign Office was concerned by the commercial advantages that the treaty would give American trade with Mexico,[22] but no new urgency was injected into the discussions concerning the renewal of Anglo-Mexican diplomatic relations. Matters of principle and diplomatic procedure transcended those of mere commercial advantage.[23] While Britain could gain some comfort by the opposition to the treaty within the American Congress, the potential American threat was considerably increased by the application of the reciprocity policy to other parts of Latin America. The most significant development was the opening of discussions in early 1884 between the United States and Spain concerning trade with Cuba and Puerto Rico. The specific American aims were the reduction of Spanish duties on American products, both agricultural and manufactured, and the settlement of long-standing claims against Cuba. However, in the longer term, Frelinghuysen saw a commercial treaty as bringing the islands "a lasting amelioration of their condition . . . which would strongly tend to restore confidence, establish healthful prosperity, and, by removing causes of discontent now only too plainly visible, ensure to those provinces the enduring well being which they deserve as the richest jewels in the Spanish crown."[24] In charge of negotiations with Spain was the experienced diplomat John W. Foster. Negotiations were arduous and lasted virtually throughout 1884. The treaty that was finally signed in Madrid in late November was described by Foster as "the most perfect reciprocity treaty our Government has ever made. . . . I am quite confident it will result in giving us the almost complete commercial monopoly of the commerce of Cuba. . . . It will be annexing Cuba in the most desirable way."[25]

Yet, earlier in 1884 Frelinghuysen had expressed reservations regarding the policy of reciprocity. He noted the strong congressional opposition to the Mexican treaty and feared that the Spanish treaty would be even more unpopular because its immediate benefits would tend to favor Cuba rather than the United States.[26] Furthermore, in contrast to the Mexican negotiations, the prospect of an early conclusion of a treaty with Spain was unlikely. In the early spring of 1884 Foster was recalled to Washington for consultations, and even in late July he was writing from Madrid that negotiations "advance slowly with no great prospects of success." It was not until September that he began to feel confident that his mission would be successful.[27]

In the meantime, Blaine had secured the Republican presidential nomination, thus effectively numbering the days in office of the Arthur administration. Nevertheless, the State Department was still headed by Frelinghuysen and until March 4, 1885, it was Frelinghuysen with whom foreign diplomats conducted official business. Among a number of these diplomats, the policy of reciprocity was a matter of growing concern. Most affected were the sugar-producing countries of Central America and the Caribbean islands who feared the loss of the American sugar market to Mexico. This was the main reason for Spain's willingness to discuss a treaty on behalf of Cuba and Puerto Rico. In the spring of 1884 Hawaiian interests appeared eager to complete negotiations leading to an extension of the 1875 reciprocity treaty. In June 1884 the minister of the Dominican Republic offered Frelinghuysen terms virtually identical to those contained in the Mexican treaty. In July and August it was learned that the sugar producers of the British West Indian Islands were requesting the British government to open reciprocity talks with Washington and that there was even discussion of the possible annexation of those islands to the United States.[28] In November the British government made a formal approach to Frelinghuysen to begin negotiations for a reciprocity treaty on behalf of these islands. By the end of the year Frelinghuysen had also discussed reciprocity with representative from El Salvador, Colombia, Venezuela, and Haiti.[29]

A policy that had begun so inauspiciously now positively radiated success. The implications of the Mexican treaty had suddenly evoked from several countries, including Britain, a clear acknowledgment of American power within the Western Hemisphere. The Spanish treaty was concluded in November and during the next month reciprocity treaties were signed with Hawaii and the Dominican Republic and the canal treaty concluded with Nicaragua. At the same time the policy was presented for the approval of the new congressional session, which began in December 1884. The administration decided to put the Spanish and the Nicaraguan treaties before the Senate and await the verdict of the House on the Mexican treaty. American press reaction to the treaties was not particularly favorable, and the victory of Cleveland over Blaine in the November presidential election had been a blow to the Republican party. The lame-duck Arthur administration was also fast losing its political influence. On the other hand, the treaties affirmed well-established American traditions and appealed to both expansionist and commercial sentiment. In the previous session the Senate had approved the Mexican treaty and the House had voted funds to send a trade commission to Latin America. Support for an active Latin American policy was not therefore lacking within Congress.

Yet, if the Arthur administration was a lame duck, so was the Forty-eighth Congress. In a brief session of only four months this body was unprepared to act decisively in any areas of policy, least of all those involving political or financial commitments to other countries. This applied to the treaties that raised the question of existing international obligations and also reopened the controversial tariff issue. Protectionist opinion continued to be suspicious of reciprocity. Moreover, the feud between the Arthur administration and Blaine now assumed the form of Blaine using his influence to persuade fellow Republicans to vote against the treaties. The Democrats preferred to await instructions from President-elect Cleveland, but he remained studiously silent. They were, however, clearly aware that the passage of the reciprocity treaties would seriously undermine the new president's freedom of action. Moreover, congressmen of both parties were subject to considerable lobbying against the treaties by the sugar and tobacco interests and by many east coast chambers of commerce. A resolution put forward by Senator Morrill of Vermont succinctly listed the arguments against reciprocity: "That so-called reciprocity treaties, having no possible basis of reciprocity with nations of inferior population and wealth, involving the surrender of enormously unequal sums of revenue, involving the surrender of immensely larger volumes of home trade than are offered to us in return, and involving constitutional questions of the gravest character, are untimely, and should everywhere be regarded with disfavor."[30]

Critics of reciprocity also claimed that the terms of the Spanish treaty so favored Cuban exports to the United States that the consequent reduction in customs revenue would turn the annual surplus into a deficit. The precedent of altering the tariff by means of treaties negotiated by the executive also threatened the powers of the House over revenue matters and thus raised a major constitutional issue. In these circumstances, it was not surprising that *Bradstreet's* was reporting early in 1885 that "the commercial treaties are, undoubtedly, defeated."[31] Only the Nicaraguan treaty was brought to a vote and it failed to secure ratification. None of the reciprocity treaties even came to a vote, and the new Cleveland administration effectively closed the debate by announcing its intention to reconsider the whole question. In practice this meant the rejection of the Spanish and Dominican treaties, and though support was given to the ratified but deferred Mexican treaty, it failed to secure congressional approval during the 1885–1886 session.[32]

Despite general agreement on the need for more trade with Latin America, powerful business lobbies and domestic political factors combined to defeat the ambitious Arthur-Frelinghuysen Latin American policy. Even the final report of the Latin American Trade Commission in 1885 failed to generate any new enthusiasm for the reciprocity idea. In fact, the history of the trade commission illustrates many of the reasons why the United States was failing to make inroads into Latin American markets and why nations such as Britain could maintain a complacent and negative attitude.[33]

The Latin American Trade Commission had received congressional approval in July 1884 through an appropriation of $25,000 included in the consular and diplomatic appropriation bill. The stated purpose of the commission was "to ascertain the best mode of securing more intimate international and commercial relations" between the United States and Latin America.[34] The congressional debates on the appropriation demonstrated, however, that the House was not entirely favorable to the idea. The Democratic spokesman, James Burnes of Missouri, argued that the United States had already enough resident officials in Latin America and that economic negotiations could be more easily conducted in Washington.[35] Congressman William Springer of Illinois declared: "You can send commissioners to South America from now until the day of judgment, and you may drink barrels of champagne with the people there, and you can never sell a wool hat to a single citizen of those countries until you can sell it as cheap or cheaper than such articles are sold by the countries of Europe."[36] The appropriation was not finally approved until the final day of the congressional session and then only as a result of political compromise.[37]

The commissioners were appointed by the administration in August. The chairman was General George Sharpe, a former surveyor of the port of New York and a personal friend of both Arthur and Grant. The two other commissioners were Thomas Reynolds of Missouri and Solon Thacher of Kansas. The Chicago journalist, William E. Curtis, was later appointed as secretary to the commission and eventually acted as a commissioner in place of Reynolds.

The appointments reflected political patronage, and the pro-Democrat *New York Herald* later described the commissioners as "men without international and scarcely even with national fame, armed with credentials giving them the diplomatic rank of Envoys Extraordinary and Ministers Plenipotentiary, but without specific powers or duties."[38] The assessment was harsh but also accurate and was reiterated by a number of English-language newspapers in South America. The *Rio News* argued that until there were changes in the American tariff, the commission could only achieve negative results. The *Buenos Ayres*

Herald regarded the commissioners as "eminent men in their respective callings," but described the whole project as "ridiculous."[39] The British minister in Washington was not so disparaging. He considered the congressional appropriation as an economic assertion of the Monroe Doctrine, and concluded that the aim of the commission was to persuade the Latin Americans to buy from the United States instead of from Europe.[40] The interest of the Foreign Office was aroused and instructions were dispatched on November 19, 1884, to its various officials in Latin America to keep the department informed of the activities of the commission.

The commission commenced its investigations in September 1884 by interviewing American businessmen in New York, Philadelphia, Baltimore, and San Francisco. West reported these events to London and expressed the opinion that no practical results were likely. Already, even within the United States, observers outlined the American tariff and the lack of regular and direct steamship communication between the United States and Latin America as major obstacles to the growth of hemispheric trade.[41] The prospects of the commission received a further blow in November 1884 with the election of a Democratic president. Possibly as a result of this, General Sharpe withdrew from active participation in its work.[42] The other commissioners continued with their task although Reynolds proceeded no further than Guatemala. The task was made no easier by congressional rejection of the reciprocity treaties. It was not only awkward diplomacy, it was also somewhat invidious and demeaning for the commissioners to argue in favor of closer commercial ties while that very same policy was being defeated in Washington. Consequently, the commission did little to promote a favorable image of the United States in Latin America. In the short term the general trend of Latin American trade remained unaffected, with the European nations and especially Britain still in control.

Diplomatic awkwardness was also reflected in the itinerary of the commission and was the result of conceiving of the mission in much too ambitious and vague terms and then compounding this error with ignorance, faulty planning, and sheer bad luck. The commissioners planned a visit to New Orleans to coincide with the New Orleans Exposition, but on arrival they discovered they were too early. Upon reaching Venezuela in January 1885 they learned that the leading Venezuelan political figure, Guzman Blanco, was absent in Europe and that without him substantive talks were not possible. The outbreak of civil war in Colombia prevented a visit to Bogotá, and by visiting Peru before Chile, the commission aroused the resentment of the Chilean government.

Nor were the susceptibilities of the Latin Americans taken into account when the new Democratic administration instructed the commission to wind up its activities and return to the United States by July 1, 1885. The commissioners cut short their stay in Chile and paid only a brief visit to Uruguay and Argentina, provoking local ridicule and indignation. The *Buenos Ayres Herald* headlined an editorial "The Argentine Republic in 35 hours" and drew an analogy with Jules Verne's story of rapid transit to the moon. After the months it had spent in Central America and the west coast of South America, the commission's brief visit to Argentina was regarded as "a shameful slight," arousing "outspoken and strong disgust."[43] In the case of Brazil the turn of events was even more poignant. In his original instructions to the commissioners, Frelinghuysen had emphasized the importance of visiting Brazil,[44] but on account of the new deadline the commissioners decided to miss Brazil even though it was necessary to pass through Rio harbor on their way to New York. But the accident of a shipwreck just outside Rio delayed their return by another twenty days and the deadline was missed. A British official in Brazil described the Rio incident as giving the commissioners "an unpleasant recollection of a mission so unfruitful in its results, and terminated by a catastrophe illustrating so aptly its failure."[45]

Thacher returned to the United States in the last days of July 1885, and the commission's final report was presented to Congress in October. It singled out the lack of direct and regular steamship communication between the United States and Latin America as the main obstacle to increased commerce. Other recommendations included an expanded and improved consular service, reciprocity treaties, the establishment of American banks and credit facilities to promote trade with Latin America, more simplified customs schedules, and, in general, more American interest in its sister republics.[46]

Furthermore, the report emphasized that if the United States was to expect tariff concessions from Latin America, then it must be prepared to import the commodities that these countries produced, especially sugar and wool. A positive step in this direction had already been taken with the treaty with Mexico, but the protectionist and sugar lobbies had shown themselves capable of preventing congressional ratification. No doubt the National Association of Wool Manufacturers would also spring into action if its members felt their interests threatened by foreign imports. The commissioners were only too clearly aware of these domestic pressures, for they deliberately avoided discussion of wool and sugar. "Had we been at liberty to bring on a discussion as to them," the report noted, "we have no doubt the result in every case, except perhaps Chile, would have been a very favorable reciprocity treaty."[47]

The action of the Cleveland administration in withdrawing the reciprocity treaties and in insisting that the commissioners return by July 1 had severely undermined their prospects of success. Even so, these prospects had never been high. The Argentine foreign minister, Luis Ortiz, had remarked to the British minister in September 1884 that commerce with Europe was long established in Argentina and could not be easily diverted into other channels. In his opinion, the commission was "one of those projects . . . which the Americans so frequently start without reflecting upon the difficulties of realization, and which seem to be put forward by their authors for the sake of notoriety or some individual interest."[48]

On the other hand, the commission had reflected the genuine interest of the Arthur administration in Latin America even though this interest was translated into a policy that took little account of the feelings and susceptibilities of the Latin American nations. The uneven organization of the commission's itinerary upset most of those governments, thus confirming their suspicions of American insincerity and ulterior motives. Nevertheless, the commission had actually visited and had been made welcome by most of those governments and had acquired a considerable amount of information that could be used to fulfill its original objective of securing closer hemispheric relations.

In 1884 the reciprocity treaty with Mexico had prompted great interest in the question of reciprocity on the part of Latin American governments. Despite various reservations the commissioners confirmed that this was still the case. "In every country that we visited except, perhaps, Chile," noted Thacher, "we found the authorities and the people desirous of strengthening the relations between their country and the United States."[49] The commercial policy inaugurated by the Arthur administration demonstrated that Latin America was eager for further contact with the United States and that some of those countries were vulnerable to American economic pressure. The execution of that policy left, however, a lot to be desired. Domestic political factors were largely responsible for this, but diplomatic naïveté and awkwardness also exacted a price. As the *Buenos Ayres Herald* noted in November 1885:

> During the last few years we have heard a great amount of talk about the encouragement of closer commercial relations between the United States and the countries of South America. Papers have printed tons of paper about this matter. Congress has created commissions, who have gone junketing about the world with no end of fur and feathers, making a loud noise—and doing nothing. . . .
>
> So long as Europe comes here with its millions and Americans come here with itinerating commissions, the business supremacy of Europe in this country will be seen.[50]

For the moment Britain did not have to fear losing its commercial preeminence in South America to the United States. As West noted in July 1885, "The inauguration of an American hemispherical policy does not seem to meet with much favour."[51] Indeed, the expansionist direction of policy unleashed by Arthur and Frelinghuysen had received a setback in 1885, but events were soon to demonstrate that this policy, far from declining in attractiveness, was growing in popularity.

The Washington Conference, 1889–1890

President Cleveland and his secretary of state, Thomas Bayard, were fully conscious of American strategic and commercial needs, but they were not prepared to become identified with a policy inaugurated by their Republican predecessors and political rivals. On occasion, steps were taken to protect American interests in Colombia, Hawaii, and Samoa, but such intervention was conservative and limited in nature. Under these circumstances, the activist role in the formulation of an expansionist policy toward Latin America was now assumed by Congress. The result was not the ratification of reciprocity treaties, for political and tariff difficulties still prevented this, but the emergence of bipartisan political support for the idea of a conference of American nations to be held in Washington.

The idea of resolving hemispheric problems by inviting the parties concerned to a conference in Washington was the natural corollary to the assumed role of the United States as leader and protector of its hemispheric sisters. In 1866 Congress had attempted to bring the belligerents in the Pacific war and the War of the Triple Alliance to discuss peace terms in Washington. The idea of a fully representative inter-American conference under United States auspices later found concrete expression in 1881, when James G. Blaine proposed this as a means of resolving inter-American disputes such as the War of the Pacific and the Mexico-Guatemalan boundary controversy by resort to arbitration under the aegis of inter-American goodwill and, no doubt, judicious pressure from the United States. But the implications of the initiative were too far-reaching for Blaine's successor, and the invitations were withdrawn in August 1882.[52]

Blaine argued in 1882 that the proposed conference was not only designed to secure hemispheric peace but also to stimulate trade between the United States and Latin America. Frelinghuysen shared Blaine's aims, but preferred to achieve them by means of reciprocity treaties rather than an international conference where the United States might be outvoted and in which sensitive issues such as the isthmian canal might be inopportunely raised. Nevertheless, there was growing pressure from Congress for increased contact and cooperation with Latin American governments and a conference was increasingly suggested as a way of facilitating this. A direct consequence was the Latin American Trade Commission, whose final report recommended closer inter-American relations and especially the negotiation of reciprocity treaties.

In the absence of positive directions from the White House, the new Democratic-controlled House in 1885 showed little interest in the trade commission's report. The Democratic view remained the same as it had been in 1882, when the *New York Herald* summed it up: "What we want of the American Republics is trade, which we can best get not by ridiculous conventions but by the repeal of bad laws that make commercial intercourse with our neighbors impossible and difficult."[53] Current Democratic political strategy was to prepare a major attack on the tariff, and despite the efforts of various individual congressmen and senators to arouse interest in Latin American affairs, such matters were not given legislative priority.[54]

In 1886 the Senate did approve Senator Frye's proposal that the United States hold an inter-American conference, but, although the House had similar measures under consideration, joint House-Senate agreement proved impossible.[55] West reported to London that Bayard regarded such ideas as "chimerical" and a Foreign Office official minuted that it was doubtful "if anything will come of this rather fantastic scheme."[56] The British minister later explained that Bayard believed that a conference was futile so long as the United States maintained its protective tariff.[57]

Circumstances had, however, changed when the new session of Congress assembled in December 1887. Both political parties now looked to the 1888 elections and sought to introduce attractive policies. The priority still appeared to be the alleviation of economic discontent, especially that of western agrarian interests. The Republicans argued that continued protection was the answer and that trade should be expanded by reciprocity treaties with Latin American nations. Under the impetus of Cleveland's tariff message to Congress in December 1887, the Democrats now advocated a major reduction of the tariff. This would lower the price of raw materials and reduce the treasury surplus, thus bringing more money into circulation and stimulating the economy. Although the attempt was defeated by Republican opposition and by internal divisions within the Democratic party, there was a general consensus in Congress that trade must somehow be encouraged. Major tariff changes were impossible, but bipartisan agreement was reached in early 1888 on a bill instructing the president to invite Latin American governments to a conference to be held in Washington in 1889.[58]

As befitting a compromise measure, the proposed agenda of the conference was extremely broad. Matters to be discussed included steamship and railroad communication, customs regulations, weights and measures, and copyright agreements, but more significantly, the project of an inter-American customs union,[59] an arbitration scheme, and the adoption of a common silver coin. The arbitration aspect evoked memories of Blaine's initiative in 1881, but Blaine took no active role in the passage of the bill. The measure reflected the widespread desire for increased trade with Latin America and appealed to Democrats and Republicans alike. Democrats saw the bill as part of their general onslaught on the tariff and believed it would stimulate the economy and win votes for their party in the forthcoming elections. Republicans welcomed the measure because it assisted business and held out the prospect of congressional aid for shipping interests. It might also divert attention from the tariff question. Democratic congressmen, such as James McCreary of Kentucky and Richard Townshend of Illinois, expressed the bill's aims in ambitious commercial terms. "The countries of Central and South America," declared McCreary, "need the products of our furnaces, of our factories, and of our farms." In traditional vein, Townshend saw the conference as a positive step toward American displacement of European commercial ascendancy in Latin America.[60]

Congress not only gave substance to the idea of a conference, but also sought to exercise some control over the choice of the American delegation. This procedure was, however, criticized as an invasion of the powers of the executive to enforce congressional laws, and was excluded from the final bill.[61] While Cleveland approved the bill,[62] he concentrated on the 1888 presidential campaign and showed no interest in scheduling the conference before the end of his term of office.[63] His defeat in the election resulted in the third consecutive lame-duck administration. In contrast to Blaine in 1881 and Frelinghuysen in 1884-1885, Bayard did not attempt to compromise his successor at the State Department. No new treaties were unveiled and it appeared that all the arrangements for the conference would be left to the new Harrison administration.[64]

Bayard did, however, take an interest in the conference and showed that he wanted it to take place even under Republican auspices. Although the selection of the American delegation was left entirely to the new administration, Bayard was concerned that some Latin American nations would not attend the conference. The attitudes of Argentina, Brazil, and Chile were particularly uncertain, and a special mission was dispatched to ascertain the opinions of these countries. The commissioner was John G. Walker, a former secretary of the Bogotá legation. His task was to tour South America and persuade all the nations to accept their invitations, a mission that he successfully completed between February and June 1889.[65]

The decision by the United States to call an inter-American conference was an event of major diplomatic significance. The London Chamber of Commerce saw the importance of the development as "hardly [to] be overestimated,"[66] and the British chargé in Washington warned of possible danger to the independence of the Central American and Caribbean countries.[67] While the Latin American nations were attracted by the commercial prospects of the conference, they were also acutely suspicious of American motives. Nor was this apprehension allayed by the election of Harrison and the prospect of the return of Blaine to the State Department. The Walker mission appeared to remove some of the fears, but doubts still remained, as dispatches from British officials in Latin America confirmed. From Mexico, Francis Denys reported that the Mexican government was showing little interest in the conference and did not expect to derive much benefit from attendance. Mexican opinion was lukewarm because of traditional distrust of its neighbor and the knowledge, underlined by the fate of the 1883 reciprocity treaty, that the United States was unlikely to alter the tariff. The issue still rankled and was inflamed in the summer of 1889 by the imposition of a new duty by the United States on silver-lead ores. This was regarded as a direct blow to the Mexican mining industry and, according to Denys, "has rendered the Mexican Government very averse to promoting or helping in any way the commerce of the United States."[68]

During the summer of 1888 Lionel West had expressed doubt as to whether Brazil would attend the conference.[69] Even after Brazil had accepted the invitation in 1889, the *Rio News* continued to reflect Brazilian fears that American policy was motivated "more by a spirit of domination and gain than of neighborly co-operation and sympathy."[70] From Peru, too, reports suggested a certain coolness on the part of that government. The British minister in Lima summed up the Peruvian attitude as welcoming more friendly inter-American relations but expecting nothing of value from the conference.[71] In Chile, the attitude was still strongly influenced by bitter memories of Blaine's meddling during the War of the Pacific. Nor did Chile's neighbor, Argentina, regard the conference as likely to be particularly productive. The *Buenos Ayres Herald* argued that few Argentines thought of or cared about the United States, and that "the International American Congress about meeting [sic] in Washington, will disclose the fact that South America will not be caught or intoxicated with American grandeur, or dinners or flattery, but will know and attend to its own interests, and the few who thought South America would make a serviceable tail for Brother Jonathan's kite will get badly left."[72]

British opinion adopted a similar attitude. The *South American Journal* believed that the conference threatened British interests in Latin America, but would encourage more vigorous British commercial effort there. Unless the United States had something concrete to offer, the journal predicted that the Latin Americans would "listen coldly to mere sympathetic and rhetorical exhortations."[73] The London correspondent of the *Boston Herald* reported that the conference had attracted little attention in Britain and that the British were supremely confident of maintaining their hold over South American markets.[74]

The exclusion of Canada and the British West Indies from the conference pointed to the anti-British nature of United States policy. The proposals to form a customs union and to establish arbitration machinery signified a continuation of Washington's attempt to exclude European political and commercial influence from the Western Hemisphere. The Foreign Office was aware of these implications, but was not inclined to counter them. The Argentine minister in Washington had suggested privately that Britain should use its influence to undermine the conference,[75] but there is no direct evidence that this was taken up. Dispatches from British officials in Latin America reported widespread suspicion of United States motives and suggested that agreement on substantial issues was unlikely. Moreover, it was not in the nature of the late nineteenth-century Foreign Office to intervene actively in commercial matters or with the course of American politics, especially so soon after the "Sackville-West" incident.[76]

Despite Latin American distrust of the United States and amid rumors of European plots, the conference did take place on schedule in October 1889. The reasons were varied. One was the sheer difficulty of refusing an invitation made by the United States, because such a refusal could be interpreted as lack of diplomatic courtesy.[77] Bayard's original invitation had stressed that the conference was "consultative and recommendatory only," and therefore no obligations were incurred by attendance.[78] The Walker mission had reiterated this and by persuading Chile to attend had virtually ensured that the conference would take place.[79]

Attendance at the conference had an attractive side too. Thacher had informed a Senate committee in 1886 that Chile would accept an invitation to an inter-American conference despite that country's apparent hostility toward the United States. He based his belief on Chile's well-known support for steamship communication with the United States and its keen interest in the proposal to establish a silver coin as common currency throughout the hemisphere.[80] Similar desires were shared by all the Latin American countries, and Brazil in particular was most eager to negotiate a commercial treaty with the United States.[81] Moreover, item eight of the agenda allowed virtually any subject to be raised at the conference and so presented valuable political opportunities. Venezuela used this to further publicize the question of its boundary dispute with Britain. Likewise, Ecuador, Colombia, and Paraguay were able to direct attention to their own special interests in the question of the right of access to the sea and the free navigation of rivers.[82]

The timing of the invitation was also opportune in that there was no major conflict pending in Latin America to prevent attendance. With the sole exception of the Dominican Republic,[83] all the Latin American countries accepted the invitation, and their delegates assembled in Washington for the opening of the conference in October 1889.[84] The agenda was that outlined in the 1888 congressional act. A Republican administration was now in office, and during the summer of 1889 extensive preparations were made for the conference. Following the instructions of the 1888 act Harrison appointed ten delegates to represent the United States. The majority of these were businessmen with Republican sympathies.[85] At the same time, Blaine and his agent, William E. Curtis, contacted various commercial groups and individual merchants for their views on the forthcoming conference. Most respondents were strongly in favor of the need for more trade, but unsure whether the conference could achieve very much in this direction. The need for improved steamship communication was widely recognized, although Andrew Carnegie expected that this would arouse strong opposition within the United States itself.[86] Another delegate pointed out the difficulties of establishing either a court of arbitration or a customs union.[87] The Philadelphia Board of Trade summed up a generally held opinion when it described commercial union as "impolitic, if not impracticable."[88]

Curtis's inquiries also emphasized the question of reciprocity treaties. In general, the response was not encouraging. He was informed that because the Latin American countries depended on customs duties as their major source of revenue, they would be reluctant to reduce these duties. Most of these countries enjoyed only a modest trade with the United States and saw little value in wide-ranging commercial agreements, especially when the American tariff only affected two of their exports, namely, sugar and wool. Curtis therefore ruled out the possibility of free trade or a general customs union and considered that the United States must bargain for trade concessions by offering tariff reductions on sugar and, perhaps, wool.[89]

Despite the concentration on commercial matters, the new Harrison administration also saw the conference as an opportunity for mounting an impressive public relations spectacle. "The constitutional centennial of this, the mother of republics," wrote Curtis in June 1889, "could not be celebrated in a more appropriate manner than by bringing her children together."[90] In an attempt to impress not only American public opinion but also the Latin American delegates, Blaine instructed Curtis to prepare a deluxe railroad tour of the United States for the visitors. The tour would commence just after the opening reception in Washington and would last for six weeks. The delegates would first visit New England and then head west to Chicago and St. Louis returning to Washington to begin the actual conference business.

The excursion illustrated many of the defects that had long bedeviled United States relations with Latin America. The achievements of the United States were undeniable and well worthy of personal observation, and the concept of an excursion by luxury train was an act of generous hospitality. But the itinerary had a somewhat limited appeal. The *Boston Journal* noted that the delegates would see "the mines and iron mills, the factories, gas wells, cotton plantations and all the other wonders of American enterprise, particular attention being paid to a full exposition of American agricultural methods."[91] As traveling companions the Latin Americans would be accompanied by the American delegates, whose business backgrounds and qualifications no doubt reinforced the commercial nature of the whole exercise. The journey would also be long—an estimated six thousand miles—but it would be completed in only six weeks, well within the capacity of the excursion's manager, Curtis, whose "flying official excursion" to South America in 1885 had not been forgotten by Latin Americans.[92] Curtis had compiled a book[93] about these travels and it had gained him the reputation in the United States of an expert on Latin America, but in Latin America itself the book had aroused considerable criticism and indignation. "The fact is," noted the *Nation*, "that many of the South Americans look upon him as a man who has heaped gratuitous insults upon their people." Moreover, his apparent insensitivity seemed to pervade the entire excursion:

> It may be said that its planning showed other motives than delicate consideration for the nation's guests. Most of them are men of mature years, for whom six weeks of life in railroad cars, in a changeable climate, is not exactly a luxury. Besides, there is in the thing almost an implication against their intelligence—as if it would be a good thing to treat them as the Government used to treat the Sioux chiefs Red Cloud and Crazy Horse—take them to Washington, show them the sights, and so impress them with Uncle Sam's power that they would see no hope in opposing him. These delegates are travelled gentlemen, who are not easily awe-stricken.[94]

On at least one occasion, some of the delegates were made to feel humiliated and insulted as local citizens treated them as foreign objects to be viewed and commented upon.[95]

The demands of traveling were such that it was widely reported that the delegates were suffering from exhaustion. Unless there was more opportunity for rest, the *Savannah News* predicted that "few, if any [of the delegates] will get back to Washington in a condition to take part in the congress."[96] Blaine reacted to these reports by sending a telegram of inquiry to Matías Romero, one of the Mexican delegates. Romero replied that there was no foundation for such rumors and that everything was well.[97]

The two delegates from Argentina, Manuel Quintana and Roque Sáenz Peña, were, however, much more critical of the way in which the United States was organizing the conference. Sáenz Peña refused to participate in the excursion, and Quintana went along only for a few days before returning to join his colleague in Washington. Later in the conference the Argentine delegates stated that they had come to the United States to discuss the specific diplomatic and commercial matters set out in their invitations.[98] These evidently did not include a six-thousand-mile excursion. An editorial in the *Rio News* reflected a similar view:

> We do not understand that these delegates have gone to
> Washington to buy a stock of goods, nor did we believe that the
> United States proposed to play the part of a professional drummer.
> We were of the opinion that this congress was designed to discuss a
> number of important international questions, some political, some
> financial, and some commercial. The delegates are for the most
> part lawyers and diplomats. . . . Had it been known that their
> appreciation and patronage was to be solicited for the cotton mills
> and iron foundries of New England and Pennsylvania, they would
> probably have taken along a few merchants and engineers.[99]

The tour demonstrated, therefore, that side of American diplomacy that was confident and generous but also somewhat insensitive and forceful. During their preparations for the conference Blaine and Curtis had come to realize the many difficulties that such a gathering would pose, but their spirits were considerably raised when the conference actually assembled.[100] Nevertheless, it was clear that the outcome of the conference would depend on what the United States offered the delegates from the south. America had, however, little experience in staging international conferences, and the men in charge, Blaine and especially Curtis, were the particular bête noires of many of the visiting delegates. If the conference was to be successful, moderation and diplomacy would be very much in demand, but would these be forthcoming from a delegation consisting primarily of businessmen? The first item of business indicated the answer. In July, Carnegie had suggested to Blaine that as a matter of goodwill the president of the conference should be a Latin

American.[101] The general view of the conference was that an American should be chosen, but there was internal disagreement among the American delegation over whether this should be Henderson or Trescot. As a compromise solution Blaine was proposed and this was approved by the whole conference although the two Argentine delegates abstained from voting on the question. They argued that it was inappropriate to appoint as presiding officer a man who was not one of the official delegates. The other delegates deferred to the wishes of the American delegation.

Questions of diplomatic protocol could be easily waived, but the results were not necessarily beneficial. Blaine's many duties as secretary of state compelled his frequent absence from the conference, and this created considerable delay and inconvenience.[102] In his absence, various Latin American delegates took the chair on a rotating system. An even greater cause of difficulty was that of language. Knowledge of Spanish had not been a prerequisite of appointment to the American delegation since only Trescot and Flint possessed this qualification. To make matters even more difficult, only a minority of the Latin Americans could speak English. The opening session of the conference was conducted entirely in English until Quintana requested that a translation be made and that two bilingual secretaries be appointed for this purpose.[103] Thereafter, all the proceedings both in plenary and committee session were greatly handicapped by the necessity of translating every speech. Translation was not simultaneous but took the form of long printed documents that could be studied between sessions. Since few delegates were bilingual, immediate reply in debate was infrequent, and the delay was further extended by the failure of the printing office to produce translations quickly enough.[104]

Putting aside clerical and procedural difficulties, the discussion of substantive issues was also considerably impaired by American internal divisions and failure to offer concrete proposals. This was a reflection of the 1888 act, which had set out the objects to be discussed in such a way as to include, noted the *Nation*, "almost everything a government can attempt."[105] Just like the excursion, the conference agenda proved to be so ambitious that it ultimately became meaningless, if not counterproductive. The idea of an inter-American customs union, which had been a major reason for calling the conference, was ruled out by Blaine and Curtis even before the conference had assembled.

Nor were Blaine and the American delegates able to provide the sense of purpose and leadership that might have given the conference a positive direction. The arguments over whether Henderson or Trescot should be conference president pointed to internal differences, and it was not uncommon for the American delegates to clash with each other in open debate. On such occasions the Latin Americans looked to Blaine to clarify the confusion, but they soon learned that his control over the American delegation was very loose indeed. Whereas the Latin American delegates were guided and bound by instructions from their governments, their American colleagues lacked similar instructions and were even allowed to express their own individual views.[106]

The result was frequent and unseemly delay and debate.[107] The Argentine delegates were particularly critical of this and from the first day of the conference they frequently raised problems of rules and procedure. Theirs was an attitude that affirmed the equality of states and the preservation of sovereignty by resisting American attempts to stage-manage and manipulate the conference. Moreover, their efforts were considerably aided by American disorganization and diplomatic ineptitude. Quintana and Sáenz Peña declared themselves bound by the original terms of the agenda, and in contrast to the American delegates, they did not feel free to discuss items outside its terms of reference. To the infuriation of the Americans they criticized the recommendation of reciprocity treaties on the grounds that the discussion of such matters had not been mentioned in the original agenda.

"Between us, the American nations," Sáenz Peña declared, "interchange is the exception, and non-communion the rule." He charged that the policy of the American delegates was determined by concern for their adverse trade balance with the Latin American nations. He understood their problem of overproduction and their consequent need for foreign markets, but he also pointed out that the tariff history of the United States belied their present attitudes.[108] The Uruguayan delegate, Alberto Nin, believed that trade with Europe was so strongly established that the difficulties presented by an inter-American customs union were insurmountable and "beyond the reach of the best of wishes and best of laws."[109] More direct support for the Argentine position came from José Alfonso, the leading delegate from Chile. Chile had attended the conference with reluctance, and it was no surprise that Alfonso generally adopted a position critical of American proposals, especially those relating to political questions.[110]

The actions of Sáenz Peña, Quintana, Nin, and Alfonso demonstrated that the South Americans were conscious of their own interests and would resist American pressure where necessary.[111] Although their interventions in debate were sometimes displeasing, if not embarrassing, to the Americans, their intention was not to disrupt the conference. They came to Washington and remained there[112] because their countries had something to gain. Increased trade with the United States, improved credit and banking facilities, better steamship communications, and a common silver coin were included among the possible benefits. On the other hand, the American delegates were not able to take advantage of this opportunity for constructive discussions because of their own internal divisions and because of domestic political pressures, especially from the American Congress, whose actions ran counter to everything the conference was trying to achieve.

By April 1890 the reports of various committees had been debated and voted upon. Several broadly worded resolutions in favor of closer hemispheric relations were accepted, but what did they mean in practical terms? The most important commercial issue, that of the customs union, had never been seriously discussed. Even the question of the recommendation of reciprocity treaties was hedged with qualifications. Just as the political implications of the tariff had restricted the activities of the Latin American Trade Commission, so they also affected the freedom of maneuver of the American delegates in 1889–1890. Further, the actions of the Argentine delegates ensured that this dilemma would not go unnoticed. When Coolidge suggested that the Latin American countries should reduce their harbor charges because it was a simple and straightforward measure, Quintana replied somewhat sarcastically that it was as easy to suggest that Argentina do such a thing as to suggest that the United States reduce its duty on wool, "which reduction, although immensely beneficial to the United States commerce, is not likely to be accomplished."[113]

The possibility of establishing a common silver coin was effectively nullified by American political factors. In open debate Coolidge admitted that both the Harrison administration and Congress opposed the proposal.[114] "As the foreign delegates understand perfectly," reported the *Nation*, "the silver question is at present such a football in our Congress that the most perfect Pan-American measure is as likely to be killed incontinently as to be endorsed."[115] Moreover, while the conference was in session, the new Republican-controlled Congress began to prepare, under the leadership of Congressman William McKinley, a tariff bill that aimed to increase rather than decrease existing duties. Curtis was later to write that this development provided the delegates "a topic of daily conversation more interesting and important than the questions under consideration in their own councils."[116] Sáenz Peña explained why this was so when he pointed out that, despite all the talk of customs unions and closer commercial relations, he might have to return home to report that American duties on Argentine products were higher than ever before.[117] "I am convinced," concluded the pro-American, Matías Romero, "that the public opinion of the United States is not yet ready to adopt liberal commercial measures with regard to its foreign trade, or even with its sister Republics of this continent."[118]

The reasons for the conference's lack of achievement lay, therefore, primarily with United States attitudes and policies. Julian Pauncefote, the new British minister in Washington, dispatched a long memorandum on this to London in February 1890. He predicted that the only "practicable" results would concern patent and trademark arrangements and the recommendation of steamship subsidies. While he agreed that American products were "more esteemed" in Latin America than those of Britain or Germany, their relative cost was also greater and the trade was basically not large enough to attract American businessmen. "South American travel and social and intellectual intercourse are with Europe and not with North America," emphasized Pauncefote, "and this social isolation of the two parts of the western continent has been strongly brought out in connection with the present conference."[119]

As with previous American initiatives toward Latin America, the Foreign Office had little occasion for alarm. London was fully informed of the developments at the conference, and this information underlined the difficulties that the United States was facing. In the British press the conference was given a low priority and references to it were few. "We never were of opinion," concluded the *South America Journal* in March 1890, "that any results of importance would flow from this conference, and the news which we have recently received from the United States proves the correctness of our prediction."[120] American newspapers took a much greater interest in the conference, but opinions on it were varied. The pro-Blaine *New York Tribune* was full of praise while the *Nation,* which was hostile to Blaine, and Democratic newspapers such as the *New York Herald* were sharply critical.[121]

As Pauncefote and his predecessors in Washington had forecast, the results of the conference were very slight. The initial cause of most European concern, the customs union, had never materialized, and only seven delegations had agreed in principle to Blaine's arbitration scheme.[122] An inter-American bank was recommended, but when President Harrison presented the proposal to Congress the response was discouraging. Transportation projects such as an intercontinental railroad and steamship communication received more congressional attention, but actual results were meager. The sole tangible achievement of the conference was the establishment of a commercial information bureau in Washington that would ultimately form the foundation of the Pan-American Union.

Nevertheless, if the primary purpose of the conference had been to promote international fellowship,[123] then a certain amount of success had been achieved. After six months together the delegates had no doubt learned more of each other's national interests. In particular, the Latin Americans now knew more about the United States, but as the *Buenos Ayres Herald* had predicted in October 1889:

> The delegates will have the best of a good time, for the United
> States as a host cannot be excelled by any country, and her guests
> will have a most cordial welcome and a princely entertainment.
> The delegates will see a little of that wonderful country, with its
> unexampled prosperity and marvellous progress, and, in so far, it
> will be mutually pleasant and beneficial, as increasing the
> knowledge which one people will have of another, and this will be
> all that will come from this Congress.[124]

The prediction was amply vindicated by succeeding events. But whether
relations between Latin America and the United States had taken a step
forward was another question. The United States had initiated and
managed the conference with a style that was marked by impressive
rhetoric but also a certain amount of awkwardness and insensitivity
toward its visitors. Since the rhetoric proved ultimately empty, it was
the awkwardness of the Americans that caused most irritation and
hindered cooperation on substantive issues. The American-owned *Rio
News* summed up:

> It is a bitter confession for an American to make, but the truth is
> that the United States has played a part in this Congress which can
> not be considered in any other light than as discreditable to her
> wealth, power and intelligence. To invite the attendance of a
> number of smaller foreign states at a congress for the purpose of
> bewildering them by an exhibition of American progress and
> wealth, and then to try and over-reach them in a commercial
> agreement, is most decidedly discreditable. While we asked for
> everything, we were prepared to yield nothing. It may be that these
> foreign guests will return home fully impressed with the wealth and
> progress of the United States, but they will also bring home with
> them an impression of American selfishness and commercial
> narrowness which will not be forgotten for many years.[125]

The very fact that the conference had taken place was a demonstration
of the power and influence of the United States within the hemisphere.
Muddled management of the conference and internal political pressures
had prevented the achievement of expansionist aims. Although the
Latin Americans had generally deferred to the wishes of the host nation,
the actions of the Argentine delegates showed that suspicion and even
resistance to American pretensions were not lacking. The British Foreign Office had regarded the conference as a "fantastic scheme" in 1886
and could take comfort in its lack of tangible achievement. The rising

power of the United States was, however, undeniable and it now took another form in the shape of the revival of the reciprocity policy.

The McKinley Tariff and Reciprocity, 1890–1894

Upon accepting his party's presidential nomination in 1888 Benjamin Harrison had placed increased trade with Latin America high on his list of priorities.[126] When he assumed office in 1889 conditions appeared most favorable for the successful implementation of that policy. As secretary of state he appointed the expansionist-minded James G. Blaine. Later in the year, the Washington conference provided an invaluable opportunity for discussion and personal contact with representatives from the Latin American nations. If the idea of an inter-American customs union was impracticable, the Republican administration had a satisfactory alternative in the shape of reciprocal trade agreements. The Brazilian delegate, Salvador de Mendonça, was particularly interested in just such an agreement, but the attitude of the Argentines prevented the conference from giving a unanimous endorsement to reciprocity in principle.[127]

An even more serious obstacle to reciprocity agreements was the new congressional tariff bill prepared by William McKinley, the chairman of the House Ways and Means Committee. The priority of the new Republican-controlled Congress was to reaffirm the party's adherence to the protective tariff. The McKinley bill proposed to raise tariff duties to a prohibitive level so that imports would fall. This would not only protect American industry and standard of living, but would also reduce customs revenue, thus diminishing the annual treasury surplus. The measure implied victory for protectionism with a vengeance, but to allay possible criticism two important concessions were also granted. First, 99 percent of the duty paid on imported raw materials could be recovered if the materials were destined for use in American exports. Secondly, raw sugar was placed on the free list though American planters were compensated for this by a federal bounty on homegrown sugar. The American manufacturer was therefore offered cheap raw materials while the American consumer was given cheap sugar.[128] In this way the Republicans hoped to satisfy their supporters and to refute Democratic charges that protection inevitably resulted in higher prices.

What Republican congressmen believed to be the most appealing aspects of the McKinley bill were, however, clearly detrimental to the Pan-American policy of the Republican administration. The higher tariff on manufactured goods did not affect trade with Latin America, but many other provisions did. For example, the increase in the duty on extract of meat alarmed Uruguay.[129] So did the proposal to take hides off the free list. Blaine wrote to McKinley that this was "a slap in the face of the South Americans, with whom we are trying to enlarge our trade."[130] McKinley responded to this appeal by reinstating hides on the free list, but he proved much less conciliatory over other matters. The policy of reciprocity was predicated upon gaining trade concessions from the Latin Americans by offering them concessions on sugar and wool. Since the tariff on wool could not be changed,[131] sugar remained the major bargaining counter. But if sugar was admitted free into the United States, it would give the Latin American sugar exporters an enormous concession without exacting anything in return. The offer of free sugar by Congress took away the American bargaining position and seriously undermined all prospect of reciprocity.

Blaine had attempted to influence the proposed legislation in a personal meeting with the House Ways and Means Committee as early as February 1890.[132] The Republican leaders were nevertheless insistent on retaining free sugar, and this was included in the bill that passed the House in late May. Despite this setback, Blaine continued his struggle to alter the bill by using his influence with the president and the Senate and by arousing public opinion to his cause. Harrison sent messages to Congress endorsing the recommendation of the Washington conference that reciprocity treaties be negotiated.[133] Senator Hale from Blaine's home state of Maine kept the issue in the forefront of Senate business. Moreover, in a series of speeches and letters leaked to the press, Blaine transformed the reciprocity question into an issue of national debate. In a calculated appeal to discontented agrarian interests he argued that "there is not a section or a line in the entire bill that will open the market for another bushel of wheat or another barrel of pork."[134]

Blaine's intervention implied that Republican congressional leaders had mistaken and misinterpreted the public mood. It was not therefore surprising that this intervention should be attributed to selfish political motives. His political rivals such as the Speaker of the House, Thomas Reed, and McKinley were growing in prestige, and Blaine's criticism of them was interpreted as a bid to regain the leadership of the Republican party. The talk of reciprocity treaties with Latin America was also seen as an attempt by Blaine to extract something from the Washington conference,[135] which, although opened with considerable public fanfare, had been somewhat barren of achievement.

The support for free sugar among Republican congressmen was such that Harrison informed Blaine in July that the provision could not be changed.[136] The administration now adopted the alternative strategy of proposing what amounted to forced rather than voluntary reciprocity. The new free list contained sugar, molasses, coffee, tea, and hides, most of which were largely imported from Latin America. Thus, the administration could not offer concessions such as those contained in the treaties negotiated by Frelinghuysen in 1883–1884. Instead, in order to extract commercial concessions from the Latin Americans, it was now proposed that the president be given power to impose duties on the items in the free list from any country which he considered was in any way unreasonably discriminating against American exports. This retaliatory provision could be put into effect after January 1, 1892.[137]

The reciprocity amendment was incorporated into the final tariff bill that Harrison signed into law on October 1, 1890. This marked not only a major achievement for the administration but also a reversal of the congressional attitude that had opposed reciprocity during the previous decade. But success had not been easy. Reed and McKinley[138] were aggrieved by what they considered to be excessive executive interference in legislative matters. Opponents of reciprocity revived the old question of whether concessions could be forthcoming from countries whose revenue was based on customs duties, many of whom would be required to extend any concessions granted to other nations with whom they had most-favored-nation commercial treaties. There was also criticism that the reciprocity provision diminished the taxing power of Congress and was therefore unconstitutional. "We do not say that liberty is in danger," declared the *Nation*, "but we do say that this is a most dangerous precedent."[139]

The administration's success was due to several factors. Despite their misgivings, Republicans could hardly defy their own president or not be moved by a cause advocated by the magnetic Blaine. Furthermore, Harrison was not a lame-duck president nor was he facing a politically hostile Congress. Though their majorities were not overwhelming, the Republican party did control both houses of Congress in 1890 in contrast to the situation in 1884–1885. Another important change was the strong support that several congressmen gave the administration on this issue. In particular, the powerful Senator Aldrich of Rhode Island steered the amendment through the Senate and used his influence to persuade House leaders to accept it. The administration also overtly and covertly lobbied for the measure. Blaine made speeches and gave interviews while administration spokesmen such as Curtis, Foster, and Flint worked behind the scenes drumming up support from congressmen and business interests.[140] They held out the vision of expanded trade with Latin America and the creation of a hemispheric commercial system ultimately dominated by Americans. It was a concept that evoked favorable responses from all sections of the nation. "Never have the South American nations been so willing as now to make concessions in the interest of increased trade between the Americas," parroted the *Troy*

Times, "and the time to deal with them is when they are ready to make terms." The *Sioux City Journal* remarked that "this immense market would largely be for the benefit of western farmers."[141]

The administration did in fact argue that agreements would be immediately forthcoming once the amendment was approved. Flint declared publicly that the time was "most favorable" for a treaty with Brazil. Foster suggested to Aldrich that both Spain and the British West Indies would be willing to conclude agreements.[142] The *Chicago Herald* saw reciprocity as a club for use not only against Spain but for wider use too against such countries as Germany.[143] The economic power of reciprocity did not thus go unnoticed. "It will show the somewhat refractory countries of Central and South America," asserted the *Boston Traveller,* "that we have a whip hung up which can be laid upon their backs at some future time, if they do not behave themselves."[144]

Even more significant in the success of the reciprocity proposal was its support from public and business opinion in general. Congressmen had not only to contend with administration lobbying; they also had to respond to pressure from their constituents in what was a midterm election year. "Mr. Blaine," commented *Export and Finance,* "has won hosts of friends for his reciprocity plan among the farmers of the northwest." The *Sacramento Bee* described Blaine's proposal as a "masterly proposition," while the *Boston Herald* argued that Blaine was "flirting with the Farmers' Alliance."[145] In doing so he was responding to a political movement that was sweeping through the West in the 1890s. With the president's support he was advocating a program that retained the protective system in principle and yet offered the prospect of increasing trade and alleviating agrarian discontent. In this way it also undermined Democratic cries for tariff reform. Its electoral popularity was undeniable, and Republican hopes of success in the November elections began to rise. Furthermore, despite internal differences the party could present a united front, for neither Harrison nor Blaine was dogmatic or rigid. They fought hard for reciprocity, but they were prepared to accept free sugar if necessary. The result was a political compromise and the enactment of the reciprocity amendment into law. It was a victory for economic and political expediency, but it was also a victory for the advocates of Pan-Americanism and an expansionist policy toward Latin America.

The amendment gave the president power to conclude reciprocal agreements by executive action and without requiring Senate ratification. Negotiations were speedily opened with Brazil. The Brazilian minister, Salvador de Mendonça, and Foster quickly concluded an agreement which the Brazilian government accepted in early 1891 and which came into effect on April 1, 1891. Foster saw the reciprocity provision as giving the United States an even stronger bargaining position than before. In previous negotiations with Brazil the United States had offered concessions only on sugar, but now these extended to coffee and hides. "Hence Brazil can afford," insisted Foster, "to grant a free or favored exemption of duties to a much larger list of articles than was at first proposed at the opening of Dr. Mendonça's negotiations."[146] In return for the benefits of the free list Brazil reciprocated by removing duties on American machinery and breadstuffs and by granting a 25 percent reduction of duty on a long list of commodities including iron, steel, cotton manufactured goods, preserved meats, lard, and dairy products.

At the same time the American minister in Spain was reporting that the Spanish government was "very anxious" to discuss a treaty on behalf of Cuba and Puerto Rico.[147] Foster arrived in Madrid at the end of March 1891 and by mid-April had satisfactorily negotiated a treaty giving the United States significant commercial advantages.[148] Within the next few months negotiations were opened with a number of other Latin American and European nations, and ultimately further reciprocal agreements were concluded with the Dominican Republic, Guatemala, Honduras, El Salvador, Costa Rica, Nicaragua, the British West Indies, Germany, and Austria-Hungary. The power of the United States, so apparent in the reciprocity negotiations of 1883–1884 and in the acceptance of the conference invitations in 1889, was therefore once again strikingly demonstrated.

In Britain, the home of free trade, these developments were regarded with dismay. The *Times* interpreted the McKinley act as the proclamation of a tariff war.[149] Business interests were most alarmed by the effects it would have on British exports to the United States, but there was also some concern over the implications of the reciprocity provision and especially the treaty with Brazil. The first reaction of the Foreign Office was to examine whether Britain possessed most-favored-nation agreements with the countries likely to conclude reciprocity agreements.[150] Where these existed, for example with Mexico, Guatemala, and Argentina, British officials were instructed to insist that these clauses be upheld. In the case of Brazil, where it was feared that the Americans were gaining a considerable trade advantage, Britain had no treaty rights. The Foreign Office attempted to remedy this by proposing a new commercial treaty, but this was not acceptable to the Brazilian government. The brief duration of the reciprocity policy, however, and the fact that neither Mexico nor Argentina entered into reciprocity agreements were to render academic the whole question of treaty stipulations.

The British government was considerably concerned about the

consequences of the tariff act upon Canada and the British West Indies. The Canadian question was a perennial dilemma in Anglo-American relations and defied immediate settlement. Carnegie informed Gladstone that "there is no use in any Canadian delegation going to Washington in the hope of effecting reciprocity."[151] The Republican administration was, however, interested, as its predecessor had been in 1884, in concluding an arrangement with the British West Indies. "The object of the United States," reported Spring-Rice, "is either to obtain differential duties in the West Indies which would put Canada and Great Britain at a disadvantage, or else to force us to refuse an offer of that nature and by the ruin of our colonies to drive them into discontent and possibly annexation." But he also believed that Britain was not entirely defenseless because Blaine was eager for as many reciprocity treaties as possible and was therefore in a more conciliatory mood than was supposed.[152] As in 1884, the threat of exclusion from the American sugar market compelled action. The British government decided to leave actual negotiations to the West Indians themselves, though reserving its ultimate sanction of whatever might be concluded. The West Indian representatives, assisted by Pauncefote, negotiated an agreement in Washington that came into effect on February 1, 1892.

Pauncefote confirmed the political motives behind the reciprocity amendment. He described the McKinley Tariff as "unpopular" and considered that Blaine had gained a "great reputation" by the passage of the amendment. The British minister did not believe the American threat to be quite so serious as was feared. Political reasons had demanded free sugar and these same reasons would prevent the president from using his retaliatory powers to reimpose a duty on this commodity. As for the other items on the free list, Pauncefote put molasses in the same category as sugar and argued that the United States could not dispense with supplies of tea from China and Japan or coffee from Brazil. Any duty on these commodities would simply raise the price for the American consumer and would be extremely unpopular. By similar logic, any tax on hides would not be well received in the marginal electoral area of the northeastern states, the home of the boot and shoe trade.

But one event completely changed this comfortable prognosis. Even though Pauncefote believed that it could resist "with impunity," Brazil in March 1891 consented to a reciprocity treaty with the United States. Since this agreement assured the United States of adequate supplies of coffee, Harrison could consequently retaliate against such coffee exporters as Mexico and Costa Rica without affecting the internal American price of coffee. "It is plain," concluded Pauncefote, "that the surrender of Brazil has crippled Costa Rica in her negotiations with the United States who can impose a duty on three quarters of her export trade to this country unless she satisfied [*sic*] the president that United States goods are not unfairly taxed."[153]

The agreement between the United States and Spain in April 1891 continued the momentum by increasing pressure on sugar exporters to accede to American demands. The *Times* had reported as early as November 1890 the "baneful influence" of the McKinley act and the resulting Spanish interest in a commercial treaty.[154] The threat of its colonies being excluded from the American sugar market forced Britain to imitate the Spanish action and agree to a reciprocity treaty with the United States on behalf of its West Indies possessions. The political acumen of Harrison and especially that of Blaine seemed therefore more than amply vindicated. The United States had indeed a club with which to beat much of the rest of the world.

The principal American negotiator, John W. Foster, described reciprocity as "a permanent policy,"[155] but the internal political factors that had brought about the defeat of the Arthur-Frelinghuysen policies of 1884–1885 would also undermine the hopes of Harrison and Blaine. Blaine had sensed that the electorate was turning against the Republican party in 1890, and the November elections proved him correct. The Republicans retained a small majority in the Senate, but suffered devastating losses in the House.[156] During the next two years the administration was further handicapped by Blaine's frequent illnesses and by the intensification of personal rivalry between the president and his secretary of state over the 1892 Republican presidential nomination.

Blaine's ill health meant his virtual complete withdrawal from active politics after the summer of 1892,[157] but Harrison continued to work vigorously for increased trade with Latin America.[158] During the election campaign of 1892 Republicans claimed that their policy of protection and reciprocity had brought prosperity:

> We point to the success of the Republican policy of reciprocity, under which our export trade has vastly increased, and new and enlarged markets have been opened for the products of our farms and workshops. We remind the people of the bitter opposition of the Democratic party to this practical business measure, and claim that executed by a Republican administration, our present laws will eventually give us control of the trade of the world.[159]

The Democratic platform on foreign trade counterattacked:

> Trade-interchange on the basis of reciprocal advantage to the countries participating is a time-honored doctrine of the Democratic faith but we denounce the sham reciprocity which

juggles with the people's desire for enlarged foreign markets and
freer exchanges by pretending to establish closer trade
relations.[160]

The electorate decided in favor of the Democrats. "All parties are
agreed that the Republican defeat was largely caused by the general
dissatisfaction with the McKinley Tariff," remarked the *Statist*. "If that
be so, then the McKinley Tariff will soon be repealed."[161]

Congress assembled in special session in August 1893 with the intention of preparing a bill to revise the tariff downward. Once again the
vagaries of the American political system threatened to reverse the
expansionist direction of American foreign policy. But had reciprocity
been all that successful? Blaine and Harrison had talked in terms of a
hemispheric commercial system. Treaties had been negotiated with
Brazil and a number of Central American and Caribbean countries, but
none had been concluded either with Mexico or the nations of Spanish
South America. After the nonratification of the 1883 treaty, Mexico was
not eager to negotiate another arrangement.[162] With the exception of
Brazil, the other South American countries showed little interest in
reciprocity. Under President Balmaceda, Chile appeared eager for an
agreement, but the outbreak of civil war in 1891 effectively closed this
possibility.[163] Ecuador, Peru, Bolivia, and Uruguay had so little trade
with the United States that they saw no advantage in pursuing the idea of
reciprocity. Argentina showed more interest, and actual negotiations
were begun in late 1891. British dispatches suggested that a treaty was
likely if the United States would put wool on its free list. The threat of a
tax on hides did not disturb the Argentines, who replied characteris-
tically that they would counter this by raising their own tariffs on imports
from the United States. As the Latin American Trade Commission in
1885 and Sáenz Pēna and Quintana in 1889–1890 had pointed out, no
reciprocal agreement between the two countries was possible without a
major American concession on wool.[164]

Under the terms of the reciprocity amendment the president was
empowered at any time after January 1, 1892, to impose duties on those
articles contained in the free list coming from countries whose duties on
American goods he considered to be unreasonable. This was the club,
but it was a weapon that Harrison chose to wield very selectively.
Argentina, Mexico, and Chile were unwilling to conclude reciprocity
agreements, but no action was taken against them. Instead, the more
vulnerable countries of Haiti, Venezuela, and Colombia were singled
out for the retaliatory penalties. Haiti was selected because it showed no
interest in negotiating a treaty. By contrast, Venezuela appeared eager
for agreement, but at the last moment attempted to drive too hard a

bargain. "I have little hopes," Blaine informed Foster, "that they [the Venezuelans] will have sense enough to adopt your suggestions, I think they are bent on being the 'awful example.' "[165]

John Abbott, the American minister in Colombia, expressed confidence that an agreement with Colombia would be secured, although various political factors made immediate agreement difficult. Blaine eventually grew impatient and instructed Abbott to remind the Colombians of the presidential deadline.[166] The Colombian government responded by claiming that a reciprocity treaty was not necessary since they were entitled to most-favored-nation treatment according to the terms of the 1846 treaty with the United States. This argument was not so much rejected as ignored by Washington, and Harrison's proclamation of March 15, 1892, imposing retaliatory duties on Haiti, Venezuela, and Colombia came as a surprise to Bogotá. "I would say," reported Abbott, "that the Foreign Office is at a loss to understand why the Argentine Republic and Mexico are not included in the President's Proclamation." A few months later he noted that the Colombian government had adopted a "course of absolute hostility" toward reciprocity with the United States.[167]

This apparently invidious operation of the reciprocity policy provoked protests from Colombia and Haiti,[168] but several of the countries that had concluded reciprocity agreements also expressed a certain amount of dissatisfaction. The British minister in Central America reported in 1894 that both Nicaragua and Guatemala were contemplating denouncing their agreements with the United States. Their customs revenue had suffered considerably, and he was informed that the arrangements were "one-sided" and "advantageous alone to the United States."[169] In Spain the Cortes responded to public criticism and appointed a committee to investigate the effects of the reciprocity agreement.[170]

The Brazilian reaction was even more critical. Despite the long-standing desire for a commercial arrangement with the United States, the reciprocity treaty was never popular in Brazil. "The Brazilian press, congress, the foreign mercantile houses, and even the Brazilians themselves," noted the protreaty *Rio News,* "are almost unanimous in condemning the recent commercial treaty with the United States."[171] The Brazilian government had at first viewed the agreement as leading the way to a virtual Brazilian monopoly of the American sugar market, but this expectation was soon destroyed by the conclusion of the United States–Spanish agreement on behalf of Cuba and Puerto Rico, which gave those sugar producers similar free access to the American market. Brazilian disappointment was such that there were even suggestions of bad faith and duplicity on Blaine's part.[172] Brazil had been the example that had initially forced the Central American and Caribbean countries to enter into reciprocity negotiations with Washington, but as the British minister in Mexico pointed out: "If one or two Republics were granted special advantages then a Reciprocity Treaty might benefit them, but as eleven of the countries produced precisely the same articles, the competition among them would remain the same and all the advantages of the Treaties would be for the United States."[173] Ironically, therefore, the Brazilians became the prime example of the one-sided nature of the reciprocity agreements.[174]

Even if the reciprocity policy produced embarrassing damaging diplomatic consequences, the treaties did appear to give American exporters tangible advantages over their European competitors in many Latin American markets. In particular, the Brazilian treaty aroused alarm among foreign merchants. British consuls in Central America and the Caribbean islands reported that European trade was seriously affected by the treaties.[175] The reciprocity policy presented an outlet for surplus American products and a means of excluding European influence from the Western Hemisphere. Moreover, it was a policy sanctioned by Congress and the Supreme Court.[176] "If the merchants and manufacturers of the United States utilize the advantages secured for them," predicted Curtis, now director of the Bureau of American Republics, "the ultimate effect will be to confine American trade almost entirely to American waters."[177]

Despite these factors, critics of the reciprocity policy were as vociferous at home as abroad. The network of reciprocity treaties had never extended far beyond the Caribbean and Central American countries whose trade was already mostly with the United States. In fact, it was argued by domestic opponents that those countries and not the United States were the chief beneficiaries of the treaties.[178] The *Nation* singled out the Brazilian treaty as "a disastrous failure" because it had stimulated imports from Brazil and thus actually widened the trade balance even further to the detriment of the United States.[179] The imposition of the retaliatory duties was also seen as provoking Latin American ill will, if not also diverting the trade of those countries toward Europe and away from the United States, a development that was the antithesis of the aims of the reciprocity policy.[180]

Moreover, the economic doubts were reinforced by political imperatives. The Democratic party was pledged to tariff reform and interpreted its electoral victories of 1890 and 1892 as a mandate for this policy. In late 1893 Congressman William Wilson of West Virginia prepared his party's answer to the McKinley Tariff.[181] The Wilson bill proposed a thorough reduction of existing tariff schedules and also included the repeal of the reciprocity amendment. The ensuing congressional debates on this latter proposal evoked all the traditional arguments for and against the reciprocity policy. Republicans such as Congressman Tawney of Minnesota saw the proposal as the "absolute destruction of the law that has achieved such a grand victory for American commerce in foreign lands." Senator Hale of Maine predicted that repeal would be detrimental to northeastern agricultural interests and would severely set back the growing trade with Cuba and Germany that had resulted from the reciprocity treaties. Senator Washburn of Minnesota confirmed that the western states were similarly alarmed. The Republican argument was ably presented by Senator Proctor of Vermont:

> Reciprocity under the existing laws has met every reasonable expectation of its friends. Its prospects for the future were even brighter. And yet, in utter disregard of the positive advantages thus secured to our producers, it is proposed to throw these advantages entirely away. It is proposed, too, to effect these changes at once, and arbitrarily, in a manner well calculated to wound the sensibilities of those neighbors with whom we ought to cultivate the most frank, consistent, and friendly relations.[182]

Democratic congressmen replied that the reciprocity policy did little to help the farmer, and that if the Republicans were really so interested in reciprocal commercial agreements, why not make one with Britain, America's best customer? It was also argued that the reciprocity amendment had given too much power to the president. "Commerce loves freedom," declared Congressman McRae of Arkansas, "and I hope that we will leave in existence no part of the law with authorizes the President to interfere with that freedom."[183] The Democratic majority in the House passed the amendment repealing the reciprocity provision in late January 1894, and the whole Wilson bill was finally approved in February.

The bill was, however, subject to numerous protectionist amendments in the Senate. Senator Gorman of Maryland defied his party's leaders and successfully organized Democratic opposition. Duties were now revised upward, and the duty on imported raw sugar was reimposed. The protectionist counterattack was therefore successful, although the attempt by Republican senators to retain the reciprocity provision was defeated.[184] Democrats would not identify themselves with what had become such a partisan political issue and, moreover, the reimposition of sugar duties, which remained in the final bill, directly undermined the existing reciprocity agreements.[185]

In fact, the passage of the Wilson bill in August 1894[186] meant the termination of the reciprocity arrangements, for the traditional American position was that a new statute repealed any stipulations of earlier treaties that were inconsistent with its terms. In the diplomatic correspondence that followed this was the answer of the United States to the protests of its former treaty partners who claimed that the imposition of a duty upon sugar was a direct violation of their rights under the reciprocity agreements.[187] On the other hand, since the retaliatory provision had also been repealed there was no reason for these countries to maintain their agreements.

The United States thus unilaterally abrogated the agreements that it had forced upon so many nations. In the opinion of the British Foreign Office, the developments of these years were a "most extraordinary series of legislative and political manoeuvres."[188] The policy of reciprocity was another manifestation of the increasing American interest in Latin America that was so much a feature of the last quarter of the nineteenth century. This interest was primarily economic, but political and strategic factors were also present. Both in formulation and execution, however, American policy was dictated by internal political pressures, and it all too often assumed an inconsistent and aggressive, if not insensitive, character. Interest vied with indifference. The executive moved one step forward while Congress moved one step backward. British and Latin American officials regarded American policy as ambitious but also as selfish and unpredictable. Friendly governments such as those of Haiti or Venezuela were punished by the reciprocity policy whereas hostile nations such as Argentina and Chile remained unaffected.

Latin American nations might criticize or even resist the pretensions of the United States, but the reality of United States power in the Western Hemisphere was indisputable. When confined to political rhetoric the battle between Latin America and the United States was on equal terms, as Sáenz Pēna and Quintana had demonstrated at the Washington conference, but when commercial diplomacy was involved, Latin America proved highly vulnerable to American pressure. The Latin Americans realized this and so did Europe. American commercial diplomacy was not immediately successful,[189] for internal political factors prevented a consistent policy, and in contrast to Britain, the United States did not yet possess the industrial and financial base to dominate Latin American markets. Nonetheless, as the exclusion of Europe from the Washington conference had demonstrated, the signs of an "American" hemisphere were not far distant.

//6//

Rivalry in Brazil

The history of relations between Brazil and the United States has been characterized by friendship and sympathetic cooperation. During the nineteenth century the bonds of commerce were the strongest and political relations were somewhat neglected. After the overthrow of the Brazilian empire in 1889, a new mood visibly emerged. The establishment of a republic with a constitution owing much to that of the United States indicated a vindication of American democratic ideals and a rejection of Old World values. More specifically, the Harrison-Blaine policy of reciprocity achieved its earliest success when a reciprocal commercial agreement was concluded between Brazil and the United States in 1891. The close interest of the United States in the affairs of the new Brazilian republic was further demonstrated by American naval intervention during the naval revolt of 1893–1894.[1]

The advance of American influence in Brazil appeared to undermine that of Europe and especially of Britain, which had long held a position of economic and, at one time, political preeminence in Brazil.[2] Late nineteenth-century Brazil was an area of growing significance in the struggle for world markets among the industrialized powers, but these powers exerted little influence upon Brazilian political developments. These were shaped primarily by internal Brazilian factors, and whatever success the United States achieved in republican Brazil was more the result of a Brazilian tendency to favor closer relations with Washington than a direct consequence of an activist "Pan-American" diplomacy. The advance of American prestige and influence in Brazil was real, but it was also part of a long-term development that stretched from the late nineteenth century into the twentieth.[3] During the 1890s the accomplishments of American diplomacy there were both fortuitous and somewhat exaggerated. American influence over Brazilian political affairs was in fact slight, and American businessmen were unable, if not unwilling, to compete effectively with their European rivals in the Brazilian market.

Nevertheless, the establishment of a republic and the conclusion of the first reciprocity agreement pointed the way to closer United States–Brazilian relations and aroused the attention of European governments. Both American ministers at Rio during this period[4] expressed the opinion that British officials and merchants desired the restoration of the monarchy in order to bring about the abrogation of the reciprocity agreement. British diplomats, merchants, and investors were concerned by the increasing instability and disorder that marked the early years of the Brazilian republic, but this did not extend to interference in Brazilian political affairs.[5] Early nineteenth-century Brazil had possessed considerable strategic and diplomatic significance for Britain, but this no longer applied in the late nineteenth century. The Foreign Office accepted the 1889 coup as a fait accompli and delayed official recognition of the republic on grounds of diplomatic procedure and protocol rather than selfish national advantage or political ideology. A similar problem was posed by the naval revolt of 1893–1894, and though British officials once more pursued a careful and legalistic policy, different circumstances produced different results, to the benefit of American diplomacy. The concept of Anglo-American rivalry was, however, rarely present in the consideration of British policy toward Brazil. British officials fully appreciated American interest in, and capacity to influence, the affairs of the Western Hemisphere. While they could not fail to be concerned by the threat of the reciprocity agreement to British commercial interests in Brazil, in effect there was little that they could do or were required to do about it. Britain could hardly prevent sovereign nations from concluding treaties with each other, and reports from Washington and Rio soon tended to allay whatever apprehensions had existed and demonstrated that diplomatic and legislative rhetoric and machinations were no substitute for well-established business practices and financial institutions.

The Establishment of the Brazilian Republic

From its inception the Brazilian empire manifested a remarkable degree of political stability in contrast to its Spanish-American neighbors. But the collapse of the empire in 1889 released latent tensions and forces that ushered in a period of chaotic instability under the guise of military rule. The leaders of the new republic displayed a marked friendliness toward the United States; the republican constitution and the reciprocity agreement were the most obvious examples of this. In contrast to the 1860s and 1870s this appeared to mark an improvement in United States–Brazilian relations. During this earlier period the United States government had been upset by Brazil's unfriendly attitude during the Civil War and by its rejection of American mediation during the War of the Triple Alliance. In return, Brazil had been dismayed by the low caliber of American ministers sent from Washington.[6] Nevertheless, an improvement in relations was clearly discernible some time before 1889 and represented much more than a sudden espousal of republican or "American" principles.

The last years of the empire were in fact marked by a foreign policy just as friendly to the United States as that pursued by the later republican governments. The emperor himself was regarded as a friend of the United States, especially after his conspicuous visit to the centennial exposition at Philadelphia in 1876. Pedro II was also an advocate of closer economic links with the United States and particularly favored improved steamship communication. The close ties of the two nations were reflected by Blaine in 1881 when he noted in his proposal to convene a congress of the countries of the Western Hemisphere that "the good friendship between Brazil and the United States is singularly strong. The ties which join them are intimate and permanent. What, then is more natural than that these two great powers should earnestly unite in a movement which, it is hoped will mark a historical epoch in America."[7] When the conference idea was later revived in 1888 the imperial government soon signified its intention to attend. "The present ministry," reported the American minister at Rio, "are very friendly to the United States."[8]

The friendly attitude of the imperial government toward the United States was based upon respect and admiration for the northern republic and also upon an awareness of economic reality. In economic terms Britain dominated Brazilian commerce throughout the nineteenth century although after 1850 the United States became the biggest purchaser of Brazilian exports.[9] In particular, the prosperity of the Brazilian sugar industry was linked with a high level of export to the United States. Consequently, during the 1880s successive imperial governments showed interest in negotiating a commercial treaty with the United States that would provide a guaranteed market for Brazilian sugar.

The American response was not encouraging. The trade commission of 1884–1885 neglected Brazil, and the State Department under Bayard appeared to show little positive interest in a commercial arrangement with that country.[10] Nonetheless, the imperial government persevered with its efforts while at the same time pursuing a very different policy toward Europe. Of the European powers Britain was the most important to Brazil even though the days of British preeminence had long since passed.[11] Rio de Janeiro still remained, along with Mexico City and Buenos Aires, the most prestigious of the British legations in Latin America, but in contrast to the early nineteenth century, British relations with Brazil toward the close of the century were very much more commercial than political.

The legacy of subordination to Europe produced an element of pride and independence that was never absent from Brazilian foreign policy throughout the nineteenth century. This manifested itself in a distinct determination to avoid entangling agreements with European countries. The imperial government also pursued a policy of tariff protection for certain industries and continually discouraged suggestions from Britain that a new commercial treaty be concluded to replace the Anglo-Brazilian treaty abrogated in 1844.[12] The Foreign Office accepted that little could be done to change the Brazilian attitude, especially so long as the tariff remained the major Brazilian source of revenue.[13] A negative policy was therefore adopted although the following standing instruction was given to British ministers: "To advocate reform in the Brazilian tariff, wherever an opportunity presents itself of doing so with prospects of good results. A measure of this nature could not fail to be advantageous to the Brazilian people and Treasury; and would also be beneficial to British trade."[14]

The policy of persuasion had no effect, but this did not lead to British interference in Brazilian internal politics. It might be argued that the time for the application of pressure was propitious because British dispatches throughout the 1880s frequently referred to the rise of republicanism and the growing weakness of the imperial form of government. The British minister, Hugh Wyndham, arrived in Rio in mid-1888, and within a few months was speculating upon "the possibility of a revolution in the no-distant future."[15]

How much interest Foreign Office officials took in Brazilian affairs was reflected by private instructions to Wyndham that his main task in Brazil would be to settle certain "troublesome claims," and that if these could "be got rid of" he "might look forward to a quiet time."[16] The British minister was, however, soon complaining that it was impossible to conduct official business amid the increasing political chaos. He noted the rapid rise in republican strength and forecast the early dissolution of the Brazilian Congress. "A general feeling of uneasiness prevails," he wrote in June 1889, "that this Empire is on the eve of a grave crisis."[17]

Wyndham's dispatches suggested that some sort of political upheaval was imminent in Brazil; this was corroborated by several other sources.[18] But because similar reports had been common throughout the decade, no special significance was attached to these remarks. Thus, when the coup occurred in November 1889, it came completely by surprise. Three days after the event Wyndham wrote that he could "hardly realise" that the emperor had been driven from the country "for which he has done so much." The successful revolutionaries were "a few discontented officers, two thousand troops and sailors, most of whom are half-castes, some obscure journalists, lawyers and agitators." What seemed to impress Wyndham most was the fact that except for the isolated action of the Baron de Ladário, not a single blow had been struck in the emperor's defense.[19]

As the British minister reported, observers were surprised not so much by the fact that a successful coup had finally taken place, but by the almost total absence of support for the monarchy when the long-anticipated event materialized. Immediately after the coup, Wyndham described Rio as "perfectly quiet." The inhabitants of the capital appeared to be indifferent to the proceedings, and he noted that they were powerless against the united military forces of Marshal Deodoro da Fonseca.[20] The American minister, Robert Adams, shared his British colleague's surprise at the turn of events and viewed them as "the most remarkable ever recorded in history. Entirely unexpected by the Government or people, the overthrow of the Empire has been accomplished without bloodshed, without riotous proceedings or interruption to the usual avocations of life."[21] The peaceful nature of the coup stirred the former British prime minister, William Gladstone, to make a speech in Manchester describing the event as "a remarkable indication of the advance that in certain important respects mankind has made." In a similar fashion Senator John T. Morgan of Alabama declared that "nothing so grand or so excellent has ever been achieved in the history of any nation."[22]

"The news from Brazil," commented the London *Daily News,* "is a thunder-clap for the whole world."[23] For Britain, the immediate concern was not the political implications of the coup, but how it affected existing British financial interests in Brazil.[24] The initial reaction of the Foreign Office was to request the Admiralty to send a warship to Rio as a protective measure, but with the arrival of reassuring reports from Wyndham it was decided that it should not remain very long at that port. In fact, the British minister's response to local developments was one of personal petulance rather than ideological concern. "It seems to be my fate to be in ports," he wrote privately, "where trouble is going on, Athens, Belgrade, and now Rio."[25] Wyndham's attitude did not cause him to neglect his duty to look to the protection of British interests. The situation was so quiet in Rio that he judged the visit of a British warship to be "unnecessary and even inexpedient." One reason was his desire to avoid arousing Brazilian suspicions of British interference. He pointed out, however, that if British subjects should be in danger he would immediately request naval protection.[26]

British naval intervention was not necessary because British citizens and their property were not at risk in Brazil. The coup was clearly successful and was, moreover, an internal Brazilian matter. Within a few days the emperor set sail to Europe in exile, and the transfer of power had been achieved in an orderly and peaceful manner. At the same time diplomatic recognition was extended to the new provisional government by Argentina, Chile, and Uruguay. Britain and the United States acted with much more circumspection. While maintaining unofficial relations with the new government, both nations decided to withhold official recognition until evidence of popular support for the new regime was apparent in Brazil.[27]

For the Foreign Office the question took the form of what procedure British warships should follow in the presence of the new Brazilian flag. "If Her Majesty's Government were precipitately and without due deliberation to recognize any Government that might be established in any Foreign Country," pointed out the Foreign Office librarian, Edward Hertslet, "they might possibly have to recognize half a dozen different and successive Governments in as many days." In his opinion, recognition of the republican flag was "contrary to precedent."[28] A further argument for caution was presented by increasing reports that the provisional government was not quite as stable as it had first appeared. Both the American and the British ministers commented that the government was more and more relying on force to impose its will. Adams expressed "serious doubts" as to the consequences of this policy, while Wyndham suggested that a mutiny was not improbable.[29] In December 1889 the anticipated mutiny broke out among a section of the Rio garrison, and Wyndham considered the situation serious enough to alert the senior British naval officer on the South Atlantic station. Although the government quickly reasserted its authority and it was not necessary for Wyndham to invoke naval assistance, the overall situation remained uncertain. Wyndham reported the rumors of Deodoro's ill health and of the separatist tendencies of the states beyond Rio. "The new form of Government which was ushered in last month with high sounding phrases of liberty for Brazil," he added, "is now apparently turning into a reign of terror."[30]

Adams was also critical of the turn of events. He regretfully concluded: "The suddenness of the change of government, the excitable character of the people and necessity of education to the new ideas all compel allowances to be made, but the method of procedure is so foreign to the American idea of founding a Republic, that it is difficult to commend all the acts of the Government."[31] Newspaper reports confirmed the precarious political situation. The *Statist* warned British investors that the republic can "scarcely be regarded as established." The *Nation* informed its readers that "it is not enough . . . to get rid of a monarch in order to set up a republic," while the *Buenos Ayres Herald* commented that "Brazil is far, very far, from true republicanism and probably no nearer under its new name than under imperial rule."[32]

In a typically unilateral manner the State Department decided to reverse its attitude of watchful waiting and to extend official recognition to the provisional Brazilian government on February 20, 1890. The action fitted in well with the Harrison-Blaine aspirations for closer hemispheric contact, but it was also somewhat impulsive coming after Senate debates that had rejected just such a step. In addition, the action was taken without either the knowledge or consultation of the American minister at Rio, and according to Wyndham, Adams was "much hurt," especially since he had only recently denied that recognition was being contemplated by his government. Adams confided to Wyndham that he believed the Harrison administration to be mistaken in recognizing what he felt to be a "military dictatorship." In the circumstances Adams decided that his only course was resignation.[33]

The American action was no doubt designed to gain short-term advantages for the United States in Brazil, but this did not persuade the European powers to reverse their policy of withholding official recognition of the provisional government. The *Rio News* argued that the United States had "taken the extraordinary step of formally recognizing a republic which does not yet exist,"[34] and this was the view maintained by British officials. Britain was not to be rushed into departing from its careful legalistic attitude. In June 1890 the Foreign Office was informed by the German ambassador in London that France was contemplating recognition. The ambassador also requested the foreign secretary's views on the subject. He was informed that Britain believed that full diplomatic recognition should wait until after the meeting of the Brazilian Constituent Assembly scheduled for November 1890.[35]

The arrival in Europe of an envoy from the provisional government raised difficulties of diplomatic protocol for the Foreign Office. Hertslet again examined the problem and advised against recognition, since until the Constituent Assembly had met, the provisional government "can scarcely be said to speak in the voice of the Nation, and it would be difficult therefore, for her Majesty to receive credentials from a Minister accredited by the Chief of a self-constituted Provisional Government without establishing a precedent which might prove to be productive of a little inconvenience hereafter."[36] The assistant undersecretary, Thomas Sanderson, instead envisaged an alternative policy, which he described as "a fresh departure." In his opinion the meeting of the Constituent Assembly had little significance since it would merely confirm the status quo in Brazil. Britain might gain, therefore, by granting immediate recognition to the provisional government. But this irregular proceeding was rejected by Salisbury and the unofficial Brazilian envoy was refused recognition.[37]

In July 1890 France decided to recognize the provisional government. Wyndham suspected that the move was dictated by a French desire for popularity and special advantage. He believed, however, that Brazil was "far more anxious" for British recognition "as it is in London that they doubtless hope to raise further loans."[38] Despite his views, the Foreign Office remained fixed to its original purpose. In September, Wyndham telegraphed that the elections for the Constituent Assembly had taken place and that the occasion for official recognition had now arrived.[39] In London the unofficial Brazilian envoy called at the Foreign Office and informed Sanderson of the elections and added that Portugal had now granted recognition. The assistant undersecretary recommended that Britain do the same, but once more was overruled by Salisbury, who minuted that "the precedents are against our acting before Assembly has met."[40]

Accordingly, Sanderson instructed Wyndham that Britain would grant official recognition as soon as the Assembly had formally and constitutionally convened. It was understood that this decision would be received in Brazil with some disappointment, but Britain would not depart from its stated principles.[41] Full diplomatic recognition by Britain of the provisional government was finally granted in May 1891. The whole episode demonstrated British concern for legal precedents rather than national advantage. Unlike that of the United States, the British decision to recognize was not made impulsively and, in contrast to the French action, the Foreign Office did not attempt to exploit the situation in order to gain preferential treatment. Nor was there any desire to interfere with the course of developments in Brazil. British officials accepted the republic as a fait accompli. British citizens and their interests in Brazil were secure and even appeared to prosper during the early months of republican rule.[42] Consequently, there was no need for British naval intervention, and despite the denial of official recognition, the British minister considered his relations with the provisional government as "excellent."[43]

The desire of the new republic for British recognition also contrasted pleasantly with the independent and noncooperative attitude frequently shown toward Britain by the imperial government. While the Foreign Office was aware of the significance attached to British recognition, this only increased the necessity for acting with more circumspection. Nevertheless, there were inherent risks in inaction and delay, however commendable or justifiable that policy might appear. This was especially apparent in a nation such as Brazil, which had long sought increased political and economic contact not with Britain but with the

United States. However awkward or impulsive, the decision by the United States to recognize the provisional government was not only a further affirmation of Western Hemispheric ideals in contrast to those of the Old World, but also one more indication of the development of an "alliance" between the United States and Brazil.

Reciprocity

Although British policy adopted a legalistic and somewhat time-consuming approach toward the question of recognizing the provisional Brazilian government, the announcement in February 1891 of the conclusion of a reciprocal trade agreement between Brazil and the United States prompted a much more vigorous British response. The acting British minister at Rio was instructed to suggest the negotiation of a similar agreement between Britain and Brazil. This was not a new departure in British policy occasioned by American pressure, for as recently as 1886 and 1887 the Foreign Office had sounded out the imperial government on the possibility of concluding a commercial treaty. Similar British approaches had met with success in Paraguay and Uruguay, but Brazil rejected the proposal on the grounds that a commercial treaty would entail a departure from its traditional policy of making such agreements only with adjoining states.[44]

The imperial government was in fact much more interested in a commercial agreement with the United States, and the American minister at Rio, Thomas Jarvis, reported certain "indirect" inquiries to this effect in 1887.[45] A year later he revealed that the Brazilian foreign minister had expressed "the most earnest desire to enter, at once, upon the necessary negotiations," but Jarvis could only reply in a "general and guarded" way since he had received no instructions on the subject from Washington.[46]

Despite this initial American indifference the Brazilian government saw the invitation to attend the Washington conference in 1889 as an opportunity to expedite its commercial policy. The American consul general in Rio noted that Brazil was "extremely anxious to secure in the United States a permanent and lucrative market for its sugar."[47] The British minister at Rio confirmed this Brazilian intention and argued that this was the reason for Brazil's recent refusal to attend a sugar convention scheduled to be held in London.[48] On the other hand, British officials understood that American trade was not a serious competitor to Britain in the Brazilian market,[49] and that because the Brazilian government relied so heavily on revenue from custom duties, extensive tariff concessions to the United States were unlikely. The Foreign Office was also in receipt of reports from Washington and Latin America that suggested that the conference would not produce anything practical and that American professions and ideals were somewhat divorced from reality. Even when the conference actually took place observers were confronted by the confusing spectacle of the delegates discussing the dismantling of trade barriers while the United States Congress prepared a bill raising the American tariff to a record prohibitive level. In the circumstances British policy adopted a careful attitude of watchful waiting.

In December 1890 the acting British minister in Brazil, Frederick Adam,[50] reported the return of Salvador de Mendonça from Washington where he had led the negotiations for a commercial treaty. The change from an empire to a republic had in no way affected Brazilian commercial aims and Adam predicted that a treaty would be shortly concluded. Because so much Brazilian produce was exported to the United States he considered that Brazil was more "directly interested" in the reciprocity amendment to the McKinley bill than any other country.[51] During February 1891 the Foreign Office received confirmation, first from Pauncefote in Washington and then from Adam in Rio, that a commercial agreement had been signed between Brazil and the United States and would come into force on April 1, 1891. In return for the privileges under section three of the McKinley act, Brazil would either abolish or reduce by 25 percent the duties on various American imported commodities.[52]

In February 1890 the United States had been the first leading international power to recognize the Brazilian republic, but with the exception of an exchange of naval visits in June of that year, the diplomats of both countries showed more preoccupation with their own internal political affairs than with closer hemispheric relations. The fact that the treaty with Brazil was the first of the reciprocity agreements to be negotiated under the McKinley act underlined, however, the friendly nature of United States–Brazilian relations and implied a considerable advance for American influence in Brazil. The new American minister at Rio, Edwin Conger, sent his congratulations to Blaine and noted enthusiastically that the "successful reciprocity negotiations have opened the doors of Brazilian trade to wonderful opportunities for our people."[53]

In Britain the result was considerable commercial pressure upon the government for action to offset the damaging effects that it was believed the treaty would have on British trade with Brazil. The Foreign Office had realized as early as June 1890 that the United States government would reject any British claim to most-favored-nation treatment. Nor was Britain in a stronger position with regard to Brazil. An official noted: "It is clear . . . that the Brazilian government intend to give preferential treatment to United States trade. This arrangement will chiefly injure UK trade as regards machinery and cotton goods. We have no treaty of commerce with Brazil and have no Treaty ground for remonstrance."[54] This was the reply given by government ministers when the issue was raised in Parliament.[55] Nevertheless, intense lobbying continued. In March the Manchester Chamber of Commerce requested a personal meeting with the foreign secretary to discuss the news from Brazil. The Glasgow Chamber of Commerce presented a petition pointing out the threat to British steel and iron exports to Brazil and suggested that the flow of British capital to that country be restricted. The London Chamber of Commerce proposed that the duty on Brazilian coffee imported into Britain be abolished in return for reciprocal concessions. In April the Foreign Office received further petitions of concern from the chambers of commerce of Middlesborough, Blackburn, and Wolverhampton.[56]

The British government faced a difficult situation. The reciprocity treaty posed a serious threat to British exports to Brazil, but Britain had no legal grounds for complaint. At the same time, the government was subject to so much pressure from business interests that inaction could not be long justified. The initial reaction of the Foreign Office was to make the Brazilian government aware of British displeasure. Adam was instructed to point out that some £4 million of Brazilian exports were admitted annually into Britain free of duty and that industrial undertakings in Brazil had been greatly assisted by British capital. He was also to convey the opinion of his government that the reciprocity agreement could not "fail to give rise to bad impressions in this country towards trade and commercial enterprises connected with Brazil."[57]

The policy of communicating vague threats was soon replaced in March 1891 by an attempt to negotiate a commercial arrangement with Brazil that would avoid for British goods the discriminations implied by the reciprocity treaty with the United States. The decision was constructive and sound, but the new Brazilian republic showed no more eagerness to comply with British wishes than had the empire. Adam described the Brazilian response as evasive and negative although he was assured that should Brazil decide to negotiate any such treaties, Britain would be the first nation with whom it would do so.[58]

The Brazilian government also informed Adam that "they had no intention of injuring British interests and only endeavoured to protect Brazilian products." Moreover, because Brazil was so dependent upon customs duties for revenue, if the concessions granted to the United States were similarly extended to Britain, "she would be almost without resources, or would have so few that it would be difficult to meet internal expenses and fulfil foreign engagements in which English capitalists are interested." The veiled British threat to curtail credit thus led to the Brazilian counterthreat of default.[59] The Foreign Office accepted the Brazilian reply as it had done in 1887 and reverted to its policy of watchful waiting.[60] This marked the end of the British attempt, never a particularly vigorous or hopeful one, to conclude a separate commercial treaty with Brazil. British business interests continued to lobby the government and questions were regularly raised in Parliament, but the government answered by repeating its statement that the Brazilian government refused to proceed in the matter.[61]

The Foreign Office was fully aware that British exports of cotton and hardware would be at a disadvantage to those imported into Brazil from the United States.[62] But it was also realized that the lack of American steamship communications with Brazil would reduce the value of the new concessions.[63] Moreover, the Brazilian foreign minister had expressed to Adam his personal regard for Britain and had remarked that the reductions of duty granted to the United States would not be sufficient to enable American manufacturers to compete successfully with those of Europe.[64] Toward the end of 1891 Wyndham dispatched a general report on the effects of the reciprocity treaty on British trade to Brazil. He noted the concern of British merchants in Rio that if the agreement became permanent it would be to the serious detriment of British interests. Consular reports were, however, conflicting in their assessments. Some alarm for British trade was expressed from Pará, although the consuls in Santos and Pernambuco felt that British interests had not been affected. In Bahia and Maranhão, British exports were declining but not because of the reciprocity agreement. "Germany rather than the United States," Wyndham agreed, "is England's great trade rival in Brazil."[65]

In spite of complaints from British merchants and some pessimistic consular reports, British trade was not so seriously threatened by the reciprocity agreement as had at first been feared. It was true that American merchants had gained definite commercial advantages over their rivals,[66] but these were not adequately exploited. The period in which reciprocity operated, from 1891 to 1894, was also a time of general economic recession in Latin America due to the collapse of Baring Brothers, the vast British merchant bank in Argentina, which had an adverse effect on commercial transactions. In fact, contemporary opinion viewed the reciprocity agreement as of more immediate advantage to Brazil than the United States.[67] Another further, though slight, comfort to British opinion was that any special advantages American goods obtained by the treaty were not extended to other countries. The Brazilian government consistently refused to negotiate a commercial treaty with Britain,[68] but it also rejected similar proposals from Britain's main commercial rivals, Germany and France.

Another development that did much to compensate British officials for their apparent powerlessness to influence events was the criticism and opposition that the agreement aroused in both the United States and Brazil. Defeats for the Republican party in the elections of 1890 and 1892 indicated that the American tariff would soon be altered. At the same time the reciprocity agreement stirred strong opposition in Brazil itself. "The Brazilian press, congress, the foreign mercantile houses, and even the Brazilians themselves," noted the *Rio News* in early February 1891, "are almost unanimous in condemning the recent commercial treaty with the United States."[69] The acting British minister reported that the action of the government in concluding such an important agreement without the apparent intention of submitting it to Congress for approval was criticized as "high handed."[70] The Congress was determined to discuss the matter, and fiercely contested debates took place. In one particularly stormy scene, the admonition that Brazilians must not become the slaves of the North Americans was greeted with applause.[71]

In March, Adam reported assurances from "competent judges" that the treaty was "doomed." This opinion was given added substance when his French colleague informed him that the Brazilian government was annoyed that the United States might grant similar commercial concessions to Cuba. Adam believed it was certain that Congress would reject the treaty.[72] The Foreign Office also received reports from a former British diplomat, William Haggard, who wrote privately to Sanderson confirming that the reciprocity treaty was considered by Brazilians "as distasteful as ever." From a conversation with the American minister, Haggard surmised that even the Americans were pessimistic about the future.[73]

Conger was indeed taken aback by the turn of events. "The reception of the reciprocity arrangement," he wrote to Blaine, "has been by no means as cordial as we had a right to expect." In April 1891 he reported with regret that the general feeling in Rio was adverse to the treaty and that Congress would vote its repeal. Short of adopting measures of military coercion the State Department was as powerless to influence Brazilian affairs as was the Foreign Office. Alvey Adee replied to Conger that Harrison would regard the defeat of the treaty as "most unfortunate for the good relations of the two countries." The American minister was instructed to point out the president's "deep interest" in this subject although he should avoid having his actions construed as interference in domestic Brazilian affairs.[74]

The friendliness and goodwill that had been such a feature of the relations between the new Brazilian republic and the United States were further undermined in May 1891 by the news of the conclusion of a reciprocity agreement between the United States and Spain on behalf of Cuba and Puerto Rico. Cuban sugar would now also enjoy the benefits of the McKinley act and, consequently, Brazilian hopes of monopolizing the American sugar market were dashed.[75] Conger reported that the Brazilian government was surprised by the development since it had been under the impression that the agreement had been a "special favor" granted to Brazil only.[76]

One factor was, however, strongly in favor of the agreement and that was President Deodoro's unwavering support for it.[77] The denouement was finally reached in September when Congress reassembled and a motion to modify the agreement was introduced. Salvador de Mendonça had been brought back from Washington to organize the campaign on behalf of the treaty, and the government mobilized all its resources of persuasion and patronage to secure congressional ratification.[78]

Indeed, the treaty was narrowly ratified by Congress, although this show of support was only temporary. Led by the influential *Jornal do comercio,* a constant campaign of criticism was directed against it.[79] In fact, Conger believed that "one of the strong grounds" of opposition to Deodoro was his support for the reciprocity treaty.[80] He was therefore alarmed by Deodoro's fall from power in November 1891. Despite some initial apprehension Conger was relieved that the new regime headed by Vice-president Floriano Peixoto made no move against the treaty. Nevertheless, when Conger returned to Rio in August 1892 after a brief leave of absence, he noted that there was only "a little improvement in the feeling" in favor of reciprocity.[81]

British dispatches conveyed the same information to London. In May 1892 Wyndham reported that the Brazilian government desired to modify the treaty. He believed: "The present Government in this country does not wish to surrender itself to the 'Pan American' policy of the United States, that the present Commercial Convention is very unpalatable to it, and that were it not for political motives connected with the Missiones Boundary Question which is shortly . . . to be referred to the arbitration of the President of the United States, they might possibly denounce it." Should Harrison suffer defeat at the forthcoming presidential election, Wyndham predicted that the Brazilian government would abrogate the treaty.[82]

Wyndham's prediction proved as mistaken as similar ones made previously by Adam. Conger argued that Floriano would maintain the treaty, and he was correct.[83] Criticism of reciprocity was by no means lacking in Brazil, but ultimately it was action by the United States that abrogated the agreement in 1894.[84] Despite all the internal misgivings and debate Brazil chose to maintain the treaty, primarily because it became clear that it was gaining more from reciprocity than the United States. Only fifteen months after the treaty went into effect the *Rio News* asserted "that Brazil is thus far getting nearly all the benefits."[85] That this trend continued was confirmed by the remarks of Secretary of State Gresham in 1894 that reciprocity had increased American imports from Brazil by nearly $17 million while American exports to Brazil had increased by less than $500,000.[86]

The United States had concluded the reciprocity agreement with Brazil for political as much as commercial reasons. The agreement drew the two nations closer together, but it also facilitated the political and commercial aims of Harrison and Blaine by enabling them to conclude further agreements with other nations. This development undermined the "special" nature of the United States–Brazilian agreement and caused some annoyance in Brazil. On the other hand, the underlying Brazilian objective was unaffected. From the 1880s onward Brazilian governments, whether imperial or republican, sought to increase exports to the United States. This aim was promoted by the reciprocity agreement, which for Brazil represented a commercial rather than a political or ideological alliance with the United States.

At the same time Brazil showed no desire to conclude similar arrangements with European countries, and the British government accepted this fact in 1887 and 1891. Even though there could be no doubt that American influence was advancing in republican Brazil, British concern was somewhat mollified by the distinct possibility that the reciprocity agreement would not pass the Brazilian Congress. In spite of the ultimate falsity of this hope, it did appear that British interests in Brazil were not affected too much by the concessions granted to the United States. "American interests in Brazil are insignificant in comparison with those of England, whether regarded from a commercial or financial aspect," stressed the *South American Journal* in 1890, and this situation was not greatly altered by the reciprocity treaty.[87] Moreover, the Foreign Office was undoubtedly confused by developments in the United States. Tariff changes were frequent, and there seemed little consistency in American foreign policy. The British attitude of watchful waiting received its full vindication in August 1894 when the United States Congress unilaterally abrogated the reciprocity treaty, and by so doing, restored the former commercial status quo in Brazil.

The Naval Revolt, 1893–1894

Within eighteen months of the 1889 coup the Brazilian republic had achieved international diplomatic recognition and had negotiated an important commercial agreement with the United States. But the new political order did not bring political stability. The *Economist* had remarked in November 1889 that "there is nothing in the Brazilian character to exempt its people from revolutions," and two years later the *Rio*

News reinforced this assessment by pointing out that Brazil had passed from a monarchy to a dictatorship, a republic, a dictatorship, and then once more to a republic. "It shows us," lamented the American-owned newspaper, "not only how ignorant of popular representative government the Brazilian people really are, but also how ready they are to act on the most absurd of theories and the most dangerous of experiments."[88]

American diplomatic recognition and the exchange of naval visits in 1890 demonstrated American support and sympathy for the new republic, but such diplomatic actions or goodwill gestures could hardly guarantee the viability of a democratic political system in a country where the army showed little disposition to give up its new-found power. "So long as the military chiefs are agreed among themselves, and retain a sufficient hold upon their men," noted the acting British minister, "they can impose any form of Government they please upon the Country, and the people will accept it submissively, as they accepted the Republic in November 1889."[89] Such military unanimity secured the election of Marshal Deodoro as the republic's first president, but divisions were soon apparent. Deodoro's personal prestige had been a decisive factor in persuading many Brazilians to accept the republic, but as president he was handicapped by ill health and lack of political skill and experience. Angered by persistent opposition from Congress, he dissolved the Assembly and declared a dictatorship in November 1891. This provoked a sudden countercoup in which the navy threatened the bombardment of Rio unless he resigned. Since he could count on the support of only a minority of the Rio garrison, Deodoro concurred and another bloodless coup was therefore effected.[90]

The American minister at Rio welcomed the end of Deodoro's "extravagant assumption of power." But Brazilian democracy was still very fragile. Although Conger described the situation in November 1891 as "perfectly quiet," he added the qualification that "the most important, and unexpected changes" might happen at any time.[91] Indeed, the new government headed by Vice-president Floriano Peixoto was to experience an existence as precarious as that of its predecessor. The dislocation of trade arising from the chronic political uncertainty resulted in a depressed economic situation. Moreover, opposition to the government increasingly took the form of separatist movements in the states beyond Rio.[92]

Another danger to the government and to the republic itself was persistent reports of plots to restore the empire. Government sources tended to exaggerate this monarchist threat in an attempt to gain both internal and external support. In particular, the efforts of Salvador de Mendonça in Washington were often directed at persuading the United

States government that the Euopean powers, especially Britain, were involved in monarchist conspiracies. British diplomats and businessmen were concerned by political developments in Brazil, but overt interference or participation in these affairs was avoided. As the *Rio News* noted:

> The Englishman may prefer the monarchy, and may have very little confidence in the present form of government, but his commercial and investment interests compel him to keep his political opinions to himself. As long as the country is settled and prosperous, he is bound to be satisfied. He wants to see an orderly and responsible government, no matter what its form may be, and as long as that government observes its contracts and protects his life and property, he will be satisfied. The story that the Englishman is plotting against the Brazilian republic is as absurd as it is false, and the quicker our American exchanges dismiss the idea the better it will be for their credit.[93]

In spite of the many ensuing political and economic difficulties, the republican coup of 1889 appeared to most observers as an irrevocable event. Considerable affection for the deposed emperor still existed, but as Wyndham remarked shortly after the coup, there was not "the slightest idea anywhere of attempting to restore the Monarchy."[94] During the next few years British official dispatches frequently noted rumors of monarchist plots, but their invariable failure to materialize must have persuaded Foreign Office officials to cast doubt on their substance. For example, after the coup that overthrew Deodoro in November 1891, Wyndham reported that strong monarchist sympathies existed in the navy, but only a day later he qualified this view.[95] Although the Brazilian people reacted with sadness to the news of the death of Pedro II in December 1891, Wyndham believed that the event could only weaken the monarchist movement by introducing further divisions among the various claimants to the throne.[96]

While he emphasized that rumors of monarchical restoration must be taken with "due reserve," this did not alter Wyndham's view that "the Central Government appears to have no real authority, to be too weak to adopt any strong line of policy either with regard to the internal state of affairs, or to the placing of the finances on a better footing, and to be moreover in a state of disintegration." Floriano's hold on power was as precarious as Deodoro's had been, and Wyndham noted that rumors of revolt were widespread.[97] His American colleague took a more optimistic view,[98] and although the government did maintain itself in power, political affairs in Brazil continued on a very uncertain course throughout 1892 and 1893. Disturbances were reported from several states, and the separatist revolt in Rio Grande do Sul assumed much more threatening proportions. It also seemed to Wyndham that Floriano did not enjoy the full confidence of the army and navy, the compliance of many officers being secured only by extensive use of government patronage.[99] The attitude of the navy was particularly ambiguous. In April 1893, Admiral Custódio de Melo confirmed rumors of cabinet dissensions by resigning from the Ministry of Marine and in July, Admiral Wandenwolk staged an unsuccessful coup against the government. "There is very strong opposition in Rio de Janeiro to the Vice-President's policy in Rio Grande do Sul, and because a very large part of the Army is now absent, engaged in the Rio Grande war," gloomily summed up Conger, "a general feeling of uncertainty and anticipation of trouble prevails here."[100] The "trouble" erupted on September 6, 1893, when under the leadership of Melo the Brazilian navy in the harbor of Rio demanded the resignation of Floriano under threat of naval bombardment of the city.

Melo was simply repeating the successful action of November 1891, and no doubt he believed that Floriano would step down as Deodoro had done on the previous occasion.[101] But Melo had seriously misjudged the character of his adversary, and the siege in the harbor was to be prolonged from September 1893 to March 1894. Foreign powers had so far refrained from interfering in Brazilian affairs because, unstable though they might be, the republican governments had maintained order and control within the country. The naval revolt was not, however, just another twenty-four-hour affair, and its continuation raised the question of how effective was the authority of the Floriano government and whether the foreign powers should grant belligerent rights to the insurgents. The problem of the protection of foreign commerce within the harbor was also a matter of particular concern to the foreign powers, especially Britain, whose total trade with Brazil and merchant shipping actually in the harbor was greater than that of any other country.

The allegation that the British were covertly supporting the insurgents was actively propagated in Washington by Salvador de Mendonça and in Rio by the new American minister, Thomas L. Thompson.[102] Suspicion of European intrigues in the New World did influence American policy toward the naval revolt, as one American senator later commented:

> The importance of a navy became manifest in the episode with Brazil. That Empire, becoming a republic, met with a rebellion, promoted and aided by European nations in the interest of their trade, which was advanced by the monarchical condition there, and was threatened with injury by American competition under the Republic. We sent to Brazil a fleet which by its presence

constituted the one formidable naval demonstration in foreign waters in our recent history, and it ended that rebellion and restored peace to Brazil.[103]

American naval intervention did not exactly "end the rebellion," but it did have a significant effect upon the fortunes of the insurgent cause. Much more misleading is the argument that the empire favored European commerce and that the naval revolt aimed to restore the monarchy. Rumors of monarchist plots had been extant since the fall of the empire, but none had materialized. What was certain during 1892 and 1893 was that Brazil was drifting into political chaos. British policy had sought unavailingly to persuade both imperial and republican governments to conclude a commercial treaty, but there had been no attempt to interfere in Brazilian political matters. In September 1893 Wyndham wrote to the foreign secretary that he had informed his diplomatic colleagues at Rio that "in the Revolution in 1889 which had resulted in the overthrow of the Empire, in that which had been made against President Deodoro da Fonseca, and in the civil war in Rio Grande do Sul, Her Majesty's Government had maintained strict reserve and in absence of any instructions from your Lordship to the contrary I proposed maintaining the same attitude of reserve, safeguarding as far as lay in my power British interests."[104] The British archives reveal no such instructions to the contrary. Throughout all the travails of the early Brazilian republic British policy did not depart from the guideline of strict neutrality, and British officials endeavored wherever possible to cooperate with the other interested foreign powers in the application of this policy. Despite the allegations of Mendonça and Thompson there is no direct evidence that Britain openly or covertly gave support to the insurgents at any stage of the naval revolt.

"It is for the Brazilians themselves," declared the *Times,* "to determine what form of government they prefer and to establish it."[105] Foreign Office officials shared this view. When there were suggestions that the British minister at Rio was showing a bias toward the insurgents, he was instructed that the "Brazilian Govt. have telegraphed privately here that they suspect you of being favourable to Mello. This of course I do not credit, but be careful to avoid giving the slightest ground for such a charge. You should be absolutely neutral."[106]

While proclaiming a policy of noninterference in Brazilian political affairs the British government could not, however, ignore the disruption of commercial operations resulting from the prolonged siege of Rio harbor. In practical terms this problem revolved around what form of naval protection could be given to British merchant shipping there. This was a contingency that had been discussed by British officials even before the outbreak of the naval revolt. At that time, Wyndham noted, the senior British naval officer at Rio, Captain Lang, had stated: "If a blockade were established he should at once notify that it could not be recognized by Her Majesty's Government, that he should demand free egress and ingress from and to the port for British vessels and should there be any impediment to such offered, he should escort them himself or with one of the vessels under his command." This view was sustained by the law officers of the crown, who recommended that unless a recognition of belligerent rights had been declared, the use of force would be justified to prevent harassment of British merchant shipping.[107]

This legal opinion, together with the overall strategy of nonintervention and concert with the other foreign powers, shaped British policy from the beginning of the naval revolt to its end. But for the officials on the spot in Rio the distinction between what was considered to be a neutral or a biased action was sometimes an exceedingly fine one. Immediately after the outbreak of the revolt Floriano requested that the foreign representatives in Rio come to the presidential palace in order to discuss measures to safeguard foreign merchant shipping. Wyndham and the other foreign diplomats refused on the grounds that such an act would imply support for the government and thus constitute a departure from the principle of strict neutrality.[108] Instead, the foreign diplomats and their naval commanders decided among themselves to present a series of notes to both Floriano and Melo stating that ships flying foreign flags were to be protected by their respective national warships.

Far away from the scene of conflict, the Foreign Office sent its approval of this arrangement: "The insurgents not having de facto established a Govt. have no legal authority to enforce [a blockade], and it becomes a question of the prudent exercise of might against might. All action should if possible be the result of concert between the Foreign Naval Commanders. . . . The naval Commanders must do what they think prudent in the circs as they arrive."[109] The position taken by the American secretary of state was substantially similar. In Gresham's view, as long as a legal blockade was not in existence, American cargoes should be landed at Rio with naval assistance if necessary, provided that the lighter "in doing so does not cross or otherwise interfere with Mello's line of fire."[110]

The implementation of both British and American policy lay, therefore, largely in the hands of the two countries' naval officers at Rio. "Although the foreign ministers and ships of war have not interfered in this Revolution," Wyndham noted, "the presence of foreign ships of war has had a most salutary effect." Acting in concert the foreign naval commanders informed Melo on October 1 that "they would oppose by force, if necessary, any enterprise against Rio de Janeiro" on the humanitarian grounds that it was an open and defenseless city.[111] This action deprived Melo of his main means of attack and thus directly favored Floriano.[112] Consequently, to maintain their policy of neutrality, the diplomatic representatives on shore secured from Floriano an assurance that he would avoid all pretexts for a bombardment by not erecting any new offensive fortifications within the city.[113]

Although Melo was prevented from bombarding the city, the frequent outbreak of sporadic firing between the rebel ships and the harbor gun batteries made commercial operations extremely hazardous, if not impossible. Unless they were prepared to intervene actively, the foreign powers could do little to prevent injury to foreign nationals and their property involved in these operations. The American commander, Captain Picking, was criticized for failing to protect American shipping, but in reply he argued that forceful action on his part must inevitably favor Floriano against Melo. "I feel that in the present state of matters here," he warned, "if any nation attempted to do as it was thought I should do that both parties, the Government and Insurgents, would join forces to prevent, and thus make a popular war and unite the people against a common enemy."[114]

To add to the difficulties of the foreign officials on the spot, the exact legal status of the insurgents remained continually in doubt. After his initial failure to bring about Floriano's resignation, Melo had formed an alliance with the separatist forces in Rio Grande do Sul, and on October 24, 1893, he announced the formation of a provisional government representing this alliance at Destêrro in the southern state of Santa Catarina. But would the foreign powers confer belligerent recognition? Two days before Melo's announcement, Thompson had telegraphed to Gresham that the position of the insurgents at Rio was "becoming desperate." On October 24 he reported that the Uruguayan government had refused to recognize deputation from the insurgents. On the basis of such information Gresham judged that recognition by the United States was not justified.[115]

The Foreign Office received similar reports and adopted an identical attitude. In early November, Wyndham argued that recognition of the insurgents was "inexpedient," and he noted that his diplomatic colleagues shared this view.[116] In December, after another request from Melo for foreign recognition of the belligerent rights of the insurgents, Wyndham reiterated that "there is yet, so far as foreign powers are informed, no adequate basis for such a recognition."[117] The insurgents were, however, given considerable encouragement at this time by the decision of Admiral Saldanha da Gama to join their cause.[118] Another request for foreign recognition was made, but Wyndham's attitude remained unchanged. He considered the basis of the new request as "very feeble" and saw no reason for the foreign powers to alter their position.[119]

Wyndham's apparent complacency was not shared by the foreign naval commanders. After the alarms of September foreign commerce had resumed a sometimes hazardous though steady activity in the harbor, but the entry of a Saldanha into the conflict resulted in a more vigorous prosecution of the siege with consequent detrimental effect on commercial operations. The foreign naval commanders attempted to find a safe landing place for their merchant shipping, but this was prevented by government objections.[120] The situation became so difficult that the senior British naval officer, Captain Lang, believed that he could no longer adhere to his earlier instructions. He announced in the middle of December: "I have informed masters of ships and agents that it is impossible for me to afford protection to ships and lighters from fire of Government and insurgent forces, as I will not risk the lives of officers and men, but that protection from seizure will still be afforded to lighters."[121]

This policy tended to be misinterpreted, and British merchants complained loudly of lack of protection, comparing the activities of the British squadron unfavorably with those of the United States and Germany. The Foreign Office came to Lang's defense and pointed out that the circumstances at Rio were "unparalleled" and constantly changing and that because total British shipping at Rio was greater than that of any other country his task was "much more onerous and difficult."[122] In a reply to a private letter the Foreign Office expressed no indication of a change in policy:

> H.M. Government whilst they regret the present deplorable state
> of affairs at Rio cannot depart from their general policy of
> non-intervention in the internal affairs of a Foreign State, or
> attempt to dictate that the hostile operations of the contending
> parties shall be restricted to suit the requirements of British
> interests, they are unable to take measures to protect British
> subjects against the danger to which they may be exposed in the
> harbour of Rio by the firing of the combatants when engaged.[123]

In Rio itself, British officials were under considerable pressure from British citizens who were requesting a much more forceful policy on their behalf. Wyndham was fully aware of the gravity of the situation,[124] but both he and Lang dismissed suggestions that they possessed instructions encompassing the possibility of armed British intervention. Despite the various rumors emanating from London, Lang categorically informed British bankers in Rio that "Her Majesty's Government will not afford protection to lives and property by landing armed men in the city of Rio de Janeiro." While approving Lang's statement, a Foreign Office official minuted: "There was a plan for landing a joint force in case the town were given up to pillage—but it was to have landed for the purpose of protecting the *removal* of foreigners and their property to a place of safety. Capt. Lang does not make this quite clear."[125] The British government did therefore have a contingency plan involving armed intervention, but only as a last resort should conditions in Rio give way to complete disorder.[126]

Tradition, experience, and custom reinforced by distance and lack of information justified the cautious approach of Foreign Office officials toward what was a very difficult and complex foreign policy problem. But a policy of scrupulous neutrality as viewed from London could be interpreted in another light by observers in Rio or Washington. This was especially so in Brazilian affairs, for the creation of the republic and the conclusion of the reciprocity agreement had stimulated American interest in that country and had focused attention on the issue of Anglo-American commercial rivalry. Moreover, events in December 1893 heightened American suspicions of British designs when Saldanha's reinvigoration of the insurgent cause coincided with reports of the withdrawal of British naval protection at Rio and allegations of British complicity in plots to restore the Brazilian monarchy.

As early as October 3, 1893, the American minister at Rio had communicated to Washington statements from the Floriano government that the insurgents were secretly planning to bring back the monarchy.[127] Two months later he informed Gresham that the Brazilian foreign minister had proof that British naval forces were giving material support to the insurgents in the harbor.[128] Gresham's reaction was to telegraph the American ambassador in London for clarification of these reports, but uppermost in his mind was how to resolve the problem of neutral shipping at Rio threatened by Saldanha's much more vigorous tactics.[129] Admiral Benham was ordered to Rio to take over command of the American squadron from Captain Picking.[130] But Gresham was not quite fully abreast of the situation because his instructions to Thompson were to do the very thing that the foreign naval commanders at Rio had already proposed and had failed to achieve because of Floriano's attitude: "Cooperate with senior commander of our naval forces and others if possible in effort to induce insurgents to designate a place, if there be such a place, where neutral vessels may receive and discharge cargoes in safety without interference with military operations." The next day, Gresham informed Thompson that unless all foreign shipping suffered common restrictions "no substantial interference with our vessels, however few, will be acquiesced in.''[131] Shortly thereafter, in mid-January 1894, the arrival of Benham with two additional American warships made the United States squadron the most powerful foreign fleet in Rio harbor.

Benham's arrival coincided with a renewed effort by Saldanha to prevent all articles of war from being landed at Rio. To achieve this the insurgents would have to search all merchant ships and seize contraband goods where found. If permitted, such action implied the establishment of an effective blockade and the de facto recognition of belligerent rights. In these circumstances the foreign naval commanders assembled on board Benham's flagship, *San Francisco*, on January 26. According to Wyndham they decided "that Admiral Saldanha had no right to stop coal etc. being landed, . . . that they should telegraph to their respective Governments for authority to use force against the insurgents, that Admiral Benham . . . was prepared to act at once, but that as his colleagues had to telegraph for further orders he had said he would do so also.''[132] On January 28 Benham informed Saldanha that he would employ the force at his command to ensure the safety of American merchant shipping in the harbor. The following day, by successfully escorting an American ship to the docks, an incident in which some shots were fired, he effectively broke Saldanha's attempt to enforce a blockade of the harbor.[133]

By persistently refusing to recognize the insurgents as belligerents, the United States claimed to be neutral; in fact, Benham's action in preventing the establishment of an effective blockade was a refusal to acknowledge the legal right of Saldanha to attempt the very thing that would secure the recognition of the belligerent rights of the insurgents.[134] Positive and forceful though Benham's action appeared, it reflected an American policy that was far from systematic and was somewhat confused. Benham no doubt understood that his task was to open the harbor to American merchant shipping. This he achieved, although in doing so he inevitably assisted Floriano at the expense of Saldanha.[135] But Gresham's telegram to Thompson dated January 30 indicated that the State Department was confused by events and that the coordination of policy between Washington and Rio left a lot to be desired:

> Is the attitude of our naval forces towards Brazil and the insurgents same as when Picking commanded? If different in what respect and why? Wherein does Benham disagree with other commanders if at all. What are your relations with him and Brazilian government? What protection if any is accorded our merchant ships that was not accorded by Picking? Are insurgents enforcing or attempting to

enforce blockade? Report fully and speedily present situation, what has occurred at Rio and in harbor.[136]

Benham's action of January 29 may have resolved the immediate problem of the protection of neutral shipping in the harbor, but the naval revolt still continued and, indeed, the question of recognition soon assumed a new urgency and significance. Saldanha's attempt to establish a blockade had prompted a reassessment of British policy, and while Wyndham understood that Britain might decide to use force against the insurgents, he also argued that it should be borne in mind that they had maintained for several months a commanding position both in Rio harbor and in southern Brazil.[137]

Officials in London responded by drafting a letter asking the opinion of the law officers of the crown

> as to whether, under the altered circumstances of the situation, Her Majesty's Naval forces would still be justified in resisting by force the action which the insurgents now propose to take; or whether, in view of the prolonged contest which is carried on by the insurgents and the apparent inability of the Govt. to suppress the rebellion, there is any objection from a legal point of view to H.M. Govt. now taking the very important step of recognizing the insurgents as belligerents—provided that they should deem it desirable to do so from considerations of policy and should find that other governments have decided to take such a course.

The possibility of a concerted recognition of the insurgents as belligerents was therefore under consideration in London, but news from Rio of Benham's action induced the Foreign Office to withhold dispatch of the letter.[138]

On January 31 Wyndham telegraphed that the insurgents had achieved important successes in southern Brazil and, in his opinion, recognition of their belligerent rights should be granted. He repeated this view on the following day and added that Benham's action had offended the Brazilians on shore as much as the insurgents in the harbor.[139] The Foreign Office, however, doubted the wisdom of Wyndham's advice, especially should the United States and/or Germany adopt a contrary attitude. "It could be preferable to follow the lead of the United States as to the use of force to protect our commerce," shrewdly summed up one official, "though it is doubtful if the necessity will arise."[140] Wyndham was consequently informed that Britain would not recognize the insurgents except in concert with the other foreign powers and that, if necessary, force would be used to protect British commerce.[141]

In spite of the reports of its minister at Rio, the British government was not prepared to depart from the principle of nonintervention unless joint action by the powers could be secured. This implied a tacit approval of Benham's action and indicated that British officials had no overt sympathies for the insurgents. But the whole question, far from resolving itself, aroused even more intense diplomatic activity during the first week of February. On Friday, February 2, the German ambassador in London visited the Foreign Office to raise the question of the recognition of the insurgents, and in another visit three days later he disclosed that his own government was considering "the advisability of an early recognition." In the circumstances whatever decision Britain chose to take would have significant consequences, and during the intervening weekend Sanderson had sought the views of leading cabinet ministers. Their opinions were unanimous. Britain would not gain anything from recognizing the belligerent rights of the insurgents, and such a decision might in fact be extremely damaging to British commerce at Rio. It was also stressed that Britain should not grant such recognition unless the United States did so too.[142]

The British minister at Rio had not, however, abandoned his view that Britain should grant recognition. On February 6 he telegraphed that the insurgent forces in southern Brazil were reported to be marching on São Paulo and that an end to the civil war was imminent.[143] The foreign secretary, Lord Rosebery, realized the significance of this development, but his policy was shaped by much more than a concern about being on the winning side. He explained to the British ambassador in Washington:

> Inquiries had been addressed to me by one or two European Governments as to whether it was not time to recognize the insurgents as belligerents. Almost immediately afterwards I received news from Brazil which seemed to place the question for the first time in a new light. The news was twofold; it represented the bay of Rio as being wholly in the control of the insurgents, and, secondly, that they had established themselves in some strength in the southern provinces. I had therefore telegraphed to your Excellency to ascertain the views of the United States Government. Your reply had shown that those views were in entire accord with the opinion held by my Legal Advisers. This was satisfactory, for I thought it most desirable that Great Britain and the United States should act in cordial concurrence. The agreement between the Powers generally having hitherto been so close . . . it would be a matter for much regret if there were to be any severance now.[144]

Throughout the naval revolt the British government had been reluctant to grant belligerent rights to the insurgents. In spite of dispatches from Wyndham reporting their continued successes, the Foreign Office had no intention of initiating a new policy unless this had the agreement of the other foreign powers. The emphasis on nonintervention and the value placed on concerted action among the foreign powers overrode all other considerations in British policy.[145]

The American minister at Rio interpreted British policy very differently. In January 1894 he repeated the allegations of the previous month that the British naval squadron was secretly supporting Saldanha. In direct contrast to Wyndham, the implication in Thompson's dispatches was that the insurgents were in a desperate position both at Rio and in the south and that the British were attempting to bolster up the insurgent cause in the hope of bringing back the monarchy and thereby regaining their former commercial privileges.[146] But Gresham was in receipt of dispatches from another source that counteracted Thompson's anti-British bias. The American ambassador in London, Thomas Bayard, discounted reports that Britain was affording aid to the insurgents. He wrote to Gresham at the end of 1893:

> I have as yet been able to obtain no information warranting the opinion that any interference in the struggle is meditated, or encouragement given to either of the contesting parties.
>
> . . . I am disposed to give it as my present judgement that the existing tension between the Governments of Europe including Great Britain excites such anxiety that all other questions in the Western Hemisphere are dwarfed by comparison, and whether Monarchies or Republics are demolished or established there is almost a matter of indifference to them.
>
> . . . I have no reason to suspect any disposition on the part of this Government to take sides in the pending struggle in Brazil, but there is doubtless a strong desire for a settled order of Government there as an essential basis for the encouragement and protection of neutral trade and commerce.[147]

Gresham appeared to accept these assurances. He informed Bayard:

> I do not believe Great Britain, or any other European Power, will attempt to re-establish the Monarchy in Brazil. The present state of things at Rio can not last much longer and I shall not be surprised at the result whatever it may be. I do not believe the Brazilian people are very patriotic. Perhaps a majority of them are indifferent to what is now going on.[148]

Gresham's dismay at Brazilian society indicated that he did not see the revolt as a simple struggle of republicans versus monarchists. Americans had welcomed the creation of the Brazilian republic, but ever since 1889 they had seen Brazil lurch from one political crisis to another. Furthermore, the new republic was dominated by military cliques rather than democratic ideals. Whatever the respective merits or demerits of the Floriano government or of the insurgents, it was clear that both sides were locked in a military stalemate in which the Brazilian people were not prepared to give vocal or moral support to either faction. In October, Captain Picking had described Brazilians as showing "little interest" in the revolt. Three months later Gresham's remarks to Bayard about Brazilian "indifference" showed that to the outsider the Brazilian attitude was unchanged.[149] Under these circumstances Gresham adopted a policy similar to that of Britain, based upon the principles of strict neutrality and noninterference in the internal affairs of foreign states.

While American diplomatic and naval officials cooperated with their European colleagues at Rio, American independence of action was always maintained. When American intervention by Benham took place, it was executed in a unilateral fashion. Its objective was not to maintain Floriano in power or to crush the insurgents, but to assert American rights to carry out commercial operations without hindrance in Rio harbor. A similar concern on behalf of their own citizens had also been the preoccupation of the European powers since the outbreak of the revolt. Where Picking and the other foreign naval commanders had held back, Benham had dared to act.[150] Consequently, his bold move was welcomed by foreign commercial interests as much as by Americans. "It is time," stated the *South American Journal*, "that the interests of foreign commerce should be protected by international law and practice more efficiently than is apparently the case at present."[151] Secretary of the Navy Hilary Herbert commended Benham's action as meeting with "universal approval" and noted that it would "have a far-reaching and wholesome influence in quite a number of countries where revolutions are so frequent as to almost constantly imperil the rights of American citizens."[152]

Whatever his intentions, Benham's action was a demonstration of the growing military power of the United States being used to assert American rights over those of Latin Americans. There was, however, little adverse comment in Brazil,[153] for Benham had dealt a severe blow to the insurgent cause and the Floriano government was very appreciative of this. Nevertheless, the events of January 29 did not wholly decide the outcome of the revolt. The decision of the British government to refuse the insurgents recognition as belligerents was just as much of a blow to their hopes of success. Saldanha did give up his attempt to establish a blockade, but this did not prevent him from launching a fierce assault on the government forts in Niterói across the bay. The insurgent forces were beaten back, and in mid-March Saldanha and his supporters decided to withdraw from Rio and so brought an end to the six-month siege of the harbor.[154] Saldanha was able to join the separatist forces in Rio Grande do Sul and desultory fighting continued until his death in June 1895.[155]

The complete ascendancy of Floriano was therefore reasserted, and his gratitude to the United States for his triumph was reflected by the observance of July 4, 1894, as a Brazilian national holiday. A rather uncertain policy and a forceful intervention that undermined Brazilian rights had resulted in the fortuitous effect of further cementing United States–Brazilian friendship. But was this a defeat for British diplomacy or a setback for British interests in Brazil? The scale of American commercial activities in Brazil was still far behind that of Britain, and Benham's action had in fact assisted British merchant shipping much more than the small number of American ships in the harbor. United States–Brazilian friendship was proclaimed on July 4, 1894, but a year later an official American commercial publication reiterated the basic weakness of any American challenge in Latin American markets: "There is not in the city of Rio de Janeiro one general American importing house, while there are thousands of English, German, French, Portuguese and other foreign houses doing business in that line, aggregating many millions of dollars annually."[156] Moreover, in August 1894 the United States government had announced the abrogation of the 1891 reciprocity agreement, thus weakening the competitive position of American merchants and ending the major grievance of British merchants in Brazil.

Another welcome development for British interests in Brazil was the inauguration of a period of peace and stability after the collapse of the naval revolt.[157] While it was a fact that Britain was no longer as prominent in Brazilian affairs as it had once been, such a position belonged very much to the past. Late nineteenth-century Brazil chose to pursue a policy of closer relations with the United States, and British officials had neither the need nor the desire to reverse this development. The Foreign Office accepted the Brazilian republic as a fait accompli and showed no support for schemes of monarchical restoration. British commercial interests in Brazil were alarmed by various developments during this period, but the Foreign Office demonstrated little disposition to intervene on their behalf. Experience had shown that in unstable situations, such as those frequently occurring in Latin American countries, a policy of neutrality and noninterference was the sensible course to pursue. In retrospect, the judicious British policy toward republican Brazil was not unsuccessful, but what was historically significant was the growing disposition of the United States to intervene actively in Latin American affairs. In Brazil, Britain appeared to accept if not approve of this development. "The attitude of the Government of the United States, and its avowed interest expressed in relation to European interference with affairs in the Western Hemisphere," Bayard noted, "is I believe quite well recognized and interpreted here."[158] But American diplomacy would not always operate in such a favorable environment as early republican Brazil.

//7//

"Its Fiat Is Law"

The turn of political events in Brazil had provided a favorable opportunity for the extension of American political and economic influence.
Similar opportunities were to emerge briefly in Argentina and Chile, but
in both instances American diplomacy was found wanting. At Buenos
Aires the American minister pressed vigorously for a reciprocity treaty,
but his superiors in Washington failed to respond to his appeals for rapid
action. In Chile there was perhaps too much American diplomatic involvement and presidential interest. The power of the United States was
asserted, but not without provoking Chilean ill will and animosity.

British diplomats observed these events with interest, but showed no
disposition to interfere. The Argentine financial situation was a delicate
one and was best left to the international bankers to resolve; this decision had been taken in late 1890 and was not changed by vague reports of
reciprocity negotiations between Argentina and the United States. The
same attitude prevailed toward Chilean affairs. British diplomatic or
military intervention in the Chilean revolution of 1891 was considered to
be neither wise nor feasible. In fact, the outcome of the revolution was
very pleasing to the Foreign Office, and the *Baltimore* dispute further
undermined any opportunity there had been for the extension of American influence in Chile.

These setbacks to the Pan-American ambitions of the Harrison administration were achieved without any diplomatic action by British officials. A traditional caution and a willingness to conciliate where necessary governed the Foreign Office response to the vagaries and unpredictability of American foreign policy. The wisdom of this attitude
was also confirmed by the twists and turns of American policy toward
the question of the annexation of the Hawaiian islands. British diplomats
could maintain a certain equanimity over the challenge posed by American diplomacy in Argentina, Chile, and Hawaii, but the American disposition to influence events in the Western Hemisphere was becoming

not only more frequent but also more irresistible. The result was direct confrontation between Britain and the United States over the Venezuela boundary dispute. The reality of American political preeminence in the Western Hemisphere then became apparent.

Argentine Finance and Reciprocity, 1890–1892

In his survey of Latin America published in 1888, William E. Curtis emphasized that the Argentine trade was "worth having."[1] Of the total Argentine trade in 1889 American merchants possessed, however, little more than 5 percent.[2] The American consul at Buenos Aires, E. L. Baker, pointed to the reason for this when he complained that his countrymen were "entirely lacking in all the facilities" that modern nations employed to promote their commerce.[3] Much more confidence was expressed by the British minister, who reported that his own country's trade was "progressing satisfactorily" and that British merchants need not fear foreign competition.[4] "This republic," affirmed the *Buenos Ayres Herald* in September 1889, "is forming closer and stronger relations with Europe, seldom thinking and not in the least caring for the United States."[5]

This attitude was well illustrated by the two Argentine delegates at the Washington conference of 1889–1890. Roque Sáenz Peña and Manuel Quintana took the United States government to task for its inadequate organization and management of the conference. They alluded to the impracticability of much of the agenda and hinted at American insincerity and high-handedness. In a proud and independent spirit the Argentine delegates adopted an unequivocal resistance to the Pan-American pretensions of the Harrison administration. Far from desiring a New World isolated from the Old, Sáenz Peña eloquently pointed out that "Europe extends to us her hand, sends us her strong arms, and complements our economic existence, after apportioning to us her civilization." As a counter to the slogan of "America for the Americans," he urged: "Let America be for humanity."[6]

Despite their severely critical attitude toward the American proposals, the significant fact was that both Sáenz Peña and Quintana were in attendance at the conference itself and that they remained throughout its entire session. Argentine links were mostly with Europe, but that did not prevent the Argentine government from desiring closer economic contact with the United States. The American minister had reported before the conference that the Argentine delegation would show "a generous spirit" toward the United States.[7] His British colleague noted the long-standing interest of Argentina in securing the admission of its wool to the American market, and he explained that the Argentine government hoped that the conference would produce measures of "decided advantage."[8] Consequently, despite the widespread approval of the actions of Sáenz Peña and Quintana,[9] there was also a careful scrutiny of all the resolutions and proposals emanating from the conference. Consul Baker reported that the Argentine press was in favor of the scheme for an international bank and the prospect of direct steamship communication with the United States. The proposal to construct a Pan-American railroad also aroused considerable interest in the Argentine Congress.[10]

Argentine hopes were disappointed when the United States Congress proved reluctant to vote the necessary funds to implement the projects proposed by the conference. The thrust of American diplomacy concentrated instead on the negotiation of reciprocal trade agreements. Such an agreement between Argentina and the United States appeared most unlikely, and Sáenz Peña and Quintana had repeatedly affirmed this at the Washington conference. Moreover, it would also arouse opposition from the powerful European, and especially British, economic interests in Argentina. Nor could the United States offer very much in return since internal political factors virtually precluded American tariff concessions on wool. The timing of the American diplomatic initiative coincided, however, with a period of political and economic crisis in Argentina and, as in Brazil, the turn of events in Argentina presented a brief but signal opportunity for the extension of American influence.

The Argentine crisis had erupted in mid-1890. In August the government of Juárez Celman was overthrown, and Pellegrini became president in the midst of a rapidly deteriorating financial situation. For too long the Argentine government had pursued a policy of high expenditure supported by massive overseas borrowing and a system of inconvertible paper money. The financial crash came in November 1890 with the collapse of Baring Brothers, the British merchant bank most involved in the Argentine loan business.[11] The close connection with Europe that Argentines had for so long welcomed and lauded soon appeared much more onerous and open to question. The apparent economic bondage to Europe aroused resentment, and Pellegrini came under increasing criticism for showing too much concern for the welfare of foreign investors.[12] Nevertheless, there was widespread apprehension that some form of European intervention was likely. The British minister at Buenos Aires commented in August 1891 that Argentines were "very touchy and irritable" over any remarks by foreigners about their internal affairs.[13]

Foreign intervention did not materialize, primarily because of the attitude of the British government. Britain was the great power most affected economically by the Argentine crisis, and without British participation or consent intervention was simply neither possible nor feasible. Despite considerable pressure from British financial interests, Salisbury refused to depart from Britain's traditional policy of nonintervention in the internal affairs of Latin American states. In his opinion, schemes involving intervention by the British government were illusory and unrealistic.[14] There was to be no attempt to create in Argentina a financial protectorate on the Egyptian model. The *Times* noted approvingly:

> It is a good thing that nothing of the kind has been seriously attempted. . . . Whatever is to be done to rehabilitate the finances of Argentina must be done mainly by the Argentine people, in the first instance, at any rate. All the wisest Argentine citizens are anxious to secure the credit of their country, and they are setting about it in the proper way. . . . The best thing for Argentina and her creditors is, we repeat, that she should be left alone for a while. European advice and aid have not been such a remarkable success in the past as to make it desirable that more should be offered now.[15]

The British government was not indifferent to events in Argentina. Concern arose not so much from the extent of British financial or commercial losses but because the collapse of Baring Brothers had initially threatened to engulf the whole British banking system. In November 1890 a collective guarantee to support Barings was organized by the Bank of England and leading British banks with the tacit sanction of the British government. A Latin American event had therefore required discussion at the highest cabinet level and had contributed to a major change in British financial and monetary policy. But this did not signify that Latin American affairs had suddenly acquired a new importance in British diplomacy. The purpose of the guarantee was to maintain the financial solvency of the city of London; the stabilization of Argentine finance was merely a secondary consideration.[16]

The Argentine government was able to negotiate a three-year moratorium on its foreign debt payments in March 1891. Outright default was thus averted, although this could not prevent foreign investment in Argentina from declining both in value and in volume.[17] Deprived of short-term funds but determined to maintain his nation's solvency, Pellegrini turned to the United States for assistance. In May a plan was privately presented to the American minister, John Pitkin, to establish an American bank in Argentina. Pitkin telegraphed to Blaine that this was a "signal opportunity to establish firm footing."[18] But no positive response was forthcoming from his superiors in Washington.

Despite its avowed expansionist aims the Harrison administration imitated the prevailing attitude of American merchants and showed little interest in Argentine affairs. In January 1891 Blaine had suggested to the Argentine minister at Washington that their governments discuss the possibility of a reciprocity agreement, but the result was a long delayed and negative reply.[19] Much more American diplomatic effort was directed into similar discussions with Brazil and later with Spain. Not until August 1891 was it decided to send instructions to Pitkin to open reciprocity negotiations in Buenos Aires.[20]

The American minister met with a rather ambiguous Argentine response, but he believed that the ultimate American threat to impose retaliatory duties on Argentine hides had already produced "a wholesome effect." He proposed, therefore, to "press matters with vigor."[21] A change of foreign ministers led, however, to delay until in December Pitkin deliberately asked the new foreign minister, Estanislao Zeballos, why no progress had been made after eleven months of discussions. The direct answer that Pitkin wanted came a few days later when Zeballos presented a lengthy explanation of his government's attitude. He stressed the "executive and transitory" nature of the McKinley bill and concluded that "prudence suggests to foreign economic systems to remain in waiting for the definite course of the economic policy of the United States." Included also were a number of well-known Argentine grievances against the United States, but the foremost complaint was the American refusal to reduce the tariff on wool. Nor was Zeballos intimidated by the prospect of American retaliatory duties on Argentine products. In a later note he mentioned to Pitkin that Argentina had retaliatory powers too and might increase the duty on wool imported from the United States.[22] Like the American delegates at the Washington conference, Pitkin now also discovered that victory in diplomatic debate was by no means an automatic prerogative of the United States and that forceful diplomatic methods would only provoke hostility and resistance rather than compliance from Argentine diplomats.

Suddenly, in January 1892, Zeballos abruptly changed course and indicated that his government was intent on arranging a reciprocity treaty with the United States as soon as possible. The foreign minister confided to Pitkin that he feared imminent European intervention and that Argentina required American assistance to "free herself from Europe."[23] A second opportunity now presented itself for the extension of American influence in Argentina, but Pitkin again met with silence from Washington. On January 22 he telegraphed that time was of the "utmost importance" and that "silence does not encourage an improved feeling." A few days later he used Zeballos's expression of support for the United States in its disagreement with Chile over the *Baltimore* incident to raise the question of a political alliance, but the State Department responded with a circumspect though essentially negative reply.[24]

Three weeks later Pitkin reported the revival of Argentine opposition to reciprocity, and discussions once again became deadlocked over the question of wool.[25] But Harrison's decision not to impose retaliatory duties on Argentine products and the friendly visit to Buenos Aires in March 1892 of the American naval squadron under Admiral Walker prompted speculation in the Argentine press of a United States–Argentine political and commercial alliance. The British minister at Buenos Aires, Arthur Herbert, was initially uncertain of exactly what was happening, but he soon assured the Foreign Office that a political alliance had never been under serious discussion. He did note the remarks of his French colleague that Pitkin had offered a $100 million loan to the Argentine government and that Admiral Walker had expressed an interest in American naval bases in Argentina. Although no formal agreements had been entered into, the power of the United States was very much in evidence, and Herbert concluded: "The United States in regard to any dispute arising among the South American States, have, it would appear, taken up the position of arbitrators in such matters."[26]

The matter that most concerned Foreign Office officials was not so much speculative political alliances or arbitration procedures but the prospect of yet another American reciprocity treaty with its possible adverse consequences for British trade. Argentina differed, however, from the other Latin American nations that had concluded agreements with the United States in that Britain possessed its own treaty with Argentina, dating from 1825 and containing a most-favored-nation clause. Consequently, Britain had a treaty basis to claim whatever concessions Argentina might grant to the United States, and this view was conveyed to the Argentine government.[27] The legalistic attitude that had moderated the British diplomatic response to the Brazilian reciprocity treaty now justified a vigorous defense of British rights in the case of Argentina. But such action was not necessary. In July 1892 George Welby, the new British minister at Buenos Aires, reported that not only had the Argentine government conceded Britain's right to most-favored-nation treatment, but that Pitkin had left for the United States without concluding a reciprocity treaty.[28]

Shortly before his departure Pitkin explained the failure of almost a year of diplomatic effort with the remark that he had "little faith in the Argentine desire for reciprocity with us."[29] Argentine policy again resumed its emphasis on close relations with Europe, and in August 1892 a commercial treaty was negotiated with France. To the chagrin of the acting American minister the treaty was concluded rapidly and without his knowledge. By contrast he noted that similar negotiations with the

United States government had been marked by constant postponement and delay.[30] But the blame for the failure of the discussions could hardly be wholly ascribed to the Argentines. After all, it had been the Argentine government that had taken the initiative in May 1891 and in January 1892 by presenting Pitkin with opportunities for the extension of American influence. However vague or ill-defined these approaches might appear in retrospect, Pitkin had urged a positive response. The attitude of his superiors in Washington was, however, uniformly negative. Such an attitude befitted the conservative and European-oriented officials of the Foreign Office, but seemed unusual in an executive headed by the expansionist-minded Harrison and Blaine. No doubt the administration was hampered by Blaine's frequent illness and by preoccupation with Chilean affairs, but whatever the explanation, its policy toward Argentina from 1890 to 1892 fell short of its avowed Pan-American aspirations.

Moreover, Zeballos's criticism of the unpredictability of American policy was vindicated after the 1892 American elections, when the vagaries of the American political system once again resulted in a change in that policy. For decades wool had been virtually a nonnegotiable commodity in commercial discussions between the United States and Argentina, but the Democratic majority in the new American Congress now removed the duty on wool in the 1894 tariff. The Argentines thus secured what they had wanted for so long without the necessity of a treaty or the granting of concessions on their part. Argentine exports to the United States soon doubled in value, but the tariff concession was short-lived and a Republican Congress reimposed the duty on wool in 1897.[31] The development of closer commercial relations between the United States and Argentina during the late nineteenth century was therefore at the mercy of American politics, and the seemingly apathetic attitude of American diplomats and businessmen reinforced this state of affairs. British diplomats adopted a similar attitude, but, unlike the United States, Britain did not proclaim Pan-American aspirations. Nor was diplomatic action considered necessary to assist British economic interests in Argentina. These interests steadily revived as the depression of the early 1890s began to recede. As Consul Baker perceptively remarked in December 1892:

> It almost seems that the English have the preference in everything pertaining to the business and business interests of the country. Nothing appears to be wanting to assist, dispatch, and infinitely augment the commerce which they now so completely control or to strengthen the industrial foothold which they already possess in the Argentine Republic. They are "in" everything, except politics, as intimately as though it were a British colony.[32]

The record of United States–Argentine relations between 1890 and 1892 demonstrated that American diplomats and businessmen lacked the will to alter this situation.

The Chilean Revolution and the Baltimore Incident, 1891–1892

Although Argentina appeared as the most vocal critic of Pan-Americanism, it was from Chile that Harrison and Blaine experienced the most inveterate hostility to their expansionist aims. William E. Curtis had expressed some hope about the prospect of closer contact between the United States and Argentina, but he was much less sanguine about American relations with Chile. From personal experience he knew that Chileans nourished "an intense prejudice" against the United States.[33] Throughout the nineteenth century Chileans had frequently felt slighted by their northern neighbor.[34] The resulting sense of resentment had been most pronounced during the War of the Pacific when the advancement of Chilean territorial aims appeared to be blocked by American diplomatic intrigue. A successful and confident Chile had overridden the opposition on that occasion, but suspicion of American diplomatic actions remained a feature of Chilean policy.[35]

The sense of diplomatic friction was reinforced by lack of economic and cultural contact for, like Argentina, Chile maintained its closest links with Europe rather than the United States. Whereas it was "rather disagreeable" for Americans to reside in Chile, Curtis noted that Europeans were welcomed and that the British and Germans had formed thriving local communities. "It should not be forgotten," remarked the British minister at Santiago in 1886, "that the traditions of this country are all in favour of sympathy with Great Britain."[36] This fact was keenly appreciated by American merchants, who complained of the obstructive if not unfair practices that British and other European merchants resorted to in order to prevent American inroads into the Chilean market. But this excuse did not entirely explain the paucity of American trade with Chile. The reality was that the channels of Chilean commerce were firmly established in the direction of Britain. The Nation underlined this fact during the Washington conference when it asked: "Why should Chile offend the customer that takes 80 per cent. of what she has to sell, for the sake of pleasing a country that grudgingly takes 2 per cent.?"[37]

Channels of trade are, however, not immutable. While the Chilean government was acutely sensitive to any American diplomatic maneuver that might upset the territorial status quo in South America, it was also aware of the economic benefits that might result from closer relations with the United States. Chile especially supported the establishment of regular steamship communication with the United States, and because of internal silver deposits was interested in the proposal to adopt silver as a common unit of currency throughout the hemisphere.[38] After a show of initial reluctance, Chile therefore decided to attend the Washington conference. But little was achieved in Washington, where the Harrison administration proclaimed its Pan-American aims but showed little direct interest in the affairs of Latin America. The task of bringing about improved relations with Chile devolved primarily upon Patrick Egan, who had been appointed American minister at Santiago in March 1889. Egan lacked diplomatic experience, but his Irish background and consequent hostility toward Britain emphasized the political nature of his appointment and suggested that he would be a vigorous agent of Pan-Americanism in Chile.[39]

The *South American Journal* judged that Egan's appointment would be regarded in Chile with "indignant displeasure,"[40] but despite the Chilean government's suspicious and uncooperative attitude toward the United States, Egan's arrival in Santiago coincided with the beginning of an auspicious period for American diplomacy in South America. As in Brazil and Argentina, events in Chile were taking an anti-European turn and were, as a result, presenting opportunities for the extension of American influence. In Chile, President José Manuel Balmaceda had launched ambitious and expensive programs stressing public works and education. This extended government intervention and created conflict with the foreign economic interests whom Chile had for so long welcomed but now increasingly criticized for possessing too much power over the economy. In particular, criticism was directed at the alleged British domination of the nitrate industry, from which a major portion of government revenue was derived. In order to finance his programs Balmaceda proposed to increase this revenue by a combination of higher taxes and schemes for increased government participation in the working of the nitrate industry itself.[41] Inevitably this policy was interpreted as anti-British and, as part of his strategy to strengthen his own position while at the same time weakening his European opponents, Balmaceda also encouraged talk of closer commercial relations with the United States. "The President and Government," reported Egan in January 1890, "are most anxious to promote more extensive trade with the United States."[42]

Balmaceda's policy not only disturbed foreign interests; it also provoked considerable political controversy within Chilean society. Criticism of the president was most pronounced in the Chilean Congress. The legislature resolutely opposed the extension of executive power implicit in Balmaceda's proposals, and constitutional conflict ultimately erupted into civil war in January 1891.[43] The foreign diplomats in Santiago adopted a neutral attitude toward the struggle. In his dispatches to Washington, Egan stressed his neutrality and his determination "to keep clear of all entanglements."[44] But his protestations notwithstanding, Egan could not avoid becoming identified with the cause of Balmaceda. In this he was the victim of his own wishful thinking since he believed that the president would not only ultimately prevail, but that this outcome would be to the benefit of American interests. In Egan's opinion, the fact that British and German residents in Chile were hostile to Balmaceda would only further impress "every Chilean patriot to the importance of cultivating closer relations, commercially as well as politically, with the United States."[45]

The British minister at Santiago, John Kennedy, was fully aware that a victory for Balmaceda might assist American political and commercial aims in Chile.[46] He believed, however, that Balmaceda's apparent friendliness toward the United States could only be a short-term aberration on the president's part. It was not only "opposed to the real interests of Chile" but also contrary to Chilean public opinion. Like Egan, the British minister sought to maintain a neutral attitude, but, in contrast to his American colleague, Kennedy's sympathies were on the side of the Congressionalists.[47] This did not result in biased reporting, for despite his private opinions, Kennedy did not neglect to point out that Balmaceda's forces were growing in strength in May and June. Moreover, at no time during the conflict did he advise that the situation warranted that Britain recognize the belligerent rights of the Congressionalists.[48] From his own personal point of view Kennedy regarded the civil war as "a nuisance," but his experience and character taught him that strict neutrality was the requisite public attitude for a diplomat to assume in disturbed and uncertain situations.[49]

The Foreign Office fully approved of its minister's conduct, and an official commented in March:

> It is very difficult to suggest—in the present vague state of our information—what further specific instructions we can wisely give to Mr. Kennedy. He seems to me to have acted with great discretion in what must be a very trying situation and it is possible he will continue to do better if he trusts as he has hitherto done to his own good sense, experience and prudence than if we embarrass and perhaps hamper him by instructions which must necessarily be founded on an imperfect knowledge of the facts at the time they are framed and which by the time they reach him may be entirely inadequate to a situation which is apparently changing from day to day.[50]

Prompt action had, however, been taken in January when news of the revolution first reached London. A British warship was dispatched to Chile but with the pragmatic proviso from Sanderson:

> We cannot send a sufficient force to the Chilean Coast to overpower the Chilean Fleet—nor is it our business to do so. But we ought to have some vessels to see that British subjects are receiving proper treatment, and to join with other neutrals in giving the necessary shelter to non-combatant fugitives in cases of threatened bombardment.[51]

Although British press and financial opinion was critical of Balmaceda,[52] the Foreign Office sought to remain neutral. The foreign secretary, Salisbury, noted on one dispatch from Santiago: "Mr. Kennedy's notion seems to be that the justice of the revolt has something to do with its character of belligerency but that is quite new doctrine."[53] Whatever their private sympathies, on no occasion during the conflict did Foreign Office officials believe that a recognition of the belligerent rights of the Congressionalists was justified. When the Congressionalist envoy at London, Augustín Ross, warned that a victory for Balmaceda would directly aid American commercial interests, he was informed by Currie that British policy was to observe "a strictly neutral attitude between the contending parties."[54] Whatever the long-term issues involved, the Foreign Office stressed what Salisbury described as a policy of "complete abstention."[55] Experience had taught officials to adopt a legalistic attitude when confronted by revolutionary disturbances in far-off countries. Reinforced by the customary caution toward Latin American affairs and the awareness that Britain had limited military ability to influence the course of events in Chile, British policy stressed a diplomatically correct approach.

The lack of precise information on events in Chile also hindered the formulation of American policy.[56] In addition, Blaine's ill health compelled his frequent absence from the State Department, although this enabled Harrison and the expansionist-minded secretary of the navy, Benjamin F. Tracy, to exercise more influence over foreign policy decisions. Nevertheless, the overall policy aim was similar to that of Britain, stressing neutrality and noninterference. "Positive results must be awaited showing the true purpose of the people of Chile," stated the assistant secretary of state, William F. Wharton, in July, "and in the meantime this Government feels bound to maintain its attitude of impartial forbearance."[57]

While both Kennedy and Egan strove to maintain an attitude of official neutrality, many of their nationals and naval personnel in Chile manifested decidedly partisan inclinations. Since Balmaceda's policies had threatened British nitrate investments, the British community in Chile was in favor of a Congressionalist victory. Furthermore, the long tradition of friendship between the British and Chilean navies meant that British naval officers were strongly sympathetic to their fellow officers of the insurgent fleet. "There is no doubt," Kennedy declared after the revolution, that "our naval officers and the British community of Valparaiso and all along the coast rendered material assistance to the opposition and committed many breaches of neutrality."[58] The overthrow of Balmaceda in late August 1891 was regarded therefore as a most favorable development for British interests in Chile.[59] Conversely, the same turn of events indicated a setback for American interests. Kennedy reported: "Patrick Egan and the United States Admiral are in very bad odour. They both counted on the success of Balmaceda and made no secret of their wishes. Pat tries hard to hedge and to curry favour with party now in power, but he'll find it difficult to remove the impression against him. We may now dismiss our fears for the safety of Tarapacá and in regard to United States influence in Chile."[60]

Thus, despite Egan's proclaimed neutrality during the civil war,[61] relations between him and the new Congressionalist government were very tense. The Congressionalists were embittered by what they regarded as numerous hostile actions committed by Egan and the American naval squadron. These included the seizure of the *Itata,* the establishment of a cable link with Peru, and the alleged spying on Congressionalist troop movements by Admiral Brown at Quinteros Bay.[62] Under these circumstances the position of the American minister was rendered very difficult, and Kennedy remarked that Egan's departure could only be to the benefit of American interests in Chile.[63]

Egan's recall was not, however, suggested at this time. The United States established diplomatic relations with the new provisional government in early September,[64] but relations between the two governments steadily deteriorated in the following months. The ostensible cause was the question of political asylum in the American legation at Santiago. During the civil war Egan had given asylum to a number of Congressionalist refugees and had declared on one occasion that he would forcefully resist any attempted infringement of this right.[65] Upon Balmaceda's defeat the American legation soon swarmed with a large number of the former president's supporters. The only change in Egan's policy was in the political sympathies of those seeking asylum, but the Congressionalists chose to interpret this as confirmation of his support for the old regime. The total number of refugees within the legation was soon reduced from eighty to fifteen, but the question was not allowed to drift into insignificance. From mid-September onward the American legation was subjected to a strict and at times pettily enforced surveillance that drew forth numerous protests from Egan.[66] Neither side was apparently willing to compromise, and the issue was transformed into a question of principle. Egan asserted what he considered to be an internationally recognized right to grant asylum to political refugees, while the Chilean government insisted on its sovereign powers to observe and if necessary to restrict the movement of people in the vicinity of the American legation.[67]

The bitterness of Egan in Santiago was also present in Washington. "The trouble with these people and their kindred seems to be that they do not know how to use victory with dignity and moderation," noted President Harrison, and he added ominously that "someday it may be necessary to instruct them."[68] By early October, Harrison was describing the Chilean attitude as "the manifestation of a most unfriendly spirit."[69] To further inflame the already existing tensions, on October 16 a group of American sailors from the *Baltimore* on shore leave in Valparaiso were involved in an affray with a Chilean mob in which one American was killed and five seriously injured. The commander of the *Baltimore*, Captain Schley, reported to Washington that his men had been unarmed and had given no provocation for the attack. In Blaine's absence, Harrison and Secretary of the Navy Tracy reacted vigorously to what they regarded as a deliberate affront to the uniform of the United States. Egan was informed that the incident was viewed as "an apparent expression of an unfriendliness" that "might put in peril the maintenance of amicable relations between the two countries." Should Schley's report be substantiated, then the United States would insist on "prompt and full reparation."[70] These views were communicated by Egan to the Chilean foreign minister, Manuel Antonio Matta, who replied diplomatically but somewhat defiantly that his government must await the report of the local authorities at Valparaiso who would shortly be instituting a full investigation of the incident.[71]

In London the *Times* expressed surprise that "intelligent and fair-minded Americans" should "raise a tavern brawl to the dignity of an international question."[72] At the Foreign Office the matter was dismissed as "merely a question of temper," and the sending of a British warship to Valparaiso was not felt to be urgent.[73] Kennedy explained that the incident was being used by Egan and the Harrison administration for their own electoral purposes. The British minister regarded it as just one more addition to Egan's many disputes with the Congressionalist government. He believed that if only Egan had made a personal call on the foreign minister to discuss the incident an official statement of regret would probably have been forthcoming. In Kennedy's opinion, Egan's decision to pursue the matter indirectly by official diplomatic correspondence and his neglect in not verifying the statements sent to Washington by Schley had only contributed to further ill feeling between Washington and Santiago.[74]

American press opinion was antagonistic toward Chile as a result of the *Baltimore* incident, but it stopped short of advocating warlike measures.[75] Harrison and Tracy were angry, but moderate counsels were also in evidence. Blaine favored restraint and his friend, Andrew Carnegie, sent a telegram to Harrison pointing out that Chile was "very weak and sorely tried" and that "her giant sister should be patient."[76] Precipitate American action was also restrained by the knowledge that a number of changes were taking place in the composition of the Chilean government. In early November, Egan reported the assembly of the new Chilean Congress and the selection of Jorge Montt as president. This development was welcomed by Egan who now expected "a more liberal policy, more leniency toward the vanquished partisans of the late Government, and a kindlier feeling toward the United States."[77]

In mid-November the *Times* confidently asserted that "the Americans and Chileans are reconciled."[78] But the calm was deceptive. The Harrison administration awaited the completion of the Valparaiso investigation with mounting impatience, and in early December, Egan reported the renewal of acrimonious relations between himself and the new government over the question of asylum. In particular, the American minister complained of the presence of secret police around the legation, an action that he considered as "personally distasteful" and showing "little respect."[79] Harrison's response was to insert into his annual message to Congress references to the *Baltimore* incident as a "savage, brutal," and "unprovoked" attack.[80] The Chileans were thereby warned that the United States still awaited satisfaction. The war of words was continued by Matta. He informed the Chilean minister at Washington that the president's statements and the information upon which they were based were "erroneous or deliberately incorrect."[81] Dispatches that impugn the integrity of a head of state are rarely allowed to become public knowledge, but Matta chose to escalate the issue even further by reading out his dispatch to the Chilean Congress. The complete text was therefore soon available to the press in Chile and in the United States.

However gratified Kennedy may have been at Egan's unpopularity with the Congressionalists, the British minister reacted to Matta's note by closing ranks with his diplomatic colleague. Far from seeking to exploit the situation for any national advantage, Kennedy urged Matta to be conciliatory. "Mr. Egan," the British minister remarked, "has managed to turn the tables on the Chilean Government who have placed themselves in the wrong by a ridiculous display of defiance and discourtesy towards the United States Government and its representative here." War was a possibility, although Kennedy believed that both Matta's resignation and the necessary apologies from the Chilean government would soon be forthcoming.[82]

Matta's rashness had in fact immeasurably strengthened Egan's position vis-à-vis the Chilean government. "Almost everyone here," Egan noted with satisfaction, "admits that the manner in which Señor Matta has involved this country in such serious complications with the United States was a terrible blunder."[83] The advantage now lay with Egan. Matta refused to retract his remarks and as a result was compelled to resign. The new cabinet that was formed on December 31 contained two ministers whom Egan described as "personal friends." They assured him that Matta's note would shortly be officially disavowed.[84]

These welcome developments were used by Blaine to moderate opinion temporarily within the Harrison administration. The president had written in his diary on December 18 that war was likely, and the consensus of a cabinet meeting held on January 1, 1892, expressed the same opinion.[85] News of the Chilean political changes intervened to suspend any decision in favor of forceful measures, but the days that followed failed to bring the anticipated Chilean disavowal of Matta's note. By chance rather than by design this same tense period also saw the publication of the Chilean investigation into the *Baltimore* incident. The report placed the blame for the affray primarily on the drunken American sailors, and the Harrison cabinet was assembled on January 19 to discuss what was regarded as yet another Chilean insult against the United States.[86] So far Blaine's advocacy of restraint had prevailed despite the strong support for retaliatory action, but moderation was no longer a tenable position on January 20 when the Chilean government suddenly requested the recall of Egan. Harrison now assumed full control of foreign policy and decided on direct diplomatic confrontation with Chile. Egan was ordered to remain in Santiago, and he was instructed to communicate his government's demand for reparation for the *Baltimore* incident and an apology for the Matta note. If these were not granted the United States would break off diplomatic relations with Chile.[87] This virtual ultimatum was followed a few days later by a special message from Harrison asking Congress to discuss the question of relations with Chile. A congressional declaration of war seemed only a matter of time.[88]

On the same day that Harrison sent his message to Congress, Egan received a reply from the Chilean government stressing its desire to cultivate the "most friendly relations" with the United States. The note regretted the delay in the completion of the investigation by the Valparaiso authorities and attributed this to the process of law over which the government could not interfere. Chile offered to accept arbitration of the *Baltimore* incident and, while denying that there had been any calculated intention to insult the United States, the Chilean government "deplored" the expressions in the Matta note that Harrison considered "offensive." Although the dispatch was conciliatory in tone, it reflected no substantive change in the position of the Chilean government.[89] But Harrison was satisfied. Congress was informed that the immediate crisis was resolved, and Blaine informed Egan that the president "has no doubt that the whole matter will soon be brought to a final and honorable conclusion under the sense of justice evinced by Chile."[90]

Tactful diplomatic language could not, however, disguise the fact that Chile had been browbeaten by the "colossus of the north." The Chilean government agreed to pay an indemnity of $75,000 to the injured sailors of the *Baltimore*. An even more galling reminder of Chilean humiliation was the continued presence of Egan as American minister at Santiago until 1893.[91] Harrison had taught the Chileans the lesson he believed they deserved. But it was more than a simple exercise in moral diplomacy. Harrison's concern over Chilean affairs was motivated not by commercial or Pan-American considerations, but by his aggrieved sense that American honor and the rights of American citizens had been infringed. For some months his instinct for forceful measures had been restrained, but ultimately his insistence on upholding national honor outweighed all other considerations.[92]

The resort to the threat of force undermined the loudly proclaimed Pan-American aims of the Harrison administration. It also made the breach between Blaine and the president even wider.[93] The *Times* noted the "destruction" of Blaine's Pan-American policy and predicted that "in future the Central and South American Republics must look for protection and mutuality of interests, both commercial and political, only among themselves."[94] The Chilean minister at Berlin, Gonzalo Bulnes, similarly remarked that "the future of South America lies with Europe."[95] This had been the theme if not the practice of most South American nations throughout the nineteenth century, but was it a credible policy for the future? After all, European powers had shown little inclination to assist Chile in its controversy with the United States. European interest in Chile was commercial and financial; political disputes, and especially the possibility of conflict with the United States, were to be avoided. The British minister at Santiago had urged the Chilean government to be conciliatory toward the United States, and Chile's hope of assistance from Germany proved similarly forlorn.[96]

Without foreign support, and in the throes of recovery from internal disunity and civil war, Chilean resistance was at a low ebb.[97] The traditional spirit of Chilean independence was maintained in diplomatic correspondence, but defiance could not be sustained indefinitely. The desires of the United States government, backed by its growing economic and naval power, could not be so easily ignored as in the days of the War of the Pacific. Matta had acted rashly and Harrison did have a justifiable cause for grievance, but the browbeating of Chile did little to enhance the American image in Latin America. British diplomats could take some comfort from this and from the fact that the channels of Chilean trade were still dominated by British merchants,[98] but British diplomatic caution and military weakness had contributed to a situation in which the United States could demonstrate its might in Chile and, by implication, its political preeminence in the Western Hemisphere. The full reckoning for Britain was still to come.

"Twisting the Lion's Tail" from Hawaii to Venezuela, 1893–1896

The policy of the Harrison administration toward Argentina and Chile had achieved little immediate commercial success, but it demonstrated the growing capacity of the United States to influence affairs in Latin America. A notable feature of this assertive policy was the part played by the American navy. The navy not only raised American prestige by "showing the flag" in distant waters, but it served as a valuable instrument of diplomacy. The exchange of naval visits between the United States and Brazil in 1890 had been used to affirm American support for the new republic; Admiral Walker's visit to Buenos Aires gave timely assistance to Pitkin's negotiations for a reciprocity treaty; and the actions of American warships formed the basis for much of the controversy between Chile and the United States.

The availability of greater naval power and the demands of supply and management created by that same phenomenon resulted in a growing American interest in and need for naval bases in the Caribbean and the Pacific. The arguments for such bases were technically valid, but their advocates seriously underestimated the diplomatic difficulties of securing these facilities. During Cleveland's first administration the United States gained the use of Pearl Harbor in Hawaii, but similar discussions involving Samoa were complicated by British and German diplomatic intervention.[99] Despite certain reservations by Blaine,[100] the Harrison administration stepped up the search for possible bases although most attention was now concentrated on the Caribbean and especially on Haiti and the Dominican Republic. As in Chile, American officials on the spot became too closely identified with local politics. Harrison and Tracy sought to remedy matters by threatening naval intervention, but this only further antagonized local politicians with the result that the desired naval facilities were not granted to the United States.[101]

A much more attractive opportunity for expansionism was presented by Hawaii. American ministers such as Pitkin and Egan had sought to promote Pan-American objectives from a position of weakness, but the American minister in Hawaii operated with the advantage of well-established American political and economic influence. American policy was also much more clearly defined in that American diplomats had long attached considerable strategic significance to the islands. "The safety and welfare of the Hawaiian group is obviously more interesting and important to the United States than to any other nation," Bayard had written in 1887, and he added: "For that reason our ties of intercourse and amity should be cherished."[102] The selection of Blaine's personal friend, John L. Stevens, as minister at Honolulu indicated the Harrison administration's desire for a closer relationship between the islands and the United States. The opportunity came, however, after Blaine had left office. In January 1893 an internal coup deposed Queen Liliuokalani and established a provisional government that immediately requested annexation to the United States. Harrison instructed that a treaty be quickly prepared to this effect. But Harrison was a lame-duck president, and the treaty could secure congressional ratification only if it was endorsed by the president-elect, Grover Cleveland. On a like occasion in 1885 Cleveland had held up the Latin American treaties proposed by the Arthur administration, and he took a similar stand in 1893 by making known his preference that no action be taken on the Hawaiian treaty. Once in office the new administration appeared to support annexation, but after a special investigation of the circumstances surrounding the January coup it was decided that American diplomatic influence had been employed unethicaly and illegally to assist the deposition of the queen. Annexation of Hawaii to the United States was rejected, and the queen was restored to power.[103]

The secretary of state, Walter Q. Gresham, was the man most responsible for this decision. "I am unalterably opposed," he declared in 1894, "to stealing territory, or of annexing a people against their consent, and the people of Hawaii do not favor annexation."[104] It was an extraordinary series of events and must have amazed European diplomats.[105] In London, British officials maintained their customary cautious attitude toward Western Hemispheric questions. Much of the American press alleged, however, that Britain was conspiring against American interests in Hawaii and that if the United States did not annex the islands then Britain would.[106] But British officials had long denied any such intention. In 1887 Salisbury had described Hawaii as "of no interest to England," and Pauncefote in 1892 had expressed the view that annexation to the United States would be of economic benefit for the Hawaiians themselves.[107]

While this negative British attitude allowed American diplomacy considerable freedom of maneuver in Hawaii, as it did also in Argentina and Chile, the results were not particularly damaging to British interests. American diplomacy made little headway in either Argentina or Chile, and Hawaii remained politically independent of the United States. Nevertheless, American suspicions of British imperialist designs in the Western Hemisphere persisted and were nourished during the last quarter of the nineteenth century by reports of alleged British intrigues in such places as Brazil, Central America, and Venezuela. In fact, for most of the century British diplomats had sought to remain detached from Latin American issues and had avoided a direct confrontation with the United States over them. But this traditional attitude was challenged during the mid-1890s, when a number of contentious Latin American issues coincided with the apparent eagerness of American diplomats to assert American "rights" and with the growing electoral popularity of "twisting the lion's tail" in the United States.

Harrison and Blaine had announced a vigorous policy toward Latin America, but their achievements fell far short of their aspirations. The emergence of the Hawaiian question, however, enabled Harrison to leave office on an expansionist note. Conversely, the rejection of Hawaiian annexation implied that Cleveland was opposed to expansionism. The passage of the 1894 tariff by the Democratic-controlled Congress and the consequent abrogation of the reciprocity treaties also indicated less official interest in Latin America and an end to the policy of Pan-Americanism.

The high principles that guided Gresham and Cleveland into denouncing the scheme to annex Hawaii did not necessarily imply a passive policy toward Latin America. The reverse was the case. For example, Gresham was confused by events in Brazil during the naval revolt of 1893–1894, but his insistence upon the right of American merchant shipping to trade without molestation led ultimately to forceful action by Admiral Benham. A similar stand on principle resulted in the exercise of American influence over the affairs of Nicaragua. Growing American trade and investment and the question of the isthmian canal were contributory factors in drawing Gresham's interest to that area, but of more immediate concern to him were the reports of British intrigues in the region of Nicaragua known as the Mosquito Reservation.[108] Gresham believed that these intrigues posed a threat to Nicaraguan sovereignty, and a study of the treaties applicable to the matter convinced him that "no foreign agency shall be permitted to dictate or participate in any administration of affairs in the Mosquito Reservation.''[109]

The conclusion was very reminiscent of Gresham's decision on Hawaiian annexation in its legalistic and moralistic undertones. It was also much more than a diplomatic warning directed against Britain, for it represented a self-denying ordinance applicable to American citizens in Nicaragua as much as to foreigners. But Britain chose not to make the question a matter of international diplomatic debate. British policy had stressed cooperation with the United States during the recent Brazilian naval revolt, and a similar attitude was adopted toward Nicaraguan affairs. Bayard reported from London that Britain had no territorial designs on Nicaragua and was willing to be guided by the advice of the United States in this matter. He quoted the foreign secretary, Lord Kimberley, as noting that the United States was ''on the spot, and, being better informed could better judge, what line of action was necessary to produce requisite and reasonable security for persons and property in that region.''[110]

When political disturbances in Nicaragua in July and August 1894 resulted in the summary deportation of two British citizens, one of whom was the acting British consul at Bluefields, the whole question suddenly transcended that of political or commercial considerations and became one of national honor. Kimberley demanded redress for what was regarded in London as a deliberate affront to a British official by the Nicaraguan government, while assuring Bayard that British action was solely motivated by the concern for national honor and that the demands on Nicaragua were in no way related to the question of the Mosquito Reservation.[111] But the intransigence of the Nicaraguan government provoked the exercise of gunboat diplomacy in April 1895 when British marines temporarily occupied the Nicaraguan port of Corinto. Although Gresham believed that the British demands on Nicaragua were harsh, he also accepted that Britain had a legal and moral right to pursue its complaint to the point of coercion if necessary. He hoped, however, that Kimberley would ''as far as possible avoid action which will embarrass us here.''[112]

Gresham was referring to the increasing criticism by Congress and the press of the administration's allegedly ''weak and un-American'' foreign policy.[113] In part, this was a direct consequence of the rejection of the Hawaiian treaty. This decision not only was interpreted as a party political attack by the Democrats upon the Republicans; it was also seen as an indictment of the character of the Harrison administration.[114] The Republicans countered by constant criticism of Cleveland's foreign policy, and this campaign was given further encouragement by Republican victories in the 1894 elections. British diplomats could take little comfort in this development because much of the criticism of the Cleveland administration also contained elements of hostility toward Britain. In 1888 the Republicans had used the "Sackville-West" incident to accuse Cleveland of being too friendly with Britain. His alleged indifference to British intrigues in Hawaii and Nicaragua now presented the Republicans with an opportunity for a similar campaign of criticism.

Gresham was perturbed,[115] but he would not intervene against Britain in Nicaragua because he believed that the United States had no justifiable legal grounds for doing so. The secretary of state was no political opportunist, but he was prepared to act promptly and vigorously where he judged it to be necessary. American warships were sent to Bluefields during the disorder of July and August 1894 and to Hawaii when a political disturbance was reported in January 1895. A vigorous diplomatic response was seen to be required a few weeks later when a Spanish ship fired on the *Alliance,* an American merchant ship suspected of carrying guns to Cuba. Because the incident was reported as occurring outside Spanish territorial waters, Gresham viewed it as an infringement of American rights. He demanded "prompt disavowal of the unauthorized act." This was strong language and the press carried rumors of war, but reassurances were soon forthcoming from Spain.[116]

A much more troublesome diplomatic issue was that relating to the boundary dispute between Venezuela and the British colony of Guiana. The question had persisted since the 1840s and attracted added significance during the 1880s when discoveries of gold were reported from the area. From 1876 onward successive Venezuelan governments frequently looked to the United States for support against Britain, but they received little more than expressions of sympathetic concern.[117] The likelihood of some form of American intervention in the dispute began, however, to look much more probable in 1895. The Venezuelan government had employed a former American diplomat, William L. Scruggs, to lobby its case in Washington. The timing was auspicious, for Scruggs's energetic campaign coincided with the already evident American sensitivity toward alleged British intrigues in the Western Hemisphere and with the Cleveland administration's growing consciousness of the rising tide of criticism against its foreign policy.[118]

Cleveland responded by mentioning the boundary dispute in his annual message to Congress in December 1894. The question was thereby raised to a new level of public importance, and the House reacted in February 1895 by recommending that the dispute be submitted to arbitration.[119] Gresham suspected that Scruggs's efforts were politically motivated and designed to "embarrass" the administration, but he was nonetheless alarmed by the information that was coming to light. He viewed the British side of the case as "contradictory and palpably unjust," and he noted: "If Great Britain undertakes to maintain her present position on that question, we will be obliged, in view of the almost uniform attitude and policy of our government, to call a halt."[120] Whereas British intervention in Nicaragua was demonstrably limited in its objectives and brief in its execution, British policy toward Venezuela appeared open to a much more sinister interpretation. Scruggs sought, in fact, to persuade Cleveland and Gresham that the real British purpose was nothing less than to establish commercial dominion over the whole of northern South America.[121]

The death of Gresham on May 28 interposed to defer action. The new secretary of state, Richard Olney,[122] believed even more firmly that the Venezuelans were the aggrieved party and that Britain had for too long deliberately delayed a settlement. On July 20 he dispatched a note to London demanding that Britain agree to submit the dispute to arbitration. The timing of the dispatch reflected the administration's desire to resolve the issue before the meeting of the Republican-dominated Congress scheduled for November 1895, but the very length and complexity of Olney's arguments precluded a quick answer. A peremptory demand had recently succeeded against Spain in the *Alliance* incident, but the cautious and legalistic-minded Foreign Office was not to be hurried. Blaine and Frelinghuysen had discovered this to their cost in their years of unproductive diplomatic correspondence over the Clayton-Bulwer Treaty. That a similar impasse might occur in 1895 was suggested by Salisbury's initial comment to Bayard that "to make proper reply to so able and profound an argument, on a subject so important in its relations, would necessarily involve a great deal of labor, and possibly of time, both of which would be certainly bestowed."[123]

The implication of Olney's note was that the United States, by reason of its geographical position, possessed an inherent right to intervene in diplomatic questions relating to the Western Hemisphere. In general, British diplomats had long recognized that the United States had a special interest in these questions. But the right to intervene that Olney claimed referred not to a peripheral or insignificant matter but to a specific issue involving a Latin American country and a British colony. This uncalled for intrusion could not be officially accepted. After examination by the law officers of the crown and by the Colonial Office, Salisbury's reply to this effect was dispatched to Washington on November 27 and arrived some days after Cleveland's annual message to Congress.

"The Government of the United States," concluded the British argument, "is not entitled to affirm as a universal proposition, with reference to a number of independent States, for whose conduct it assumes no responsibility, that its interests are necessarily concerned in whatever may befall those States simply because they are situated in the Western Hemisphere."[124] The argument was sound although it had long been belied by British diplomatic practice. However, it represented a direct challenge to the validity of the Monroe Doctrine, and this was most unlikely to go unanswered. The long delay in replying to the July note had also upset Olney's original intention of settling the matter before Congress assembled. This added grievance intensified the sense of irritation and anger within the administration against Britain.

As Hayes had done in 1879 and Harrison in 1891, Cleveland now transformed a minor Latin American question into one of pressing domestic importance by sending a special message to Congress on December 17, 1895. In it he resoundingly reaffirmed the Monroe Doctrine and requested funds for a commission to investigate and decide the boundary dispute. The message was directed at Britain and its tone was authoritative and assertive. Right was assumed to be assuredly on the side of the United States, and there was no place for compromise. Salisbury's statesmanlike reply had only provoked an ultimatum from the United States and with it also the possibility of war.

Salisbury reacted impassively to Cleveland's threat. He was not inclined to give way to American bluster, especially in a matter that involved a British colony and the rights of British citizens. The policy of delay and conciliation had defused many previous Anglo-American crises, and it was instinctively pursued once more. But in this case policy was no longer the exclusive prerogative of the Foreign Office. The Venezuelan boundary dispute had been transformed from a peripheral question of minor significance into one urgently requiring the attention of the full cabinet. A much broader decision-making element was consequently introduced. Conscious of pressing problems in the Near East and in Africa, the cabinet overruled Salisbury on January 11, 1896, and decided that Britain should seek an "honourable settlement" with the United States. The American claim to intervene in the dispute was thus officially recognized by the British government.[125]

Almost a year of negotiations was required before Britain and Venezuela came to an agreement on the exact procedure of arbitration. The award was ultimately announced in October 1899 and granted Britain most of the area under dispute. From the standpoint of 1895 this indicated a humiliation for American diplomacy, but there was no outcry in the United States, for the boundary dispute had ceased to be an issue of political concern. As in the case of the *Baltimore* incident five years previously, the administration appeared to be completely satisfied when the refractory government in question signified its official acceptance of the American arguments. Despite the apparent mood of antagonism and hostility, Anglo-American diplomatic relations soon achieved a remarkable degree of friendly accord. This did not date simply from 1896, for Britain had long recognized the political predominance of the United States in Western Hemispheric questions. What occurred in 1896 was that for the first time this was officially and publicly acknowledged by Britain. While this marked a diplomatic defeat for Britain, there were also important gains. Friendship with the United States eased Britain's fear of international isolation and formed an integral element of British foreign policy in the twentieth century. The crisis of 1895–1896 only confirmed what had been apparent for many years: In the eyes of British diplomats, Latin America was politically and strategically expendable.

For the United States the episode represented an important historic victory.[126] The Monroe Doctrine was vindicated and American political preeminence in the Western Hemisphere was recognized by Britain and by implication, Europe too. Ironically, this same success raised apprehension in Latin America. The United States claimed to be acting selflessly on behalf of its Latin American sisters in defeating European imperialism, but this apparent idealism was strongly tinged with self-interest. It was also exercised in a unilateral and arrogant manner. Olney and Cleveland did not consult the Venezuelan government over their policy, and the arbitration procedure was virtually imposed upon a reluctant Venezuela. Olney claimed the preeminence of the United States in Latin America, but Europe, and especially Britain, still maintained a substantial economic and cultural relationship with those countries and the United States could barely challenge this as yet.

Nevertheless, Britain's political disengagement from Latin America visibly ended the system of international relations that had lasted in that part of the world for most of the nineteenth century. The United States saw its past as a fight against Europe, and primarily against Britain, on behalf of American values and ideas that it believed were shared by Latin America. For many decades that fight had been something of an illusion because British diplomats had no intention of provoking political conflict with the United States over Western Hemispheric questions. The issue of Anglo-American rivalry had merely disguised the real struggle for preeminence in the Western Hemisphere. This revolved around the response of the Latin American nations to the growing economic, military, and cultural power of the United States. By the middle of the nineteenth century, the nations of Central America and the Caribbean had fallen under the sway of the United States. Mexico and the more distant countries of South America were capable of stronger resistance, but their vulnerability to American pressure was demonstrated by their attendance at the Washington conference of 1889–1890 and, in the 1890s, by the reciprocity policy and the *Baltimore* incident. But American power, substantial though it might be, was not absolute.

Despite the recognition of United States hemispheric predominance, the constraints that had hampered the exercise of American policy in the late nineteenth century persisted into the twentieth. British intrigues were a thing of the past, but the frequent reassessment of Latin American policy in Washington from President Woodrow Wilson onward brought into question the veracity of Olney's statement that "the fiat of the United States was law" in Latin America.

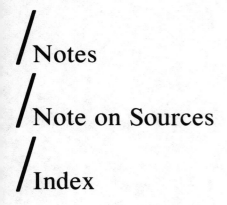

Notes

Note on Sources

Index

//

Notes

Chapter 1: British Policy Toward Latin America

1. The figures are from Albert H. Imlah, *Economic Elements in the Pax Britannica* (Cambridge, Mass.: Harvard University Press, 1958), pp. 70–75.

2. The historical debate on British "imperialism" was stimulated by John Gallagher and Ronald Robinson, "The Imperialism of Free Trade," *Economic History Review*, 2nd series, 6 (1953): 1–15. More extensive treatments of "imperialism" in an international context and with specific relation to Latin America are Stanley J. Stein and Barbara Stein, *The Colonial Heritage of Latin America* (New York: Oxford University Press, 1970); and Andre Gunder Frank, *Capitalism and Underdevelopment in Latin America* (New York: Monthly Review Press, 1969).

3. Compiled from Brian R. Mitchell, *Abstract of British Historical Statistics* (Cambridge, Eng.: Cambridge University Press, 1962), pp. 321–22.

4. See Henry S. Ferns, *Britain and Argentina in the Nineteenth Century* (Oxford: Clarendon Press, 1960); and D. C. M. Platt, *Latin America and British Trade 1806–1914* (London: A. and C. Black, 1972), p. 306.

5. Irving Stone, "British Long Term Investment in Latin America, 1865–1913," *Business History Review*, 42 (1968): 319. Another study estimated total nominal British investment in Latin America for 1890 at £425.7 million. See J. Fred Rippy, *British Investments in Latin America, 1822–1949* (Minneapolis: University of Minnesota Press, 1959), p. 37.

6. Stone estimated that one-fifth of British foreign investment before 1914 was in Latin America; Feis has shown that in a table of British foreign investment for 1914, Argentina would rank sixth after the United States, Canada, Australia, India, and South Africa. See Herbert Feis, *Europe, the World's Banker, 1870–1914* (New Haven: Yale University Press, 1930), p. 23.

7. During the French revolutionary wars Britain had attempted to gain possession of Buenos Aires and Montevideo in 1806 and 1807. See Ferns, *Britain and Argentina*, pp. 18–51. For Castlereagh's memorandum of May 1807 on the River Plate policy see ibid., p. 47.

8. In the sense that throughout the nineteenth century the Latin American nations demonstrated a degree of military resistance sufficient either to defeat or to deter projects involving foreign military invasion.

9. This refers to the Venezuelan boundary dispute.

10. Robert T. Nightingale, "The Personnel of the British Foreign Office and Diplomatic Service, 1851–1929," *American Political Science Review*, 24 (1930): 310–31.

11. The number of permanent officials in the Foreign Office actually decreased from forty-three in 1858 to forty-one in 1902–03. See Valerie Cromwell and Zara S. Steiner, "The Foreign Office Before 1914," in Gillian Sutherland, ed., *Studies in the Growth of Nineteenth-Century Government* (Totowa: Rowman and Littlefield, 1972), p. 172.

12. A property qualification of £400 was required of all applicants to the diplomatic service, and a continued private income was a necessity for most diplomats. Foreign Office officials could rarely afford to become diplomats, but even so, as one writer has noted, "no positive inducement in either pay or promotion was offered to facilitate such exchanges, despite the repeated recommendations of various select committees." See Zara S. Steiner, *The Foreign Office and Foreign Policy, 1898–1914* (London: Cambridge University Press, 1969), p. 21.

13. The term "cinderella service," implying the neglect and drudgery suffered by British consuls, is from D. C. M. Platt, *The Cinderella Service* (London: Longman, 1971). The consular service remained even into the twentieth century "a harbour of refuge for retired army officers and for failures whose only recommendation is aristocratic, official or personal influences, or an easy source of reward for persons to whom the Government of the day is in some way indebted." Ibid., p. 22.

14. On one occasion Salisbury confided to the queen that insufficient parliamentary funding was gravely hindering the effective execution of British foreign policy. See Salisbury to Queen Victoria, August 29, 1886, cited in George E. Buckle, ed., *The Letters of Queen Victoria,* 3rd series (London: John Murray, 1930), 1: 193–94.

15. This was a direct consequence of the lack of expansion in the overall number of Foreign Office personnel and also of the tradition that diplomatic officials supplement their salaries from their own private incomes.

16. An international crisis would require discussion by the cabinet, and even less important diplomatic matters might be the direct concern not only of the Foreign Office but also the Colonial Office, India Office, or the Admiralty.

17. Such issues did emerge from time to time as was illustrated by Gladstone's Midlothian campaigns of 1879 and 1880 concerning the Bulgarian atrocities.

18. This belief was shared by such widely diverse prime ministers as Gladstone and Disraeli. See Kenneth Bourne, *The Foreign Policy of Victorian England 1830–1902* (Oxford: Clarendon Press, 1970), p. 124; and Stanley R. Stembridge, "Disraeli and the Millstones," *Journal of British Studies,* (1965): 136.

19. July 11, 1867, *Parliamentary Debates,* 3rd series, 188: 1394.

20. For example, see the debate of April 2, 1886, cited in ibid., 3rd series, 304: 609–43.

21. See "Final Report of the Royal Commission on Depression of Trade and Industry," *Parliamentary Papers,* 23 (1886). See also the memorandum by the undersecretary for foreign affairs, James Bryce, July 17, 1886, cited in D. C. M. Platt, *Finance, Trade, and Politics in British Foreign Policy, 1815–1914* (Oxford: Clarendon Press, 1968), appendix 5, p. 405.

22. Circular by Lord Rosebery, July 31, 1886, London, Public Record Office, Foreign Office Records, 16/244. Hereafter cited as F.O.

23. The *Times* [London], August 6, 1886.

24. See Platt, *Finance, Trade, and Politics,* p. xxxv.

25. Ibid., p. 83.

26. Gerald S. Graham, *Tides of Empire* (Montreal: McGill-Queen's University Press, 1972), pp. 71–88. The economical aspect of British diplomacy has also been commented upon in Harold Sprout and Margaret Sprout, "The Dilemma of Rising Demands and Insufficient Resources," *World Politics,* 20 (1968): 660–94.

27. Cited in William L. Langer, *European Alliances and Alignments, 1871–1890* (New York: Vintage Books, 1950), p. 122.

28. See Public Record Office, *The Records of the Foreign Office 1782–1939* (London: Her Majesty's Stationery Office, 1969), p. 14. The American Department was renamed the American and Asiatic Department in 1882. American and Asiatic affairs were finally separated in 1899.

29. The possibility that the United States might exploit any apparent British weakness was keenly appreciated during the 1850s, especially while Britain was involved in the Crimean War. See Bourne, *Foreign Policy of Victorian England*, pp. 86–87. For a general study of Anglo-American relations see Harry C. Allen, *Great Britain and the United States* (New York: St. Martin's Press, 1955).

30. Cited in C. C. Eldridge, *England's Mission* (Chapel Hill: University of North Carolina Press, 1974), p. 73. Kimberley was lord privy seal at the time.

31. See Kenneth Bourne, *Britain and the Balance of Power in North America, 1815–1908* (Berkeley and Los Angeles: University of California Press, 1967). The Atlantic fleet continued to provide a British military presence in the area although Bourne has noted that the various bases which supported this fleet were "generally neglected" throughout the 1860s and 1870s. Ibid., p. 313.

32. See Robin A. Humphreys, *Tradition and Revolt in Latin America* (New York: Columbia University Press, 1969), p. 143.

33. This is not meant to imply that the treaty was a British surrender, although it might be argued that it was an indication of the growth of American "superiority" in the area. See ibid., p. 185.

34. The *Alabama* was a British-built cruiser used by the Confederates to attack Northern shipping during the Civil War. After the war the United States government made claims upon Britain for the damages caused by the *Alabama*. The dispute was resolved in 1871. See Adrian Cook, *The Alabama Claims* (Ithaca: Cornell University Press, 1975).

35. "Except for the period of the Revolution and a short time thereafter, admiration for the British and their ways has been almost endemic." See Edward M. Burns, *The American Idea of Mission* (New Brunswick: Rutgers University Press, 1957), p. 41.

36. Pauncefote to Salisbury, July 24, 1896, cited in Humphreys, *Tradition and Revolt*, p. 205. For the incident involving Lionel Sackville-West see Charles S. Campbell, "The Dismissal of Lord Sackville," *Mississippi Valley Historical Review*, 44 (1958): 635–48. A good example of West's bruised feelings is provided in West to Salisbury, November 15, 1888, F.O. 5/2020.

37. The most notorious example of this was Salisbury's reply to Olney's note of July 20, 1895, on the Venezuela boundary dispute. Salisbury eventually replied in November and sent the message by sea so that it did not arrive in Washington until December.

38. See minute on Pauncefote to Kimberley, no. 72, March 22, 1894, F.O. 5/2238.

39. The United States presented not only vast commercial opportunities but also political and legal stability. This obviated the kinds of pressure that merchants and investors placed on the Foreign Office on behalf of African, Asian, Latin American, and even European claims. See, for example, the attitude of the Manchester merchants in Arthur Redford, *Manchester Merchants and Foreign Trade* (Manchester: Manchester University Press, 1956), 2: 90–91.

40. The *Economist*, November 3, 1888.

41. For general accounts of this development see Alexander E. Campbell, *Great Britain and the United States, 1895–1903* (London: Longmans, 1960); and Bradford Perkins, *The Great Rapprochement* (New York: Atheneum, 1968).

42. Although Guatemala, Venezuela, and Argentina continued to dispute British jurisdiction over British Honduras, British Guiana, and the Falkland Islands respectively.

43. From 1865 to 1895 such examples were limited to Haiti in 1877, 1883, and 1887 and Nicaragua in 1895. See Dexter Perkins, *The Monroe Doctrine, 1867–1907* (Baltimore:

Johns Hopkins Press, 1937), pp. 117–18.

44. In 1885, when an Italian citizen was released from arrest in Colombia by a landing of Italian marines, Pauncefote noted: "This will be an interesting case as showing what an exhibition of force can get out of a S. American Republic." Minute on O'Leary to the foreign secretary, no. 60, August 24, 1885, F.O. 55/311. Julian Pauncefote served as permanent undersecretary at the Foreign Office until his appointment as minister to Washington in 1889.

45. See the debate, May 15, 1866, cited in *Parliamentary Debates,* 3rd series, 183: 965–86.

46. August 7, 1877, ibid., 3rd series, 236: 567–85.

47. Memorandum by the permanent undersecretary, Thomas Sanderson, January 13, 1891, F.O. 16/268.

48. Although the selection of such a senior official as Pauncefote for the Washington legation in 1889 signified an awareness of the growing importance of the United States. See Ernest R. May, *Imperial Democracy* (New York: Harcourt, Brace & World, 1961), p. 5. For a view of the same appointment, but one emphasizing internal Foreign Office considerations, see Ray Jones, *The Nineteenth-Century Foreign Office* (London: Weidenfeld and Nicolson, 1971), p. 77.

49. Rio de Janeiro, with its court and resident aristocracy, was sometimes considered to be an exception. On Latin America as a diplomatic "graveyard" see Sutherland, *Growth of Nineteenth-Century Government,* p. 187; and Zara S. Steiner, "Finance, Trade and Politics in British Foreign Policy, 1815–1914," *Historical Journal,* 13 (1970): 551. For identical German views see Lamar Cecil, *The German Diplomatic Service, 1871–1914* (Princeton: Princeton University Press, 1976), pp. 168–71.

50. From the British minister in Colombia, Frederick St. John, to Jervoise, December 23, 1884, F.O. 55/303. H. S. C. Clarke-Jervoise was a clerk in the American department of the Foreign Office.

51. Kennedy to Salisbury, May 12, 1890, and minute by Sanderson, August 4, 1890, F.O. 16/259. Second-class rank meant that the minister in charge had the position of envoy extraordinary and minister plenipotentiary. The position most common in Latin America was minister resident.

52. Report by Consul Gollan, March 12, 1873, cited in *Parliamentary Papers,* 65 (1873): 733; Fraser to Rosebery, no. 5, June 17, 1886, F.O. 16/244.

53. For the text of the speech see the *Times,* July 30, 1891.

54. Memorandum by Pauncefote, February 15, 1884, F.O. 55/307.

55. Minute by Sanderson on Gosling to Rosebery, no. 17, February 12, 1893, F.O. 15/274.

56. *South American Journal,* March 31, 1881.

57. The *Times,* November 30, 1891.

58. For some interesting comments see Victor G. Kiernan, "Diplomats in Exile," in Ragnhild Hatton and Mathew S. Anderson, eds., *Studies in Diplomatic History* (London: Longmans, 1970), p. 305.

59. The visitor was the British minister to Peru, Spenser St. John. See his report on his official mission to Bolivia, January 25, 1876, F.O. 97/442.

60. See, for example, the lack of an "honest government" in St. John to Granville, no. 111, December 27, 1881, F.O. 61/334. The weakness of Peruvian commerce is outlined in Barrington to Granville, no. 2, April 24, 1885, F.O. 61/361.

61. The comments of the British minister in Chile. See Fraser to Rosebery, no. 44, June 3, 1886, F.O. 16/242.

62. Such occasions were frequent because of the long waiting period between the dispatch and receipt of a minister's instructions. The introduction of the telegraph in the

1870s only slightly altered this situation since a telegram might cost as much as nine shillings per word in the 1880s. See Hatton and Anderson, *Studies in Diplomatic History,* p. 315.

63. See Victor G. Kiernan, "Foreign Interests in the War of the Pacific," *Hispanic American Historical Review,* 35 (1955): 32.

64. Memorandum by the Foreign Office's legal adviser, Davidson, March 4, 1891, F.O. 16/267.

65. See various dispatches from the British minister in Guatemala, Gosling, to the Foreign Office in F.O. 15/264.

66. Memorandum, March 30, 1867, F.O. 55/196.

67. Hammond to Bunch, January 1, 1867, F.O. 55/195.

68. See F.O. 61/232 and 233.

69. The Commercial Department of the Foreign Office has been described as "scarcely more than a post office for the Board of Trade." See Platt, *Finance, Trade, and Politics,* p. 371. See also his comprehensive appendix on this subject in ibid., pp. 371–97.

70. "The vetting and presentation of claims," Platt has noted, "formed a major, if not *the* major, preoccupation of British diplomacy in Latin America, whether at the Legations or at the Foreign Office itself." Ibid., p. 331.

71. Although the negotiation of treaties of friendship, commerce, and navigation between Britain and most of the Latin American countries during the first half of the nineteenth century had provided encouragement and important legal safeguards for the establishment of British commercial relations with Latin America.

72. See Platt, *Finance, Trade, and Politics,* pp. 54–72.

73. Haggard to the foreign secretary, Lord Iddesleigh, no. 52, September 21, 1886, F.O. 13/619. William Haggard was the secretary of the British legation at Rio. For his instructions from the Foreign Office see F.O. 13/617.

74. Memorandum by Davidson, January 16, 1888, F.O. 13/636.

75. He added: "I have advised and continue to advise all persons interested in such matters to do everything they can to come to an arrangement directly before they appeal to us." See Currie to Haggard, September 20, 1887, F.O. 13/642.

76. See ibid., and also Haggard to Currie, September 19, 1887.

77. Minute by Davidson on Haggard to Sanderson, January 11, 1891, F.O. 13/684.

78. See memoranda by Pauncefote, October 20, 1884, F.O. 13/600, and by Salisbury, July 22, 1887, F.O. 13/638. The definition of what constituted "unofficial" action varied according to the personality of the minister involved and the particular circumstances of the case in question. However vigorously or indifferently "unofficial" action might be implemented, the aim was to prevent the issue becoming a subject of "official" correspondence between the British government and the government concerned.

79. Minute by Davidson on Wyndham to the foreign secretary, no. 38, May 17, 1889, F.O. 13/657. See also the memorandum by Davidson, December 21, 1887, F.O. 13/638.

80. August 22, 1887, *Parliamentary Debates,* 3rd series, 319: 1348–49. See also the F.O. memorandum, August 18, 1887, F.O. 13/642.

81. Minute by Sanderson on Wyndham to Salisbury, no. 56, June 15, 1889, F.O. 13/657; Wyndham to Sanderson, private, December 17, 1889, F.O. 13/658. The large settlement in the Waring claim had also caused scandal in Brazil. "It is commonly stated and universally believed here," wrote Haggard from Rio, "that £70,000 far exceeded the fair amount of indemnity due to Messrs Waring for the recision of their contract and the granting of this large sum was the result of a pecuniary transaction between that firm and the then Brazilian Minister of Agriculture." See Haggard to Iddesleigh, no. 52, September 21, 1886, F.O. 13/619. For an interesting dispatch on the general difficulties attending this type of claim see Monson to Salisbury, no. 37, January 8, 1886, F.O. 83/932.

82. Memorandum by Davidson, January 25, 1888, F.O. 13/642.
83. Minute on Wyndham to Salisbury, no. 133, November 13, 1889, F.O. 13/658.
84. Memorandum by Davidson, September 23, 1889, F.O. 13/664. The British archives contain no evidence as to whether the Brazilian government took up this statesmanlike suggestion.
85. See minute on Wyndham to Salisbury, no. 53, February 28, 1890, F.O. 13/666.
86. The *Economist,* August 17, 1872; *South American Journal,* January 8, 1879. This is not to deny that the nineteenth century saw a considerable amount of descriptive literature on Latin America produced by British writers. For a bibliographical guide see Bernard Naylor, *Accounts of Nineteenth-Century South America* (London: Athlone Press, 1969).
87. See minute on Wyndham to Salisbury, no. 205, November 27, 1890, F.O. 13/667.
88. The liberal M.P. for Glasgow, George Anderson, asked twenty-five questions on Latin American affairs between 1870 and 1884; his successor, Hugh Watt, asked thirty similar questions between 1886 and 1892. Another prominent spokesman on Latin America was the conservative M.P. Charles Howard Vincent, who asked twenty-two questions on this subject between 1887 and 1895.
89. See, for example, the letter of the M.P. for Kilmarnock, Stephen Williamson to Fergusson, April 16, 1891, F.O. 16/271, asking the Foreign Office to consider mediating in the Chilean revolution. James Fergusson was the parliamentary undersecretary for foreign affairs.
90. The Corporation of Foreign Bondholders was formed in 1869. It had a general council, but most of its activities were directed by separate committees representing investments in a specific country. Thus, British holders of Mexican bonds were represented by the committee of Mexican bondholders. Other committees acted similarly on behalf of British bondholders in other Latin American countries. See Corporation of Foreign Bondholders, *Annual Report of the Council of the Corporation of Foreign Bondholders* (London, 1874–).
91. For these petitions see F.O. 13/687.
92. This attitude was clearly expressed in the circulars prepared by Palmerston and later by Granville cited in Platt, *Finance, Trade, and Politics,* pp. 398–402.
93. Hammond to Bunch, April 30, 1867, F.O. 55/195. Hammond was permanent undersecretary at the Foreign Office.
94. Minute on Welby to Jervoise, February 15, 1893, F.O. 6/249.
95. Certain loans such as those given to Greece, Turkey, and various Asian enterprises involved important strategic considerations, and the British government involved itself in their negotiation and guarantee. See Platt, *Finance, Trade, and Politics,* pp. 10–33.
96. The most frequent form of assistance was to include communications from the bondholders to the local government among the Foreign Office mail. On occasion, in isolated areas such as Latin America, British officials were permitted to receive and to remit payments made by the local government on behalf of the British bondholders.
97. See "Report from Select Committee on Loans to Foreign States," *Parliamentary Papers,* 11 (1875).
98. These implications were clearly pointed out in the *Economist,* November 9, 1867.
99. As Platt has noted, the bondholders had some cause to feel aggrieved. "The bondholders were particularly unfortunate in three respects: a clear policy of nonintervention had been laid down from the beginning; their claims were always readily distinguishable from the general interests; and, by the end of the century, even the term 'bondholder' itself tended to evoke an automatically hostile response from officials and the public alike." See Platt, *Finance, Trade, and Politics,* p. 41.
100. British protests were designed not to support "the claims of the Bondholders as such, but merely to protest against a portion of Peru being annexed by Chile, without the

latter taking a proportionate part of the Peruvian National Debt." Memorandum by Pauncefote, June 22, 1883, F.O. 61/351. See also Platt, *Finance, Trade, and Politics,* pp. 336–39.

101. Although British policy, in this case, stressed conciliation and political withdrawal rather than an attempt to assert Britain's power in a manner commensurate with its economic power.

102. This "great debate" was well illustrated in the "Final Report of the Royal Commission on Depression of Trade and Industry," *Parliamentary Papers,* 23 (1886).

103. April 2, 1886, *Parliamentary Debates,* 3rd series, 304: 637. Bryce was parliamentary undersecretary for foreign affairs.

104. The *Times,* August 6, 1886.

105. See Samuel B. Saul, *Studies in British Overseas Trade 1870–1914* (Liverpool: Liverpool University Press, 1960), p. 38; and Platt, *Latin America and British Trade,* pp. 274–313.

106. *South American Journal,* January 27, 1894.

107. The *Board of Trade Journal* began monthly publication in 1886; in 1898 a commercial intelligence branch was established within the Commercial Department of the Board of Trade. See Platt, *Finance, Trade, and Politics,* pp. 377–78.

108. The trend toward the decline of British influence and power in the Western Hemisphere was also assisted by the growing authority and economic and military power of the major Latin American nations during the last quarter of the nineteenth century. For an interesting analysis of diplomatic developments emphasizing the role of the Latin American nations themselves see Robert N. Burr, *By Reason or Force* (Berkeley and Los Angeles: University of California Press, 1965).

Chapter 2: United States Policy Toward Latin America

1. See, for example, Thomas A. Bailey, "America's Emergence as a World Power: The Myth and the Verity," *Pacific Historical Review,* 30 (1961): 1–16.

2. Although Argentina, in particular, made a determined effort to challenge American pretensions to predominance in the late nineteenth century. See Thomas F. McGann, *Argentina, the United States and the Inter-American System, 1880–1914* (Cambridge, Mass.: Harvard University Press, 1957).

3. On the Monroe Doctrine see especially the three volumes by Dexter Perkins, *The Monroe Doctrine, 1823–1826* (Cambridge, Mass.: Harvard University Press, 1927), *The Monroe Doctrine, 1826–1867* (Baltimore: Johns Hopkins Press, 1933), and *The Monroe Doctrine, 1867–1907* (Baltimore: Johns Hopkins Press, 1937). For a collection of important articles on Anglo-American rivalry in Latin America see Robin A. Humphreys, *Tradition and Revolt in Latin America* (New York: Columbia University Press, 1969), pp. 130–215.

4. Cited in James D. Richardson, ed., *A Compilation of the Messages and Papers of the Presidents, 1789–1897,* 10 vols. (Washington, D.C.: GPO, 1896–1899), 7: 990.

5. The secondary literature on late nineteenth-century American foreign policy is extensive and has been considerably stimulated by recent works stressing the economic aspects of American expansionism. See William A. Williams, *The Roots of the Modern American Empire* (New York: Random House, 1969); and Walter LeFeber, *The New Empire* (Ithaca: Cornell University Press, 1963). For an interpretive synthesis of the recent literature see Robert L. Beisner, *From the Old Diplomacy to the New, 1865–1900* (New York: Crowell, 1975).

6. See Albert K. Weinburg, *Manifest Destiny* (Baltimore: Johns Hopkins Press, 1935); and Frederick Merk, *Manifest Destiny and Mission in American History* (New York: Knopf, 1963).

7. Cited in LaFeber, *New Empire*, p. 27. William H. Seward served as secretary of state from 1861 to 1869.

8. International American Conference, 1889–1890, *Minutes of the Conference* (Washington, D.C., 1890), p. 872. Henderson was one of the leading American delegates at the conference. See chapter 5.

9. Richardson, *Messages and Papers,* 6: 688.

10. Ibid., 2: 219.

11. Olney to Bayard, no. 804, July 20, 1895, *Foreign Relations [of the United States]* (1895), p. 558. Richard Olney was secretary of state from 1895 to 1897.

12. Compiled from Department of Commerce, Bureau of the Census, *Historical Statistics of the United States* (Washington, D.C.: GPO, 1960), pp. 550–53.

13. Richardson, *Messages and Papers,* 8: 327. For Blaine's views on Latin American markets see James G. Blaine, *Political Discussions* (Norwich, Conn.: Henry Bill, 1887), pp. 411–19.

14. Olney to Bayard, no. 804, July 20, 1895, *Foreign Relations* (1895), p. 557.

15. Cited in Perkins, *Monroe Doctrine, 1867–1907,* p. 16.

16. Palmerston to Clarendon, December 31, 1857, cited in Kenneth Bourne, *Britain and the Balance of Power in North America, 1815–1908* (Berkeley and Los Angeles: University of California Press, 1967), p. 202.

17. "Relative strength gives the United States an enormous advantage, but relative distance gives these southern states considerable protection." See Nicholas J. Spykman, *America's Strategy in World Politics* (New York: Harcourt, Brace and Co., 1942), p. 61.

18. As Morgenthau has noted: "In the Western Hemisphere we have always endeavored to preserve the unique position of the United States as a predominant power without rival." Hans J. Morgenthau, *In Defense of the National Interest* (New York: Knopf, 1952), p. 5.

19. In October 1891 sailors from the American vessel *Baltimore* were set upon by a group of Chileans in Valparaiso. One sailor was killed and five badly hurt. The resulting diplomatic friction almost brought about a state of war between the United States and Chile. See chapter 7.

20. See the *Nation,* October 17, 1889; Worthington C. Ford, *Reciprocity Under the Tariff Act of 1890* (Washington, D.C., 1893), p. 33.

21. *Congressional Record,* 52nd Congress, 1st session, p. 3671. Blount was Democratic chairman of the House Committee on Foreign Affairs. On American attitudes in general Commager has written: "The moral superiority of his country was equally axiomatic to the American. The assumption of superiority was accompanied by a sense of destiny and mission. . . . Successive generations were equally eager to spread the American ideas over the globe and exasperated that foreign ideas should ever intrude themselves into America." See Henry S. Commager, *The American Mind* (New Haven: Yale University Press, 1950), p. 11.

22. See Arthur P. Whitaker, *The Western Hemisphere Idea* (Ithaca: Cornell University Press, 1954).

23. Olney to Bayard, no. 804, July 20, 1895, *Foreign Relations* (1895), p. 558.

24. The remark of Don Dickinson, the postmaster general in the Cleveland cabinet, cited in *Boston Daily Globe,* October 14, 1895.

25. For an outline of Latin American economic development toward the end of the nineteenth century see Sanford A. Mosk, "Latin America and the World Economy, 1850–1914," *Inter-American Economic Affairs,* 2 (1948): 53–82; and William P. Glade, *The Latin American Economies* (New York: Van Nostrand Reinhold, 1969), pp. 211–47.

26. Cited in Richardson, *Messages and Papers,* 7: 77.

27. See *Commercial Relations [of the United States]* (1894 and 1895), 1: 76–78.

28. *Buenos Ayres Herald,* November 21, 1885. The reference was to the Latin American Trade Commission of 1884–1885.

29. See International American Conference, *Minutes,* p. 324.

30. Edwardes to Salisbury, no. 221, June 15, 1888, F.O. 5/2024.

31. See Richardson, *Messages and Papers,* 7: 612.

32. With the exception of the Ten Years in Cuba, 1868–1878, which was not regarded as a case of European aggression since Spanish possession of the island long antedated the Monroe Doctrine. The European powers also acquiesced in the leading role accorded the United States in the attempts to mediate the conflict.

33. The remark of Congressman John D. Long of Massachusetts cited in Robert Seager II, "Ten Years Before Mahan," *Mississippi Valley Historical Review,* 40 (1953): 497. The period after 1865 has been described as "sixteen years of drift and inattention, stagnation in shipbuilding, and confusion in thinking about naval policy." See Leonard D. White, *The Republican Era, 1869–1901* (New York: Macmillan, 1958), p. 157.

34. See Kenneth J. Hagan, *American Gunboat Diplomacy and the Old Navy, 1877–1889* (Westport: Greenwood Press, 1973), p. 127. He describes the South Pacific squadron as almost nonexistent by 1875.

35. Harold Sprout and Margaret Sprout, *The Rise of American Naval Power, 1776–1918* (Princeton: Princeton University Press, 1967), pp. 194–95; Williams, *Modern American Empire,* p. 238.

36. *Congressional Record,* 48th Congress, 2nd session, p. 613.

37. Pletcher has described the State Department as "stunted and amateurish in comparison with the major foreign offices of Europe." See David M. Pletcher, *The Awkward Years* (Columbia: University of Missouri Press, 1962), p. 18.

38. Adee served as third assistant secretary of state from 1882 to 1886 and as second assistant secretary of state from 1886 to 1924.

39. William E. Curtis, *The United States and Foreign Powers* (New York: C. Scribner's Sons, 1899), p. 21. Curtis was a journalist who was considered an expert on Latin American affairs. He served several Republican administrations in the latter capacity.

40. See Allan Nevins, *Hamilton Fish* (New York: F. Ungar, 1957), p. 118.

41. George M. Towle, "The American Consular Service," *North American Review,* 149 (1889): 758.

42. See John W. Foster, "Pan-American Diplomacy," *Atlantic Monthly,* 89 (1902): 490.

43. *Congressional Record,* 52nd Congress, 1st session, p. 3849.

44. Logan to Frelinghuysen, September 13, 1883, cited in Henry C. Evans, *Chile and Its Relations with the United States* (Durham: Duke University Press, 1927), p. 127.

45. See John W. Foster, *Diplomatic Memoirs,* 2 vols. (New York: Houghton Mifflin, 1909), 1: 5. Foster had originally asked for the Swiss mission as one of the "lowest and least important of the diplomatic posts." He described Mexico as "the highest and most difficult mission on the American hemisphere." Ibid.

46. See Bunch to Clarendon, no. 4, January 14, 1870, F.O. 55/249.

47. Thornton to Salisbury, no. 68, March 24, 1879, F.O. 5/1681.

48. Hurlbut to Blaine, no. 26, November 9, 1881, *Foreign Relations* (1881), pp. 947–48.

49. Bayard to Pendleton, April 28, 1888, cited in Charles C. Tansill, *The Foreign Policy of Thomas F. Bayard, 1885–1897* (New York: Fordham University Press, 1940), p. 306. Bayard complained further: "I have six treaties pending consideration, and postponement, defeat, or obstructive amendment describes the treatment they have met so far." Ibid.

50. See Pletcher, *Awkward Years,* p. 278.

51. Letter from Wilson cited in *Bradstreet's,* February 28, 1885.

52. Alfred T. Mahan, *The Influence of Sea Power upon History, 1660–1783* (Boston:

Little, Brown, 1890). See also John A. S. Grenville and George B. Young, *Politics, Strategy, and American Diplomacy* (New Haven: Yale University Press, 1966), pp. 1–38.

53. Bayard to Pendleton, September 9, 1885, cited in Tansill, *Foreign Policy of Bayard*, p. 31.

54. Blaine, *Political Discussions*, p. 419. For a general account of Blaine's diplomatic activities see Alice F. Tyler, *The Foreign Policy of James G. Blaine* (Minneapolis: University of Minnesota Press, 1927).

55. Blaine, *Political Discussions*, pp. 413–14.

56. Andrew Carnegie, *Triumphant Democracy* (New York: Scribner, 1886), p. 1.

57. For example, Gustavus Goward was sent on a special mission to inspect American consulates in Latin America in 1880. His instructions also stressed: "The interest which the Department has taken in the development and enlargement of trade of the United States, suggests also that you should make all reasonable investigations into the best means for promoting this object at the various places which you may visit and it will be expected that you should embrace this subject in your reports." See John Hay to Goward, no. 1, June 30, 1880, National Archives, Records of the Department of State, Record Group [hereafter RG], 59, *Special Agents, Dispatches,* 30.

58. David A. Wells, "Evils of the Tariff System," *North American Review,* 139 (1884): 276. Wells was much more than an advocate of increased agricultural exports. His numerous and well-researched publications stressed the need for structural reform of the tariff system.

59. See David M. Pletcher, *Rails, Mines and Progress* (Ithaca: Cornell University Press, 1948), p. 72.

60. *Congressional Record,* 53rd Congress, 2nd Session, p. 3966.

61. International American Conference, *Minutes,* p. 505. Estee was one of the American delegates at the conference.

62. See International Monetary Commission, RG 43, Boxes 930, 930A.

63. Ibid. The Monetary Commission resolved "that before long another Commission may meet which shall reach an agreement that will secure the adoption of a uniform monetary system between the nations of America, advantageous to each and all." No invitations were issued, however, for the proposed conference.

64. The *Nation,* February 20, 1890.

65. See Richardson, *Messages and Papers,* 9: 313.

66. Frelinghuysen to John F. Miller, March 26, 1884, cited in West to Granville, no. 116, April 16, 1884, F.O. 5/1869.

67. Josiah Strong, *Our Country* (New York: Baker and Taylor, 1889), p. 175. See also LaFeber, *New Empire,* p. 78.

68. See Blaine, *Political Discussions*, pp. 411–19 for his defense of the foreign policy of the Garfield administration.

69. Cited in Kirk H. Porter and Donald B. Johnson, comps., *National Party Platforms, 1840–1964* (Urbana: University of Illinois Press, 1966), p. 93.

70. On Bayard's policy see Tansill, *Foreign Policy of Bayard,* passim.

71. See Gresham to Overmeyer, July 25, 1894, Library of Congress, Gresham Papers.

72. In the late nineteenth century from 70 to 80 percent of American exports were destined for Europe while 50 percent of imports came from that source. Little more than 10 percent of the American export trade was with Latin American countries. See Bureau of the Census, *Historical Statistics,* pp. 550–53. On the importance of the European market see Mathew Simon and David Novack, "Some Dimensions of the American Commercial Invasion of Europe, 1871–1914," *Journal of Economic History,* 24 (1964): 591–605.

73. West to Salisbury, no. 189, July 17, 1885, F.O. 5/1910.

74. See Eugene Schuyler, *American Diplomacy and the Furtherance of Commerce*

(New York: C. Scribner's Sons, 1886), p. 104.

75. The decline of the American merchant marine after the Civil War was a continual source of complaint by Republican administrations. As late as 1889 Harrison was still describing the situation as "humiliating to the national pride and hurtful to the national prosperity." See Richardson, *Messages and Papers*, 9: 56–57.

76. Report of Consul Frank D. Hill, Montevideo, March 21, 1891, *United States Consular Reports*, 37 (1891): 124. Although American businessmen were in a much stronger economic position in Central America than in South America, it is interesting to note that the banana enterprises of Minor C. Keith were initially financed by British rather than American sources. See Frederick U. Adams, *Conquest of the Tropics* (Garden City: Doubleday, Page, 1914), pp. 66–67.

77. See memorandum by Pauncefote, February 15, 1890, F.O. 5/2085. Pauncefote was referring to the Washington conference of 1889–1890, and he added that "this social isolation of the two parts of the western continent has been strongly brought out in connection with the present Conference."

78. Spanish dominion in the Americas came, of course, to an end in 1898.

Chapter 3: Divergent Responses to Conflict

1. Despite the local expectations of United States or British intervention that the presence of these ships frequently aroused.

2. The Spanish squadron had in fact precipitated a war with Peru in 1864 though peace arrangements had been concluded in January 1865. For an account of the war see William C. Davis, *The Last Conquistadores* (Athens: University of Georgia Press, 1950).

3. The *Times*, January 7 and November 27, 1865.

4. See Clarendon to Thomson, no. 23, December 16, 1865, F.O. 16/133. Thomson was the British chargé d'affaires in Chile. See also Clarendon to John Crampton, the British minister in Madrid, November 18, 1865, *Parliamentary Papers*, 76 (1866). Clarendon assumed office on November 3, 1865.

5. Clarendon to Thomson, no. 2, November 17, 1865, F.O. 16/133. A copy of this dispatch was also sent to the Admiralty for transmission to the British naval commander in the Pacific.

6. The *Times*, November 30, 1865. The *New York World* of December 4, 1865, predicted that "British merchants . . . are not to be lightly interfered with," especially now that Clarendon was British foreign secretary.

7. Clarendon to Thomson, no. 23, December 16, 1865, F.O. 16/133. See also Davis, *Last Conquistadores*, pp. 75, 133.

8. Clarendon to Thomson, no. 6, November 30, 1865, F.O. 16/133.

9. The Foreign Office also sent copies of the relevant British dispatches to Bismarck. See Clarendon to Francis Napier, the British ambassador in Berlin, November 29, 1865, *Parliamentary Papers*, 76 (1866).

10. "You will act in entire concert with your French colleague, who will receive similar instructions." Clarendon to Thomson, no. 23, December 16, 1865, F.O. 16/133.

11. Unlike most Latin American issues this was one that was discussed at cabinet level. No doubt this was a reflection of concern for the stability of the Spanish government. A number of the dispatches were also transmitted to Queen Victoria because of her personal concern for the fate of her fellow queen.

12. Sr. Carvallo was a frequent visitor to the Foreign Office at this time.

13. These events had taken place in November 1865 even before the Spanish acceptance of the Anglo-French good offices.

14. See Clarendon to Barton, January 30, 1866, *Parliamentary Papers*, 76 (1866).

Barton was British chargé d'affaires in Peru. The involvement of another government in the war hampered the peace efforts still further by adding to the problems of distance and communications. Peru's agreement to peace efforts was now necessary too.

15. Chile and Peru were also joined in the war by Ecuador in February 1866 and by Bolivia in March 1866.

16. See Thomson to the foreign secretary, Lord Russell, no. 30, September 16, 1865, F.O. 16/134.

17. See Thomson to Myers, Bland and Co., September 29, 1865, Parliamentary Papers, 76 (1866).

18. Indeed, the American minister, Thomas Nelson, noted in December that "the war has begun to stimulate commercial transaction." Nelson to Seward, December 1, 1867, Foreign Relations [of the United States] (1866–1867), 2: 363. Thomson described the situation as "a partial blockade." See Thomson to Russell, December 2, 1865, Parliamentary Papers, 76 (1866). See D. C. M. Platt, Latin America and British Trade 1806–1914 (London: A. and C. Black, 1972), pp. 316–23 for statistics suggesting that there was no major reduction in British exports and imports to Chile during these years.

19. Thomson to Rouse, September 30, 1865, F.O. 16/134. Rouse was British consul in Valparaiso.

20. Clarendon to Thomson, January 11, 1866. These views were communicated by Thomson to the British merchants on March 3, 1866. See Parliamentary Papers, 76 (1866).

21. Ibid. Denman to the secretary of the Admiralty, March 3, 1866.

22. Ibid. Thomson to Clarendon, March 9, 1866. For the reactions of the Foreign Office and the Admiralty see the secretary of the Admiralty to Hammond, April 13, 1866; Clarendon to Thomson, April 16, 1866; and Hammond to the secretary of the Admiralty, May 1, 1866. Denman appeared to have anticipated this criticism in his belated revelation that he had established an accord with Rodgers, but that this had long since lapsed. "It seemed unimportant to mention it, but on further consideration I think it better to do so," he wrote to the secretary of the Admiralty, March 29, 1866.

23. On this latter point see Seward to Koerner, May 19, 1864, cited in Davis, Last Conquistadores, pp. 133–34. Koerner was the American minister in Spain.

24. Ibid., pp. 75, 133, 143, 281.

25. "The mainland of South America interested him not at all as a field for territorial expansion, and while Secretary of State he made no effort in that direction." For this comment on Seward's foreign policy see Ernest N. Paolino, The Foundations of the American Empire (Ithaca: Cornell University Press, 1973), p. 21.

26. See Davis, Last Conquistadores, p. 282.

27. No doubt with the Alabama dispute in mind. This neutral policy considerably annoyed Chilean agents in the United States; see ibid., p. 289.

28. "In the opinion of the President," summed up Seward, "the most beneficial policy which this government can practice with reference to foreign states is to abstain from all authoritative or dictatorial proceedings in regard to their own peculiar affairs, while it employs at all times whatever just influence it enjoys to promote peace, and to recommend to them, by its own fidelity to justice and freedom, the institutions of free popular government." Seward to Kilpatrick, May 5, 1866, Foreign Relations (1866–1867), 2: 411.

29. See James W. Cortada, "Diplomatic Rivalry Between Spain and the United States over Chile and Peru, 1864–1871," Inter-American Economic Affairs, 27 (1974): 57.

30. Seward to Nelson, December 5, 1865, Foreign Relations (1866–1867), 2: 364. See also Seward to Adams, December 8, 1865, ibid., 1: 29. It is also interesting to note that Thomson proposed a "joint accord of the neutral Powers" in his dispatch to Russell of November 16, 1865, Parliamentary Papers, 76 (1866).

31. He had the rank of envoy extraordinary and minister plenipotentiary whereas

Britain was represented by a chargé d'affaires.

32. Crampton to Clarendon, November 23, 1865, *Parliamentary Papers,* 76 (1866). See also Davis, *Last Conquistadores,* p. 236.

33. Nelson to President Pezet, March 12, 1866, *Foreign Relations* (1866–1867), 2: 384. This also probably explains Seward's instruction to Nelson of December 5, 1865, that he treat Spain and Chile "with equal consideration and respect." Ibid., p. 364.

34. Kilpatrick to Seward, June 15, 1866, ibid., p. 414. The *New York World* of December 4, 1865, had described Kilpatrick's appointment as "so alarming and so unseasonable."

35. The cannons protecting the harbor had been removed early in the war so as not to provoke Spanish bombardment.

36. Kilpatrick to Seward, April 2, 1866, *Foreign Relations* (1866–1867), 2: 386–93.

37. Thomson to Clarendon, March 29, 1866, *Parliamentary Papers,* 76 (1866).

38. Kilpatrick to Seward, April 16, 1866, *Foreign Relations* (1866–1867), 2: 408. Anti-American feeling persisted, and in May Kilpatrick reported the prevalent Chilean belief that the United States was more friendly to Spain than to Chile. See Kilpatrick to Seward, May 2, 1866, ibid., p. 410.

The Chilean Department of Foreign Affairs issued a statement, dated April 1, 1866: "It was natural to believe that although the Spanish squadron might attempt the bombardment, the naval forces of the United States and Great Britain would prevent the consummation of an act of such useless barbarity which would involve the ruin of many British subjects and North American citizens." Ibid., p. 422.

39. Kilpatrick to Seward, April 2, 1866, ibid., p. 393.

40. Indeed, Kilpatrick even believed that war between Spain and the United States was a distinct possibility. "I could not risk the certainty of a war with Spain," he noted to Seward on April 2, 1866. See ibid., pp. 390–91. The risks of the late nineteenth-century American system of foreign service appointments have rarely been more vividly illustrated.

41. Denman to the secretary of the Admiralty, April 2, 1866, *Parliamentary Papers,* 76 (1866).

42. See Davis, *Last Conquistadores,* p. 304.

43. Parliamentary undersecretary for foreign affairs.

44. May 15, 1866, *Parliamentary Debates,* 3rd series, 183: 980.

45. See Clarendon to Crampton, April 23 and May 16, 1866, *Parliamentary Papers,* 76 (1866). Clarendon was especially upset because the Spanish government appeared to have sent instructions to Mendez Nuñez for bombardment while simultaneously encouraging Anglo-French efforts at mediation.

46. See Davis, *Last Conquistadores,* pp. 324–27. The seizure of these guano islands by Spain in 1864 had been the initial cause of the war.

47. The offer was made by Seward in response to a House resolution; see *Congressional Globe,* 39th Congress, 2nd session, p. 152. The Anglo-French attempt at mediation had been withdrawn in favor of that of the United States. See Cortada, "Diplomatic Rivalry Between Spain and the United States," p. 55.

48. The Washington conference did result in the declaration of an armistice on April 11, 1871, although the actual peace treaties with Spain were signed between that country and Peru (April 1879), Bolivia (August 1879), Chile (June 1883), and Ecuador (January 1885).

49. The *Times,* January 29, 1866.

50. For a survey of internal Spanish developments at this time see Raymond Carr, *Spain 1808–1939* (Oxford: Clarendon Press, 1966), chapter 7. In 1863 "Chile and Bolivia stood on the threshhold of bloodshed." See Robert N. Burr, *By Reason or Force* (Berkeley and Los Angeles: University of California Press, 1965), p. 90.

51. Harold F. Peterson, "Efforts of the United States to Mediate in the Paraguayan

War," *Hispanic American Historical Review,* 12 (1932): 2–17.

52. Ibid., p. 17.

53. See Mathew to Stanley, April 6, 1867, *British and Foreign State Papers,* 66 (1874–1875): 1291. Mathew was the British chargé d'affaires in Argentina. The allies also rejected the good offices of Chile and Peru. On this see Burr, *By Reason or Force,* pp. 104–06.

54. H. Gaylord Warren, *Paraguay* (Norman: University of Oklahoma Press, 1949), pp. 247–48.

55. See Peterson, "United States in the Paraguayan War," pp. 11–15.

56. "There is no doubt that the image of the United States in Brazil suffered during Webb's eight years as minister." See Norman T. Straus, "Brazil in the 1870's as Seen by American Diplomats" (Ph.D. diss., New York University, 1971), p. 8. For financial scandals involving Webb see Allan Nevins, *Hamilton Fish* (New York: F. Ungar, 1957), pp. 642–46.

57. After a conversation with the Brazilian foreign minister, the British minister reported: "The war with Paraguay was upon a point of honour, and that it was impossible for any but themselves [i.e., the allies] to decide when and by what means their honour would be satisfied." Thornton to Stanley, April 8, 1867, *British and Foreign State Papers,* 66 (1874–1875): 1290.

58. The *Times,* July 18, 1868. "With regard to the war in Paraguay," stated Lord Stanley, "Her Majesty's Government have at present no inducement to interfere, at least as far as British interests generally are concerned; and there seems little likelihood that any tender of intervention on their part, with a view to the restoration of peace, would be sincerely accepted by both, even if it were by either of the belligerents." Stanley to Stuart, July 7, 1868, *Parliamentary Papers,* 73 (1867–1868). Stuart was the British chargé d'affaires in Argentina. See also Stanley's reply to a question on mediation, March 27, 1868, *Parliamentary Debates,* 3rd series, 191: 359–60.

59. Thornton to Stanley, no. 6, January 7, 1867, F.O. 13/445. Thornton also noted that Webb might be jealous of other attempts at mediation. See also Seward's views on the role of the United States in the Western Hemisphere cited in Peterson, "United States in the Paraguayan War," pp. 4–5.

60. Stanley to Lyons, April 4, 1867, cited in Kenneth Bourne, *Britain and Balance of Power in North America, 1815–1908* (Berkeley and Los Angeles: University of California Press, 1967), p. 302. Lyons was the British ambassador in France.

61. See Christopher J. Bartlett, "British Reaction to the Cuban Insurrection of 1868–1878," *Hispanic American Historical Review,* 37 (1957): 297–98.

62. May 9, 1870, *Parliamentary Debates,* 3rd series, 201: 394–95.

63. See Bartlett, "British Reaction to the Cuban Insurrection." The *Virginius* was an arms smuggler seized by the Spanish authorities outside Spanish territorial waters in 1873. The summary execution of the crew, consisting of American and British citizens, provoked a major diplomatic controversy.

64. See Herbert Millington, *American Diplomacy and the War of the Pacific* (New York: Columbia University Press, 1948); and William J. Dennis, *Tacna and Arica* (New Haven: Yale University Press, 1931). For a contemporary British though anti-Chilean account, see Clements R. Markham, *The War Between Peru and Chile, 1879–1882* (London: S. Low & Co., 1883). The war had begun initially between Bolivia and Chile, but Bolivia played little part in the later proceedings. Indeed, Britain had broken off diplomatic relations with Bolivia in 1853, and these were not fully restored until 1903.

65. See the brief survey of the "Anglo-Chilean connection" in Harold Blakemore, *British Nitrates and Chilean Politics, 1886–1896* (London: Athlone Press, 1974), pp. 10–14. After Brazil, Peru was the next most favored area of British investment in Latin America in 1880. See J. Fred Rippy, *British Investments in Latin America, 1822–1949*

(Minneapolis: University of Minnesota Press, 1959), p. 25.

66. Spenser St. John to Salisbury, no. 101, July 21, 1879, F.O. 61/319. St. John was the British minister in Peru.

67. Minute by Pauncefote, dated March 2, 1881, F.O. 61/333. At this time Pauncefote was assistant undersecretary at the Foreign Office.

68. In the case of the attack on Lima, all the foreign representatives in that city participated jointly in contingency plans to protect foreign property. Naval cooperation between the powers was also strongly in evidence. A recent study has noted: "American naval operations during the War of the Pacific were very similar to those of the European squadrons. To a remarkable degree, American and European naval ship movements coincided with one another." See Kenneth J. Hagan, *American Gunboat Diplomacy and the Old Navy, 1877–1889* (Westport: Greenwood Press, 1973), p. 140.

69. See F.O. 61/232 and 233. British companies did, however, supply military equipment to both sides, and British citizens also fought on both sides.

70. F.O. to Blest Gana, June 3, 1880, F.O. 16/210. Blest Gana was the Chilean minister in Britain.

71. Graham to Granville, no. 61, August 15, 1882, F.O. 61/340. See also the minute by Pauncefote on this dispatch. Graham was the British chargé d'affaires in Peru.

72. The New York newspapers tended to award praise or criticism to Blaine according to their own respective party political viewpoints. Most newspapers had little but criticism for the activities of the various American ministers who served in Peru and Chile during the war. One modern historian has commented that the failure of American diplomacy "stemmed almost entirely" from the failings of the American ministers on the spot. See Millington, *American Diplomacy and the War of the Pacific,* pp. 38–39.

At the outset of the war, the American ministers were Isaac Christiancy in Peru and Thomas A. Osborn in Chile. The Garfield administration replaced these men in 1881 with Judson Kilpatrick in Santiago and Stephen Hurlbut in Lima. The deaths of both Kilpatrick and Hurlbut upset American diplomacy at the critical moment of the Trescot mission. Cornelius Logan was then assigned to Chile and James Partridge to Peru. Partridge was later recalled to be replaced in 1882 by Seth L. Phelps. Kiernan has commented that American diplomacy was "far too poorly equipped," while the British ministers were "adequate to their task." The British officials possessed greater diplomatic experience and more explicit standing instructions. Moreover, both Pakenham in Chile and Spenser St. John in Peru had competent deputies in Drummond-Hay and Alfred St. John. See Victor G. Kiernan, "Foreign Interests in the War of the Pacific," *Hispanic American Historical Review,* 35 (1955): 32.

73. See Salisbury to Spenser St. John, no. 14, April 14, 1879, F.O. 61/317; and minute by Salisbury, April 15, 1879, F.O. 16/201.

74. Spenser St. John to Salisbury, no. 49, April 23, 1879, F.O. 61/318.

75. Memorandum by Jervoise, April 24, 1879, F.O. 16/202.

76. The *Times,* October 10, 1879. In May 1879 Pauncefote argued "that it is almost worth making another attempt at pacification in the interests of British commerce which must suffer very much by a continuance of hostilities between such fiery and unscrupulous belligerents." See memorandum by Pauncefote, May 20, 1879, F.O. 16/201. The *Times* appeared, however, to be unaware of British attempts at mediation during 1879. Note also the comment of the *South American Journal,* June 24, 1880: "European nations are too much engrossed by their own political complications to trouble themselves much with what transpires in those distant countries."

77. Memorandum by Pauncefote, May 20, 1879, F.O. 16/201.

78. Thornton to Salisbury, no. 138, June 20, 1879, F.O. 5/1683. At the time Evarts had received a dispatch from the Department of the Navy reporting that "the war will soon die

of sheer inanition." Cited in Gary A. Pennannen, "The Foreign Policy of William M. Evarts" (Ph.D. diss., University of Wisconsin, 1968), p. 369. For the desultory character of the fighting in the early months of the war, see William F. Sater, "Chile During the First Months of the War of the Pacific," *Journal of Latin American Studies,* 5 (1973): 133–58.

79. Evarts is described as "impartial in thought and deed" by Pennannen, "Foreign Policy of Evarts," p. 364.

80. See Dennis, *Tacna and Arica,* pp. 92–93.

81. Spenser St. John to Salisbury, no. 107, August 5, 1879, F.O. 61/319.

82. Thornton to Salisbury, no. 202, September 29, 1879, F.O. 5/1683.

83. See minute on Spenser St. John to Salisbury, no. 147, October 7, 1879, F.O. 61/319.

84. Piérola had been acclaimed in Lima as the new dictator of Peru after the flight of President Prado in December 1879.

85. Spenser St. John to Granville, no. 62, June 14, 1880, F.O. 61/326.

86. See minute by Pauncefote on Barclay to Dilke, May 18, 1880, F.O. 61/330. James Barclay was M.P. for Forfarshire. It is interesting to note that the Foreign Office considered that British mediation might only prolong the war and that American mediation would have a better chance of success at this time. See memorandum on Armitstead to Dilke, May 20, 1880, ibid. Armitstead was M.P. for Dundee.

87. See memorandum by the Foreign Office librarian, Edward Hertslet, September 29, 1880, ibid.

88. Pakenham to Granville, no. 50, August 2, 1880, F.O. 16/207. Pauncefote minuted on July 16 that "the time for mediation has not arrived but is approaching." See minute on Spenser St. John to the foreign secretary, no. 58, June 7, 1880, F.O. 61/326. Pauncefote's opinion was prompted by news of decisive Chilean victories at Tacna and Arica. At about the same time, in early August 1880, the American ministers received their instructions to offer mediation. See Millington, *American Diplomacy and the War of the Pacific,* p. 69.

89. Spenser St. John to Granville, no. 80, September 13, 1880, F.O. 61/326.

90. Spenser St. John to the foreign secretary, no. 58, June 7, 1880, ibid. Although a sense of Anglo-American rivalry was present, Christiancy was on good terms with his British colleague. Note the comment of Christiancy's successor: "Mr. Christiancy was in the questionable habit of calling together the diplomatic corps and taking counsel on almost all questions, which practically emasculated the United States and deprived them of their proper leadership." See Hurlbut to Blaine, August 27, 1881, *Foreign Relations* (1881), p. 927.

91. Spenser St. John to Granville, no. 84, September 18, 1880, and no. 96, October 30, 1880, F.O. 61/326. The peace talks were held in October 1880 on board the U.S.S. *Lackawanna* and are generally referred to as the "Lackawanna conference." For an account of the conference see Millington, *American Diplomacy and the War of the Pacific,* pp. 69–79.

92. See his circular telegram, November 20, 1880, F.O. 61/330.

93. The Foreign Office was, however, concerned by reports of concessions granted to the United States by Peru in return for intervention favorable to the Peruvian cause. These reports had originated from the British consul general in New York and were passed on to London. In November 1880, it was reported that the "guano ring" had no official backing in the United States. Consequently, Pauncefote minuted that "this matter does not seem to call for any further action." See Spenser St. John to Granville, no. 1, January 1, 1881, F.O. 61/333; Drummond to Granville, no. 307, November 5, 1880, F.O. 5/1724.

94. See Kiernan, "Foreign Interests in the War of the Pacific," p. 21.

95. Circular to Paris, Berlin, and Rome, December 2, 1880. See also memorandum by Pauncefote, January 3, 1881, F.O. 16/206. The Chilean troops arrived outside Lima on January 12, 1881, and had captured the city by January 17.

96. With the result that Germany came to be regarded as a benefactor and friend of Chile. It was believed in Chile that Germany's attitude had prevented European intervention against Chile. See Frederick B. Pike, *Chile and the United States, 1880–1962* (Notre Dame: University of Notre Dame Press, 1963), pp. 47, 49.

97. As one writer has noted: "Those which thrust themselves forward, usually found England hanging back." See Kiernan, "Foreign Interests in the War of the Pacific," p. 21.

98. Memorandum by Pauncefote, June 14, 1887, F.O. 61/372. Grévy was president of France from 1879 to 1887 when he resigned as a result of a scandal concerning the sale of honors.

99. Blaine replaced Evarts in March 1881.

100. See Kiernan, "Foreign Interests in the War of the Pacific," p. 22; and Dennis, *Tacna and Arica,* pp. 157–58.

101. Blaine manifested a "rather intransigent attitude toward European chancelleries in general and the British Foreign Office in particular." See David S. Muzzey, *James G. Blaine* (New York: Dodd, Mead, 1934), p. 24.

102. These remarks were made before a congressional inquiry in 1882. Cited in Perry Belmont, *An American Democrat* (New York: Columbia University Press, 1940), pp. 258–60.

103. *New York Times,* January 30, 1882, cited in Russell H. Bastert, "A New Approach to the Origins of Blaine's Pan-American Policy," *Hispanic American Historical Review,* 39 (1959): 395.

104. West to Granville, no. 42, January 31, 1882, F.O. 5/1785. Lionel Sackville-West had replaced Edward Thornton as British minister in Washington in June 1881.

105. Thornton described his first official meetings with Blaine as "amiable and friendly" though he underlined that the secretary of state was also "impulsive" and "of rather a quick temper." See Paul Knaplund and Carolyn Clewes, eds., *Private Letters from the British Embassy in Washington to the Foreign Secretary Lord Granville, 1880–1885* (Washington, D.C.: American Historical Association, 1942), p. 121.

106. For a view stressing Blaine's pragmatic approach to Latin American affairs see Bastert, "Origins of Blaine's Pan-American Policy," p. 380.

107. Blaine to Morton, no. 30, September 5, 1881, *Foreign Relations* (1881), p. 427.

108. See Blaine to Hurlbut, June 15, 1881, ibid., pp. 914–15.

109. "One might search the whole list of Congress, Judiciary, and Executive during the twenty-five years 1870 to 1895," wrote Henry Adams, "and find little but damaged reputation." Cited in John A. Garraty, *The New Commonwealth, 1877–1890* (New York: Harper & Row, 1968), p. 2.

110. Mulligan had accused Blaine of using his official position as Speaker of the House to promote railroad interests. Blaine gained disputed possession of the letters alleging this and successfully defended himself in the House of Representatives.

111. A feud that split the Republicans into "stalwarts" (pro-Conkling) and "half-breeds" (pro-Blaine).

112. See Russell H. Bastert, "Diplomatic Reversal: Frelinghuysen's Opposition to Blaine's Pan-American Policy in 1882," *Mississippi Valley Historical Review,* 42 (1956): 653–71.

113. See Bastert, "Origins of Blaine's Pan-American Policy," p. 397. For an excellent summary of the three claims see David M. Pletcher, *The Awkward Years* (Columbia: University of Missouri Press, 1962), pp. 51–58.

114. In a dispatch to Hurlbut, August 4, 1881, Blaine insisted that even if Chile annexed the Peruvian territory in question, there must be adequate compensation made for the Landreau claim. See ibid., p. 54.

115. The claims "came close enough to Blaine's own hope for helping Peru that his

policy disastrously became identified in many minds with theirs." See Bastert, "Origins of Blaine's Pan-American Policy," p. 399.

116. Martínez to the Chilean Ministry of Foreign Affairs, October 26, 1881, cited in Pike, *Chile and the United States,* pp. 52–53.

117. Pletcher, *Awkward Years,* p. 50. He notes that Kilpatrick's wife was the niece of the archbishop of Santiago.

118. The *Nation,* November 24, 1881. Pletcher has described Hurlbut as "a minister completely unsuitable for the delicate assignment of persuasion and consolation." See *Awkward Years,* pp. 47, 58. Note also that Evarts had blocked all suggestions of appointing Hurlbut to diplomatic office during the Hayes administration; see Pennannen, "Foreign Policy of Evarts," p. 84.

119. Spenser St. John to Granville, no. 74, August 9, 1881, F.O. 61/334.

120. "He [Hurlbut] is denouncing the Government of Señor Piérola and supporting that of Señor Calderón, which may account for the marked desire shown by the Chileans to force the latter to resign." See Spenser St. John to Granville, no. 92, September 28, 1881, F.O. 61/334. García Calderón had replaced Piérola, who had fled to Europe after the fall of Lima in January 1881.

121. See Hurlbut to Blaine, no. 16, October 4, 1881, *Foreign Relations* (1881), pp. 935–37.

122. Hurlbut to Blaine, no. 26, November 9, 1881, ibid., pp. 947–48.

123. The *Times,* October 11, 1881, noted that Blaine had left Washington for Maine to rest. "He is broken down by the terrible siege of worry and physical unrest through which he has passed since the fatal 2d of July." Ibid.

124. Hurlbut to Blaine, no. 23, October 26, 1881, *Foreign Relations* (1881), pp. 942–44.

125. Spenser St. John to Granville, no. 104, November 9, 1881, F.O. 61/334.

126. Spenser St. John to Granville, no. 105, November 24, 1881, ibid. Hurlbut had acquired a concession to complete the construction of a railroad at Chimbote. He had also been offered Chimbote harbor for lease as a naval coaling station.

127. The *Nation,* November 17, 1881.

128. Drummond to Granville, October 22, 1881, F.O. 5/1755.

129. Blaine to Hurlbut, no. 19, November 22, 1881, *Foreign Relations* (1881), pp. 948–51.

130. "The Chilians," noted St. John, "are talking and writing freely of a prolonged occupation of Peru." Spenser St. John to Granville, no. 104, November 9, 1881, F.O. 61/334.

131. Spenser St. John to Granville, no. 105, November 24, 1881, ibid. The American railroad promoter, George E. Church, noted in early October that the Chileans were "now proud enough" to think of fighting the United States. See Church to Blaine, October 2, 1881, Records of the Department of State, RG 59, *Special Agents,* 30.

132. Spenser St. John to Granville, no. 105, November 24, 1881, F.O. 61/334.

133. This refers to the attempt of the House of Representatives to bring an end to the war in the Pacific between Spain and the west coast republics of Chile, Peru, Bolivia, and Ecuador.

134. See Blaine to Trescot, no. 2, December 1, 1881, *Foreign Relations* (1881), pp. 143–49. Various arguments have been put forward to explain the reasons for this move by Blaine. He justified his policy on the grounds that he was trying to arrange a settlement by honorable means and within purely American terms of reference. He also emphasized his desire for closer links between all the nations of the Western Hemisphere. See James G. Blaine, *Political Discussions* (Norwich, Conn.: Henry Bill, 1887), pp. 411–19. For the view that Blaine was attempting "a last and brilliant effort" to add achievement to his record as secretary of state see Bastert, "Origins of Blaine's Pan-American Policy," pp. 403–05.

135. Spenser St. John to Granville, no. 12, January 11, 1882, and no. 14, January 11, 1882, F.O. 61/339. In an earlier dispatch St. John predicted that, after the failure of the "Lackawanna conference," the prestige of the United States would greatly suffer should Trescot's mission also fail. See St. John to Granville, no. 6, January 4, 1882, ibid.

136. Frelinghuysen replaced Blaine on December 20, 1881.

137. Trescot to Frelinghuysen, no. 2, January 13, 1882, *Foreign Relations* (1882), pp. 58–59. Trescot later stated that his instructions from Blaine were to obtain "an amicable settlement" of the war, to prepare the way for the forthcoming Washington peace conference, and to "establish such relations between the republics of the two Americas, as would prevent the possibility of future war." Trescot to Blaine, July 17, 1882, Library of Congress, Blaine Papers.

138. See Bastert, "Diplomatic Reversal," pp. 660–61.

139. Frelinghuysen to Trescot, no. 6, January 9, 1882, *Foreign Relations* (1882), p. 57.

140. Bastert, "Origins of Blaine's Pan-American Policy," p. 406.

141. See Pakenham to Granville, no. 6, January 18, 1882, F.O. 16/218. The mission was, however, not completely ignored. Trescot had a number of interviews with the foreign minister, Balmaceda, and with tacit Chilean support Trescot traveled to Peru for discussions with various Peruvian leaders, including Montero.

142. Spenser St. John to Granville, no. 20, February 8, 1882, and no. 26, March 26, 1882, F.O. 61/339. See also West to Granville, no. 133, March 26, 1882, F.O. 5/1786.

143. St. John's request for leave was granted.

144. Graham to Granville, no. 39, May 15, 1882, F.O. 61/339. After conversations with the Chilean minister in Washington, Lionel West also confirmed that the Chileans appeared to be reconciled to an indefinite occupation of Peru. See West to Granville, no. 261, June 24, 1882, F.O. 5/1787.

145. For example, see the letter from a London barrister, Edward Pollard, to Pauncefote, August 18, 1882, F.O. 61/343.

146. Memorandum by Pauncefote, August 18, 1882, F.O. 61/343.

147. Drummond-Hay to Pauncefote, private, August 30, 1882, F.O. 16/219; Graham to Granville, no. 68, August 30, 1882, F.O. 61/340. Admiral Patricio Lynch was the commander of the Chilean occupational forces in Peru.

148. Spenser St. John to Pauncefote, October 11, 1882, F.O. 61/340.

149. Graham to Granville, October 18, 1882, ibid. This was confirmed by his successor, Alfred St. John, who described the situation as "complete anarchy" and wrote that even a temporary union of the various rival factions "appears altogether hopeless." Alfred St. John to Granville, no. 85, October 25, 1882, ibid. Alfred St. John was a nephew of Spenser St. John.

150. Drummond-Hay to Granville, no. 82, September 25, no. 83, October 7, no. 84, October 8, no. 94, December 5, 1882, F.O. 16/219. On Logan's mediation see Millington, *American Diplomacy and the War of the Pacific,* pp. 128–37. Dennis has described Logan as "merely a messenger in the dismemberment of Peru instead of her moral defender." See Dennis, *Tacna and Arica,* p. 178. The days of active American diplomacy had ended.

151. Alfred St. John to Granville, no. 1, January 3, 1883, F.O. 61/346.

152. Spenser St. John to Pauncefote, January 23, 1883, ibid.

153. Alfred St. John to Granville, no. 3, January 13, 1883, ibid.

154. He added that "it is highly improbable that the American Diplomatists on this coast will now keep in the background, in spite of the uselessness of their endeavours to induce the belligerents to come to terms." See Alfred St. John to Granville, January 23, 1883, ibid.

155. Frelinghuysen granted Partridge the term of leave that the minister had previously requested. See Dennis, *Tacna and Arica,* pp. 182–83.

156. Alfred St. John to Granville, no. 24, February 28, 1883, F.O. 61/346. The British

chargé regretted the recall of Partridge, whom he considered to be "very popular." In contrast to British opinions of the other American ministers, there was no trace of rivalry or dislike in St. John's comment on Partridge: "In laying himself open to blame for having departed from the traditional policy of his country, he was only moved by an earnest desire to help in averting the utter ruin of this country." See Alfred St. John to Granville, no. 31, March 21, 1883, ibid.

157. Alfred St. John to Granville, no. 56, July 3, and no. 60, July 13, 1883, F.O. 61/347.

158. Memorandum by West to Granville, April 8, 1883, F.O. 5/1831.

159. Alfred St. John had noted in January 1883 that the Chileans were giving Iglesias "their support in a secret but very effective manner." Alfred St. John to Granville, no. 5, January 22, 1883, F.O. 61/346.

160. Frelinghuysen to Phelps, no. 6, July 26, 1883, *Foreign Relations* (1883), pp. 709–11.

161. Alfred St. John to Granville, no. 86, September 13, 1883, F.O. 61/347.

162. Although the treaty had still to be ratified by the respective legislatures.

163. Alfred St. John to Granville, no. 115, November 3, 1883, F.O. 61/347.

164. See memorandum by Jervoise, December 13, 1883, and by Currie, December 14, 1883, F.O. 61/345.

165. Known as the Treaty of Ancón.

166. Mansfield to the foreign secretary, no. 68, September 16, and no. 72, October 1, 1885, F.O. 61/360. Mansfield's attitude provides a striking contrast to that taken up earlier in Peru by Hurlbut.

167. The *Times*, February 1, 1882.

168. Before the war, the payment on the Peruvian debt had been guaranteed by revenues on the nitrate lands in southern Peru. See Robert G. Greenhill and Rory M. Miller, "The Peruvian Government and the Nitrate Trade, 1873–1879," *Journal of Latin American Studies*, 5 (1973): 107–31.

169. European diplomats might have had in mind the recent precedent of the transfer of Alsace-Lorraine from France to Germany in 1871.

170. Memorandum by Pauncefote, June 22, 1883, F.O. 61/351.

171. See Pauncefote to the law officers of the crown, January 22, 1884; law officers of the crown to Pauncefote, February 2, 1884, F.O. 61/357. The protests were to be made prior to the ratification of the Treaty of Ancón scheduled for March 1884.

172. Pauncefote summed up: "We are not supporting the claims of the Bondholders qua Bondholders. We are supporting a principle applicable to all cases of cession of territory, namely that private rights should be respected." Pauncefote to Granville, April 2, 1884, ibid.

173. The intervention would be directed against Chile rather than against Peru. It was believed that it was the Chileans who were responsible for the intransigence shown by Iglesias.

174. See minute by Pauncefote on Waddington to Granville, April 8, 1884, F.O. 61/357. Waddington was the French ambassador in London.

175. Memorandum by Pauncefote, August 30, 1887, F.O. 61/372.

176. See D. C. M. Platt, *Finance, Trade, and Politics in British Foreign Policy 1815–1914* (Oxford: Clarendon Press, 1968), pp. 336–39.

177. The *Times*, February 1, 1882.

178. *New York World*, December 5, 1881.

179. As one historian has noted: "Few of the wider consequences of the war could have been foreseen when it began." See Kiernan, "Foreign Interests in the War of the Pacific," pp. 35–36.

180. Although Anglo-American rivalry was strongly in evidence in Lima, especially during Hurlbut's tenure of office. See Pletcher, *Awkward Years*, p. 49, note 22.

Chapter 4: The Isthmian Canal

1. From a speech delivered in New York on February 23, 1869, cited in G. E. Baker, ed., *The Works of William H. Seward*, 5 vols. (Boston: Houghton Mifflin, 1884), 5: 590. Seward also believed that the canal must be an American enterprise. "Time will sooner or later satisfy the Colombian government," he predicted, "that the Darien canal must be an American work and can in no case become a distant enterprize." Seward to Sullivan, no. 57, September 17, 1868, Records of the Department of State, RG 59, *Colombia,* Instructions, 16. Peter Sullivan was the American minister in Bogotá.

2. See Charles R. Williams, ed., *Diary and Letters of Rutherford Birchard Hayes*, 5 vols. (Columbus: Ohio State Archaeological and Historical Society, 1922–1926), 3: 586.

3. Kirk H. Porter and Donald B. Johnson, comps., *National Party Platforms, 1840–1964* (Urbana: University of Illinois Press, 1966), p. 108.

4. Nineteenth-century canal projects involved numerous promoters, routes, and governments. Ultimately, the United States government chose the Panama route. Construction work began in 1904 and the Panama canal was eventually completed and opened in 1914.

5. For a general survey of canal projects see Gerstle Mack, *The Land Divided* (New York: Knopf, 1944); and Miles Du Val, *From Cadiz to Cathay* (Palo Alto: Stanford University Press, 1947). See also E. Taylor Parks, *Colombia and the United States, 1765–1934* (Durham: Duke University Press, 1935), chapter 11.

6. New Granada was renamed the United States of Colombia in 1863 and shall be referred to as *Colombia* here.

7. This undertaking was described as the guarantee of the "neutrality" of the isthmus and after the opening of the Panama railroad in 1855 involved the United States in at least ten military interventions during the second half of the nineteenth century. See Parks, *Colombia and the United States,* chapters 13–15.

8. The treaty was negotiated at a time when a Nicaraguan canal project appeared likely. Article 1 stipulated that neither power "will ever obtain or maintain for itself any exclusive control over the said Ship Canal," nor seek to obtain "any rights or advantages in regard to commerce or navigation through the said canal, which shall not be offered, on the same terms, to the subjects or citizens of the other." Article 8 added that the terms of the treaty extended to "any other practicable communications, whether by canal or railway, across the isthmus which connects North and South America." See Mary W. Williams, *Anglo-American Isthmian Diplomacy, 1815–1915* (Washington, D.C.: American Historical Association, 1916).

9. The term *American* will be used here to refer to a policy in which the United States government sought to involve itself directly in the construction, funding, operation, and ownership of the canal project.

10. See Rolt Hammond and C. J. Lewin, *The Panama Canal* (London: F. Muller, 1966), chapters 2–3. The authors have argued that the scheme proposed by Godin de Lépinay in 1879 had a much greater chance of success. Ibid., pp. 29–31.

11. Bunch to Clarendon, no. 4, January 14, 1870, F.O. 55/249. Robert Bunch served as British chargé d'affaires in Colombia from 1866 to 1872 and as minister from 1872 to 1878. The American minister referred to was Stephen Hurlbut.

12. Bunch to Stanley, private, November 3, 1868, F.O. 55/248. Bunch was referring to Peter Sullivan, who failed to negotiate the treaty.

13. See Jackson Crowell, "The United States and a Central American Canal, 1869–1877," *Hispanic American Historical Review,* 49 (1969); pp. 42ff. On the 1884 negotiations see David M. Pletcher, *The Awkward Years* (Columbia: University of Missouri Press, 1962), chapter 15. The 1884 treaty proposed a loan of $4 million to Nicaragua. See ibid., p. 278.

14. Thornton to Stanley, no. 70, December 14, 1868, F.O. 55/248. Seward was referring to Peter Sullivan.

15. Thornton to Salisbury, no. 68, March 24, 1879, F.O. 5/1681.

16. See Mansfield to the foreign secretary, no. 15, August 4, 1879, F.O. 55/271 and no. 13, April 5, 1880, F.O. 55/273. Relations became so strained between the United States and Colombia that there was no Colombian representation at Washington from February 1881 to October 1884 although an American minister arrived at Bogotá to replace Dichman in September 1881.

17. For example, the accession of General Santos Gutiérrez to the Colombian presidency in April 1868 disrupted the canal negotiations then in progress. See Bunch to Stanley, no. 57, November 2, 1868, F.O. 55/248. The problem of Central American union and the various boundary disputes between the countries of Central America also affected negotiations at certain times. See Crowell, "The United States and a Central American Canal," p. 33; and J. Fred Rippy, "Justo Rufino Barrios and the Nicaraguan Canal," *Hispanic American Historical Review,* 20 (1940): 190–97.

18. Seward to Burton, no. 134, November 9, 1869, RG 59, *Colombia,* Instructions, 16.

19. This occurred in 1869, 1870, 1876, and 1879. The British attitude toward the treaty did not change until 1899, and ultimately the Hay-Pauncefote Treaty of 1901 abrogated the 1850 agreement.

20. For Grant's views see Crowell, "The United States and a Central American Canal," p. 50.

21. Evarts appeared pessimistic that the Panama canal would even be started. See Thornton to Salisbury, no. 169, July 21, 1879, F.O. 5/1683.

22. For the Republican platform see Porter and Johnson, *National Party Platforms,* p. 82.

23. See Dexter Perkins, *The Monroe Doctrine, 1867–1907* (Baltimore: Johns Hopkins Press, 1937), chapter 2.

24. The *Nation,* January 12, 1882.

25. Bayard to Senator Gray, April 28, 1894, cited in Charles C. Tansill, *The Foreign Policy of Thomas F. Bayard, 1885–1897* (New York: Fordham University Press, 1940), p. 680.

26. Ibid.

27. Pletcher, *Awkward Years,* pp. 275–76. See also West to Granville, July 15, 1884, F.O. 55/320.

28. A treaty with Nicaragua signed in 1860 added to British rights in this respect.

29. The *Times,* April 7, 1885.

30. Reports from British officials in Bogotá generally described Colombia as "miserably poor." See Bunch to Stanley, no. 6, February 4, 1868, F.O. 55/204A. On Colombian economic development in general see Frank Safford, "Foreign and National Enterprise in Nineteenth-Century Colombia," *Business History Review,* 39 (1965): 503–26; and William P. McGreevey, *An Economic History of Colombia, 1845–1930* (Cambridge, Eng.: Cambridge University Press, 1971).

31. Rippy's figures of British total nominal investment in Latin America for 1890 show that only £12 million was invested in the Central American area—around 3 percent of total investment. See J. Fred Rippy, *British Investments in Latin America, 1822–1949* (Minneapolis: University of Minnesota Press, 1959), p. 37.

32. Memoranda by Jervoise and Pauncefote, February 15, 1884, F.O. 55/307. American ministers serving in Colombia frequently expressed similar views. For example, Allan Burton noted in 1866 that "law is a dead letter, and the strongest ties of society, are the sympathies arising from degradation and crime on the one hand, and misfortune and oppression on the other." Burton to Seward, no. 197, November 3, 1865, RG 59, *Colom-*

bia, Dispatches, 21. Ernest Dichman commented that the "normal state" of Colombia was either "civil war" or "armed peace." Dichman to Evarts, no. 118, August 1, 1879, RG 59, *Colombia,* Dispatches, 33.

33. Hammond to Bunch, April 30, 1867, F.O. 55/195.

34. The foreign secretary, Kimberley, added: "These affairs are always of the same sort; and the difficulty of dealing with these wretched Republics is very great." See minutes on Jenner to Kimberley, no. 6, March 12, 1894, F.O. 55/362. George Jenner was British minister in Colombia from 1892 to 1897.

35. Memorandum, July 12, 1875, F.O. 55/234. Bunch had joined his American colleague, William L. Scruggs, in making joint representations to the Colombian president.

36. Although Britain did intervene by force at Corinto in 1895 to protect the Mosquito Indians in their dispute with the government of Nicaragua.

37. F.O. to Bunch, January 1, 1867, F.O. 55/195. The following paragraph was prepared, but then deleted from the final draft of the dispatch: "Her Majesty's Government, are prepared to support this view of the subject by force if necessary; but they trust that the Colombian Government on reconsideration will not compel them to have recourse to measures of a forcible character towards a Country with which it is their sincere desire to maintain the most friendly relations."

38. For concern over the attitude of the United States see memorandum by Bergne, February 12, 1867, F.O. 55/201. The postal decree was suspended after a protest by the United States government, and the whole issue was "set at rest" by the outbreak of civil war in 1867. Henry Bergne was chief clerk of the Treaty Department. See Bunch to Stanley, no. 40, April 8, 1867, F.O. 55/197A.

39. Hammond to Bunch, April 30, 1867, F.O. 55/195.

40. These disturbances took the form of anti-American rioting and represented a local reaction to the much more visible American presence on the isthmus resulting from the opening of the Panama railroad in 1855.

41. If Britain gave the required guarantee and if Colombia became involved in war with the United States, then Britain would have to join the war on the Colombian side. See memoranda June 21 and July 29, 1865, F.O. 55/194. On the Panama riot of 1856 see Parks, *Colombia and the United States,* pp. 221–24, 288–302. Foreign Office officials were also aware that their refusal to give a guarantee enhanced the importance of the 1846 treaty. Nonetheless, when approached by the Colombian government in 1887, they advised against Colombian abrogation of that treaty. See Dickson to Salisbury, no. 47, August 2, 1887, and memorandum by Hertslet, September 23, 1887, F.O. 55/336. William Dickson was British minister in Colombia from 1885 to 1892.

42. See memorandum dated November 17, 1868, F.O. 55/248. Cullen seemed more persuasive to Seward; see Ernest N. Paolino, *The Foundations of the American Empire* (Ithaca: Cornell University Press, 1973), p. 130.

43. Memorandum by Pauncefote, August 17, 1886, F.O. 55/336.

44. See minute on Knight to Currie, January 8, 1892, and memorandum by Sanderson, December 6, 1892, F.O. 55/356. Knight was a canal promoter who was attempting to interest the Foreign Office in supporting his project.

45. West to Granville, no. 94, March 2, 1885, F.O. 55/320.

46. Memoranda by Villiers, January 10 and 17, 1895, F.O. 55/385. The matter under discussion was the progress of the Nicaraguan canal bill in the United States Senate.

47. Memorandum by Sanderson, May 22, 1889, F.O. 55/346. The "pressing question" was possibly the Bering Sea arbitration, or perhaps Britain's involvement in the Suez canal question, which made the Foreign Office reluctant to enter into public discussion of canal issues during the 1880s.

48. F.O. to Thornton, no. 156, April 29, 1870, F.O. 55/249.

49. See Paolino, *Foundations of the American Empire,* pp. 128–29; and Perkins, *Monroe Doctrine, 1867–1907,* p. 66.

50. Paolino, *Foundations of the American Empire,* p. 142.

51. The 1846 treaty expired in June 1868 although the terms remained in force until either party gave twelve months notice of termination. The rumors that Colombia would terminate the treaty proved unfounded. The Panama railroad successfully renegotiated its contract in 1867.

52. See Burton to Seward, no. 250, July 1, 1866, RG 59, *Colombia,* Dispatches, 22.

53. See Parks, *Colombia and the United States,* p. 340.

54. Ibid., pp. 341–44.

55. Paolino, *Foundations of the American Empire,* pp. 129–32. Seward did, however, envisage that the project would require the assistance of "capitalists of all countries" and not only those of the United States. See Seward to Sullivan, no. 57, September 17, 1868, RG 59, *Colombia,* Instructions, 16.

56. Bunch to Stanley, no. 2, January 16, 1869, F.O. 55/248. Cushing had served as attorney general from 1853 to 1857 and had been given various special missions to China in 1844 and to Mexico in 1847.

57. In the sense that the United States granted terms to Colombia that had been rejected in the previous months of negotiation. See Parks, *Colombia and the United States,* pp. 345–46.

58. This was a period in which "the anti-expansionists . . . defeated every annexationist project of the Johnson administration except the purchase of Alaska." See Donald M. Dozer, "Anti-Expansionism During the Johnson Administration," *Pacific Historical Review,* 12 (1943): 275.

59. Bunch to Hammond, private, February 17, 1869, F.O. 55/248.

60. "In plain words, if his [Hurlbut's] own account is to be depended upon," reported Bunch, "he must have threatened the Colombians with the loss of the Isthmus if they do not accede to his terms whatever they may be." Bunch to Clarendon, no. 4, January 14, 1870, F.O. 55/249.

61. With the exception of an added provision giving United States warships free use of the canal at all times. See Parks, *Colombia and the United States,* p. 348.

62. Bunch to Clarendon, no. 46, May 16, 1870, F.O. 55/249. The amendment undermined the special role of the United States in isthmian affairs resulting from the 1846 treaty.

63. Thornton to Granville, no. 169, September 12, 1870, ibid. See also Parks, *Colombia and the United States,* p. 350.

64. Burton to Seward, no. 250, July 1, 1866, RG 59, *Colombia,* Dispatches, 22; Sullivan to the secretary of state, no. 119, March 15, 1869, ibid., 27.

65. With the exception of Bunch's statement approved by the Foreign Office in December 1868. See below, note 71.

66. Official dispatches took from six to eight weeks to reach their destination.

67. See Parks, *Colombia and the United States,* p. 342; Bunch to Stanley, no. 41, August 14, 1868, F.O. 55/248.

68. Ibid.

69. See minute on Bunch to Stanley, no. 3, January 16, 1869, ibid. It was also noted that a British protest would make the United States more favorable to the treaty.

70. Memorandum by Bergne, August 14, 1870, F.O. 55/249. The foreign secretary, Lord Granville, minuted that it was "unnecessary to do anything on the subject at present."

71. Bunch to Stanley, no. 57, November 2, 1868; F.O. to Bunch, no. 47, December 30, 1868, F.O. 55/248.

72. See Stanley to Lyons, no. 62, October 14, 1868, ibid.

73. Thornton to Clarendon, no. 16, January 18, 1869, ibid.
74. F.O. to Torres Caicedo, January 27, 1869, ibid.
75. F.O. to Thornton, January 30, 1869, ibid.
76. F.O. to Lyons, no. 127, January 30, 1869; Lyons to Clarendon, no. 168, February 9, 1869, ibid.
77. Bunch to Clarendon, no. 7, January 29, 1870, F.O. 55/249.
78. F.O. to Thornton, February 26, 1870, ibid.
79. See Lyons to Clarendon, no. 220, March 14, 1870, ibid.
80. Memoranda by Bergne, April 1 and 22, 1870, ibid. On April 22 he noted that, in contrast to the efficiently operated American railroad company, "all the trouble Her Majesty's Government had with regard to the conveyance of mails across the Isthmus arose from the proceedings of the Colombian Government." Ibid.
81. Rear Admiral Daniel Ammen was a personal friend of President Grant and became one of the most prominent enthusiasts of the Nicaraguan route in the late 1870s and 1880s.
82. Bunch to Granville, no. 70, September 9, 1870, F.O. 55/249.
83. Bunch to Granville, no. 39, July 4, 1871, F.O. 55/250. This was a reference to the surveys of the Darien isthmus carried out by Commander Thomas Selfridge.
84. Thornton to Granville, no. 169, September 12, 1870, F.O. 55/249.
85. See O'Leary to Granville, no. 30, July 1, 1873, F.O. 55/256. Charles O'Leary held various British consular offices in Bogotá from 1864 to 1878. Hurlbut's successor, William L. Scruggs, was instructed by Fish to avoid discussion of the canal question. See Scruggs to Fish, no. 74, November 17, 1874, RG 59, *Colombia,* Dispatches, 29.
86. For these approaches to Fish see Parks, *Colombia and the United States,* pp. 352–54; and Crowell, "The United States and a Central American Canal," pp. 32–33.
87. The American-owned steamer *Montijo* had been seized by Colombian rebels in 1871. See Fish to Hurlbut, no. 55, December 19, 1871, RG 59, *Colombia,* Instructions, 16.
88. F.O. to O'Leary, no. 5, April 25, 1873, F.O. 55/226.
89. See Thornton to Granville, no. 128, April 6, 1874, and Mallet to the foreign secretary, no. 27, December 21, 1875, F.O. 55/250. Mallet was the British consul at Panama.
90. See Crowell, "The United States and a Central American Canal," p. 32.
91. Ibid., p. 39. The route selected also adjoined Costa Rican territory and would involve negotiations with that government.
92. See Thornton to the foreign secretary, Lord Derby, no. 86, March 27, 1876, F.O. 55/250.
93. Memorandum on ibid.
94. See Crowell, "The United States and a Central American Canal," p. 50.
95. For a survey of American press opinion see ibid., p. 36.
96. "Desultory negotiations" were begun with Nicaragua; see Pletcher, *Awkward Years,* p. 8. See also Kenneth J. Hagan, *American Gunboat Diplomacy and the Old Navy, 1877–1889* (Westport: Greenwood Press, 1973), p. 151.
97. His diplomatic exploits and especially his successful efforts to bring about the completion of the Suez canal in 1869 made Ferdinand de Lesseps (1805–1894) one of the most celebrated French personalities of the nineteenth century. It should be noted that his experience was in diplomacy and administration and that he had no qualifications in engineering.
98. See Parks, *Colombia and the United States,* pp. 356–58.
99. Aniceto G. Menocal, a civil engineer from the U.S. Navy, was a close associate of Admiral Ammen and became involved in a number of surveys of the isthmus. These convinced him of the superiority of the Nicaraguan route over all others.
100. To be known as the Universal Interoceanic Panama Canal Company.
101. See Thornton to Salisbury, no. 156, July 7, 1879, F.O. 5/1683.

102. *New York Herald*, July 3, 1879. For a similar view see the *Nation*, July 31, 1879, and for a general survey of the American attitude at this time see Perkins, *Monroe Doctrine, 1867–1907*, pp. 69–74.

103. See the editor's preface to Aniceto G. Menocal, "Intrigues at the Paris Canal Congress," *North American Review*, 129 (1879): 289. The idea of an isthmian canal had long been a dream of the former French emperor, Louis Napoleon.

104. Evarts to Dichman, no. 57, July 9, 1879, RG 59, *Colombia*, Instructions, 17.

105. See Thornton to Salisbury, no. 36, February 2, 1880, F.O. 5/1720.

106. Thornton to Salisbury, no. 177, August 11, 1879, F.O. 5/1683.

107. See James D. Richardson, ed., *A Compilation of the Messages and Papers of the Presidents, 1789–1897*, 10 vols., (Washington, D.C.: GPO, 1896–1899), 7: 569.

108. Thornton to Salisbury, no. 36, February 2, 1880, F.O. 5/1720, and no. 45, February 16, 1880, F.O. 55/281.

109. Williams, *Diary and Letters of Hayes*, 3: 587–89. On February 7, 1880, Hayes noted: "The most important subject now under consideration is as to the canal across the isthmus." Ibid., p. 586.

110. The Maritime Canal Company of Nicaragua, in which Admiral Ammen and Captain Seth Phelps played a leading role. Phelps undertook a special mission to Nicaragua in 1882; see RG 59, *Special Agents*, Dispatches, 32.

111. The *Times*, March 20, 1880.

112. The American minister, Ernest Dichman, sailed to Colombia in May 1880 on board the U.S. warship *Tennessee*. Thornton suggested a "demonstration of force" was intended. See Thornton to Salisbury, no. 132, April 26, 1880, F.O. 5/1721.

113. Dichman to Evarts, no. 183, July 3, 1880, RG 59, *Colombia*, Dispatches, 34. Note also that Hayes's message to Congress had aroused anti-Americanism in Colombia. See Gary A. Pennannen, "The Foreign Policy of William M. Evarts," (Ph.D. diss., University of Wisconsin, 1968), pp. 345, 353.

114. Negotiations were begun in January 1881 and then broken off. Trescot rushed to New York and negotiated the protocol with Santo Domingo Vila just before the minister set off for Colombia. See Parks, *Colombia and the United States*, pp. 366–68.

115. See Evarts to Dichman, no. 153, February 18, 1881, RG 59, *Colombia*, Instructions, 17. The protocol is usually referred to as the Santo Domingo–Trescot Protocol.

116. The protocol was negotiated in February 1881, and the Colombian reply was not known until May. The Hayes administration had of course already left office by then.

117. Parks, *Colombia and the United States*, pp. 368–69. See also Dichman to Blaine, no. 268, May 6, 1881, RG 59, *Colombia*, Dispatches, 35.

118. Evarts had been a founder of the Isthmus Canal Company in September 1868. See Paolino, *Foundations of the American Empire*, p. 132.

119. See Thornton to Salisbury, no. 169, July 21, 1879, F.O. 5/1683, and no. 45, February 16, 1880, F.O. 55/281. As early as July 1879 the *Times* reported that "strong business influences, including the Pacific Railroads, are being exerted against the French scheme." See the *Times*, July 11, 1879. On Evarts's diplomatic caution see Chester L. Barrows, *William M. Evarts* (Chapel Hill: University of North Carolina Press, 1941), p. 346.

120. See the *Nation*, July 31, 1879.

121. The *Times*, March 20, 1880.

122. Parks, *Colombia and the United States*, p. 363. See also George Edgar-Bonnet, *Ferdinand de Lesseps* (Paris: Librairie Plon, 1959), pp. 140–63.

123. See Thornton to Granville, private, December 14, 1880, Granville Papers, Public Record Office, 30/29/154.

124. Ferdinand de Lesseps, "The Interoceanic Canal," *North American Review*, 130 (1880): 8.

125. The Nicaragua scheme was advocated by Ammen and Phelps of the Maritime Canal Company of Nicaragua. The "ship-railway" was proposed by James B. Eads, who had successfully constructed a similar project involving the Mississippi River. See Pletcher, *Awkward Years,* p. 24.

126. Ibid., pp. 24–28. A route by way of Darien was also considered. This was advocated by Commander Selfridge, who had surveyed the isthmus in 1870 and 1873. See Hagan, *American Gunboat Diplomacy,* pp. 145–46.

127. Stokes to Salisbury, May 19, 1879, F.O. 55/271. Lord Derby had expressed little confidence in the Gogorza project in 1876. See minute on Bunch to Derby, no. 38, May 1, 1876, F.O. 55/250.

128. Thornton to Salisbury, no. 169, July 21, 1879, F.O. 5/1683.

129. See Mansfield to the foreign secretary, no. 50, August 4, 1879, F.O. 55/271.

130. This was caused by the return of ex-prime minister William Gladstone to active politics in late 1879 and the ensuing general election of April 1880, which resulted in victory for the Liberals over the Conservatives.

131. On this see Ronald Robinson, John Gallagher, and Alice Denny, *Africa and the Victorians* (London: Macmillan, 1961), chapter 4.

132. Thornton to Salisbury, no. 132, April 26, 1880, F.O. 5/1721; and memorandum by Hertslet, May 20, 1880, F.O. 55/281.

133. Cited in Richardson, *Messages and Papers,* 8: 11.

134. Memorandum by Pauncefote, May 9, 1881, F.O. 55/281.

135. Memorandum by Pauncefote, July 4, 1881, ibid. The Colombian minister had specifically renewed his request for a British guarantee in June 1881. See memorandum by Pauncefote, June 10, 1881, ibid.

136. Granville to Lyons, July 5, 1881, ibid.

137. Granville to Paget, July 5, 1881, ibid. Paget was the British ambassador in Italy.

138. Dichman to Blaine, no. 269, May 9, 1881, RG 59, *Colombia,* Dispatches, 35.

139. See Blaine to Lowell, no. 187, June 24, 1881, *Foreign Relations [of the United States]* (1881), pp. 537–40. Lowell was the American minister in Britain.

140. Granville to Adams, no. 775b, August 10, 1881, F.O. 55/282.

141. Law officers of the crown to Granville, August 15, 1881, ibid.

142. See the circular by Granville, no. 399, September 23, 1881, ibid.

143. Granville to Mounsey, November 10, 1881, ibid.

144. Granville to Hoppin, November 10, 1881, ibid.

145. See West to Granville, December 14, 1881, ibid.; and Blaine to Lowell, November 19 and 29, 1881, *Foreign Relations* (1881), pp. 554–59, 563–69.

146. The *Economist,* December 24, 1881.

147. See West to Granville, no. 353, December 8, 1881, and no. 377, December 19, 1881, F.O. 55/282.

148. Memorandum by Hertslet, December 30, 1881, ibid. According to Hertslet, if the 1850 treaty had not been made, then Britain would not have given up the Bay Islands and would not have withdrawn its influence from other parts of South America. "Under these circumstances," argued Hertslet, "it would be manifestly unjust for the United States Government to demand officially that the Clayton-Bulwer Treaty should be abrogated." Ibid.

149. Granville to West, January 7, 1882, F.O. 55/290. The idea of an international convention was taken from a proposal made by Fish in February 1877 after the breakdown of his discussions with Nicaragua.

150. West to Granville, no. 19, January 17, 1882, ibid.

151. West to Granville, no. 73, February 19, 1882, ibid.

152. Frelinghuysen to Lowell, May 8, 1882, *Foreign Relations* (1882), pp. 271–83.

153. Law officers of the crown to Granville, received August 30, 1882; Granville to

West, December 30, 1882, F.O. 55/291.

154. Memorandum by Hertslet, June 22, 1883, F.O. 55/299; Granville to West, August 17, 1883, ibid. See also Frelinghuysen to Lowell, May 5 and November 22, 1883, *Foreign Relations* (1883), pp. 418–21, 529–32. "Since neither side had retreated," Pletcher has commented, "*status quo* carried the day, but alas, in this case after two full years of argument a return to *status quo* meant a British victory." See Pletcher, *Awkward Years*, p. 105. A sound examination of the whole debate is contained in Ella P. Levett, "Negotiations for Release from the Inter-Oceanic Obligations of the Clayton-Bulwer Treaty" (Ph.D. diss., University of Chicago, 1941).

155. Blaine apprised the British minister of his views; see West to Granville, no. 421, December 5, 1882, F.O. 55/291.

156. By way of the banking company of Grant and Ward, Grant became heavily involved in the Nicaraguan scheme. He also was active in the company's general lobbying activities. For example, see Grant's article, "The Nicaragua Canal," *North American Review*, 132 (1881): 107–16.

157. See the *Nation*, January 19 and February 16, 1882. An Admiralty report dated November 29, 1883, stated that the canal would not be completed in the century. See F.O. 55/320.

158. West to Granville, no. 78, March 11, 1883, and no. 340, November 2, 1883, F.O. 55/299; and no. 189, June 11, 1884, F.O. 55/320. On the negotiation of the treaty, usually referred to as the Frelinghuysen-Zavala Treaty, see Pletcher, *Awkward Years*, pp. 112–15, 270–83.

159. In contrast to the treaties of 1869 and 1870, the 1884 treaty did come to a vote and received a majority in its favor albeit an insufficient one for ratification.

160. He informed West that the treaty would not pass the Senate. See West to Granville, no. 373, December 26, 1884, F.O. 55/320.

161. West to Granville, no. 11, January 12, 1885, and no. 61, February 3, 1885, ibid. See also Pletcher, *Awkward Years*, p. 331; and Tansill, *Foreign Policy of Bayard*, p. 676.

162. West to Granville, July 15, 1884, F.O. 55/320.

163. *New York Sun*, December 3, 1884.

164. Pletcher, *Awkward Years*, pp. 282–83.

165. *New York Times*, December 17, 1884. See also Pletcher, *Awkward Years*, pp. 330–31; and Tansill, *Foreign Policy of Bayard*, p. 676.

166. West to Granville, no. 94, March 2, 1885, F.O. 55/320. The Foreign Office declined to take any action because most of the information received about the Nicaraguan treaty was in newspaper form rather than in official communications from the State Department. Unless an official request to abrogate the treaty was made by the United States government, the Foreign Office considered the Clayton-Bulwer Treaty to be in force.

167. Bayard to Stevens, August 25, 1885, cited in Tansill, *Foreign Policy of Bayard*, p. 676.

168. Scruggs to Bayard, no. 203, April 23, 1885, RG 59, *Colombia*, Dispatches, 39.

169. Scruggs's dispatches were filed and remained unanswered. See Parks, *Colombia and the United States*, p. 376.

170. Most of the claims arose from the burning of the city of Colón by the rebels. Bayard defended his policy toward the claims on the grounds that "as a general rule of international law a government is not responsible for the consequences of acts of rebellion against its authority." Ibid., pp. 310, 376.

171. O'Leary to the foreign secretary, no. 60, August 24, 1885, F.O. 55/311. On the Cerruti incident see Raimundo Rivas, *Historia diplomática de Colombia 1810–1934* (Bogotá: Imprenta Nacional, 1961), pp. 554–59.

172. See Tansill, *Foreign Policy of Bayard*, pp. 670–71.

173. Rosebery to Pauncefote, March 10, 1886, F.O. 55/336.

174. Memorandum by Hertslet, September 23, 1887; memorandum by Pauncefote, August 17, 1886; and St. John to Rosebery, no. 52, June 10, 1886, ibid. See also Dickson to Salisbury, no. 47, August 2, 1887, F.O. 55/330.

175. West to Salisbury, no. 374, December 20, 1887, F.O. 55/336, and no. 15, January 13, 1888, F.O. 55/346.

176. The concession of the Nicaraguan company headed by Ammen and Phelps had lapsed in 1884 because of its failure to begin actual construction work. Menocal secured a new concession in 1887 and reorganized the company as the Nicaragua Canal Construction Company. See Parks, *Colombia and the United States,* p. 379.

177. Usually referred to as "the Edmunds resolution" after its sponsor, Senator George F. Edmunds of Vermont.

178. The House did not, however, adopt the resolution. The Committee on Foreign Affairs reported the resolution favorably although a minority report was issued critical of the resolution. See 50th Congress, 2nd session, House report no. 4167.

179. The charter gave legal status to the company. Although this implied congressional approval and encouragement of the company, no financial support was involved.

180. Porter and Johnson, *National Party Platforms,* p. 82. See also Herbert to Salisbury, no. 375, December 21, 1888, F.O. 55/346.

181. The *Nation,* January 15, 1891.

182. Memorandum by Hertslet, May 19, 1889, F.O. 55/246. He also noted that should the United States abrogate the treaty, Britain would be justified in reverting to the status quo ante "but they would have great difficulty in enforcing that right, without entering into a conflict with the United States, which have shown recently a greater determination than ever to carry out the 'monroe doctrine' [*sic*]." Ibid.

183. Memorandum by Sanderson, March 31, 1893, F.O. 55/360.

184. Memoranda January 10 and January 17, 1895, F.O. 55/385.

185. Pauncefote to Kimberley, May 15, 1894, F.O. 55/365; Kimberley to Pauncefote, no. 12, January 16, 1895, F.O. 55/385.

186. *South American Journal,* May 26, 1894.

Chapter 5: Expansion and Reciprocity

1. Official diplomatic relations between Britain and Bolivia were suspended in 1853 and those with Mexico in 1867. On the renewal of relations between Britain and Mexico see Alfred Tischendorf, *Great Britain and Mexico in the Era of Porfirio Díaz* (Durham: Duke University Press, 1961), chapter 1; and Victor C. Dahl, "Business Influence in the Anglo-Mexican Reconciliation of 1884," *Inter-American Economic Affairs,* 15 (1961): 33–51. On the mission of Spenser St. John to Bolivia in 1875 see his report in F.O. 97/442. As late as 1892, Lord Rosebery was asserting that "we might as well send an ambassador to a volcano as a minister to Bolivia." See minute on memorandum, August 30, 1892, F.O. 11/32. A consular official was eventually sent to La Paz in 1903.

2. West to Granville, no. 91, February 28, 1885, F.O. 5/1902.

3. See James D. Richardson, ed., *A Compilation of the Messages and Papers of the Presidents, 1789–1897,* 10 vols. (Washington, D.C.: GPO, 1896–1899), 7: 77.

4. James G. Blaine, *Political Discussions* (Norwich, Conn.: Henry Bill, 1887), p. 411.

5. Merze Tate, *Hawaii* (East Lansing: Michigan State University Press, 1968), p. 117.

6. See the dispatches of Gustavus Goward, who visited Latin America as a special agent for the State Department in 1880–1881. "Although it is very proper and useful for consuls to give commercial information," he noted, "yet it is somewhat doubtful if their knowledge of credits and mercantile standing has particular value." The priority for consuls was

consular business; in commercial matters they were vulnerable to gossip, misjudgment, fear of incurring too much publicity, and out-of-date information. See Goward to Hitt, August 29, 1881, Records of the Department of State, RG 59, *Special Agents,* Dispatches, 30.

7. For an example of interest in Latin American trade see Hayes's first annual message to Congress cited in Richardson, *Messages and Papers,* 7: 469. For Evarts's lack of interest in reciprocity see Gary A. Pennannen, "The Foreign Policy of William M. Evarts," (Ph.D. diss., University of Wisconsin, 1968), pp. 313–14.

8. Richardson, *Messages and Papers,* 8: 251.

9. For an outline of relations with Mexico see Karl M. Schmitt, *Mexico and the United States, 1821–1973* (New York: Wiley, 1974), chapter 4; on the role of American entrepreneurs in Mexico see David M. Pletcher, *Rails, Mines, and Progress* (Ithaca: Cornell University Press, 1948). As an example of business pressure see the statement by John Kasson that the proposal for a Latin American trade commission came from the businessmen of the Mississippi Valley. *Congressional Record,* 48th Congress, 1st session, p. 6098.

10. See 48th Congress, 1st session, House report no. 1445; and David M. Pletcher, "Inter-American Shipping in the 1880s," *Inter-American Economic Affairs,* 10 (1956): 14–41.

11. The British minister in Washington remarked that foreign policy issues were being raised in order to divert attention from more troublesome domestic issues. See West to Granville, no. 171, May 30, 1884, F.O. 5/1870.

12. The *Economist,* December 13, 1884; *South American Journal,* March 4, 1885.

13. Remarks of Adee cited in Edward P. Crapol, *America For the Americans* (Westport: Greenwood Press, 1973), p. 122.

14. Frelinghuysen to the commissioners, August 27, 1884, cited in *Commission on Relations with Latin America,* 49th Congress, 1st session, House executive document no. 50, p. 6. He also described the United States as "the senior of this family of nations," to which they "may naturally look for example and for disinterested counsel and aid." Ibid.

15. Frelinghuysen to John F. Miller, March 26, 1884, cited in West to Granville, no. 116, April 16, 1884, F.O. 5/1869.

16. See Pletcher, *Rails, Mines and Progress.*

17. Although Romero was not appointed until 1882.

18. The United States commissioners were Grant and Trescot. Romero and Cañedo represented Mexico.

19. Frelinghuysen to Grant and Trescot, January 13, 1883, Library of Congress, Frelinghuysen Papers.

20. West to Granville, no. 219, November 19, 1882, F.O. 5/1796, and no. 19, January 19, 1883, F.O. 5/1838.

21. See Frelinghuysen to Foster, no. 146, March 14, 1884, RG 59, *Spain,* Instructions, 19.

22. See Tischendorf, *Great Britain and Mexico,* p. 129.

23. The long delay in resuming relations was considerably influenced by the fact that each government considered that the other side had been responsible for originally breaking off relations, and that it was for that side to take the initiative in asking for renewal. Hence the resulting diplomatic impasse.

24. Frelinghuysen to Foster, no. 146, March 14, 1884, RG 59, *Spain,* Instructions, 19.

25. Foster to Gresham, September 28 and October 26, 1884, cited in David M. Pletcher, *The Awkward Years* (Columbia: University of Missouri Press, 1962), pp. 296–67.

26. Frelinghuysen to Foster, no. 146, March 14, 1884, RG 59, *Spain,* Instructions, 19.

27. Foster to Frelinghuysen, telegram, July 25, 1884, and September 11, 1884, RG 59,

Spain, Dispatches, 110. "I was destined to delays and disappointment," Foster noted in his memoirs, "and to learn over again the lesson of my Mexican experience that the Spanish temperament does not admit of celerity in the dispatch of public business." See John W. Foster, *Diplomatic Memoirs,* 2 vols. (New York: Houghton Mifflin, 1909), 1: 243–44.

28. Foster to Frelinghuysen, no. 247, August 19, 1884, and no. 252, August 25, 1884, RG 59, *Spain,* Dispatches, 110.

29. See Pletcher, *Awkward Years,* chapter 16.

30. *Congressional Record,* 48th Congress, 2nd session, p. 231.

31. *Bradstreet's,* January 3, 1885.

32. A treaty with Hawaii was ultimately ratified in 1887, but all the Latin American treaties signed in 1884 were consigned to an early demise. The British government had decided against a reciprocity treaty on behalf of the West Indian colonies, but American congressional action rendered this decision rather academic.

33. See Joseph Smith, "The Latin American Trade Commission of 1884–5," *Inter-American Economic Affairs,* 24 (1971): 3–24.

34. *Congressional Record,* 48th Congress, 1st session, p. 4957.

35. Ibid., p. 6098.

36. Ibid., p. 6100.

37. The final version of the appropriation bill contained funds for the commission, but deleted was Frelinghuysen's earlier request for expenses under the neutrality act. See Pletcher, *Awkward Years,* pp. 275–76.

38. *New York Herald,* June 29, 1885.

39. *Rio News,* September 15, 1884; *Buenos Ayres Herald,* March 4, 1885.

40. West to Granville, no. 178, July 16, 1884, F.O. 5/1878.

41. West to Granville, no. 245, November 3, 1884, F.O. 5/1879.

42. Sharpe never in fact left the United States, and he eventually resigned his commission in February 1885.

43. *Buenos Ayres Herald,* June 11, 1885.

44. See *Commission on Relations with Latin America,* p. 9.

45. Haggard to Granville, no. 19, July 10, 1885, F.O. 13/614.

46. *Commission on Relations with Latin America,* pp. 21–33.

47. Ibid., p. 27.

48. Cited in Monson to Granville, no. 12, September 9, 1884, F.O. 6/381. Edmund Monson was the British minister in Buenos Aires.

49. Extract from an interview published in the *New York Herald,* July 29, 1885.

50. *Buenos Ayres Herald,* November 21, 1885.

51. West to Salisbury, no. 189, July 17, 1885, F.O. 5/1910.

52. See Russell H. Bastert, "Diplomatic Reversal: Frelinghuysen's Opposition to Blaine's Pan-American Policy in 1882," *Mississippi Valley Historical Review,* 42 (1956): 653–71; and the same author's, "A New Approach to the Origins of Blaine's Pan-American Policy," *Hispanic American Historical Review,* 39 (1959): 375–412.

53. *New York Herald,* February 1, 1882.

54. A number of measures relating to inter-American cooperation were introduced in these years, most notably by McCreary and Townshend in the House and by Frye in the Senate. See A. Curtis Wilgus, "James G. Blaine and the Pan American Movement," *Hispanic American Historical Review,* 5 (1922): 685–90; and Tom E. Terrill, *The Tariff, Politics, and American Foreign Policy, 1874–1901* (Westport: Greenwood Press, 1973), chapters 4 and 5.

55. Ibid.

56. West to Rosebery, no. 151, May 28, 1886, F.O. 5/1943.

57. West to Iddesleigh, no. 261, September 25, 1886, F.O. 5/1944.

58. Pauncefote later commented that the bill "was passed by the concurrent action of the Democratic majority in the House and the Republican majority in the Senate, the former hoping that it might strengthen the cause of freer trade, and the latter that it might help alleviate pressure upon the protective system." See memorandum by Pauncefote, February 15, 1890, F.O. 5/2085. The activities of the American Peace Society also put pressure on Congress to pass the measure. See Edson L. Whitney, *The American Peace Society* (Washington, D.C.: American Peace Society, 1928), pp. 154–57.

59. The project of a customs union was more usually referred to as an attempt to establish an American *Zollverein*. The Harrison administration abandoned this project in favor of reciprocal trade agreements.

60. *Congressional Record,* 50th Congress, 1st session, pp. 1656, 1658, appendix p. 308.

61. It was initially proposed that of the ten American delegates, the president should appoint six, the Senate two, and the House two.

62. It has usually been argued that Cleveland did not sign the bill. For a contrary view see James F. Vivian, "The Pan American Conference Act of May 10, 1888," *The Americas,* 27 (1970): 185–92.

63. Invitations were dispatched to the Latin American governments in July 1888 notifying them that the conference would take place in October 1889.

64. The acting British minister in Washington noted that "the project will doubtless be vigorously taken up by the incoming administration." See Herbert to Salisbury, no. 18, January 24, 1889, F.O. 5/2058.

65. For Walker's instructions see Bayard to Walker, January 18, 1889, RG 59, *Argentine Republic,* Instructions, 16.

66. See *South American Journal,* July 27, 1889.

67. Edwardes to Salisbury, no. 77, April 12, 1889, F.O. 5/2058.

68. Denys to Salisbury, no. 27, July 11, 1889, and no. 21, September 6, 1889, F.O. 50/469. See also the *Nation,* October 3, 1889.

69. West to Salisbury, no. 174, May 14, 1888, F.O. 5/2024.

70. *Rio News,* June 3, 1889. There was also strong criticism of Walker's visit to Rio in an editorial dated May 27, 1889.

71. Mansfield to Salisbury, no. 30, April 29, 1889, F.O. 61/374.

72. *Buenos Ayres Herald,* September 7, 1889.

73. *South American Journal,* September 14, 1889.

74. *Boston Herald,* November 4, 1889.

75. See Edwardes to Salisbury, no. 221, June 15, 1888, F.O. 5/2024 and no. 77, April 12, 1889, F.O. 5/2058.

76. West was recalled after his alleged intervention in the presidential election of 1888. The fact that such a senior Foreign Office official as Julian Pauncefote was appointed as his successor indicated that Britain greatly desired to keep good Anglo-American relations.

77. In June 1888 the Argentine minister in Washington, Quesada, had told his British colleague that, although he personally disapproved of the idea of a conference, it would be difficult to decline an invitation made by a government as powerful as the United States. See Edwardes to Salisbury, no. 221, June 15, 1888, F.O. 5/2024.

78. See Wilgus, "Blaine and the Pan American Movement," p. 692.

79. Walker to Blaine, no. 1, April 5, 1889, RG 59, *Argentine Republic,* Dispatches, 27. Chile's acceptance was important because without it Peru would not attend the conference.

80. See International American Conference, 1889–1890, *Reports of Committees and Discussions Thereon,* 4 vols. (Washington, D.C., 1890), 4: 331.

81. *Rio News,* July 1, 1889.

82. See International American Conference, 1889–1890, *Minutes of the Conference* (Washington, D.C., 1890), pp. 116, 137–38. The British minister at Buenos Aires, George Jenner, speculated that Argentina might use the conference to secure American mediation in its dispute with Britain over the Falkland Islands. See Jenner to Salisbury, no. 15, August 30, 1888, F.O. 6/399.

83. The Dominican Republic argued that its commercial relations with the United States had been settled by the 1884 reciprocity treaty, which still awaited American ratification. Attendance at the conference was therefore regarded as futile.

84. Brazil, Colombia, and Venezuela were represented by three delegates each. Argentina, Chile, and Mexico each sent two while Bolivia, Costa Rica, Ecuador, El Salvador, Guatemala, Haiti, Honduras, Nicaragua, Paraguay, Peru, and Uruguay each sent one. A representative from Hawaii attended the later sessions of the conference.

85. The two nonbusinessmen were ex-senator John B. Henderson and William H. Trescot, the diplomat. The other delegates were Cornelius Bliss, Andrew Carnegie, T. Jefferson Coolidge, Henry G. Davis, Morris Estee, Charles Flint, John F. Hanson, and Clement Studebaker.

86. Carnegie to Blaine, July 22, 1889, RG 43, *International American Conference*, Box 14.

87. Coolidge to Blaine, July 22, 1889, ibid.

88. Board of Trade, Philadelphia, to Blaine, September 16, 1889, cited in 51st Congress, 1st session, Senate executive document no. 59.

89. See the various letters in RG 43, *International American Conference*, Box 19; see also William E. Curtis, *Trade and Transportation Between the United States and Spanish America* (Washington, D.C.: GPO, 1889), pp. 285–86.

90. Anonymous article by Curtis in *Frank Leslie's Illustrated Newspaper*, June 8, 1889.

91. *Boston Journal*, July 26, 1889. Curtis was also quoted as remarking that American agricultural methods would be a "big novelty" to the visitors since they still used the "primitive methods of centuries ago." Ibid.

92. *Rio News*, October 14, 1889.

93. *The Capitals of Spanish America*, published in New York by Harper and Brothers in 1888.

94. The *Nation*, October 17, 1889.

95. This incident occurred in Philadelphia. See *New York World*, November 16, 1889.

96. *Savannah News*, November 18, 1889.

97. Romero's diplomatic reply was no doubt influenced by the demands of diplomatic courtesy and protocol. The failure to visit the southern states was to be remedied by a similar excursion there after the conference had ended. Only two delegates attended and the tour was canceled at Richmond.

98. See Thomas F. Mc Gann, *Argentina, the United States and the Inter-American System, 1880–1914* (Cambridge, Mass.: Harvard University Press, 1957), pp. 141–43.

99. *Rio News*, October 14, 1889. The *Rio News* added that, had the delegates known "that they were to be chaperoned by a man who has made himself a laughing stock because of his flying official excursion around South America and his blundering attempt to transform his fleeting impressions into serious descriptions, they would probably have taken the affair less seriously than they have done." Ibid. See also *New York Star*, November 26, 1889.

100. The *Boston Post*, August 23, 1889, reported that "few final results are looked for" by the State Department. For Blaine's views in October 1889 see his opening address to the conference cited in International American Conference, *Minutes*, pp. 10–13.

101. Carnegie to Blaine, July 22, 1889, RG 43, *International American Conference*, Box 14.

102. See Matías Romero, "The Pan-American Conference," *North American Review,* 151 (1890): 408.

103. See Mc Gann, *Argentina and the Inter-American System,* pp. 137–38. Quintana's request for the appointment of bilingual secretaries was an attempt to exclude Curtis, whose knowledge of Spanish was known to be deficient. Blaine retained Curtis by giving him the position of "executive" secretary. See also Romero's statement that the "success" of the conference was threatened by language difficulties. Romero, "Pan-American Conference," p. 361.

104. The Ecuadorian delegate, Plácido Caamaño, complained that the translation of documents took days and days. See International American Conference, *Minutes,* p. 170.

105. The *Nation,* September 12, 1889.

106. Not only had Blaine no prearranged plan, but he "even refused to express opinions on any subject, or even to give instructions to his delegates when called on for them." See Romero, "Pan-American Conference," p. 410. Quintana asked on one occasion, after Estee and Coolidge had expressed opposing views over the question of silver coinage: "Is this a conference of private individuals speaking for themselves, or is it a diplomatic conference in which each delegate represents the idea of his government?" Cited in Mc Gann, *Argentina and the Inter-American System,* pp. 141–42.

107. Ibid., p. 147. During the debate on arbitration Blaine actually left the chair and personally intervened in the discussion.

108. Sáenz Peña pointed out that Argentina was not opposed to reciprocity treaties in principle. In fact, the United States had rejected just such a proposal from Argentina in 1870. Nevertheless, according to the original agenda, he argued that they had no place in the deliberations of the conference. See International American Conference, *Minutes,* pp. 293–334.

109. Ibid., p. 179.

110. The British minister in Chile reported that Chile had entered into an agreement with Argentina and Brazil to oppose discussion of noncommercial matters at the conference. Brazil's departure from this understanding aroused "a general feeling of intense indignation" in Chile. See Kennedy to Salisbury, no. 36, April 27, 1890, F.O. 16/259, and no. 3, June 6, 1890, F.O. 5/2087.

111. One writer has concluded that the conference was "a diplomatic victory for the Spanish Americans." See Alejandro Magnet, *Orígenes y antecedentes del panamericanismo* (Santiago de Chile: Talleres gráficos "Horizonte," 1945), p. 331.

112. With the exception of Nin, who left in February 1890. See the *Nation,* February 20, 1890.

113. International American Conference, *Minutes,* pp. 366–67. In its platform the Republican party had promised "full and adequate protection" to the wool industry. See Kirk H. Porter and Donald B. Johnson, comps., *National Party Platforms, 1840–1964* (Urbana: University of Illinois Press, 1966), p. 80; and the *Times,* July 15, 1890.

114. International American Conference, *Minutes,* pp. 492–93.

115. The *Nation,* February 20, 1890.

116. William E. Curtis, *The United States and Foreign Powers* (New York: C. Scribner's Sons, 1899), p. 73.

117. McGann, *Argentina and the Inter-American System,* pp. 152–53.

118. Romero, "Pan-American Conference," p. 574.

119. Memorandum by Pauncefote, February 15, 1890, F.O. 5/2085.

120. *South American Journal,* March 1, 1890.

121. At the close of the conference the *New York Tribune* remarked that "the way has been opened for securing united action on the part of the eighteen commonwealths which will promote the enlightened self-interest of each and the common wealfare of all." The

Nation adopted a different view: "The closing scene of the Pan-American Conference is said to have been extremely affecting, Mr. Blaine being almost moved to tears when he gave the word of parting. If the emotions of the Conference were due to the small results achieved, they were fully justified." Cited in Wilgus, "Blaine and the Pan American Movement," pp. 700–01.

122. See McGann, *Argentina and the Inter-American System*, pp. 145–47.

123. This had been claimed by Curtis's article in *Frank Leslie's Illustrated Newspaper*, June 8, 1889.

124. *Buenos Ayres Herald*, October 10, 1889. See also Romero, "Pan-American Conference," pp. 420–21.

125. *Rio News*, April 28, 1890.

126. See Harrison to Estee, September 11, 1888, cited in Charles Hedges, ed., *Speeches of Benjamin Harrison* (New York: United States Book Co., 1892), p. 114.

127. Blaine claimed that fifteen of the seventeen foreign delegations were in favor of reciprocity agreements. See Blaine to Harrison, June 19, 1890, 51st Congress, 1st session, Senate executive document no. 158.

128. Import duties were also to be taken off molasses, coffee, and tea. This political strategy of lowering the prices of certain basic foodstuffs was known as the "free breakfast table."

129. *South American Journal*, June 14, 1890.

130. Blaine to McKinley, April 10, 1890, cited in Ida M. Tarbell, *The Tariff in Our Times* (New York: Macmillan, 1911), p. 204.

131. The national party platform of 1888 committed the Republicans to an increase in the tariff on wool. This was duly incorporated into the McKinley bill.

132. See Foster, *Memoirs*, 2: 4.

133. For Harrison's views see Harry J. Sievers, *Benjamin Harrison: Hoosier President* (Indianapolis: Bobbs-Merrill, 1968), pp. 163–66.

134. Blaine to Frye, July 11, 1890, cited in Tarbell, *Tariff in Our Times*, p. 205.

135. See *Albany Argus*, June 26 and 27, 1890.

136. Harrison to Blaine, July 23, 1890, cited in Albert T. Volwiler, ed., *The Correspondence Between Benjamin Harrison and James G. Blaine, 1882–1893* (Philadelphia: American Philosophical Society, 1940), p. 112.

137. Pauncefote described the policy as "a threat rather than a bribe." See memorandum by Pauncefote, July 1, 1891, F.O. 5/2120.

138. See Margaret Leech, *In the Days of McKinley* (New York: Harper, 1959), pp. 46–47.

139. The *Nation*, September 4, 1890. See also *Export and Finance*, July 26, 1890; and *New York Commercial Bulletin*, September 3, 1890.

140. See Terrill, *Tariff, Politics and American Foreign Policy*, p. 171. For a critical review pointing to the need for more research into the tariff issue see Lewis L. Gould, "Tariffs and Markets in the Gilded Age," *Reviews in American History*, 2 (1974): 266–71.

141. *Troy Times*, June 20, 1890; *Sioux City Journal*, June 27, 1890.

142. Interview with Flint cited in *Boston Globe*, July 28, 1890. See Foster to Aldrich, September 4, 1890, Library of Congress, Aldrich Papers, and Aldrich's statement in *Congressional Record*, 53rd Congress, 2nd session, p. 6992.

143. *Chicago Herald*, August 12, 1890. It was suggested that Germany might remove its restrictions on American pork imports as part of a reciprocity agreement.

144. *Boston Traveller*, July 26, 1890.

145. *Export and Finance*, August 2, 1890; *Sacramento Bee*, June 28, 1890; and *Boston Herald*, August 5, 1890. Note also the comments of Robert La Follette, who had attended the Ways and Means Committee meeting with Blaine in February 1890. In his opinion,

Blaine at that time "had begun to see clearly the path along which the high protective tariff was driving us and to realize the necessity of developing our foreign markets." See Robert M. La Follette, *La Follette's Autobiography* (Madison: Robert M. La Follette Co., 1913), p. 111.

146. See undated memorandum by Foster on the most-favored-nation clause in the Foster Papers, Library of Congress.

147. See Grubb to Blaine, no. 44, March 7, 1891, RG 59, *Spain,* Dispatches, 122.

148. Herminio Portell Vilá, *Historia de Cuba en sus relaciones con los Estados Unidos y España,* 4 vols. (Havana: J. Montero, 1938), 3: 76.

149. The *Times,* October 3, 1890.

150. A protest to the United States was considered, but was rejected since the basis of any British claim, the Anglo-American convention of 1815, could be terminated by either nation at twelve months' notice, and the Foreign Office assumed that the United States "would doubtless do so if we pressed any claim in an inconvenient manner." See minutes on Pauncefote to Salisbury, no. 121, June 20, 1890, F.O. 5/2088.

151. Carnegie to Gladstone, March 28, 1891, Library of Congress, Carnegie Papers.

152. Spring-Rice to Lowther, October 26, 1891, F.O. 800/28. Cecil Spring-Rice held various secondary diplomatic offices in Washington from 1886 to 1895. In 1913 he was appointed British ambassador to the United States.

153. See Pauncefote to Salisbury, no. 154, July 10, 1891, F.O. 5/2120.

154. The *Times,* November 1, 1890.

155. See undated memorandum by Foster on reciprocity in Foster Papers.

156. The Republicans retained a majority of 8 in the Senate, but in the House they numbered only 86 in comparison to 235 democrats. See Sievers, *Harrison,* p. 181. One notable individual result was the defeat of McKinley in Ohio.

157. For most of 1891 Blaine was in a state of "almost complete collapse." See Alan Spetter, "Harrison and Blaine: Foreign Policy, 1889–93" (Ph.D. diss., Rutgers University, 1967), p. vii. On the rivalry with Harrison that predated Blaine's resignation as secretary of state in June 1892, see Sievers, *Harrison,* pp. 213–25. Blaine died in January 1893.

158. See especially his vigorous exhortations in speeches on his tour of the Western states during April and May 1891 cited in Hedges, *Speeches of Harrison,* pp. 388–468.

159. Porter and Johnson, *National Party Platforms,* p. 87.

160. Ibid., p. 93.

161. The *Statist,* November 12, 1892.

162. See Pauncefote to Salisbury, no. 154, July 10, 1891, F.O. 5/2120.

163. The Chilean foreign minister informed the British chargé in Santiago in 1892 that "whenever the United States supplied better and cheaper goods than other countries they would gain the advantages they desired without any Treaty." See Maude to Salisbury, no. 27, March 24, 1892, F.O. 16/276.

164. See George Welby, the British minister in Buenos Aires, to Salisbury, no. 16, July 12, 1892, F.O. 6/425; Pauncefote to Salisbury, no. 82, March 18, 1892, and no. 86, March 31, 1892, F.O. 5/2152. On the Argentine threat of retaliation see the *Nation,* October 9, 1890. The official dispatches between Washington and Buenos Aires do not confirm that any such threat was made, but the Argentine attitude of defiance is well expressed in Zeballos to Pitkin, December 24, 1891, RG 59, *Argentine Republic,* Dispatches, 29.

165. Blaine to Foster, December 5, 1891, Foster Papers.

166. See *Report of the Committee on Ways and Means Concerning Reciprocity and Commercial Treaties,* 54th Congress, 1st session, House report no. 2263, pp. 11–12. See also Abbott to Blaine, no. 22, April 28, 1891, RG 59, *Colombia,* Dispatches, 46; no. 256, September 7; no. 276, October 19; and no. 289, November 13, 1891, ibid., 47; and Blaine to Abbott, telegram, February 8, 1892, ibid., 48.

167. Abbott to Blaine, no. 337, April 23, 1892, RG 59, *Colombia,* Dispatches, 48; Abbott to Foster, no. 372, August 3, and no. 394, August 23, 1892, ibid., 49. Colombia chose to retaliate in its own way by negotiating commercial agreements with France and Germany in 1893. The Colombian protest at Harrison's action was later sustained by the report of the 1918 United States Tariff Commission that: "The protests of Colombia and Haiti against the imposition of the penalty duties appear to have been justified. . . . Colombia and Haiti were entitled to the free enjoyment of such advantages as were enjoyed by those states [i.e., Mexico and Argentina]." See United States Tariff Commission, *Reciprocity and Commercial Treaties* (Washington, D.C.: GPO, 1919), p. 38.

168. No protest was received from Venezuela.

169. Gosling to Kimberley, no. 16, July 16, 1894, F.O. 15/286.

170. The *Nation,* February 4, 1892. The reciprocity treaty particularly affected the export of Spanish flour to Cuba. See John B. Osborne, "Reciprocity in the American Tariff System," The *Annals,* 23 (1904): 65.

171. *Rio News,* February 10, 1891.

172. See Matías Romero, *Mexico and the United States* (New York: G. P. Putnam, 1898), pp. 661–62. For the debate on Blaine's alleged deception of Mendonça see the *Nation,* October 8, November 19, December 3, 1891, April 7 and 14, 1892.

173. Spenser St. John to Salisbury, no. 4, February 25, 1892, F.O. 50/484.

174. For the Argentine position see Welby to Salisbury, no. 20, July 31, 1892, F.O. 6/425.

175. See Gosling to Rosebery, April 30, 1893, *Reports from H. M. Diplomatic and Consular Officers Abroad on the Subject of Trade and Finance* [hereafter *Trade Reports*] (1893), no. 1245, Guatemala; Coen to Salisbury, February 27, 1892, *Trade Reports* (1892), no. 1030, Dominican Republic; and Ramsden to Rosebery, August 30, 1892, *Trade Reports* (1892), no. 1132, Spain, Santiago de Cuba.

176. A majority of the United States Supreme Court sustained the constitutionality of the reciprocity provision on April 30, 1892. See *Ways and Means Report on Reciprocity,* pp. 17–19.

177. Curtis to Foster, December 20, 1892, cited in *2nd Annual Report of the Bureau of American Republics, 1892,* 52nd Congress, 2nd session, Senate executive document no. 84, p. 20.

178. "So far," the British chargé in Washington noted, "Brazil, Cuba, and Puerto Rico have been the chief gainers from the Treaties but the anticipation of largely increased markets for the agricultural and manufactured products of the United States have yet to be fulfilled." See memorandum by Herbert, dated February 2, 1893, F.O. 5/2192. Even the proreciprocity F. W. Taussig predicted that "the gain to the United States will not be great in degree, simply because the volume of our trade with the South American countries is not large, nor likely for some time to become large." Frank W. Taussig, *Free Trade, the Tariff and Reciprocity* (New York: Macmillan, 1920), p. 133. See also Worthington C. Ford, *Reciprocity Under the Tariff Act of 1890* (Washington, D.C., 1893), pp. 30–33.

179. The *Nation,* April 27, 1893.

180. Ibid., March 24, 1892; see also the memorandum from Cartagena by Consul Smyth, September 10, 1894, *United States Consular Reports* (1894), 46: 379–81.

181. While the Wilson bill was not in principle opposed to an expansionist policy toward Latin America, other Democratic measures were. In particular, James Blount of the House Committee on Foreign Affairs advocated an isolationist policy that brought about reduced appropriations for the proposed Pan-American railroad, the Bureau of American Republics, and diplomatic expenses in United States legations in Latin America. For example, see the debate on H. R. 7624 in *Congressional Record,* 52nd Congress, 1st session.

182. Ibid., 53rd Congress, 2nd session, pp. 1418, 3663, 3962–63, 5437.

183. Ibid., p. 1423. See also ibid., pp. 1420, 1422, and 4024 for other representative Democratic views.

184. The amendment introduced by Senator Hale to retain the reciprocity treaties was defeated by thirty-four votes to twenty-six on June 6, 1894.

185. The response of the Democratic senators to the Wilson bill generated considerable intraparty strife. According to one British view, "No principle is settled by the Tariff Act, the arrangement is purely one of expediency." See the *Statist,* August 25, 1894.

186. President Cleveland allowed this bill to become law without his signature.

187. See U.S. Tariff Commission, *Reciprocity,* p. 159; and *Ways and Means Report on Reciprocity,* pp. 21–25. Protests were received from Germany, Guatemala, Brazil, Nicaragua, Costa Rica, and the Dominican Republic. Although Foster had regarded the reciprocity policy as "permanent," he had pointed out during negotiations that the agreements were not binding on the United States Congress. See Foster to Blaine, telegram, April 17, 1891, RG 59, *Spain,* Dispatches, 122.

188. See minute on Pauncefote to Kimberley, August 21, 1894, F.O. 5/2238. Earlier in the year an official had minuted that "it is no use to go through the Tariff . . . as it changes almost every day." See Pauncefote to Kimberley, no. 72, March 22, 1894, ibid.

189. The reciprocity agreements were in operation for such a short period that their effects cannot be determined. See Lincoln Hutchinson, "The Results of Reciprocity with Brazil," *Political Science Quarterly,* 18 (1903): 282–303. Pauncefote concluded: "It cannot be said therefore that the arrangements in question have contributed much to the development of trade or that the United States will lose much by their abrogation beyond the power they gave of discriminating against countries who refused to become parties to them." See Pauncefote to Kimberley, no. 72, March 22, 1894, F.O. 5/2238.

Chapter 6: Rivalry in Brazil

1. Another example of the close relations between the two countries was Brazil's choice of the president of the United States to arbitrate the Missiones boundary dispute between Brazil and Argentina. President Cleveland delivered his decision on this in 1895.

2. See Alan K. Manchester, *British Preeminence in Brazil* (Chapel Hill: University of North Carolina Press, 1933); and Richard Graham, *Britain and the Onset of Modernization in Brazil, 1850–1914* (Cambridge, Eng.: Cambridge University Press, 1968).

3. On the formative period of these relations see E. Bradford Burns, *The Unwritten Alliance* (New York: Columbia University Press, 1966).

4. Edwin H. Conger served as American minister to Brazil from 1890 to 1893 and was succeeded by Thomas L. Thompson, who held this position until 1897.

5. The scale and nature of British trade and investment with Brazil was such that British merchants and financial institutions were actively involved in Brazilian economic affairs. During the early years of the republic it was alleged that British banks were manipulating the Brazilian foreign exchange rate for political and commercial purposes. See Wyndham to Salisbury, no. 138, November 6, 1891, F.O. 13/677.

6. See E. Bradford Burns, *A History of Brazil* (New York: Columbia University Press, 1970), p. 169; and Norman T. Straus, "Brazil in the 1870's As Seen by American Diplomats" (Ph.D. diss., New York University, 1971), passim.

7. Blaine to Osborn, no. 9, December 1, 1881, Records of the Department of State, RG 59, *Brazil,* Instructions, 17.

8. Adams to Blaine, no. 9, September 4, 1889, RG 59, *Brazil,* Dispatches, 48. Robert Adams served as American minister to Brazil from March 1889 to February 1890.

9. For a general discussion of this subject see Graham, *Britain and Onset of Modernization,* chapter 3.

10. See, for example, the lack of instructions mentioned in Jarvis to Bayard, no. 143, August 27, 1888, RG 59, *Brazil,* Dispatches, 48.

11. This had been underlined by the abrogation of the Anglo-Brazilian commercial treaty in 1844 and by the failure of coercion in the Christie incident of 1863. For the latter see Richard Graham, "Os fundamentos da ruptura de relações diplomáticas entre o Brasil e a Grã-Bretanha em 1863," *Revista de história,* 24 (1962): 117–38, 379–402.

12. Britain made a specific effort in 1886 and 1887 to revive discussion of this subject even though there had been numerous prior attempts. See Clarendon to Thornton, no. 3, January 24, 1866, F.O. 13/438.

13. A British report estimated that 70 percent of Brazilian revenue was derived from customs duties. See MacDonell to Salisbury, August 6, 1887, *Parliamentary Papers,* 100 (1888).

14. F.O. to Corbett, no. 15, September 24, 1883, F.O. 13/590.

15. Wyndham to Salisbury, no. 140, December 19, 1888, F.O. 13/647.

16. Currie to Wyndham, August 21, 1888, F.O. 13/645.

17. Wyndham to Salisbury, no. 45, June 3, 1889, and no. 47, June 5, 1889, F.O. 13/657. Congress was in fact dissolved and riots were reported from Bahia, but at the end of June, Wyndham reported a decrease in republic agitation. See Wyndham to Salisbury, no. 64, June 28, 1889, ibid.

18. For example, the *South American Journal* reported on July 13, 1889, that the "signs of the times" could not be disregarded in Brazil.

19. Wyndham to Salisbury, no. 137, November 18, 1889, F.O. 13/658. The reference is to the Baron of Ladário's unsuccessful attempt to resist arrest. See José Maria Bello, *A History of Modern Brazil, 1889–1964,* translated by James L. Taylor (Stanford: Stanford University Press, 1966), p. 52. On the 1889 coup see Charles W. Simmons, *Marshal Deodoro and the Fall of Dom Pedro II* (Durham: Duke University Press, 1966). There was some opposition to the republic from recently emancipated blacks; see Gilberto Freyre, *Order and Progress,* translated by Rod W. Horton (New York: Knopf, 1970), p. 8.

20. Wyndham to Salisbury, no. 137, November 18, 1889, F.O. 13/658.

21. Adams to Blaine, no. 20, November 19, 1889, RG 59, *Brazil,* Dispatches, 48.

22. See Gladstone's speech cited in the *Times,* December 5, 1889; and Morgan's statement of December 20, 1889, in *Congressional Record,* 51st Congress, 1st session, p. 315.

23. *Daily News,* November 18, 1889.

24. "Although interesting to the political student," noted a leading British financial journal, "the revolution in Brazil would have attracted comparatively little attention in this country and on the continent had it not been for the great financial interests involved." The *Economist,* November 23, 1889.

25. Wyndham to Sanderson, November 25, 1889, F.O. 13/658.

26. Although Wyndham observed that in a serious emergency the small British ships of the South Atlantic squadron "would be quite unequal to inspiring awe to the forts or ironclads at Rio de Janeiro." See Wyndham to Salisbury, no. 138, November 18, 1889, ibid. In his opinion, the arrival of H.M.S. *Nymphe* demonstrated that Britain "is not indifferent to what is occuring in this country" and that "it would produce a very good general effect if a powerful ship or two were to look in here now and then." See Wyndham to Salisbury, no. 156, November 25, 1889, and Wyndham to Sanderson, November 25, 1889, ibid.

27. Blaine to Adams, November 30, 1889, RG 59, *Brazil,* Dispatches, 49; F.O. to Wyndham, no. 7, November 29, 1889, F.O. 13/659. See also J. Fred Rippy, "The United States and the Establishment of the Republic of Brazil," *Southwestern Political Science Quarterly,* 3 (1922): 39–53.

28. Memorandum by Hertslet, November 25, 1889, F.O. 13/664. The problem of recognition was well summed up by the *Rio News* on January 6, 1890, when it described the provisional government as "nothing but a military usurpation, with a self-appointed chief and cabinet." Recognition could not be accorded until "a legal form of government" had been established and "until that is done, foreign governments will very properly hold aloof and await the result not through unfriendly motives but through the mere obligation of leaving the Brazilian people alone in the settlement of their domestic affairs."

29. Adams to Blaine, no. 26, December 17, 1889, RG 59, *Brazil,* Dispatches, 49. Wyndham to Salisbury, no. 176, December 8, 1889, and Wyndham to Sanderson, December 17, 1889, F.O. 13/658.

30. See Wyndham to Salisbury, no. 186, December 19; no. 188, December 22; and no. 201, December 30, 1889, F.O. 13/658.

31. Adams to Blaine, no. 30, December 28, 1889, RG 59, *Brazil,* Dispatches, 49.

32. The *Statist,* February 8, 1890; the *Nation,* January 2, 1890; and *Buenos Ayres Herald,* February 1, 1890.

33. See Wyndham to Salisbury, no. 45, February 24, 1890, and no. 52, February 26, 1890, F.O. 13/666.

34. *Rio News,* February 24, 1890.

35. See memorandum by Sanderson, June 12, 1890, F.O. 13/665.

36. Memorandum by Hertslet, June 28, 1890, F.O. 13/672.

37. Memorandum by Sanderson, June 28, 1890, ibid. See also F.O. to Wyndham, July 8, 1890, F.O. 13/665.

38. Wyndham to Salisbury, no. 53, July 24, 1890, F.O. 13/666. A F.O. minute on this dispatch indicated that British policy was not affected by the French decision and that British recognition would follow only after the meeting of the Constituent Assembly.

39. Wyndham to Salisbury, no. 44, September 18, 1890, F.O. 13/667.

40. See memorandum by Sanderson, September 22, 1890, F.O. 13/665.

41. F.O. to Wyndham, no. 2, October 2, 1890. Wyndham was to soften the British decision by stating that the recent elections had shown "unmistakably the acquiescence of the great mass of the population in the new form of government." The decision to recognize was, however, further delayed until after the election and installation of the first president of the republic.

42. British exports to Brazil increased during this period. See D. C. M. Platt, *Latin America and British Trade, 1806–1914* (London: A. and C. Black, 1972), p. 292.

43. Wyndham to Salisbury, no. 53, July 24, 1890, F.O. 13/666. Wyndham was referring to the settlement of various financial claims. In this respect, it should be noted that the republican government did not attempt to denounce or reject financial commitments and obligations undertaken by the imperial regime.

44. See memorandum February 9, 1891, F.O. 13/687.

45. Jarvis to Bayard, no. 104, September 20, 1887, RG 59, *Brazil,* Dispatches, 48.

46. Jarvis to Bayard, no. 143, August 27, 1888, ibid.

47. Report from H. Clay Armstrong, June 1, 1889, *United States Consular Reports,* 30 (1889), p. 221.

48. Wyndham to Salisbury, no. 139, December 19, 1888, and no. 65, November 26, 1888, F.O. 13/649.

49. Much more disturbing was the German threat. See, for example, Haggard to Rosebery, no. 17, April 25, 1886, F.O. 13/621.

50. Wyndham was on leave of absence from December 1890 to September 1891, and Adam served as acting British minister in his place.

51. Adam to Salisbury, no. 60, December 12, 1890, F.O. 13/669.

52. Pauncefote to Salisbury, no. 19, February 6, 1891, F.O. 5/2119; Adam to Salisbury,

no. 4, February 6, 1891, F.O. 13/681.

53. Conger to Blaine, no. 27, February 26, 1891, RG 59, *Brazil,* Dispatches, 50. On the treaty in general see Steven C. Topik, "Informal Empire? The U.S.-Brazilian Trade Treaty of 1891" (M.A. thesis, University of Texas, 1974).

54. Minute on Pauncefote to Salisbury, no. 19, February 6, 1891, F.O. 5/2119.

55. See the statement of James Fergusson, the undersecretary for foreign affairs, February 9, 1891, *Parliamentary Debates,* 3rd series, 301: 207.

56. These various petitions dated March and April 1891 are contained in F.O. 13/687.

57. F.O. to Adam, February 20, 1891, F.O. 13/680.

58. The Brazilian foreign minister also described the reciprocity agreement as an experiment that should be allowed to go into operation for at least one year. See Adam to Salisbury, no. 17, March 21; no. 18, March 22; and no. 19, March 22, 1891, F.O. 13/681.

59. Adam confirmed that an agreement with Britain similar to the reciprocity treaty would result in "a serious and immediate loss of revenue to the Brazilian Treasury." Adam to Salisbury, no. 22, April 4, and no. 34, May 16, 1891, ibid.

60. Adam was instructed to send a report on the reciprocity agreement after it had been in operation for six months. See F.O. to Adam, no. 10, June 9, 1891, F.O. 13/680.

61. See June 8, 1891, *Parliamentary Debates,* 3rd series, 353: 1823; February 19, 1892, ibid., 4th series, 1: 823–24; May 26, 1892, ibid., 4th series, 4: 1884–85; February 14, 1893, ibid., 4th series, 8: 1368–69; and March 7, 1893, ibid., 4th series, 9: 1231–32.

62. See the statement of the undersecretary for foreign affairs, James Lowther, February 26, 1892, ibid., 4th series, 1: 1384–85.

63. "For the present," wrote Adam, "the great disproportion between freight rates from Europe to Brazil, and those from the United States, will tend to check to some extent the importation of goods from the latter country." See Adam to Salisbury, no. 5, February 9, 1891, F.O. 13/681. The *Rio News* noted on February 10, 1891: "In regard to cotton and hardware, our English friends may rest content—the treaty will work no great changes in this respect." This comforting opinion was quoted in the *Economist* on March 7, 1891.

64. Adam to Salisbury, no. 18, March 22, 1891, F.O. 13/681. Clermont's successor Cabo-Frio repeated a similar assurance; see Adam to Salisbury, no. 39, June 2, 1891, ibid.

65. Wyndham to Salisbury, no. 118, December 8, 1891, F.O. 13/682.

66. The reductions were not always completely put into effect, and some Brazilian customs houses continued to levy duties on American imports in defiance of the reciprocity agreement. For example, see Hearn to Kimberley, April 30, 1894, *Reports from H. M. Diplomatic and Consular Officers Abroad on the Subject of Trade and Finance* (1894), no. 1425, Brazil, Rio Grande do Sul.

67. See the report by the British consul Frederic Harford enclosed in Wyndham to Rosebery, November 7, 1893, ibid., no. 1321, Brazil. The *Nation* described reciprocity with Brazil as "a disastrous failure." See the *Nation,* April 27, 1893. The historians of reciprocity concluded: "In the case of Brazil, it does not appear that we were able to develop our export trade to any considerable extent." See James L. Laughlin and H. Parker Willis, *Reciprocity* (New York: Baker and Taylor, 1903), p. 218. A more favorable view of reciprocity was argued by Lincoln Hutchinson, "The Results of Reciprocity with Brazil," *Political Science Quarterly,* 18 (1903): 282–303, but Topik has concluded that "the treaty had little significance." See Topik, "Informal Empire," p. 94.

68. "Her Majesty's Government have done all they can," summed up one Foreign Office official in November 1892, "but the Brazilian Republic is obdurate." Memorandum by the Foreign Office clerk, Warburton, November 16, 1892, F.O. 13/701.

69. *Rio News,* February 10, 1891.

70. Adam to Salisbury, no. 5, February 9, 1891, F.O. 13/681. The government maintained initially that the agreement was a purely executive matter, but later gave way to

pressure and submitted it for congressional ratification.

71. See the speech by Assis Brazil, February 11, 1891, *Annaes do Congresso Nacional,* 3: 94.

72. Adam to Salisbury, no. 18, March 22; no. 19, March 22; and no. 21, March 30, 1891, F.O. 13/681.

73. Haggard to Sanderson, private, May 17, 1891, F.O. 13/684.

74. Conger to Blaine, no. 30, March 6, 1891, and no. 40, April 2, 1891, RG 59, *Brazil, Dispatches,* 50; Adee to Conger, May 23, 1891, ibid., *Brazil,* Instructions, 17.

75. See Adam to Salisbury, no. 39, June 2, 1891, F.O. 13/681.

76. Conger to Blaine, no. 76, July 7, 1891, ibid., *Brazil,* Dispatches, 51. The question whether Salvador de Mendonça had been given certain special assurances by Blaine became something of a newspaper *cause célèbre,* especially in the anti-Blaine *Nation.* See the *Nation,* October 8, November 19, December 3, 1891; April 7 and 14, 1892. For Mendonça's view see his letter to the New York *Evening Post,* April 5, 1892.

77. "He has all the time been a true friend of this policy," noted Conger of Deodoro, "and has fought loyally for the arrangement, even against almost overwhelming odds." See Conger to Blaine, no. 159, November 13, 1891, RG 59, *Brazil,* Dispatches, 51.

78. Conger to Blaine, no. 123, September 17, 1891, ibid. Bribery was also used by the government to secure congressional support for the treaty. See Lawrence F. Hill, *Diplomatic Relations Between the United States and Brazil* (Durham: Duke University Press, 1932), pp. 271–72.

79. Ibid.

80. Conger to Blaine, no. 159, November 13, 1891, RG 59, *Brazil,* Dispatches, 51.

81. Conger to Blaine, no. 300, August 15, 1892, ibid., 53. Before leaving Rio Conger had reported that Floriano was believed to be an opponent of the treaty. See Conger to Blaine, no. 185, January 11, 1892, ibid., 52.

82. Wyndham to Salisbury, no. 88, May 6, 1892, F.O. 13/695.

83. Conger to Blaine, no. 192, January 22, 1892, RG 59, *Brazil,* Dispatches, 52.

84. This was achieved by the passage of the Wilson tariff bill in August 1894. See *Foreign Relations [of the United States]* (1894), pp. 77–82.

85. *Rio News,* July 5, 1892.

86. Gresham to Mendonça, October 26, 1894, *Foreign Relations* (1894), p. 82.

87. *South American Journal,* February 15, 1890.

88. The *Economist,* November 23, 1889; *Rio News,* December 1, 1891.

89. Adam to Salisbury, no. 59, May 15, 1891, F.O. 13/676. On the activities of the Brazilian military during this period see June E. Hahner, *Civilian-Military Relations in Brazil, 1889–1898* (Columbia: University of South Carolina Press, 1969).

90. See Wyndham to Salisbury, no. 158, November 25, 1891, F.O. 13/677.

91. Conger to Blaine, no. 165, November 28, 1891, RG 59, *Brazil,* Dispatches, 51.

92. The most significant separatist movement was in Rio Grande do Sul. See Joseph L. Love, *Rio Grande do Sul and Brazilian Regionalism, 1882–1930* (Stanford: Stanford University Press, 1971).

93. *Rio News,* December 29, 1891.

94. Wyndham to Salisbury, no. 169, December 3, 1889, F.O. 13/658.

95. Wyndham to Salisbury, no. 165, November 28, 1891, and no. 166, November 29, 1891, F.O. 13/677. In November 1891 when Deodoro justified his dissolution of Congress as necessary to forestall a monarchist conspiracy, Wyndham commented that it was merely a pretext with "no real foundation." See Wyndham to Salisbury, no. 138, November 6, 1891, and no. 141, November 9, 1891, ibid. Earlier in the year Adam had suggested that monarchist plots were the result of "random expressions of ill-humour on the part of the disappointed politicians and speculators." See Adam to Salisbury, no. 59, May 15, 1891, F.O. 13/676.

96. Wyndham to Salisbury, no. 185, December 23, 1891, F.O. 13/677. Such was the unpopularity of Pedro's daughter, Princess Isabel, that some monarchists favored the claim of her nephew, Augusto of Saxe-Coburg.

97. Wyndham to Salisbury, no. 7, January 23; no. 12, February 9; and no. 13, February 10, 1892, F.O. 13/689.

98. See Conger to Blaine, no. 191, January 22, 1892, RG 59, *Brazil,* Dispatches, 52.

99. Wyndham to Salisbury, no. 32, March 14, 1892, F.O. 13/689.

100. Conger to Gresham, no. 446, May 26, 1893, RG 59, *Brazil,* Dispatches, 54.

101. See the comments of Percy A. Martin in A. Curtis Wilgus, ed., *Argentina, Brazil and Chile* (Washington, D.C.: George Washington University Press, 1935), p. 229.

102. The Brazilian minister called almost daily at the secretary of state's house during the revolt. See Matilda Gresham, *The Life of Walter Quintin Gresham, 1832–1895,* 2 vols. (Chicago: Rand, McNally and Co., 1919), 2: 777. For an example of Mendonça's public relations activities see his articles "Republicanism in Brazil" and "Latest Aspects of the Brazilian Rebellion," *North American Review,* 158 (1894): 8–15, 164–74. Thompson superseded Conger as American minister at Rio on September 9, 1893, three days after the outbreak of the naval revolt. He became convinced that the British supported the insurgents out of a desire to defeat the reciprocity treaty. See Thompson to Gresham, no. 150, February 1, 1894, RG 59, *Brazil,* Dispatches, 54.

103. See the comments of Senator Anthony Higgins of Delaware, March 2, 1895, *Congressional Record,* 53rd Congress, 3rd session, p. 3109. For a general guide to the secondary literature on the naval revolt see Joseph Smith, "Britain and the Brazilian Naval Revolt of 1893–4," *Journal of Latin American Studies,* 2 (1970): 175, note 1.

104. Wyndham to Rosebery, no. 122, September 18, 1893, F.O. 13/705. Earlier dispatches show that Wyndham had refused to become involved in anti-Floriano plots during July 1893. See Wyndham to Rosebery, no. 88, July 22, 1893, F.O. 13/704.

105. The *Times,* November 17, 1893.

106. Rosebery to Wyndham, no. 20, October 6, 1893, F.O. 13/708.

107. See Wyndham to Rosebery, July 26, 1893, F.O. 13/704; and the opinion of the law officers of the crown, no. 8, n.d. [probably August 1893], F.O. 420/142.

108. Wyndham to Rosebery, September 10, 1893, F.O. 13/704. The American minister supported his diplomatic colleague in this decision. See Thompson to Gresham, September 7, 1893, RG 59, *Brazil,* Dispatches, 54. Complete unanimity on the part of the foreign diplomats was, however, prevented by the attitude of the German minister, who refused to participate in any collective actions or statements.

109. Rosebery to Wyndham, no. 15, September 29, 1893, F.O. 13/708.

110. Gresham to Thompson, November 1, 1893, RG 59, *Brazil,* Instructions, 17. No American warship was actually present at Rio when the naval revolt began, but a number of ships were soon dispatched. By January 1894 five American warships were stationed within the harbor. This was the biggest single foreign naval presence and gave American policy the significant option of the availability of military power to influence events.

111. Wyndham to Rosebery, September 10, 1893, and no. 143, October 9, 1893, F.O. 13/705. The acting commander of the U.S. naval forces at Rio, Captain Picking, joined in the actions of the foreign naval commanders. See Pauncefote to the F.O., October 3 and 4, 1893, F.O. 5/2189.

112. Melo had initially assumed control of all the government ships in the harbor, comprising the ironclad *Aquidabã,* a dozen cruisers and gunboats of varying size, and a number of armed merchant ships. He controlled some of the fortified islands in the bay, but he had no support on the mainland and had no more than fifteen hundred men under his command. By contrast, Floriano lacked immediate naval power and was forced to place orders for ships in the United States. These arrived too late to influence the course of the revolt, but Floriano's military position was always strong since he controlled all the

mainland fortifications and had from seven to eight thousand loyal troops. For an account of the military aspects of the revolt see William L. Clowes, *Four Modern Naval Campaigns* (London: Unit Library, 1902), pp. 191–231. On the military orders placed by Floriano in the United States see Charles R. Flint, *Memories of an Active Life* (New York: G. P. Putnam's Sons, 1923); for the view that the action of the foreign naval commanders was favorable to Floriano see Joaquim Nabuco, *A intervenção estrangeira durante a revolta de 1893* (São Paulo: Companhía editora nacional, 1939), p. 48.

113. Wyndham noted, however, that Rio "can hardly be considered a defenceless town as the quays are lined with troops and guns." See Wyndham to Rosebery, September 10, 1893, F.O. 13/705. When two American naval officers later discovered that Floriano had gone back on his assurance, a conference of naval commanders assembled and insisted that the guns in question be dismounted. See Wyndham to Rosebery, no. 143, October 9, 1893, ibid.

114. Picking to Herbert, December 28, 1893, National Archives, Records of the Department of the Navy, Record Group [hereafter Navy Records RG] 45, Area 4, microfilm roll no. 26. See also Picking to Herbert, December 23, 1893, cited in Walter LaFeber, "United States Depression Diplomacy and the Brazilian Revolution, 1893–1894," *Hispanic American Historical Review*, 40 (1960): 110–11.

115. Thompson to Gresham, October 22 and October 24, 1893, RG 59, *Brazil*, Dispatches, 55; Gresham to Thompson, October 25, 1893, ibid., Instructions, 18.

116. Wyndham to Rosebery, no. 189 and no. 190, November 2, 1893, F.O. 13/706.

117. Wyndham to Rosebery, December 5, 1893, F.O. 13/707. On the previous day President Cleveland had informed the United States Congress that he "failed to see that the insurgents can reasonably claim recognition as belligerents." See James D. Richardson, ed., *A Compilation of the Messages and Papers of the Presidents, 1789–1897*, 10 vols. (Washington, D.C.: GPO, 1896–1899), 9: 435.

118. Saldanha was head of the prestigious naval school. He was known to have monarchist sympathies, but he was greatly respected for his loyal service to both the empire and the republic. Personal differences with Melo perhaps dissuaded Saldanha from joining the naval revolt in its initial stages, but on December 1, 1893, Melo left Rio for Rio Grande do Sul and this opened the way for Saldanha to join the insurgents and to assume command of their ships in the harbor on December 9. Since Melo did not return to Rio, Saldanha remained in effective command.

119. Wyndham to Rosebery, no. 273, December 28, 1893, F.O. 13/707. Ironically, in view of Thompson's partiality for Floriano, Gresham appeared to believe that success for the insurgents was imminent in mid-December. See Gresham to Straus, December 14, 1893, Library of Congress, Oscar S. Straus Papers.

120. The government insisted that cargoes be landed at the customs houses. "The object of their refusal was very apparent," commented Lang, "as, so long as the foreigners used this landing, the Marine Arsenal and Custom House were protected from the fire of the insurgents, who would not like to fire into foreign boats if it could be avoided." See Lang to the Admiralty, December 17, 1893, F.O. 13/733.

121. Ibid. See also his explanation of his policy in a letter to the Foreign Office dated March 9, 1894, F.O. 13/734.

122. See draft of letter from the Foreign Office to the Clyde Shipowners' Association, January 13, 1894, F.O. 13/733.

123. Foreign Office to Humphrey Sturt, M.P. for East Dorset, January 20, 1894, ibid.

124. "The continuation of the present state of things," he noted, "must entail severe losses, and in many cases ruin." See Wyndham to Rosebery, no. 260, December 20, 1893, F.O. 13/706.

125. London and Brazilian Bank to Lang, November 14, 1893; Lang to London and

Brazilian Bank, November 14, 1893, F.O. 13/717.

126. Even if a resort to force was necessary the Foreign Office did not intend to act unilaterally. When the same complaints over the lack of naval protection arose in February 1894 the assistant undersecretary, Francis Bertie, underlined the value to Britain of concerted action with the other naval powers. He suggested to the Admiralty that: "The best thing to do would be that Captain Ripon should propose in the council of naval commanders that combined force should be used in the event of the formal protest being disregarded. If the other powers or a majority of them refuse to concur we shall have as a defence against the complaints of merchants the plea of desiring to preserve the concert of the Powers with whom we have been acting. If the other powers agree to use force we may be pretty well sure that there will be no occasion for its application." See Bertie to the Admiralty, February 21, 1894, F.O. 13/733. Captain Ripon had replaced Lang as the senior British naval officer at Rio.

127. Thompson to Gresham, October 3, 1893, RG 59, *Brazil,* Dispatches, 54.

128. Thompson to Gresham, December 13, 1893, ibid.

129. On December 14 Thompson sent the following cryptic telegram: "Da Gama informed Commanders he will endeavor to prevent landing merchandise. British Naval Officers have withdrawn protection." Three days later he reported that the foreign naval commanders had withdrawn their protection too and that Picking had apparently joined in this action. The information in Gresham's possession about affairs in Brazil was therefore misleading. For the telegrams see Thompson to Gresham, December 14 and December 17, 1893, ibid.

130. Admiral Stanton had assumed command of the American squadron at Rio in October, but by firing a salute to Melo he was accused by the Floriano government of supporting the insurgents. Stanton was recalled and Picking assumed temporary command. See Picking to Herbert, November 4, 1893, Navy Records, RG 45, Area 4, microfilm roll no. 26.

131. Gresham to Thompson, January 9 and January 10, 1894, RG 59, *Brazil,* Instructions, 18.

132. See Wyndham to Rosebery, no. 34, January 30, 1894, F.O. 13/724; Captain Rolleston to the Admiralty, January 28, 1894, F.O. 13/734. The exact nature of Benham's instructions is unknown, but it does appear that he attempted to mediate between Floriano and Saldanha before deciding on his action of January 29. See Picking to Herbert, January 26, 1894, Navy Records, RG 45, Area 4, microfilm roll no. 26; and Michael B. McCloskey, "The United States and the Brazilian Naval Revolt, 1893–1894," The *Americas,* 2 (1946): 313–17.

133. For a description of Benham's action see Picking to Herbert, January 29, 1894, Navy Records, RG 45, Area 4, microfilm roll no. 26. See also Clowes, *Four Naval Campaigns,* pp. 221–23.

134. See John B. Moore, *A Digest of International Law,* 8 vols. (Washington, D.C.: GPO, 1906), 2: 1113–20; and Charles E. Martin, *The Policy of the United States As Regards Intervention* (New York: Columbia University Press, 1921), pp. 118–23.

135. Benham's action also assisted British commerce at Rio and was welcomed by the *Times,* February 1, 1894, and the *South American Journal,* February 3, 1894. While the action allowed five American ships to proceed to the dockyard, the way was also opened for over a hundred British merchant ships to do the same. See the statement by Thompson, October 12, 1895, *Consular Reports,* 51 (1896): 92.

136. Gresham to Thompson, January 30, 1894, RG 59, *Brazil,* Instructions, 18.

137. Wyndham to Rosebery, no. 34, January 30, 1894, F.O. 13/724. A certain amount of anti-American feeling also entered Wyndham's dispatches at this time. On January 29 he telegraphed: "U.S. minister appears to favour the Govt. side which makes me oppose

recourse to force and to think that recognition would be preferable." See Wyndham to Rosebery, January 29, 1894, F.O. 13/728.

138. Draft letter to the law officers of the crown, January 30, 1894, F.O. 13/733.

139. See Wyndham to Rosebery, January 31, February 1, and February 2, 1894, F.O. 13/728. On February 2 Wyndham reported that Benham's action had "produced a bad impression here and even amongst the supporters of the Government, the Brazilians being very jealous of intervention on the part of foreigners in their internal affairs." Ibid.

140. Minute on Wyndham to Rosebery, February 1, 1894, ibid.

141. Rosebery to Wyndham, February 2, 1894, ibid.

142. See memorandum February 2, 1894; Sanderson to the lord chancellor, Herschell, February 3, 1894; Herschell to Sanderson, February 5, 1894, F.O. 13/733. British officials were aware that if Britain recognized a blockade at Rio then British shipping would have to leave the harbor. Consequently, British commerce would be totally disrupted. In this sense, Benham's action resolved an exceedingly difficult problem.

143. Wyndham to Rosebery, no. 29, February 6, 1894, F.O. 13/728. The insurgents had captured Curitiba, the capital of Paraná, but the success was short-lived and the report of a march on São Paulo was no more than a threat.

144. Rosebery to Pauncefote, no. 194, February 6, 1894, F.O. 420/152.

145. The various European powers were informed on February 9, 1894, that: "H.M.G. had come to the conclusion that it did not appear that the insurgents had yet constituted any such Govt. as would entitle them to such recognition." See Rosebery's circular to the various British ambassadors, February 9, 1894, F.O. 420/152.

146. Thompson to Gresham, December 13, 1893, RG 59, *Brazil,* Dispatches, 55; Thompson to Gresham, January 12 and February 1, 1894, ibid., 56.

147. Bayard to Gresham, no. 126, December 30, 1893, RG 59, *Great Britain,* Dispatches, 176.

148. Gresham to Bayard, January 21, 1894, Library of Congress, Gresham Papers.

149. Picking to the secretary of the navy, October 14, 1893, Navy Records, RG 45, Area 4, microfilm roll no. 26; Gresham to Bayard, January 21, 1894, Gresham Papers.

150. Picking approved Benham's action of January 29 as "perfectly right in my judgement." See his report to Herbert, January 31, 1894, Navy Records, RG 45, Area 4, microfilm roll no. 26. Note his earlier and much more cautious view in Picking to Herbert, December 28, 1893, ibid.

151. *South American Journal,* February 3, 1894.

152. Cited in *Report of the Secretary of the Navy,* 53rd Congress, 3rd session, House executive document no. 1, p. 23.

153. The most notable exception to this attitude was Eduardo Prado, *A illusão americana* (Paris: A. Colin, 1895). Although not directly concerned with the naval revolt, Prado's theme was that "a fraternidade americana é uma mentira." Ibid., p. 4.

154. Mendonça informed Gresham that the British naval squadron assisted the insurgent withdrawal from Rio. See Gresham to Bayard, no. 342, April 6, 1894, and no. 411, June 4, 1894, RG 59, *Great Britain,* Instructions, 30. The Foreign Office informed Wyndham that there was "no reason" for British interference. See F.O. to Wyndham, no. 27, March 13, 1894, F.O. 13/728.

155. Melo withdrew from an active role in the revolt in April 1894 when he sought political asylum in Argentina.

156. Bureau of the American Republics, *Monthly Bulletin* (Washington, D.C., July 1895).

157. Despite the many rumors to the contrary Floriano did step down from power in November 1894 and was succeeded by the legally elected candidate, Prudente de Morais. An era of civilian presidents was thus begun. The resulting political stability did stimulate

Brazilian commerce, but note the report that the naval revolt, although adversely affecting trade at Rio, had led to an increase in the trade of other Brazilian ports. See Bureau of American Republics, *Monthly Bulletin* (Washington, D.C.: January 1894).

158. Bayard to Gresham, no. 180, March 16, 1894, RG 59, *Great Britain,* Dispatches, 176.

Chapter 7: "Its Fiat Is Law"

1. William E. Curtis, *The Capitals of Spanish America* (New York: Harper and Brothers, 1888), p. 552.

2. See Thomas F. Mc Gann, *Argentina, the United States and the Inter-American System, 1800–1914* (Cambridge, Mass.: Harvard University Press, 1957), p. 167.

3. Report by Consul Baker, December 13, 1888, *Commercial Relations [of the United States]* (1887–1888), pp. 73–74.

4. Jenner to Salisbury, no. 35, May 13, 1889, F.O. 6/405.

5. *Buenos Ayres Herald,* September 7, 1889.

6. See International American Conference, 1889–1890, *Minutes of the Conference* (Washington, 1890), p. 324.

7. Hanna to Bayard, no. 207, March 2, 1889, Records of the Department of State, RG 59, *Argentine Republic,* Dispatches, 27.

8. Jenner to Salisbury, no. 16, August 31, 1888, F.O. 6/399.

9. For example, see the article by a special correspondent at Buenos Aires cited in the *Times,* July 15, 1890.

10. See report by Baker dated November 17, 1890, *United States Consular Reports,* 35 (1891): 7.

11. On the crisis see A. G. Ford, "Argentina and the Baring Crisis of 1890," *Oxford Economic Papers,* new series, 8 (1956): 127–50.

12. See John E. Hodge, "Carlos Pellegrini and the Financial Crisis of 1890," *Hispanic American Historical Review,* 1 (1970): 509. An editorial in the *Times,* dated August 21, 1891, admitted: "To European influence . . . must a large part of the responsibility for the present condition of Argentina be attributed."

13. Herbert to Sanderson, August 31, 1891, F.O. 6/418. Herbert predicted that his position would become "very much strained" when the references to Latin America made by Salisbury in a recent speech became generally known in Buenos Aires. For this speech, see the *Times,* July 30, 1891.

14. Ibid. See also Henry S. Ferns, *Britain and Argentina in the Nineteenth Century* (Oxford: Clarendon Press, 1960), pp. 465–66.

15. The *Times,* August 21, 1891. The *Statist* commented in similar fashion: "It is quite right that the European creditors of Argentina should not press too hardly upon the Argentine people." See the *Statist,* August 29, 1891.

16. See L. S. Pressnell, "Gold Reserves, Banking Reserves, and the Baring Crisis of 1890," in Charles R. Whittlesey and John S. G. Wilson, eds., *Essays in Money and Banking* (Oxford: Clarendon Press, 1968), pp. 167–228.

17. D. C. M. Platt, *Latin America and British Trade 1806–1914* (London: A. and C. Black, 1972), pp. 283–84.

18. Pitkin to Blaine, June 2, 1891, RG 59, *Argentine Republic,* Dispatches, 29. See also Hodge, "Pellegrini and the 1890 Crisis," pp. 519–20.

19. Mc Gann, *Argentina and the Inter-American System,* pp. 170–71.

20. Wharton to Pitkin, no. 136, August 3, 1891, RG 59, *Argentine Republic,* Instructions, 16.

21. Pitkin to Blaine, no. 156, October 7, 1891, ibid., Dispatches, 29.

22. See Pitkin to Blaine, no. 158, October 28; no. 164, December 5; and telegram, December 29, 1891, ibid. Zeballos's reply to Pitkin is enclosed in Pitkin to Blaine, no. 175, January 9, 1892, ibid., and also reprinted in Ministerio de Relaciones Exteriores República Argentina, *Reciprocidad comercial* (Buenos Aires: Impr. J. Peuser, 1892), pp. 29–39. Zeballos was critical of the brevity of the Latin American Trade Commission's visit to Buenos Aires in 1885, and he was particularly scathing of what he regarded as insulting references to Argentina contained in Curtis's *Capitals of Spanish America*.

23. Pitkin to Blaine, telegram, January 17, and no. 177, January 20, 1892, RG 59, *Argentine Republic,* Dispatches, 29. See also Mc Gann, *Argentina and the Inter-American System,* p. 172.

24. Pitkin to Blaine, telegrams, dated January 22 and 30, 1892. See also the comment by Blaine in margin of latter telegram, RG 59, *Argentine Republic,* Dispatches, 29. Zeballos suggested that Argentina would give material support to the United States should a war break out between the latter nation and Chile. Argentina was currently involved in a boundary dispute with Chile and, no doubt, Zeballos's proposal was tinged with ulterior motive. See Robert N. Burr, *By Reason or Force* (Berkeley and Los Angeles: University of California Press, 1965), pp. 195–97.

25. Pitkin to Blaine, no. 182, February 20, and no. 183, February 26, 1892, RG 59, *Argentine Republic,* Dispatches, 30.

26. The rumors of an impending United States-Argentine alliance were reprinted in the *Times,* March 21, 1892. See also Herbert to Salisbury, no. 17, March 23; no. 18, March 28; no. 22, March 30; and no. 34, May 3, 1892, F.O. 6/423. See also his telegram to Salisbury, dated March 29, 1892, F.O. 6/425. Dispatches from British ministers in Chile and Peru also mentioned the rumor of an imminent alliance. See Kennedy to Salisbury, no. 27, March 24, 1892, F.O. 16/276; and Jenner to Salisbury, no. 14, April 3, 1892, F.O. 61/391. In contrast to Pitkin, who appears to have had direct personal contact with Zeballos, Herbert depended upon somewhat anonymous and indirect sources for much of his information. Nevertheless, his prediction that a political alliance would not materialize was proved correct.

27. F.O. to Herbert, no. 10, June 8, 1892, F.O. 6/425.

28. Welby to Salisbury, no. 16, July 12, and no. 20, July 31, 1892, ibid.

29. Pitkin to Blaine, no. 205, July 11, 1892, RG 59, *Argentine Republic,* Dispatches, 30.

30. Fishback to Foster, no. 211, August 23, 1892, ibid.

31. See Mc Gann, *Argentina and the Inter-American System,* pp. 174–75.

32. Report by Baker, December 26, 1892, *Consular Reports,* 47 (1893): 536.

33. Curtis, *Capitals of Spanish America,* p. 454.

34. See Harold Lindsell, *The Chilean-American Controversy of 1891–1892* (New York: New York University, 1943), p. 1.

35. Chilean diplomats feared most of all that the United States might assist Peru, Bolivia, or Argentina in their respective boundary disputes with Chile.

36. Curtis, *Capitals of Spanish America,* p. 455; Fraser to Rosebery, no. 45, June 7, 1886, F.O. 16/242.

37. The *Nation,* March 13, 1890. The most commonly voiced grievance by American merchants was that British steamship companies levied higher freight charges on Latin American cargoes shipped via the United States than via Europe. See Curtis, *Capitals of Spanish America,* p. 456. Even so, total American trade with Chile during the late 1880s was little more than $6 million annually while British trade amounted to over $80 million. Curtis concluded that "there is little hope of extending our export trade" in Chile. See William E. Curtis, "Our Commercial Relations with Chile," *North American Review,* 154 (1892): 360–63.

38. See the remarks of Thacher cited in International American Conference, 1889–1890, *Reports of Committees and Discussions Thereon,* 4 vols. (Washington, 1890), 4: 331.

39. The British minister at Santiago later summed up that Egan's aim was "to improve the politics and commercial relations between Chile and the United States, to the detriment of Great Britain and Germany." See Kennedy to Rosebery, no. 42, July 17, 1893, F.O. 16/282. For a general view of Egan's diplomatic and commercial activities in Chile see Osgood Hardy, "Was Patrick Egan a 'Blundering Minister'?" *Hispanic American Historical Review,* 8 (1928): 65–81.

40. *South American Journal,* April 6, 1889.

41. On the nitrate question see Joseph R. Brown, "Nitrate Crises, Combinations, and the Chilean Government in the Nitrate Age," *Hispanic American Historical Review,* 43 (1963): 230–46; and Harold Blakemore, *British Nitrates and Chilean Politics, 1886–1896* (London: Athlone Press, 1974). For Balmaceda's policy see Hernán Ramírez Necochea, *Blamaceda y la contrarrevolución de 1891* (Santiago de Chile: Editorial Universitaria, 1969); and for a guide to the literature in English see Harold Blakemore, "The Chilean Revolution of 1891 and its Historiography," *Hispanic American Historical Review,* 45 (1965): 393–421.

42. Egan to Blaine, no. 38, January 13, 1890, RG 43, *International American Conference,* Box 19.

43. The civil war quickly developed into a military stalemate that was not broken until late August 1891. The army remained loyal to the government so that Balmaceda retained control of the capital. The opposition forces—known as the Congressionalists—gained the support of the navy and established their initial base at Iquique in northern Chile. For an account of the military aspects of the war see William L. Clowes, *Four Modern Naval Campaigns* (London: Unit Library, 1902), pp. 133–85.

44. Egan to Blaine, no. 185, July 30, 1891, *Foreign Relations [of the United States]* (1891), pp. 149–50.

45. See Egan to Blaine, no. 143, March 17, and no. 154, April 23, 1891, ibid., pp. 106–07, 111. With the approval of the State Department Egan did, however, attempt to mediate between the contending forces. See Egan to Blaine, no. 164, May 18, 1891, with enclosures, ibid., pp. 123–30.

46. Kennedy to Salisbury, no. 61, June 23, 1891, F.O. 16/265.

47. Kennedy believed that Chilean opinion was "very clearly against any agreement which might subject Chile in any way to the programme proposed by Mr. Blaine." See Kennedy to Salisbury, no. 48, May 21, and no. 62, June 23, 1891, ibid. See also Kennedy to Sanderson, private, June 9, 1891, ibid. Kennedy predicted in January that the "fleet will win" although his later reports pointed out the growing strength of the government forces. See Kennedy to Sanderson, private, January 24, 1891, F.O. 16/264, and compare with his later dispatch to Sanderson, June 9, 1891, F.O. 16/265.

48. Kennedy to Salisbury, no. 61, June 23, 1891, ibid.

49. Kennedy to Sanderson, February 3, 1891, F.O. 16/270. The same dispatch also reported his rejection of the Chilean foreign minister's request for British naval assistance against the Congressionalists.

50. Memorandum by Davidson, March 4, 1891, F.O. 16/267.

51. Memorandum by Sanderson, January 13, 1891, F.O. 16/268. Davidson also noted that since the conflict appeared to be a purely political movement, "we should not interfere at all unless the lives or property of our subjects was directly threatened." See minute on Kennedy to Salisbury, telegram, January 13, 1891, F.O. 16/267.

52. For example, see the *Times,* January 19, 1891, and the *Statist,* January 24, 1891.

53. See minute on memorandum by Kennedy enclosed in Kennedy to Salisbury, no. 10, January 29, 1891, F.O. 16/264.

54. F.O. to Kennedy, no. 59, July 6, 1891, F.O. 16/263.

55. F.O. to Duncan, July 18, 1891, F.O. 16/272.

56. See the comments on the difficulty of receiving accurate information from Chile in the *Statist*, August 29, 1891.

57. Wharton to Egan, no. 120, July 21, 1891, *Foreign Relations* (1891), p. 147.

58. Kennedy to Sanderson, September 15, 1891, F.O. 16/266. See also Maurice H. Hervey, *Dark Days in Chile* (London: Arnold, 1892), p. 155.

59. Sanderson noted: "This is charming—as things have turned out." See his minute on no. 91, Kennedy to Salisbury, September 2, 1891, F.O. 16/266. "In England, and probably in most other civilized countries," stated the *Times*, "the intelligence of Balmaceda's downfall will be received with a feeling of very general relief." See the *Times*, August 31, 1891.

60. Kennedy to Sanderson, private, September 4, 1891, F.O. 16/266. The reference to Tarapacá related to a rumor that Balmaceda might sell nitrate concessions to American interests.

61. The charges that Egan was sympathetic to Balmaceda were balanced somewhat by his granting of political asylum to two Congressionalist leaders and by his sincere attempts to mediate between the two contending parties.

62. Kennedy to Salisbury, no. 104, October 6, 1891, F.O. 16/266. The *Itata* had received arms shipments purchased by Congressionalist agents in the United States, but became the subject of a detention order by the United States government. The arms and the ship were returned to the United States under American naval guard in July 1891. See Osgood Hardy, "The Itata Incident," *Hispanic American Historical Review*, 5 (1922): 195–226. The other major grievance of the Congressionalists related to Balmaceda's apparent prior knowledge of their troop movements, a fact that they attributed to Admiral George Brown's presence at Quinteros Bay when they were preparing for the attack on Valparaiso. See Egan to Blaine, no. 203, September 17, 1891, *Foreign Relations* (1891), p. 163.

63. Kennedy to Salisbury, no. 105, October 8, 1891, F.O. 16/266.

64. Britain established diplomatic relations at the same time. See F.O. to Kennedy, telegram, September 6, 1891, F.O. 16/267.

65. Egan claimed that he would personally shoot the first man who attempted to enter the legation by force. See Egan to Blaine, no. 193, August 20, 1891, *Foreign Relations* (1891), p. 153.

66. See Egan to Blaine, telegram, October 8, 1891, and no. 205, September 29, 1891, ibid., pp. 168–77, 184. The harassment of the legation continued spasmodically until January 1892. On one occasion Kennedy described Egan as "the object of tremendous persecution." See Kennedy to Sanderson, private, October 25, 1891, F.O. 16/266.

67. John Bassett Moore, who served as third assistant secretary of state during the Chilean revolution, later argued that Egan's claim of extraterritoriality was "obviously too broad." See John B. Moore, "Asylum in Legations and Consulates and in Vessels," *Political Science Quarterly*, 7 (1892): 229.

68. Harrison to Blaine, September 26, 1891, cited in Albert T. Volwiler, ed., *The Correspondence Between Benjamin Harrison and James G. Blaine, 1882–1893* (Philadelphia: American Philosophical Society, 1940), pp. 195–97.

69. See Wharton to Egan, telegram, October 1, 1891, *Foreign Relations* (1891), pp. 177–78.

70. Wharton to Egan, telegram, October 23, 1891, ibid., pp. 196–97. For a general account of the *Baltimore* incident see Albert T. Volwiler, "Harrison, Blaine and American Foreign Policy, 1889–1893," *Proceedings of the American Philosophical Society*, 79 (1938): 637–48; and Frederick B. Pike, *Chile and the United States, 1880–1962* (Notre Dame: University of Notre Dame Press, 1963), pp. 73–85.

71. Matta to Egan, October 27, 1891, *Foreign Relations* (1891), pp. 209–10. Matta did not question the accuracy of Schley's report, but in order to assert Chilean independence

and rights of sovereignty, he added that "by duty and in compliance with international rules and customs never denied by civilized nations, he abides by and will abide by, the jurisdiction of the authority of his own country, which are the only ones which have full right and will have sufficient power to judge and punish the guilty whoever they may be and wherever they may be found in the territory of Chile." Ibid., p. 209. Note also the comment by Moore that the United States government had denied liability in similar cases. See John B. Moore, "The Late Chilean Controversy," *Political Science Quarterly,* 8 (1893): 490. In connection with the death of eleven Italians at the hands of a New Orleans mob in March 1891 Harrison himself commented: "It is very appalling, but under our federal system, while the United States is responsible to other nations for injuries done to their citizens, it is without jurisdiction to interfere for their protection, except by suggestion, or appeal, to the State authorities." See Volwiler, *Harrison-Blaine Correspondence,* pp. 141–43.

72. The *Times,* October 27, 1891.

73. Sanderson did not believe in the report of "a serious quarrel" between the United States and Chile. See minute on Kennedy to Salisbury, November 9, 1891, F.O. 16/267. A British warship did not arrive at Valparaiso until January 1892. See the comments on the lack of British naval protection in Robley D. Evans, *A Sailor's Log* (New York: D. Appleton and Co., 1901), p. 272.

74. Kennedy to Salisbury, no. 124, November 9, and no. 137, December 20, 1891, F.O. 16/266. Kennedy noted: "As regards British and European commercial interests . . . it is desirable that Mr. Egan should remain in Chile because this Government show their hatred of Mr. Egan by acts of hostility against United States commerce, independently of the affronts heaped upon the United States legation and ships." See Kennedy to Salisbury, no. 123, November 8, 1891, ibid.

75. Excitement reached such a height that the body of the murdered American sailor, Riggins, lay in state at Independence Hall, Philadelphia. See Henry C. Evans, *Chile and Its Relations with the United States* (Durham: Duke University Press, 1927), p. 152. One study has, however, concluded that the controversy with Chile from 1891 to 1892 "never really touched the American people nor did it arouse in them a jingoistic sentiment for aggressive action." See Lindsell, *Chilean-American Controversy,* pp. 12–14.

76. Carnegie to Harrison, October 26, 1891, Library of Congress, Carnegie Papers. An editorial in the *Times,* dated October 30, 1891, argued: "The larger objects of Mr. Blaine's Pan-American policy, the acquisition of a predominant influence over the Republics of South America and their inclusion in a commercial union, are not likely to be promoted by threats, still less by an actual declaration of war."

77. Egan to Blaine, no. 229, November 11, 1891, *Foreign Relations* (1891), p. 227.

78. The *Times,* November 16, 1891.

79. Egan to Blaine, telegram, December 3, 1891, *Foreign Relations* (1891), p. 250.

80. See James D. Richardson, ed., *A Compilation of the Messages and Papers of the Presidents, 1789–1897,* 10 vols. (Washington, D.C.: GPO, 1896–1899), 9: 185.

81. For the text of Matta's statement see *Foreign Relations* (1891), pp. 268–69.

82. Kennedy to Salisbury, nos. 142 and 143, December 31, 1891, F.O. 16/266. In view of the undoubted rivalry between the two ministers Kennedy remarked rather magnanimously that Egan "certainly deserves credit for the firmness and ability which he has displayed under circumstances of unusual difficulty." Ibid.

83. Egan to Blaine, no. 256, December 28, 1891, *Foreign Relations* (1891), pp. 276–78. President Montt, in particular, stressed the need for conciliation. See William R. Sherman, *Diplomatic and Commercial Relations of the United States and Chile, 1820–1914* (Boston: R. G. Badger, 1926), p. 184.

84. Egan to Blaine, telegram, December 31, 1891, *Foreign Relations* (1891), p. 284.

85. See Volwiler, "Harrison, Blaine and Foreign Policy," p. 643.

86. Ibid., p. 645. Volwiler has described this as a "grave" meeting.

87. Blaine to Egan, January 21, 1892, *Foreign Relations* (1891), p. 307.

88. Tracy had also been preparing the navy for possible action in Chile throughout the whole period of the controversy over the *Baltimore* incident. See Walter R. Herrick, Jr., *The American Naval Revolution* (Baton Rouge: Louisiana State University Press, 1966), pp. 126–27.

89. Egan to Blaine, telegram, January 25, 1892, *Foreign Relations* (1891), pp. 309–12. See also Pike, *Chile and the United States,* p. 80.

90. Blaine to Egan, telegram, January 30, 1892, *Foreign Relations* (1891), pp. 312–13.

91. Egan even attempted to press for a reciprocity treaty in March 1892 although this was rejected by the Chilean government. See Maude to Sanderson, no. 27, March 24, 1892, F.O. 16/276.

92. In a strict legal sense the American demands on Chile had little justification. The *Economist* summed up: "Chile only yields because it is too small to resist." The editorial went on to argue that if the American demand was upheld then governments must warn their citizens "to fly whenever they see American sailors approaching, lest in the heat of argument or bargaining an international question should be raised." The American insistence that Egan remain at his post was also compared to the "much slighter grounds" used by the United States to demand the recall of Lionel West in 1888. See the *Economist,* January 30, 1892.

93. Blaine's bitterness toward Harrison's Chilean policy became something of a minor scandal. See the *Washington Post,* January 30, 1892.

94. The *Times,* February 8, 1892.

95. Cited in Pike, *Chile and the United States,* p. 85.

96. Ibid., p. 78.

97. Chile was also apprehensive that its neighbors, Argentina, Peru, and Bolivia, might exploit its difficulties with the United States to press their territorial claims against Chile. See Burr, *By Reason or Force,* pp. 192–203.

98. Despite the sympathy and support of local British interests for the Congressionalist victory over Balmaceda, the new government pursued an unchanged policy of increasing the tax burden on nitrate producers. Chile was not therefore a "satellite" of the British-based nitrate interests. See Blakemore, *British Nitrates and Chilean Politics,* p. 226; and Brown, "Nitrate Crises," pp. 236–37.

99. See Charles C. Tansill, *The Foreign Policy of Thomas F. Bayard, 1885–1897* (New York: Fordham University Press, 1940), pp. 3–119, 359–409. On foreign policy in general see George R. Dulebohn, *Principles of Foreign Policy Under the Cleveland Administrations* (Philadelphia: University of Pennsylvania Press, 1941); on the question of Samoa see Paul M. Kennedy, *The Samoan Tangle* (New York: Barnes and Noble, 1974).

100. In 1891 Blaine stated that only three places were of "value enough to be taken." These were Cuba, Puerto Rico, and Hawaii. See Blaine to Harrison, August 10, 1891, cited in Volwiler, *Harrison-Blaine Correspondence,* pp. 173–74.

101. Herrick, *American Naval Revolution,* pp. 86–107. The reference is to the diplomatic activities of Frederick Douglass in Haiti and John Durham in the Dominican Republic. On the former see Rayford W. Logan, *The Diplomatic Relations of the United States with Haiti, 1776–1891* (Chapel Hill: University of North Carolina Press, 1941), pp. 408–25.

102. Bayard to Merrill, January 8, 1887, cited in Tansill, *Foreign Policy of Bayard,* pp. 382–83.

103. For a general account see William A. Russ, *The Hawaiian Revolution (1893–94)* (Selinsgrove: Susquehanna University Press, 1959).

104. Gresham to Overmeyer, July 25, 1894, Library of Congress, Gresham Papers.

105. Similar surprise outside the United States must have been generated by the 1894 tariff, which reversed the reciprocity policy so fervently pursued by the Harrison administration.

106. See Merze Tate, "Twisting the Lion's Tail over Hawaii," *Pacific Historical Review*, 36 (1967): 27–46. Russ has commented that: "It would be nearer the truth to say that London favored American annexation." See Russ, *Hawaiian Revolution*, p. 18.

107. See memorandum by Herbert Bismarck, August 24, 1887, cited in Tansill, *Foreign Policy of Bayard*, pp. 46–47; Pauncefote to Salisbury, no. 110, April 29, 1892, F.O. 5/2148.

108. Britain had long maintained friendly relations with the Mosquito Indians of eastern Nicaragua although Britain recognized Nicaraguan sovereignty over the Mosquito territory in the Anglo-Nicaraguan treaty of 1860.

109. Gresham to Bayard, no. 374, April 30, 1894, RG 59, *Great Britain*, Instructions, 30. See also Mary W. Williams, *Anglo-American Isthmian Diplomacy, 1815–1915* (Washington, D.C.: American Historical Association, 1916), pp. 288–99.

110. Bayard to Gresham, no. 224, May 28, 1894, RG 59, *Great Britain*, Dispatches, 177.

111. See memorandum by Bayard, dated November 23, 1894, cited in Tansill, *Foreign Policy of Bayard*, pp. 683–84.

112. Gresham to Bayard, April 23, 1895, Library of Congress, Bayard Papers. On Gresham's response to the British action see Matilda Gresham, *The Life of Walter Quintin Gresham, 1832–1895*, 2 vols. (Chicago: Rand, McNally and Co., 1919), 2: 784–85. The Philadelphia correspondent of the *Times* reported: "The British statement of the case is generally regarded in official circles as unassailable. Great Britain's demands are considered to be reasonable and not to require the intervention of the United States, being only what this country would make in similar circumstances." See the *Times*, March 30, 1895.

113. See Festus P. Summers, ed., *The Cabinet Diary of William L. Wilson, 1896–1897* (Chapel Hill: University of North Carolina Press, 1957), p. 5.

114. Cleveland's action in accepting the report of his special commissioner, James Blount, implied that the Harrison administration was implicated in the intrigues that precipitated the coup of January 1893.

115. See Russell to Bayard, December 8, 1895, cited in Gerald C. Eggert, *Richard Olney* (University Park: Pennsylvania State University Press, 1974), p. 357.

116. Gresham to Taylor, March 14, 1895, *Foreign Relations* (1895), p. 1177. The *New York Times*, March 17, 1895, remarked: "It is gratifying, moreover, that these insolent and ignorant Spaniards are to be taught a lesson in manners as well as morals, as the result of this incident. They are entirely too much given to strutting." Senator Frye of Maine was reported as regretting the peaceful settlement of the affair since he had hoped for war so that the United States might take possession of Cuba. See the *Times*, March 22, 1895.

117. For a general account of the dispute see Tansill, *Foreign Policy of Bayard*, pp. 621–65. Of the many articles on this subject see Walter LaFeber, "The Background of Cleveland's Venezuelan Policy," *American Historical Review*, 46 (1961): 947–67; and Robin A. Humphreys, "Anglo-American Rivalries and the Venezuela Crisis of 1895," cited in Robin A. Humphreys, *Tradition and Revolt in Latin America* (New York: Columbia University Press, 1969), pp. 186–215.

118. See John A. S. Grenville and George B. Young, *Politics, Strategy, and American Diplomacy* (New Haven: Yale University Press, 1966), pp. 125–40.

119. Richardson, *Messages and Papers*, 9: 256. Scruggs was the initiator of the House resolution. See Grenville and Young, *Politics, Strategy and American Diplomacy*, pp. 141–45.

120. Gresham to Bayard, March 31 and April 23, 1895, cited in Tansill, *Foreign Policy of Bayard*, pp. 695–96.

121. See Walter LaFeber, *The New Empire* (Ithaca: Cornell University Press, 1963), p. 253.

122. See Eggert, *Richard Olney*, passim.

123. For Olney's dispatch—known as the "Olney memorandum"—see Olney to Bayard, July 20, 1895, *Foreign Relations* (1895), pp. 545–62. Salisbury had recently succeeded Kimberley as foreign secretary. His reply was reported in Bayard to Olney, August 9, 1895, cited in Tansill, *Foreign Policy of Bayard*, p. 709.

124. Ibid., p. 717.

125. See Humphreys, *Tradition and Revolt*, p. 209.

126. One cabinet member believed that the crisis had "done us good politically." See Summers, *Cabinet Diary of Wilson*, pp. 4–5. But such hopes were disappointed in 1896 when Cleveland failed to secure the Democratic presidential nomination and when a Republican won the presidential election.

//

Note on Sources

Bibliographies

The essential bibliographical source is the *Handbook of Latin American Studies* (Cambridge, Mass.: Harvard University Press, 1936–51; Gainesville: University of Florida Press, 1961–). On American relations with Latin America see David F. Trask, Michael C. Meyer, and Roger R. Trask, eds., *A Bibliography of United States–Latin American Relations Since 1810* (Lincoln: University of Nebraska Press, 1968). There is no similar bibliography for British relations with Latin America; for British external relations in general see H. J. Hanham, *Bibliography of British History 1851–1914* (Oxford: Clarendon Press, 1976), chapter 3.

An excellent guide to the vast secondary literature on late nineteenth-century American foreign relations is the bibliographical essay in Charles S. Campbell, *The Transformation of American Foreign Relations, 1865–1900* (New York: Harper & Row, 1976), pp. 339–77. Other useful bibliographical essays are Robert L. Beisner, *From the Old Diplomacy to the New, 1865–1900* (New York: Crowell, 1975), pp. 140–50; and Alexander DeConde, *American Diplomatic History in Transformation* (Washington, D.C.: American Historical Association pamphlet no. 702, 1976), pp. 5–14, 21–23.

Primary Sources

The fundamental manuscript sources used in this study were the diplomatic records of the Foreign Office and the Department of State. Extensive use was made of the F.O. records located in the Public Record Office, London. Especially valuable were the files on British relations with individual Latin American countries; many of these files have never been fully utilized by previous writers on this subject. A more selective examination was made of the State Department files in the National Archives, Washington, D.C. The private papers of many leading American political and diplomatic figures are available in the Manuscript Division of the Library of Congress, Washington, D.C., but their value for this study proved uneven.

Printed Documentary Material

A considerable amount of F.O. diplomatic and, in particular, commercial material was reprinted annually in *Parliamentary Papers* and in *Reports from H. M. Diplomatic and Consular Officers Abroad on the Subject of Trade and Finance* [cited as *Trade Reports*]. Latin American affairs were rarely discussed at length in Parliament; nevertheless,

Parliamentary Debates are a useful source of information on British policy and attitudes toward the Western Hemisphere.

By contrast, American political debate gave more prominence to relations with Latin America so that the *Congressional Globe* and *Congressional Record* provide more pertinent material than their British counterparts. During the late nineteenth century the United States government also published more diplomatic material on a regular basis than did the British government. In this respect, the annual series of the Department of State, *Papers Relating to the Foreign Relations of the United States,* is an invaluable and convenient supplement to the State Department archives.

Material relating to Latin America can also be found in Department of State, *Commercial Relations of the United States* (Washington, D.C., 1881–83); and Department of State, *United States Consular Reports* (Washington, D.C., 1883–). Another important source of commercial information is the International Bureau of the American Republics, *Bulletin* (Washington, D.C., 1891–). Several executive documents and reports of the House of Representatives and the Senate also provided essential material for this study. James D. Richardson, ed., *A Compilation of the Messages and Papers of the Presidents, 1789–1897,* 10 vols. (Washington, D.C., 1896–99) proved to be an indispensable source for official statements on relations with Latin America.

Newspapers and Periodicals

The source most extensively consulted was the *Times* [London]. More selective reference was made to the *New York Times, New York Tribune, New York World,* and *Buenos Ayres Herald.* Two extremely valuable sources on Anglo-American policy and attitudes toward Latin America were the *South American Journal* and the *Rio News.* Important articles and information were found in the *Economist,* the *Nation, North American Review,* and the *Statist.* The William E. Curtis Papers at Princeton University also contain a very comprehensive collection of American newspaper clippings on political developments during the late nineteenth century.

Index

Abbott, John T., 151
Adam, Frederick, 164–70 *passim*
Adams, Robert, 157, 159, 160, 161
Adee, Alvey A., 33, 167
Alabama dispute: and Anglo-American relations, 10, 11, 58; and War of the Pacific, 15, 60; description of, 215*n34*; mentioned, 224*n27*
Aldrich, Nelson A., 145, 146
Alduñate, Luis, 76
Alfonso, José, 139
Ammen, Daniel, 98, 100, 101, 237*n81*
Anglo-American relations: British conciliation and, xiv, 9–10, 24, 45, 91–92, 113, 184, 203, 207; commercial rivalry in, 7, 22–23, 31, 45, 118; description of, 9–12; diplomatic cooperation in, 10, 59, 180; friction in, 10, 25–26, 44, 53–54, 65, 112, 134, 203, 207; and *Virginius* incident, 59. *See also* Clayton-Bulwer treaty
Argentina: and relations with Britain, 4, 147, 185–88, 190, 191–92, 213*n6*; and Baring crisis, 22, 185–88; and Washington conference, 31–32, 133, 134, 139, 186, 187, 189; and War of the Triple Alliance, 57–58; visited by Latin American Trade Commission, 128; and reciprocity with United States, 150, 151, 154, 185, 187, 189, 191, 201; trade with United States, 186, 191; desires closer commercial relations with United States, 186–87, 188, 189–90, 192; mentioned, 160, 193, 203
Arthur, Chester A.: political reputation of, 119; as president, 119–20

Arthur administration: policy of, 32, 43, 119–26, 129; and Blaine, 43, 65, 71–72, 109, 119–20, 124, 125; lame-duck, 85, 124–25; mentioned, 37, 111, 202
Asboth, Alexander, 58

Baker, E. L., 186, 187, 191–92
Balmaceda, José Manuel: friendly toward United States, 150, 193–94; as president of Chile, 193–96; British views on, 195, 196; mentioned, 231*n141*
Baltimore incident: and Harrison administration, 29, 44, 197–201; description of, 197, 220*n19*; British views on, 197, 200; and Germany, 200; mentioned, 32, 185, 189, 207, 208
Bayard, Thomas F.: on Congress, 36; suspicions of Germany, 39, 43; and Washington conference, 43, 131, 132, 134; and Clayton-Bulwer treaty, 86, 113; on isthmian canal, 86, 102, 112, 116; as ambassador to Britain, 177, 181, 182, 184, 204, 206; on Hawaii, 202; mentioned, 130, 157
Benham, Admiral Andrew E. K., 177–83 *passim*, 203, 257*nn132, 135, 258n139*
Bergne, Henry, 95, 97, 235*n38*
Blaine, James G.: and United States expansionism in Latin America, xiv, 37, 39, 43, 114, 117–20 *passim*, 155, 157, 161, 188–89, 201; anti-British attitude, 10, 65, 68, 77, 79, 229*n105*; and War of the Pacific, 35, 61, 65–72, 77, 80; and reciprocity, 42, 122, 125, 144–51 *passim*; political reputation of, 61, 66; and Washington conference, 70–71,

PITT LATIN AMERICAN SERIES

Cole Blasier, Editor